# SOCIAL ADMINISTRATION

## A CLIENT-CENTERED APPROACH

**CHARLES A. RAPP AND JOHN POERTNER**

University of Kansas

Longman

New York & London

**Social Administration: A Client-Centered Approach**

**Longman, 10 Bank Street, White Plains, N.Y. 10606**

Associated companies:
Longman Group Ltd., London
Longman Cheshire Pty., Melbourne
Longman Paul Pty., Auckland
Copp Clark Pitman, Toronto

Senior editor: David J. Estrin
Production editor: Kailyard Associates
Cover design: Renée Kilbride Edelman
Production supervisor: Richard C. Bretan

Library of Congress Cataloging in Publication Data

Rapp, Charles A.
    Social administration : a client-centered approach / Charles Rapp
and John Poertner.
        p.   cm.
    Includes index.
    ISBN 0-8013-0435-0
    1. Social work administration.   I. Poertner, John.   II. Title.
HV40.R3   1992
361'.0068—dc20                                          90-19564
                                                            CIP

6 7 8 9 10-MA-99 98

*To our social administration students past, present, and future, with whom the welfare of so many rests.*

# Contents

# Foreword

Every so often a book appears on the scene that raises the state of the art of administrative practice in social welfare to a new level. This is such a book. Hereafter, those who study social administration will see this practice domain in a new way.

The proposition that energizes the book is a deceptively simple one: Since social agencies exist primarily to benefit clients, administrators should practice in ways that facilitate this outcome. This is hardly a startling idea. Indeed, for all the years that social workers have been concerned with administration as professional practice there has been a rhetorical recognition that managers were ultimately responsible for how their agencies performed. Until recently, however, the vital link between managerial action and the effectiveness of services to clients was not well understood or even appreciated. There were several reasons for this.

Low cost, easily replicable technologies for evaluating service outcomes were slow to evolve in social welfare. Lacking such technologies, administrators (like their clinical colleagues) found it difficult to reliably assess the relationship between managerial behavior and client outcomes. Without this critical source of information about the ultimate consequences of practice, it is not surprising that more readily observable performance indicators emerged, such as the amount of service provided, funds raised, retention and satisfaction of subordinates, and the like. These and similar surrogates of agency performance could be directly observed and measured; more importantly, the consequences of practice related to these objectives could be assessed. As a result, administrative practice was shaped around these types of performance indicators, which were often equated with organizational effectiveness.

Add to this, as Rapp and Poertner argue, that social agencies have a number of constituencies more powerful than clients (e.g., legislative and funding bodies, other service providing agencies, professional staff), who tend to judge agency performance by criteria other than service effectiveness. Under these circumstances it is not difficult to understand why administrative practice has tended to focus on performance criteria that have little to do with client outcomes.

There has also been a persistent tendency in social work and other human service professions to view administrators as somehow distant from the essential service functions of the agency. This view, and the fact that administrators often focus their attention on issues that have little direct bearing on the delivery of service, has perpetuated the idea that the best managers provide a benignly supportive context for service providers so that the service providers can ply their craft relatively unfettered by organizational interference.

The tendency of human service managers and students of social administration to draw heavily upon extant theories of organization and administration (mostly derived from the business and public administration fields) to construct models of practice, reinforced the tendency to think of administration as divorced from the essential service of the agency. With few exceptions, these theories were not developed in the nonprofit human service sector and consequently contained no concept of service effectiveness that was specific to these types of organizations. What these theories of administration did provide was guidance about what administrators should do and how, based typically on the assumption that if the manager did the right things this would contribute to general organizational effectiveness. But there was little guidance about how managerial action should support and improve the quality and effectiveness of services and realize intended benefits for clients. In the formative years then, when administration was being shaped in the field and in academia, the principal focus was on the *what* and *how* of practice, not the *why*. We learned a good deal about leadership, managing personnel, budgeting, and strategic planning, for example, but the ultimate purpose of administrative behavior, that which gave it direction, remained illusive.

It was not until the early 1980s that Rapp and Poertner and several others concerned with social administration rediscovered what had become obscured in the quest to develop technically proficient managers, that is, that the purpose of human service management is to see that conditions and processes in and around the agency support the delivery of competent services that result in intended benefits for clients. This rediscovery provided the basis for a new paradigm of practice that focused attention on the relationship between what managers do and the service objectives of the organizations.

There remained the demanding task of filling out the paradigm. This is the achievement of Rapp and Poertner. They have provided us with the first relatively comprehensive model of management that traces the pathway from managerial behavior to worker empowerment and the delivery of effective services to clients. The model provides not only richly detailed guidance for administrative practitioners who seek to build client-centered agencies but an extensive array of propositions that scholars concerned with managerial effectiveness in social welfare will be studying for years to come.

The basic elements of the client-centered model of management are a program design with clearly specified service goals, objectives, and service technologies; an information system targeted to key performance indicators; a personnel system that seeks through recruitment, training, supervision and reward to mesh the needs and values of workers with the goals and objectives of the agency; and, a systematic process of resource acquisition and allocation that is guided by the program design. These components of the model are cumulative and interactive and resonate through the entire discussion. Various aspects of management are woven together in a fabric that reflects the organic nature of this practice. Moreover, at each step of the way, the authors return to the basic question: how does it help clients?

Although the book is a scholarly achievement, the authors have managed to make it eminently readable, practical, and concrete. It speaks to the reader in a personal voice that is supportive, instructive, and encouraging. The authors appreciate the complexity of agency management and confront this directly by providing the reader with helpful suggestions for dealing with the constraints and problems that are likely to be encountered as the administrator moves to create a client-centered agency. Particularly helpful is an extended treatment of strategies and tactics that can be employed to create an agency culture that enables and supports service effectiveness. Rapp and Poertner realize that in order to effect so fundamental a change in agencies, administrators must nurture a social-psychological climate congruent with the new goals and objectives.

In summary, we have here a book on management that speaks to the crucial and inseparable relationship between administrative practice and the essential service function of social agencies. It offers a way to orchestrate the efforts of managers and direct-service practitioners toward seeing that clients live happier and more fulfilled lives.

Rino J. Patti

# Preface

For most authors, the preface is written last, not first, despite its location in the book. A preface allows authors to reflect on the voyage that led to the final manuscript.

Like many books, this one grew out of our disenchantment with current writing in the field. We had developed a deep appreciation for the importance of management in both business and human services. We had been participants in and admirers of well-managed systems: management that made a positive difference in the lives of people who were both employed and served by these organizations. We had also witnessed the opposite: management that made the work life of employees miserable, disheartening, and unproductive, and programs that seemed to dehumanize, neglect, and even exacerbate the pain for which clients sought assistance.

The portrayals of "good management" in texts, in our perception, were not what was making the difference. Often these texts failed to provide specific instruction in management behavior and rather relied on general descriptions of management technology. More important, the management methods proferred by these books did not seem to derive from social work values, nor did they seem to help them operate.

Much management literature seemed to forget, ignore, or neglect the *raison d'être* of human services: the client. In fact, as we argue in Chapter 1, management literature has too often contributed to the separation of human service managers from clients and the staff who work with them. Techniques reflected those taught in business or public administration.

What, we began to ask, is distinctive about social work practice at the management level? Why should a school of social work teach administration, rather than refer its students to a school of business or public administration?

*Clients* is the answer to this question. Social workers share a defined set of values and a clear concern that clients obtain mutually determined benefits. Current human service literature fails to explain why some programs produce significant benefits for clients and others do not. The literature fails to explain how two offices, or even two teams within the same office, can affect clients in widely divergent ways.

Management texts tend to imply that knowledge of organizational theory and management methods like program budgeting, information systems, and management by objectives are determinant. Practicing managers frequently explain differences in terms of quality and size of staff, the financial stability of the program, the difficulty or uniqueness of the client population, or the amount of support provided by the chief executive of the program. But none of these factors account for the differences among programs. We have seen effective programs operated under indifferent or even hostile executives; we have seen effective programs run with virtually no resources and poorly credentialed staff. We have seen managers who have never heard of information systems use information creatively and skillfully to enhance the welfare of their clients and staff. The current literature in the field does not explain this phenomenon.

What does explain it? We propose that a lexicon like the following is what makes the difference.

| | |
|---|---|
| client-centered | fun and joy |
| learning for a living | manager as educator |
| empowerment | client outcomes |
| clients as heroes | clients as people |
| healthy disrespect for | celebrations |
|    the impossible persistence | persistence |
| flexibility/invention/ | risk-taking |
|    experimentation | management as performance |
| learning environment | vision |
| opportunity-finding | reciprocal responsibilities |
| inverted hierarchy | culture |
| program design | symbols/stories/language |
| forms as tools | reward-based environment |
| values | |

You won't find these terms playing a significant role in most current management texts. We believe that this book is different. We believe that there are ideas in this volume that extend present thinking in the field in such a way that our human service organizations can help clients in better, more efficient ways. We do this by blending specific instruction in "hard-core" management methods and technologies with attempts to make sense out of the "fuzzies" of social work management and organizational life. And all of it is done from the perspective of improving the outcomes for the people whom we serve. It is this single proposition that drives this book and provides its unifying theme.

## HOW THIS BOOK IS ORGANIZED

We have divided this book into seven chapters. The first, Client-Centered Management, describes the current state of human services management and the principles that underlie the model we propose. Chapter 2, Social Program Design, provides a step-by-step set of analytical procedures for developing human services programs. These procedures are designed to help practitioners avoid a major cause of program failure: inadequate conceptualization and design.

In Chapters 3 through 5 we look at what managers manage: information, people, and resources. Each chapter explores ideas and methods for managing in these three areas, which are keyed to enhancing client benefits.

In Chapter 6, we focus on the skills managers need to move the ideas and methods presented in the preceding chapters from the drawing board to reality. Finally, in Chapter 7, with the inverted hierarchy, we seek to integrate our model, procedures, and principles into a coherent framework for viewing the job of social work management. Included also are a handful of new ideas for which a "home" could not be found earlier in the book.

The primary audience for this book is supervisors, managers, and administrators in human services organizations, and graduate students aspiring to these positions. We make no major distinctions among supervisors, managers, and administrators, because regardless of title, these people do not directly serve clients. Their impact on clients is through the intermediary of the direct-service worker, and in some cases other levels of management. The only justification for these positions, then, is that they help front-line personnel do their jobs more effectively and efficiently than would otherwise be possible.

Management positions may have different emphases (chief executives, for example, may spend more time managing resources, while supervisors spend more time managing people). But all these positions have essentially the same purpose— to improve services to clients—and to meet that purpose, all those who occupy management positions must be skillful in program design, in managing information, people and resources, and in affecting change in organizations. For these reasons, we treat these organizational positions as if they were interchangeable.

The material in this text has formed the basis of the Social Administration curriculum at the University of Kansas School of Social Welfare for almost a decade. It has been the foundation for both course work and field practicum, and the ideas have been revised, refined, altered, and elaborated upon as a result of our work with students and agencies.

As in any effort of this scope, numerous people have influenced the conception and content of this book. Our students deserve credit for their audacity in demanding clarity and coherence in our lectures. Our students operate in a wide variety of agencies in virtually all fields of practice, and they have demanded that our teaching be applicable for all of them. Their demands were our encouragement. They urged us to write this book, and their successful application of the ideas in it to the exigencies of real life human service organizations gave us confidence. Their encouragement became our inspiration. As they graduated and assumed management positions themselves, we have been able to see their difficulty in moving their agencies to increased levels of client-centeredness, but, despite numerous obstacles, many of them have prevailed—and they have demonstrated that client-centered management will produce more humane and effective service to clients. Many of our students became our heroes.

We also owe a debt of gratitude to those social administrators who may never have heard of client-centered management. So many ideas gleaned from their practice have found their way into this text. These managers have made a profound difference in the lives of their clients, often in the face of limited resources and indifferent or unsupportive environments. Our contact with them has been based on their requests for our help through consultation, training, systems development, and so on; we only hope that we have given them half of what we received in return. Among those who taught and inspired us are Estelle Richman, Marti Knisely, Pam Hyde, Tom Wernert, Ginny Ferree, Jack Hunter, Linda Carlson, Cheryl Runyan, Leslie Young, Margaret Hayes, Phil Bruner, Sandy Vasco, Norm Jacobs, Janie Fields, and Sue Marshall.

We particularly acknowledge the contributions of Elizabeth Gowdy, Merlin Taber, and Rino Patti. Liz was both student and colleague, and much of her scholarly and professional work has been devoted to developing and refining the perspectives and methods of client-centered management. We have learned much from her. Merlin Taber was our initial management mentor at the University of Illinois and in many ways launched us on the voyage that culminates in this book. Rino Patti, Dean of the School of Social Work at the University of Southern California, is among the most respected scholars in human service management. Not only has he honored us by writing the foreword to this book, but more importantly, when we weren't sure we had anything to say, he told us that we did. He encouraged, stimulated, and helped us to become clearer about our recommendations for this complex field.

To Rosalee Neibarger, Crystal Cunningham, and Marian Abegg, many thanks for such competence and good humor while typing the seventy-second draft of each chapter.

Sue Pearlmutter deserves special recognition for writing the chapter on resource management. Based on her many years of administering social agencies which symbolize the best in client-centered management, Sue's chapter is rich in concepts and strategies for successful resource acquisition and use. Thank you, Sue, for sharing your knowledge with us and our readers.

To each of these people, our sincerest thanks, and our hopes that this book does justice to all of you.

Charles A. Rapp<br>John Poertner

# CHAPTER 1

# Client-Centered Management

This chapter describes the basic framework of client-centered performance management in the human services. The framework rests on the assumption that the principal justification for a human service agency is to improve the lives of the clients it serves. This chapter argues that the separation between managers and clients causes the program results to be less than desired. A taxonomy of human service performance is presented to help managers focus their efforts. And finally, the four principles of client-centered performance management that act as the core of the model are described with case examples.

Wanda Jones enters the building and is greeted by the receptionist with a smile and a handshake. Since she is five minutes early, the receptionist shows her to the reception area and offers her a cup of coffee. Ms. Jones glances through a recent issue of *People* magazine in a room tastefully decorated with framed pictures of children, table lamps, and comfortable chairs. A bulletin board in the waiting room contains information on other community services, jobs, and housing opportunities. To the left of the bulletin board is a one foot square wooden box with a poster above it. The poster has a group picture of the agency staff and says, "Please tell us how we could do better!" Taped to the box is a list of fifteen suggestions in which changes were made, the dates of the suggestion, and the date of the change. In all but one case the change was made within one week of the time of the suggestion.

Sally, the agency worker, comes to the waiting room, shakes hands with the client, and escorts Ms. Jones to her office. On the way, they pass Carol, the executive director, who is headed for an executive staff meeting. Carol is introduced by the worker to Ms. Jones. Carol says, "We will try to do all we can to help you, and Sarah here is one of our finest staff members. If there is anything I can do please let me know." Ms. Jones and Sally go off to Sally's office.

Entering the executive staff meeting, Joe, a new supervisor, immediately notices the smiles, energy, and courtesy with which the staff interact. Carol begins the meeting by

1

distributing the monthly reports on client outcomes. The supervisors receive reports for their teams and an agency-wide report. The next ten minutes are devoted to the executive director indicating the specific achievements by each team and expressions of appreciation. On one occasion, the entire group spontaneously and lightheartedly applauded one team's radical improvement. The director then asked that supervisor to describe the actions that contributed to such a change. Revised case review procedures, two meetings with Judge Landis, and an all day in-service training were highlighted. The other supervisors asked detailed questions about the meetings with Judge Landis with one supervisor saying that he should have similar discussions with the judge from his county.

The next agenda item was a review of last week's suggestions from clients, which had been typed on two pages and distributed to each supervisor. Two clients were concerned about the lack of evening hours and the difficulty of meeting with staff between eight and five. This issue had been raised by clients before and discussed but no changes had been made. The executive director stated that she wanted the agency opened at least four hours a week beyond five o'clock and asked the supervisors for ways it could be done. A list of obstacles was generated, and each supervisor was delegated responsibility to produce a series of solutions to each obstacle for the next meeting in two weeks. The supervisors were asked to involve as many staff as possible and to include "wild" ideas.

On the way back to her office, Carol stops for a cup of coffee and meets a staff member who had helped a woman get a job in the local shoe factory. "Congratulations on getting Martha the job. With the child care and transportation arrangements and Martha's lack of past employment, that was no small accomplishment. Would you be willing to describe the case to the board members at Friday's meeting?" The staff person said she would be happy to report her experience to the board.

Upon entering her office, Carol examines the graphs of each team's client outcomes. Based on the reports just received, she writes a few complimentary notes to staff, calls one staff member, and asks her secretary to update her graphs. She calls the board president to arrange for a staff member to make a special presentation at the next meeting.

This is a client-centered social agency. This is an agency in which clients ubiquitously intrude on managerial and organizational behavior. In this agency clients experience a pleasant waiting room and receptionists who behave more like hosts and hostesses. Suggestion boxes, client feedback cards, and client satisfaction measures are in constant use. Client goals are solicited, clarified, blended, recorded, and monitored. Clients experience program modifications to meet their individual and collective needs. Social service clients experience the agency like guests of an expensive hotel experience being pampered.

At staff meetings the social work staff smile, laugh, and attend to each other. Reports of client outcome dominate the agenda. Problems are framed in terms of removing barriers to gain a desired outcome. Budget decisions are examined in light of contributions to client welfare. Policies are adopted and evaluated in terms of client benefits. Staff learn from each other and leave meetings energized and ready to confront the next difficult case.

Imagine a social agency where clients even dominate hallway and coffee pot conversations. Signs communicating the client outcome goals of the agency are conspicuously posted. Board meetings include case examples of client successes and client outcome data, and the executive director spends time every day making sure the staff know they are special and appreciated. The manager's channeled, single-minded obsession with clients creates and maintains the agency's work environment.

Such focus is rare, however. In this chapter, we will explore what we mean by management, how management typically functions today in the realm of social work practice, and how it functions in client-centered social practice. Since the driving force of this book is client-centered management, we need first to examine just what we mean by management.

## MANAGEMENT AS PERFORMANCE

A manager's performance is virtually inseparable from the performance of the organizational unit to which the manager is assigned. We assume that managers are responsible for the performance of the domain they manage, whether it is a team, an office, an area, a program, a division, or an agency. We assume that this is why the organization is paying the manager. Rarely, therefore, do we find a "superior" manager overseeing an inadequate program, or a superior team being run by an "inferior" manager. Manager and unit are interchangeable 80 to 90 percent of the time.

This notion is prevalent in business, where excellence in top-level management is equated with organizational performance: profit, market share, growth. Sam Walton of Wal-Mart, Stephen Jobs formerly of Apple, and Lee Iaccoca of Chrysler have achieved high visibility in large part through the performance of their organizations. In *In Search of Excellence,* Peters and Waterman (1982) first identifies the high-performing companies and then finds the managers who made it happen.

The notion that management is performance is much more alien in the human services. A typical initial response is to identify factors that are seemingly beyond the influence and control of managers and that affect organizational performance. Common examples include civil service or patronage appointments; less than adequate community services; unsympathetic judges, physicians, and other gate-keepers and decision makers; and insufficient quantity or quality of staff. The most frequent response is "we don't have enough resources." For each manager the obstacles to performance are numerous and vary in terms of type of obstacle and the degree of influence. Human service managers, however, are responsible for mitigating obstacles their units confront or take them as unchangeable and seek performance despite them.

## WHAT IS HUMAN SERVICE PERFORMANCE?

If management is performance then a clear definition of human service performance is necessary. The client-centered performance model posits five performance areas: *client outcomes, productivity, resource acquisition, efficiency,* and the *job satisfac-*

*tion of employees.* The client-centered manager produces performance in each of these areas.

## 1. Client Outcomes

The centerpiece of agency and managerial performance is the benefits accrued by clients as a result of our prodigious efforts. Client outcomes seek to capture the improvement in the *client's* situation or the curbing of a deteriorating *client* situation. Client outcomes act as the bottom line of human services in much the same way profit serves business. The business executive needs to closely monitor production, acquisition of component parts, and employee morale but would never assume that happy employees who seem to be diligently working guarantees an adequate profit. In much the same way, human service managers need to perform in a variety of areas but adequate performance in these areas is neither sufficient nor a proxy for client outcomes. It is this notion that leads Patti (1985) to argue that effectiveness, meaning client outcomes, should be the "philosophical linchpin" of human service organizations.

The following taxonomy applies across human services and provides a unifying framework for human service management. It proposes five types of outcome measures: *affective changes, learning, behavior changes, status mainte-nance or change,* and *environmental modification.* Most programs are complex, producing more than one type of change. Many programs employ a theory of intervention that links changes in some way. For example, a parent education program might link changes in feelings about parenting with changes in knowledge about parenting, with both outcomes being necessary before parents can demonstrate the behavior.

*Affective Changes.*  Many people seek to change the way they feel about something or the way they emotionally respond to a situation. Historically, social workers have been concerned with this dimension. People seek to change the grief and sadness they feel after a loss such as a death or divorce. People seek to regain the feelings of love and acceptance that used to accompany a particular relationship. Occasionally society identifies the need for an affective change as in the case of the angry adolescent who is acting violently. A client's feeling of empowerment is central to many human services.

*Learning.*  People or society may seek to change the way individuals think about themselves, others, or a situation. The educational aspects of human services are quite pervasive. In an extensive review of service outcomes Taber (1980) identified cognitive changes or the educational aspects as primary in those services that seem to be effective. The parent who uses excessive physical punishment on his or her young child may think that this is the most effective way to shape the behavior of the child. Society intervenes in situations of this type to help the parent learn more effective and less harmful methods of discipline. Others seek to learn new ways of relating to their spouses or their bosses. For these types of programs, one outcome is the knowledge clients gained. Do they know more after service than they did upon entrance?

***Behavior Changes.***  Behavior change is frequently the most desired client outcome. Society has an interest in a parent ceasing to abuse his or her child and the adolescent stopping stealing car stereos. Many people seek social services to learn new behavior or eliminate troublesome behavior. Many programs for the chronically mentally ill and developmentally disabled are focused on teaching daily living and vocational skills. Urging an adolescent in foster care to acquire independent living skills or stopping someone from committing suicide are other examples.

***Status Maintenance or Change.***  Individuals and society frequently have an interest in the maintenance or change in a person's status. Older people frequently seek services that assist them with daily living activities so that they can maintain their ability to live within their home and community. Society has repeatedly expressed an interest in certain vulnerable populations such as those with mental and physical disabilities living in the most normal or least restrictive environment.

***Environmental Modifications.***  Programs can improve living conditions, change policies, or produce more constructive public attitudes and beliefs. Some scholars are uncomfortable making environmental modification a separate outcome because it could move the client's well-being away from center stage. A change in policy that does not demonstrate subsequent positive impact on clients has not been a success. A policy like the deinstitutionalization of the mentally ill, for example, was supported by some of the most client-centered people in the field, but it has led to ten to fifteen years of pain and suffering by the majority of clients. (Bassuk & Gerson, 1978) Can deinstitutionalization be considered a success? If a program improves the living conditions in an apartment complex but those improvements are not reflected by the clients in one of the four ways described above, is the program a success? In such situations should client *satisfaction* be the ultimate test rather than behavior, status, cognitive, or affective changes? We have no intention here of entering into an argument of "if the tree falls in the woods and nobody hears it, did it make a sound?" or to even argue that environmental modification itself is an adequate or inadequate criterion. These questions must yet be decided.

## 2. Productivity

Productivity is traditionally viewed as the amount of service provided and is measured in units of service. Units of service reflect program effort and imply little about the quality of the service. Every human service organization has some method for reporting the amount of service provided. Funding sources demand a certain level of activity as the *sine qua non* for continued support. It is the dominant basis for virtually all forms of funding whether through government appropriations, fees for service, or grants and contracts. Internally, managers often use this information to balance caseload sizes.

Productivity is usually identified in one of four ways: client count, service episodes, service events, and elapsed time. Client counts, the most prevalent productivity measure, give the number of individuals who receive service. Service episodes are a complete period of service provision from intake to termination. Service events are a tally of specific actions on the part of the worker, client or both, such as an interview or a home visit. Elapsed time measures productivity in terms of the amount of time devoted to service as in the case of a day of nursing home care or the number of hours in therapy.

For the client-centered performance manager, productivity data can also be used to enhance client outcomes. Identifying key service events that have produced specific client outcomes, systematically monitoring these events, and feeding back this data to staff can be a powerful method for linking worker behavior to client outcomes. The chapter on managing information will discuss this method in detail.

## 3. Resource Acquisition

A third performance area is the acquisition of resources needed by the agency to produce client benefits. A human service organization needs funds, personnel, technology, clients, and public support and influence. Top-level managers devote the majority of their time to resource acquisition activities, but even at the supervisory level, much activity is devoted to obtaining the materials needed to do the job.

Money is the lifeblood of an organization and can involve such activities as grant-writing, legislative testimony, private fund-raising, and program advocacy within a larger organization. The ability of a manager to acquire funds is currently a major criteria for performance.

Human services are labor intensive with, for example, 85 percent of mental health expenditures used for salaries and benefits. It is through the organization's personnel that clients are helped. This makes the acquisition of personnel a critical responsibility. Considerations include the number of people needed, their character-istics, and their qualifications and talents. An agency may want to recruit and hire minority staff to better match personnel with clients being served. Another agency may require a certain level of educational credentials in order to be reimbursed for services. Others may require people with particular experiences or training. Personnel may also include the use of volunteers.

Managers are also responsible for providing the information and training needed to use the most powerful helping technologies. If money is the lifeblood of a human service organization then information is its intelligence. This area would include such diverse activities as incorporating the most effective helping methods into program designs, offering preservice and continuous training of staff, providing quality supervision, and designing information systems that provide meaningful feedback to organizational personnel.

Clients are also a resource to be acquired. Any social program needs a continuous flow of "appropriate" people coming to the intake gates. Appropriate generally means that referrals are consistent with the program goals and methodologies to be used. This area requires clear expectations and good relations with referral sources, a good service reputation, accessibility of service, and clear program specifications.

A human service organization also requires high levels of public support if client outcomes are to be maximized. Public support often translates into influence, which makes it possible to alter a program's environment to better assist clients. This area involves the ability of the manager to influence the behavior of important players such as juvenile judges, physicians, or personnel in other agencies. It also involves the ability to produce more supportive policies from state and local elected officials, other agencies, and within the manager's own organization.

## 4. Efficiency

This performance area is simply a ratio between resources acquired and outcomes. The most common measure of efficiency is the dollar cost of a unit of service. The cost of a counseling hour or a day of nursing home care are frequently computed and used as a basis for funding.

Although seldom considered beyond these examples, another useful indicator of efficiency might be the ratio of clients served to the total target population. Every social program is aimed at a particular target population. Normally the service provider cannot serve all of the clients in the target group. Therefore, the percentage of the target population served is a helpful indicator of efficiency. If as a result of program changes this percentage increases, it can be said that the program is more efficient. Since clients are helped primarily while in contact with an agency person, a potentially powerful measure of efficiency would be the percentage of direct-service worker-time that is devoted to direct client or collateral contact.

## 5. Staff Morale

This performance area deals with the job satisfaction of employees. The rationale for including this as a separate dimension is that work is an important part of life for most adults in the United States. In its attempts to help clients, the social service organization should concurrently contribute to the personal satisfaction and fulfillment of its employees. The recent attention to burnout among human service personnel testifies to this concern. While the evidence linking job satisfaction and productivity is equivocal; there are few attempts to link job satisfaction and the outcome for clients. One recent study does link burnout with workers' perceptions of their clients. (Corcoran, 1986) As expected those who experienced a higher level of burnout had less positive impressions of clients. It is difficult to imagine a tired, angry, cynical front-line worker facilitating improved client outcomes. If management is judged by performance, and performance equals client outcomes, productivity, resource acquisitions, efficiency, and staff morale, do social practice managers measure up? Unfortunately, the answer is too often "no."

## THE SEPARATION OF MANAGEMENT AND CLIENTS

The separation of management from clients characterizes current management practice. Buttressed by management theory and methods, management education programs, and public tolerance, human service managers have been systematically separated from the clients they are charged to serve. Miringoff (1980) states,

> As social welfare has grown, there has been an increasing recognition that management is needed, but such management has often been perceived, even by its own practitioners, as an activity almost divorced from the quality of service itself. In this view management is concerned almost exclusively with an organization's maintenance and political functioning; the quality and substance of service provided is seen to be outside the purview of management. Hence managerial measures of efficiency and budgetary concerns have often been viewed by service practitioners as being counterproductive to service delivery. (p. 10)

The separation of clients and management occurs despite the practice of promoting the best direct service staff to managerial levels. The separation is pervasive, shaping what managers do and how they do it.

### Common Manifestations of Management/Client Separation

*Goals.* The establishment of organizational or unit goals is a universally accepted task of management. The goals of a human service organization are to achieve "the desired and intended ends." (Etzioni, 1964) "The ultimate purpose or goal of human service organizations is by definition some form of benefit for the persons being serviced." (Neugeboren, 1985, p. 27) The current goal-setting practice, however, is dominated by means not ends. The most common form of goals begins with "to provide" or "to teach" or "to establish." These kinds of statements speak to the means the program will use to attain some yet unmentioned client benefit. For example, the goal of "to teach 30 parents nonphysical methods of discipline" can be easily achieved by a person lecturing to 30 parents for a couple of hours. But it does not suggest the real purpose, which could be that the parents actually learn the techniques or that a parent actually uses the techniques or that the children are not abused.

Another prevalent goal-setting practice is to state goals in abstract and lofty terms by using such phrases as "best interest of the child," or "improved quality of life." Some argue that this practice is politically wise since "under the umbrella of pietistic generalities, diverse interests can form working alliances as if there were agreement." (Gruber, 1986, p. 3) Unfortunately, such political "wisdom" does not seem to hold in practice. Human services are still attacked for being ineffective and self-serving. Platitudes, in fact, can be used against an organization if it has not fulfilled its promises. (Hasenfeld, 1983) The juvenile court's use of the "best interests of the child" standard has in no way reduced criticism of the court's functioning and in some places it has been exacerbated. Furthermore, frontline practitioners tend to minimize the importance of goals. (Neugeboren, 1985)

The current goal-setting practice of separating client and manager led Perrow (1978) to describe the goals of human service organizations as regulating deviants, absorbing part of the workforce, and providing resources to other organizations. Managerial effectiveness, he says, is based on the following:

> the growth of her or his organization, the size of the budget, the contracts with elites, the accommodations it has with other powerful organizations, and the number of programs it has . . . extracting resources from a sometimes stingy environment, delivering goods to interested parties without having scandals, and meeting at a minimal level—the ongoing rate for the locality—the official goals of the agency. (pp. 113–115)

*Daily Agency Practices.* The separation of managers and clients can be seen through a manager's actual behavior. The examination of manager's behavior has produced few insights. (Mintzberg, 1973; Patti, 1977) Lewis and Stewart's (1958) assessment seems to be as accurate today as it was thirty years ago: "We know more about the motives, habits and most intimate arcana of the primitive peoples of New Guinea or elsewhere, than we do of the denizens of the executive suites. . . ." (p. 17) Given the lack of helpful, systematic results, a few common examples of management practice will have to suffice.

One event common to virtually all human service organizations is the staff meeting. Most of these meetings are dominated or exclusively focused on policies and procedures, paperwork compliance, staff questions, funding concerns, and a variety of announcements. The relationship between these issues and clients, or specific discussions of "how well we are doing" in terms of clients is rare. Managers usually set the agendas.

Every agency has an information system to collect, store, and retrieve data on service operations. The manager is the one who works with system technicians to design the system. Managers use information system products to evaluate their agency's performance. These systems are inevitably dominated by financial and productivity (e.g., amount of service provided, number of clients served) data. Rarely does an agency information system collect and systematically report on client outcomes.

Most agencies have some procedure for employee performance appraisal. Few agencies use a results-oriented method of appraisal (Wiehe, 1980). Lawler, Mohrmon, and Resnick (1985) in a study of performance appraisal in a large corporation reported large discrepancies between the appraiser's perception and the appraisee's perception of an event. The person being appraised reported being a passive recipient whose needs were not met. The supervisor reported a positive, helpful event where important concerns were discussed. When describing this study to groups of social workers in agencies, affirmative nods and smiles of recognition are the rule. When asked if they have experienced a really positive and helpful performance appraisal, no more than one hand in thirty is raised.

Current supervisory practice seems to fare no better. Since the late 1930s, the principal focus of supervision has shifted from the case to the worker. (Burns, 1958) The notion is that by supporting and educating the worker, clients will be better assisted. Unfortunately the evidence suggests that worker perceptions of supervisory helpfulness are not associated with planning cases or developing practice skills (Shulman, Robinson, & Lucky, 1981), that worker satisfaction with supervision is uncorrelated with worker performance (Olmstead & Christensen, 1974), and that case discussions may be the smaller part of supervision. (Kadushin, 1974; Munson, 1979). In fact, Shulman, Robinson, and Lucky (1981) found case consultation representing only 43 percent of supervision, and Kadushin (1974) found that case discussion-dominated supervision was practiced by less than 20 percent of the supervisors.

*The Management Research.* The management literature fares no better. A recent review of the literature in human service management found that less than half of the articles contained *any* mention of an outcome variable. (Rapp, Hardcastle, Rosenzweig, & Poertner, 1982) In only 7 percent of the articles was a dependent variable related to client outcomes—the assumed reason for the agency's existence.

> The sampled literature, in its selection of dependent variables, often ignored the centrality of organizational performance as the crucible of management. It assumed the topic being presented was worthwhile if it was logical, reasonable, and had some relationship to organizations or human services. A higher standard than this is needed for management research so that we don't reify the means without considering the ends. (p. 97)

Supervision has had a hallowed position in social work for almost a century. Despite this stature, there has only been one study that seeks to ascertain the effects supervisory behavior has on client outcomes. This study found that supervisory behavior may in fact have a positive affect on client outcomes (Harkness, 1987). This finding makes it all the more disappointing that researchers have not found this area futile ground for study.

## Consequences of Manager/Client Separation

The separation between manager and client has had severe consequences. It has produced chronic and acute goal displacement whereby the means of an organization become its end. "Thus the activities that the organization engages in (interviewing clients, supervising staff, managerial tasks such as budgeting and personnel selection, etc.) are used as criteria to judge the success of the organization." (Neugeboren, 1985, p. 28) Concern for survival or program expansion and the loss of purpose characterize this process. Helfgot's (1974) description of the Mobilization for Youth project and Scott's (1967) discussion of sheltered workshops for the blind both trace this concern nicely.

Another result of the separation has been managers frequently engaging in reactive management practice, premature embracing of "sexy" new management practices that consume large amounts of resources before they atrophy and are discarded. They employ problem-solving modes that seem to solve problems but which never seem to lead to improved performance. The separation of management and clients also is a primary reason why management is seen as either irrelevant or as an obstacle to better service delivery in so many agencies. Management continues to be seen as a major contributor to low morale and job satisfaction, and a major source of "burnout." (Karger, 1981)

The most profound consequence is felt by clients. Clients bring their problems, needs, pain, and suffering to the human service agency seeking help, direction, relief, and an increased sense of control and power. Too often their feelings of impotence are exacerbated in the face of rules, policies, and protocols seemingly unresponsive to their problems. At times the process is dehumanizing whether because of the physical setting or because of personnel behavior. Too often our services are ineffective; they fail to produce benefits for the clients.

In terms of the social work profession, the separation of managers and clients has had a profound impact. Patti (1985) writes:

> Administration has never been fully accepted in social work in part, I suspect, because the goals of this method have been perceived, rightly or wrongly, as either in conflict with, or only tangentially related to, the profession's main business of changing people and social conditions. The intellectual and educational distance between administration and direct practice, always uncomfortably large, promises to grow even larger as those who teach and practice administration become increasingly preoccupied with such things as management control and efficiency improvement. (pp. 4–5)

The profession continues to be unable to exploit its marginal advantage over other management disciplines (e.g., public or business administration) in terms of its knowledge of clients, programs, and service systems. The profession is unable to muster the data necessary to recommend that social workers are the preferred leadership for human service organizations. The increasing intrusion of graduates from business and public administration into management positions within the human services reflects a major threat to the profession and to services. The small cadre of M.S.W. students enrolled in management specializations and the continued tension between clinical and management social workers does not augur well for the future leaders of human services. (Patti, 1985)

## Contributing Factors

The separation of clients and managers has been provoked by three major factors: (1) a *misguided response to threats,* the continued legacy of the 1970s retrenchment;

(2) the *multiple constituencies dilemma;* and (3) *politics as diversion,* the importance of political effectiveness.

***Misguided Response to Threats.*** Administration and social work have historically been reluctant partners. Despite rhetorical support since the earliest days of the profession, administration as a valued and respected specialty within social work has been slow to occur. Administration was thought of as an extension of social casework in terms of values and methods with a resultant emphasis on enabling individuals and groups in the agency to increase their respective contributions through democratic processes. (Trecker, 1946) The focus became facilitating interpersonal skills of staff, and the prominent theoretical and methodological tools were derived from the human relations school of management. "The unique character of social work administration was thought to flow from its central preoccupation with quality of service, as reflected in the "adequacy of benefits and services, client-centeredness, professional competencies, effectiveness of programs, and efficiency of operations." (Kidneigh, 1950, p. 57)

This view of management, based on the strengths of social work and closely aligned with its core beliefs, became eroded as the society and the profession responded to the turmoil of the 1970s. The phenomenal growth of the social welfare enterprise in the 1960s, buoyed by an optimistic belief that the economy would continue to grow, was stopped by the reality that economic growth and social welfare would not and could not continue to be unbridled. The politics of scarcity brought with it new priorities and a new language: efficiency, cost effectiveness, accountability, program evaluation. Management technologies like PPBS, management by objectives, zero-based budgeting, PERT, cost-benefit analysis, and management information systems began to be seen as indispensable for the competent human service administrator. These tools were all developed in industry and the military. They were not a part of social work curricula and were seen as alien in many ways to social work; they were the proper province of M.B.A. and M.P.A. programs. Administrative jobs under civil service were declassified—no longer to require social work training. The result was the increased hiring of nonsocial workers in critical managerial positions.

The response of the profession was to significantly increase the number of specialized administration programs within schools of social work. By 1976, over half of the schools reported such a specialization. Many of the programs, however, were joint programs with M.B.A. or M.P.A. programs or replicated these courses in social work programs. These management technologies were not evaluated for their usefulness. They were adopted without regard to the unique needs of human service organizations.

These developments have driven a wedge between managers and clients. This technological perspective eschews humanitarian values in favor of rationalism. Social work has not been able to infuse this point of view with the value that the client is paramount. The uncritical acceptance of these managerial methods has led to the blurring of distinctions between managers who are trained social workers and those who have general management training. The technological perspective also reinforces the notion that human service managers are different from the professionals delivering the service. The agendas, the language, the priorities are different. So the wedge is not only between social administrator and clients but social administrator and direct-practice social workers.

*Multiple Constituency Dilemma.* Human service organizations are embedded in a larger political and economic environment that serves as a second major force in separating clients and managers. "The organization is an arena in which various interest groups, external and internal, possessing resources needed by the organization, compete to optimize their values through it." (Hasenfeld, 1983, p. 44) These political struggles have profound effects on the design and operation of the organizations. (Perlmutter, 1984; Zald, 1970)

One way to view the political influences is in terms of the multitude of parties that make demands upon the manager. Figure 1–1 delineates these relationships. Internal constituencies include staff, support and maintenance staff, other managers, and agency clients. External constituencies include government officials, local elected officials, courts, private agencies, employee unions, the media, and private citizens. Each of these groups needs to have their expectations met in some fashion.

Some have argued that human service organizations are not really "the rational instruments of announced goals." (Perrow, 1978, p. 105) Instead,

> announced goals are one of the least important constraints on organizational behavior; organizations can be rational instruments of announced goals only to a very limited extent. They have more important things to do. Instead, organizations are resources for a variety of group interests within and without the organization; they are used by a multitude of interests, and the announced purposes, while they must be met to some limited degree in most cases, largely serve as a legitimating device for these interests, or a mystification of the reality. (p. 106)

For example, well-established community mental health agencies are guaranteed a certain amount of clients and dollars without the benefit of well-established and tested programs. The closing of a major mental hospital will be resisted if an area's economy is dependent on it. The federal government has traditionally required states to feed them mountains of information, little of which is actually used. The result, however, is the maintenance of jobs for federal employees. Reduction in work force is always resisted by employee unions and others.

The human service manager is also responsible for juggling the demands and expectations of internal constituencies, such as staff and the board. Upper management levels expect the middle manager to get favorable or no media attention, stay within budget allocations, and consistently provide accurate information on a wide range of program operations. Common expectations of staff include salary and fringe benefits, comfortable offices, opportunities for professional growth and career advancement, prestige, adequate secretarial support, freedom to

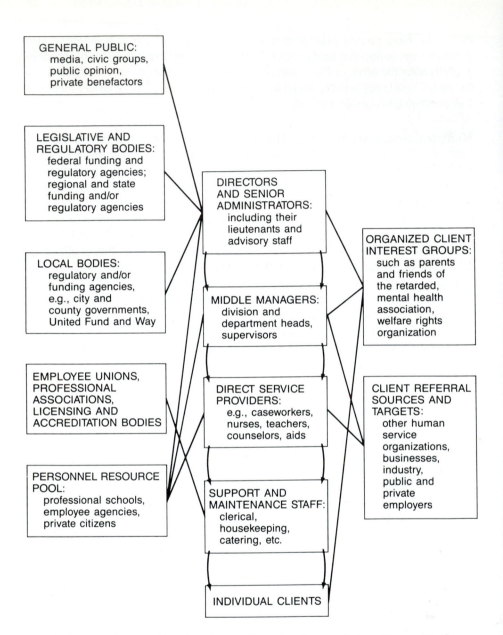

**Figure 1–1.** Relationships Among Constituencies (Source: Patricia Yancey Martin, "Multiple Constituencies, Dominant Social Values, and the Human Service Administrator: Implications for Service Delivery," *Administration in Social Work*, Vol. 4(2), Summer 1980, p. 17.)

use the skills and perspectives they bring to the job, reasonable caseloads, and participation in agency decisions that will affect their work life. The professional interests of staff frequently diverge from agency and client interests. The professional desire for autonomy confronts the organizational need for some level of control and consistency. Staff and client agendas conflict over working hours and service setting. Evenings and weekends are often more convenient for clients yet staff tend to desire the more standard eight to five hours. Service effectiveness can often be enhanced if staff visit clients' homes and workplaces yet staff often desire their work to take place in their offices. As Slavin (1980) notes:

> The administrator of a social agency always functions in a dynamic field of forces in which conflicting constituency interests contest for attention and response. The varying pressures and demands that result place powerful constraints on administrative authority. Power and influence tend to be unequally distributed among constituencies and make purely rational behavior by administrators problematical. Organizational-maintenance needs contend with the perceived requirements of clients and practitioners. (p. 13)

The human service manager is confronted with myriad constituencies who make demands on the organization. Clients are but one of these groups—and in terms of power, they are usually the most impotent. While the list can be easily extended, the major point we want to make is

EVERY MANAGER IS CONFRONTED WITH
A HOST OF CONSTITUENCIES,
EACH OF WHOM MAKES DEMANDS
WHICH ARE OFTEN UNSUPPORTIVE OF
OR INCOMPATIBLE WITH
OR IRRELEVANT TO
ORGANIZATIONAL GOAL ATTAINMENT AND CLIENT WELFARE.

These demands can and often do act as obstacles or diversions to performance. But human service programs hire and pay their managers to perform despite the particular array of obstacles each confronts, and this holds true from upper management through frontline supervisors. The difference between high-performing, client-centered managers and poor-performing managers may be that the high performers continue to be performance oriented despite the constraints.

***Politics as Diversion.*** The ubiquity of politics has led some to argue that political effectiveness is of primary importance to client outcomes as a measure of managerial performance. (Gruber, 1986) The focus of the political effectiveness criterion is often on survival (Perlmutter, 1984; Perlmutter, 1985–86) or maintenance management (Miringoff, 1980).

There are several problems with the political effectiveness school of management performance. First, it fails to recognize that the demands made by the external constituencies are often unsupportive of or incompatible with or irrelevant to client well-being. In our quest for "survival" or positive opinion by elites (Perrow, 1978), we may waste precious time that could be better spent helping clients, or more importantly, we could be unwittingly joining a coalition that will harm clients.

The political effectiveness school directs the protective service supervisor to please the judge, the district attorney, and the police. This supervisor is torn between placing children in foster care and overspending the foster care allocation. This supervisor is torn between workers' demands that a petition be filed on Johnny Jones and the district attorney's refusal to do so. The protection of children and the rights of parents somehow never get adequate attention, and children may be physically harmed or families inappropriately disrupted. The survival or mainte-nance-managed organization "does not necessarily help clients nor alleviate social problems nor contribute to the survival and development of the social welfare institution." (Miringoff, 1980, p. 9)

The literature on client outcome or rational management virtually ignores the influence and importance of organizational environments on performance and the role of the manager in this arena (Millar & Millar, 1981) or simplistically asserts that if effective with clients, environmental support will be forthcoming. (Turem, 1974; Briar, 1973) The political manager school ignores consideration of client well-being or implicitly assumes that if we survive as a program, clients will be helped.

## PRINCIPLES OF CLIENT-CENTERED MANAGEMENT*

The distinctions between managers and politicians are becoming increasingly blurred. (Aberbock, Putnam, & Rockman, 1981) The interaction with an organiza-tion's multiple constituencies is a major task of management requiring considerable skills. (Gummer, 1984) But it is also true that the *raison d'être* of the social administrator is client well-being and that the principal task of the manager is to facilitate that well-being. These perspectives need not be viewed as competing. The challenge of the client-centered manager is therefore to make clients' welfare the centerpiece of political activity. The authors contend that managers will be better politicians as well as better facilitators of client well-being once the two sets of perspectives are blended.

The principle task of management theory, methods, education, and practice is to breach the current chasm between clients and managers. Solving intractable social problems with inadequate resources that depend on satisfying everyone is an impossible assignment. Yet the vision of the client-centered agency described at the beginning of this chapter is within reach of most social administrators. A model of

---

*Much of this section has been based on a monograph, *Managerial Behavior: The Common Denominators of Effective Community-Based Programs* by Elizabeth A. Gowdy and Charles A. Rapp, published by the University of Kansas School of Social Welfare, 1988.

social administration should demonstrate that the ideal can be created out of current realities and a set of attitudes that directs the administrator in managing the client-centered agency. The following four principles of client-centered performance management are the foundation required to build the ideal. They form the basis for the management tasks and technologies that are discussed in the remaining chapters.

## Principle #1: Venerating the People Called Clients

Managers play a key role in communicating the values of the program to those who use it, those who work for it, and to the community in which it operates. Whether consciously or unconsciously, managers communicate, in their daily words and actions, how people will be viewed and treated by the program. Managers whose programs show effective results for those it serves are managers who create helping environments wherein consumers are seen and treated humanely—as people and less like patients or clients, or welfare mothers, or prisoners. (Gowdy & Rapp, 1989) They are seen as "whole" people; each individual has a life beyond the program, comprised of a variety of interests, relationships, and histories. While a mental disability, for example, might bring a person to a mental health center, that person is much more than "a schizophrenic." He or she is a person who happens to experience schizophrenia, along with many other life events.

Central to seeing people as individuals is the view that people have strengths and can grow and change over time. This belief embraces the whole experience of a person and is not limited to defining the person as "client" only. A strengths perspective (Rapp, in press; Weick, Rapp, Sullivan, & Kisthardt, 1989) is directly related to seeing people as individuals since knowing the unique wholeness of a person necessarily includes knowing his or her special strengths, abilities, and resources. From such a perspective, individuals are valued and respected for their ability to survive and adapt, and there is a sense of hope regarding each person's capacity to continue to learn and develop over time in relationship with others.

How do managers view people as having strengths and abilities? How do managers reflect the value that people are unique, are whole individuals with lives beyond their connection to the program? *First, they know the people who use the program*—they know their stories, their history, their families. They are on a first-name basis with clients and know the details of their lives. They can talk specifically about strengths, interests, and needs of the people in the program and can relate stories about many of them with warmth and excitement. There is a courtesy, a friendliness between staff and clients, and even joy in some programs. These managers model a behavior and demand the same from their staff.

*Second, they promote the idea that clients are heroes*. Their achievements, in the face of numerous obstacles and barriers, should be viewed as truly Herculean. Their resiliency is in itself a cause for a celebration of the human spirit whether it's the young single mother trying to care for her children on meager welfare subsidies, or the abused child trying to adapt to a new family, new school, and new friends, or a blind person trying to compete with nondisabled people in the workplace. These managers help their staffs to remember clients as heroes even while confronting the often chaotic and frustrating job demands. Award ceremonies for clients and pictures of clients and their achievements become regular parts of agency operation.

*Third, they manifest a client advocacy perspective toward their own jobs.* The paradox confronting the human service manager is that client welfare is the central purpose of the organization and its reason for being, but clients, who are usually the least powerful, are only one of many constituencies making demands upon the organization and manager. This paradox requires the manager to choose the client. The "client perspective becomes the focal point of orientation whereby both organization, managers and practitioners are constrained to pursue their interests in light of their impact on the integrity of client services." (Slavin, 1980, p. 16)

The manager-as-client-advocate rests not only on an ethical justification but also on pragmatic considerations. A human service manager is in a unique position to act as a client advocate because of three indispensable attributes: *formal authority to act, control over resources,* and *control over information.* (Richan, 1980) Formal authority is intrinsic to the manager's role and codified in job descriptions, policies and procedures, and tables of organization. This authority provides an increment of predisposition by others to be influenced by the manager. A manager also has control and access to resources. Managers tend to have access to a variety of people whose influence can be brought to bear to further support a client's cause. They also have responsibility for the acquisition and allocation of resources such as money and time.

While formal authority and control over resources are critically important to advocacy efforts, they are constrained in part because the manager is still largely dependent on others for these assets; they can be taken away or undermined. (Richan, 1980) The manager's control over information, however, is less susceptible to outside influence. Kaufman (1973) identified myriad internal sources of information available to the manager and therefore the manager has great control over what gets communicated to whom. (Wager, 1972) The manager also has more contact and sanction to interact with external constituencies and has more responsibility for the design and operation of formal information systems. It is the manager, therefore, who has the most control over the use of the power of information.

This fact has led Taber and Finnegan (1980) to propose a definition of human service accountability that places information as its centerpiece: "the process of providing adequate and relevant information to each party . . . in such a way as they can fulfill their role within the program." (p. 1) Simply, do funders have the information needed to allocate money to the program in a way that enhances client welfare? Do staff have adequate information to do their jobs effectively? Do referral sources have clear information about the services and client population to be served? Does the information system provide meaningful information to a variety of internal and external constituencies?

Control over information is a potent attribute of the manager-as-client-advocate, whether as social action and confrontational strategies (Ohlin, Coates, & Miller, 1974) or, more prevalently, as the basis for educational approaches.

Together with formal authority and control over resources, control over information places the manager in a uniquely powerful position to enhance client-centered human services.

## Principle #2: Creating and Maintaining the Focus

The organization that performs is the one that has clearly defined its mission, purpose, and performance and commits all its knowledge, resources, and talents to getting it done. The high-performance agency is conscientiously myopic and single-minded. It systematically excludes the irrelevant and limits the domain of organizational concern. Basically, *the performers* set out to do one or two things and to do them well. For the client-centered performance manager that focus is defined in terms of clients and client outcomes.

### NORM

The regional office of a state child welfare agency with the lowest use of out-of-home placement was also the site of the most economically disadvantaged city. Questions seeking to understand this finding were repeatedly answered, "Norm." A visit to the office and with Norm found an administrator who repeatedly reviewed every case of a child in placement. Norm was always asking "What will it take to return Karen home? When will Joey be adopted? When will Susan go home?" The persistent attention to permanency produced consistently superior results.

### DANE COUNTY MENTAL HEALTH

Not long ago, the Dane County, Wisconsin, Mental Health Center singled out chronically mentally ill patients and gave almost exclusive attention to reducing inpatient hospitalization among this population. The county spent over 80 percent of its budget on chronic patients. A broad-based, multi-agency system of community care developed. The result, only 17 percent of its mental illness dollars are spent on inpatient care compared to a national average of 70 percent. Rehospitalizations have been virtually eliminated. Approximately 25 percent of patients discharged from hospitals are readmitted within a year compared to the national average of 60 percent. It is important to note that this nationally recognized program for chronic psychiatric patients is not especially well endowed with funds to run a model program. In fact, Dane County receives less than the average Wisconsin county per capita for its mental health programming. As Disraeli penned, "Success is a product of unremitting attention to purpose."

The examples above suggest the following rules:

1. Selecting and establishing an organizational focus is the job of management.
2. The focus should be defined in terms of client outcomes.
3. Defining a focus requires *the elimination* of other potentially worthwhile goals and activities.
4. Defining a focus requires a *commitment,* a preoccupation, an obsession with achieving that focus.

The last rule deserves explanation. The cognitive possession of a focus is of little importance if it cannot be translated into behavior. A focus on maintenance of community placement and improved independent living status for persons with severe mental illness, for example, means that meetings and memos are dominated by discussion of relevant issues, obstacles, and successes; that rewards are based on increases in maintenance of community placements; that data is distributed that speaks to independent living status change. It means that once maintenance of community placement is established as a priority, it can be reinforced constantly and consistently by managerial behavior. The criteria becomes how will this meeting contribute to lower rates of rehospitalization? Even "coffee pot" conversations are opportunities for the manager to ask about how "John is doing since he was matched with a volunteer and began attending the psychosocial club" or to express pleasure at some recent performance. The focus must dominate a manager's thinking and allow him or her to apply intelligence, skills, and resources to its enhancement.

## Principle #3: A Healthy Disrespect for the Impossible

Human services suffer from a chronic lack of funds, staff, community interest, and public support. This lack of resources is simultaneously coupled with incessant demands from the program's multiple constituencies. (Martin, 1980) Thus, a manager's daily work life is often typified by a continual stream of needs and demands from consumers, staff, funders, providers, courts, regulatory agents, and advocates. There are deadlines to meet, reports and grants to be written, meetings to attend, phone calls to take, questions to be answered, and crises to attend to.

In the face of such a chaotic milieu, managers seem to evidence two responses: they surrender to such constraints and be satisfied maintaining the status quo, or they persist in finding opportunities to improve the program in the midst of chaos. *Both groups may work equally hard, but they work differently.* The effective managers are those who take the second course of action. Rather than remain inactive behind excuses of "not enough money," "not enough time," or "not enough staff" exceptional managers are those who say, "This is needed. Let's make it happen." They are people who instill a "make do" attitude in the workplace, in which program participants and staff become actively involved in making good things transpire in the face of seemingly overwhelming odds. As such, the manager removes barriers to action: needless procedures, policies, meetings, and processes. The manager is willing to go with a promising idea and willing to drop one that hasn't worked, yet is pleased with the attempt. As Franklin D. Roosevelt stated, "But above all, try *something*." The results of this perspective are programs that are flexible and changing, sprouting innovations based on emerging consumer needs.

Five characteristics seem to be at the root of these action-oriented managers:

1. A perception of self as powerful and responsible in the situation at hand
2. Flexibility and invention based on a clear focus on people's needs
3. Highly developed problem-solving skills with a premium on partializing
4. The ability to blend agendas of seemingly disparate interests
5. Persistence (Gowdy & Rapp, 1989)

*Perception of Self.*  An individual manager's perception of self in relation to his or her environment is central to "disrespecting the impossible." It was clear in the language and actions of effective managers that they perceive themselves (and their programs) as personally responsible for meeting the current and fluctuating needs of those they serve. Coupled with their sense of responsibility is their sense of personal power to meet the need; these managers are people who feel capable and hopeful and who believe in their ability to make a difference in a given situation.

This contrasts starkly with managers who defer their power to some external obstacle, who "pass the buck" or "go by the book," saying, "that is not my area of authority," "nice idea, but . . . ," "we should study that first in committee," "if only we had the money, the staff, a supportive executive and board." Such remarks reveal tendencies toward passivity that come from a sense of powerlessness within one's environment. (Kanter, 1979; Kanter & Stein, 1985) This is saddening to see in managerial positions, for if a program's leaders evidence powerlessness in their lives, how can we expect a staff and consumers to do any differently? In fact, frontline staff members' perception of power and influence was found to parallel that of their supervisor or manager. (Gowdy & Rapp, 1989) A sense of power is highly contagious.

*Flexibility and Invention.*  Another characteristic of successful managers is flexibility and invention based on a clear focus of people's needs and goals. One manager calls it "tiptoeing around the edges" where solutions are found to obstacles often contrived by organizations. For instance, a manager of a community support program was successful in setting up an arrangement with the local family support group to hold funds for projects for participants. This gets around the barrier that the nonprofit mental health center cannot sponsor "for profit" activities wherein participants make and sell some product in the community. Thus, the manager "tiptoes around the edge" by having participants present project proposals to the family group, which then provides seed money. Any profits from the project are then returned to the family group to be held for future needs, and everyone is satisfied.

*Problem-Solving Skills.*  Foremost among the skills needed for a healthy disrespect for the impossible is the use of a problem-solving approach to one's practice. While it starts with a sense of individual responsibility, power, and flexibility, it moves quickly to skills of partializing. In this way, seemingly overwhelming projects become a series of manageable steps completed over time. The ability of effective managers to "break it down and do it" seems to flow logically from their positive approach to their work, in which problems are reframed into opportunities or challenges. Although one may want to deny or escape a situation seen as problematic, an event perceived as an opportunity is infinitely more approachable.

*Blending Disparate Agendas.*  These same managers have an ability to blend the agendas of seemingly disparate interests without compromising the welfare of clients. Furthermore, they seem to do this by using generic social work skills, such as attending to multiple constituents, determining the basic needs of each audience, maximizing need satisfaction, and reframing. They can be seen doing this in interactions with staff and external constituencies, in designing programs, and in developing information systems and using its products. They are persuasive; they listen and take seriously what they hear and perceive.

*Persistence.* Another key to the healthy disrespect-for-the-impossible principle is an almost blithe indifference to feedback that something cannot be done. There is, among effective managers, an inability or even stubbornness to take "no" for an answer. Such persistence is a hallmark of their practice and seems born from their sense of responsibility, enthusiasm, and belief in people. Their ability to persist in seeing projects through also stems from the use of a step-by-step, problem-solving approach to their work. The proclivity to do a "little bit" each day lends itself to feeling capable of "seeing something through" much more than when one is overwhelmed by an apparently massive project.

The following case example demonstrates how managers are using this management principle in their practices. The case illustrates the dynamic interaction of the five elements comprising the principle, which allows one to gain a more complete understanding of the synergistic qualities of the skills this principle requires.

### CARLSON AND THE BOARDING HOME

Linda Carlson created community-based services where none previously existed for people with long-term mental illness residing in a rural boarding home.

It all started with a phone call from the state hospital, telling Linda about a small boarding home in a tiny town thirty miles from her program. The home had changed ownership, and people were being discharged from the hospital to this residence. Despite a clubhouse program staff of only two, Linda never questioned her responsibility and interest in getting services to these people. It was also a given that the boarding home manager was initially hesitant and defensive about an "outsider" coming in with offers of assistance. Linda's approach was to start slow.

We had a large dance with their people and our people. The manager was there, and I chatted with her at the dance. The next call I got was, "What are you doing?" because we were talking about using volunteers to do some social activities so I could do case management, and we had chatted briefly about that. She didn't know what was going on, so I wrote her a letter of explanation, and we set up a time to talk about it.

I went down there, and she didn't show up. I then wrote a letter going over what had happened and sent copies to the hospital and Ronna (state community mental health office) because I thought it was important we started communicating. She wrote back, saying it wasn't her understanding we had a meeting, and she had the option of not showing up. That was fine. We set a date and had the meeting. I asked her, "What are your concerns?" She said I was overbearing. I said, "I really appreciate your feedback. I don't realize I'm doing those things. What is important to me is that these people are getting served, and we need to write out a plan." Through the process, we talked out all the different issues. Working together was the best thing that ever happened.

Through a series of meetings Linda and the boarding home manager worked out a mutual plan to provide case management and social activities to residents. They also discussed increasing services over time and the use of volunteers.

That boarding home had had a bad reputation and that's why she was concerned about volunteers coming in from the community. We talked about how that would help the reputation rather than harm it. I was sure to say, "I want and need your input." I'd write a synopsis of every meeting I went down for, including the basics of what I was working on with the people (boarding home residents) and what we did together.

We also planned a meeting in Columbus with the Family Life Center since the people at the boarding home go to the psychiatrist there, even though the home is in our county. So, what's going to happen is that when they go to Columbus to see the psychiatrist, Pat Shipman will have a support group for them on that day. Also, when I was in Chetopa last week working with case management, the manager called and said she was going to bring five or six people up to the CSP every week! I said, "Wonderful, the more the better!"

This "problem" started when neither community program could get the clients involved in either program, and in the course of a few months, Linda had successfully started a cluster of support services: individual case management with three people; social and recreational activities with five or six people; medication maintenance; a support group; and clubhouse involvement once a week. How did she do it? Step-by-step, using resources at hand, devoting some time, influencing and paying attention to various key people, blending agendas, and keeping a direct focus on the need to reach out to some isolated individuals. Not taking no for an answer and feeling like something needed to be done, Linda set out to do it, with nothing more than determination, persistence, and hope. And she made something from "nothing."

## Principle #4: Learning for a Living

Managers are challenged to continue learning more effective ways of helping people throughout their work lives. The ability and desire to self-assess and self-correct one's practice, on both individual and program levels, is central to professional practice. Given that we live in an "information age" where almost daily new practice and research information is disseminated, it is imperative that managers remain open to new ideas and feedback about how to work effectively. At the same time information is coming from outside the program, rich sources of information about how to work more effectively exist within the program, for example, getting feedback from program participants, family members, self, and staff. The ability to observe, evaluate, and learn from the process of daily helping interactions is as important to effective management as learning from external sources.

Managers whose programs show effective results are those who seem to "learn for a living" rather than "work for a living." (Gowdy & Rapp, 1989) They actively seek out input and feedback on program performance from program participants, staff, publications, performance reports, funders, and consultants. Their programs are open to visitors and observers; their offices are open to continual streams of clients and staff; their conversations are laced with stories about what they have learned from reflecting upon their own practice. These managers evidence the critical skills of learning, including a total lack of defensiveness about evaluating their work; a drive to critically examine minute helping interventions and decisions to glean their impact; and the ability to brainstorm with others so truly creative ideas can be identified and pursued.

*Open to Experimentation.* Rather than deifying existing practice interventions or program models, these managers are people who approach life with the question, "What can I learn today?" They are open to experimentation. They create learning environments for their staff by paying attention to client-outcome data (see case study), by constantly putting the work of the program under a critical (but nonblaming) microscope, by encouraging contact with a diversity of people, and by providing support for risk-takers.

One component of the principle "learning for a living" includes managerial activities that "put the work under a microscope." This is a real commitment to critically evaluating minute practice interventions and practice behaviors. This is not an overly conscious decision as much as an automatic or reflex response to the managers' real desires to understand and learn from a situation.

Underlying the examination of daily work is the realization that neither helping nor learning occurs in a vacuum; just as clients often use the helping relationship to learn new behaviors and skills, the effective manager helps staff learn from their work through the supervisory relationship. They realize learning will not occur magically. They help others learn by reviewing the work together. These managers pay serious attention to the daily process of program performance as it unfolds in the relationships of consumers and workers. That is what is meant by putting the work under the microscope—unremitting attention to the critical details.

Learning managers act as if every event were an opportunity to teach. They see their jobs as teachers in classrooms without walls. Look, for example, at Cheryl Runyan, former director of the Horizon Mental Health Center Community Support Program in Hutchinson, Kansas. Ms. Runyan almost singlehandedly transformed the entire town of Hutchinson into a community support program for people with severe mental illness by educating citizens and professionals about the needs of her clients. Hutchinson residents who have been educated range from convenience store managers and police officers to employers, service providers, church members, physicians, and community college students. Education was a primary strategy for changing the system and organizing the community.

Leslie Young uses information about clients' vocational and living statuses to reexamine current programming with Karen Croman, her residential program director. As she talks, it becomes apparent that Leslie is looking beyond the numbers to the lives they represent. Karen and Leslie's ability to reflect upon the human meaning of such data and so readily identify program gaps seems linked to a keen observation of the "whole." A recurring theme of this story has to do with the simultaneous linking of "gut feelings" or intuitive knowledge with externally generated knowledge to result in integrated definitions of the practice implications of such information:

> The thing that struck Karen (Croman) about the data was the gap in the vocational area. We have a good group of people working pretty solidly, then we have a good

group in prevocational, then we have this in-between gap. So what do people do if they're done with prevocational activities but not ready for a full job? What struck me was the number of people still living with their families. That probably comes from my own personal experiences and my own feelings. What occurred to me is, perhaps we need to work on housing. We have a lot of people in their own apartments, and we have some really good facilities here, but when I saw the large number of people still living at home with their parents, to me that translates into an enormous amount of stress on families. And I'm real sensitive to family stress.

So I looked at that report and thought this is what we have to decrease—the number of people living with their families. Other people look at it and say there are other things we need to do, like Karen zeroing in on vocational stuff, which is real accurate. In fact, the interesting thing is we've had several meetings with Vocational Rehab, and with others, where we've been saying this is where we have a gap in our program. And that was without the stats. Then the stats come back and tell you what you were sensing is absolutely accurate. It told us our gut feelings were on target with some things we were concerned about, or what felt difficult to us. It felt difficult to move someone from prevocational activity to a regular job. It feels hard, it feels not as successful as it could be, it feels like clients don't always successfully make that transition, so it's clear to us (and to others) there's a missing piece there.

Another aspect of this example is Leslie Young's response to the idea of sharing the program's client-outcome data with the family group. As she discussed how she uses the data reports, the question arose regarding whether the families knew about it. Her immediate response was, "That's a good idea. I could write an article for their newsletter and let them know that. That is a neat idea, I'll do it. They'd be real interested." Such a response is a stark contrast to managerial behaviors of excuses, defensiveness, or "stonewalling" in the face of a new idea. Leslie Young speaks directly to this issue of receptivity versus close-mindedness:

I want creative people to staff this program. When I first came here, people were giving the standard answers, like "We've done it this way," "This is how we always do it," "But we don't do things that way." Being creative is when staff says, "How can we do it?" "Let's try this." That's the difference.

## SUMMARY

In this chapter, we laid out the basic perspectives to which we will adhere throughout the remainder of this book: the belief that performance is management and that client-centered management provides the best performance. We began by suggesting five areas in which performance may be measured: client outcomes, productivity, resource allocation, efficiency, and staff morale. Then we explored the current state of social practice management in which too often manager and client are separated. The multiple-constituency dilemma, the perceived need for political effectiveness, and the retrenchment of the 1970s and 1980s have led to a widening gulf between managers and both clients and frontline personnel. The separation, in turn, has led to less than optimal service, a dissatisfied workforce, and continued attacks on the social practice sector for being inefficient, self-serving, and ineffective.

Finally, we began to link performance and client-centered management by establishing four principles for the client-centered performance manager: venerating clients, creating and maintaining focus, demonstrating a healthy disrespect for the impossible, and learning for a living.

In the remainder of this book, we focus on the skills, technologies, and perspectives that social administrators need to move their organizations toward increased client-centeredness and improved performance.

## REFERENCES

Aberbock, J. D., Putnam, R. D., & Rockman, B. A. (1981). *Bureaucrats and politicians in western democracies*. Washington, DC: Howard University Press.

Bassuk, E. L., & Gerson, S. (1978). Deinstitutionalization and mental health services. *Scientific American, 232*(2), 46–53.

Briar, S. (1973, January). The age of accountability. *Social Work, 18*(1), 2.

Burns, M. (1958). *The historical development of the process of casework supervision as seen in the professional literature of social work*. Unpublished doctoral dissertation, University of Chicago.

Corcoran, K. J. (1986, Fall). The association of burnout and social work practitioners' impressions of their clients: Empirical evidence. *Journal of Social Service Research, 10*(1), 57–66.

Etzioni, A. (1964). *Modern organizations*. Englewood Cliffs, NJ: Prentice-Hall.

Fischer, J. (1976). *The effectiveness of social casework*. Springfield, IL: Charles C. Thomas.

Gowdy, E., & Rapp, C. A. (1989). Managerial behavior: The common denominator of effective community-based programs. *Psychosocial Rehabilitation Journal, 13*(2), 31–51.

Gruber, M. L. (1986, Fall). A three-factor model of administrative effectiveness. *Administration in Social Work, 10*(3), 1–14.

Gummer, B. (1980). Organizational theory for social administration. In F. D. Perlmutter & S. Slavin, (Eds.), *Leadership* (pp. 22–49). Philadelphia: Temple University Press.

Gummer, B. (1984). The social administrator as politician. In F. D. Perlmutter, (Ed.), *Human Services at Risk* (pp. 23–36). Lexington, MA: Lexington Books.

Harkness, D. R. (1987). *Social work supervision in community mental health: Evaluating the effects of normal and client focused supervision on client satisfaction and generalized contentment*. Unpublished doctoral dissertation, University of Kansas, Lawrence, KS.

Hasenfeld, Y. (1983). *Human service organizations*. Englewood Cliffs, NJ: Prentice-Hall.

Helfgot, J. (1974). Professional reform organizations and the symbolic representation of the poor. *American Sociological Review, 39*, 475–491.

Hogarty, G. E. (1979). Aftercare treatment of schizophrenia: Current status and future direction. In H. M. Pragg, (Ed.), *Management of Schizophrenia* (pp. 19–36). Assen, Netherlands: Van Gorcum.

Hogarty, G. E., et al., (1979). Fluphenazine and social therapy in aftercare of schizophrenia patients. *Archives of General Psychiatry, 36*, 1283–1294.

Kadushin, A. (1974). Supervisor-supervisee: A survey. *Social Work, 19*(3), 288–297.

Kanter, R. M. (1979). Power failure in management circuits. *Harvard Business Review, 56*.

Kanter, R. M., & Stein, B. A. (1985). Improving productivity and QWL together. In K. A. Bubok & M. K. Grant, (Eds.), *Quality of Work Life: Health Care Applications* (89–100). St. Louis, MO: The Catholic Health Association of the United States.

Karger, H. J. (1981, June). Burnout as alienation. *Social Service Review, 55*(2), 270–283.

Kaufman, H. (1973). *Administrative feedback*. Washington, DC: The Brookings Institute.

Kazmershi, K. J., & Macarr, D. (1976). *Administration in the social work curriculum: Report of a survey*. New York: Council on Social Work Education.

Kidneigh, J. (1950, April). Social work administration: An area of social work practice? *Social Work Journal, 31*(2), 57.

Lawler, E. E., III, Mohrmon, A. M., Jr., & Resnick, S. M. (1985, Fall). Performance appraisal revisited. *Organizational Dynamics, 13*(1), 20–35.

Levinson, D. J., & Klerman, G. L. (1967, February). The clinician-executive: Some problematic issues for the psychiatrist in mental health organizations. *Psychiatry, 30*(1), 3–5.

Lewis, R., & Stewart, R. (1958). *The boss*. London, England: Phoenix House.

Martin, P. Y. (1980). Multiple constituencies, dominant social values, and the human services administrator: Implications for service solving. *Administration in Social Work, 4*(2), 15–27.

Millar, R. and Millar, A. (eds.) (1981). *Developing client outcome monitoring systems*. Washington, DC: The Urban Institute.

Mintzberg, H. (1973). *The nature of managerial work*. Englewood Cliffs, NJ: Prentice-Hall.

Miringoff, M. L. (1980). *Management in Human Service Organizations*. New York: Macmillan.

Munson, C. (1979). An empirical study of structure and authority in social work supervision. In C. Munson, (Ed.), *Social Work Supervision* (pp. 286–296). New York: Free Press.

Neugeboren, B. (1985). *Organization, policy, and practice in the human services*. New York: Longman.

Ohlin, L. E., Coates, R. B., & Miller, A. D. (1974). Radical correctional reform: A case study of the Massachusetts youth correctional system. *Harvard Educational Review, 44*, 74–111.

Olmstead, J., & Christensen, H. (1974). *Research report no. 2—Effects of agency work contexts: An intensive field study* (SRS No. 74-05416). Washington, DC: U.S. Government Printing Office.

Patti, R. (1977, Spring). Patterns of management activity in social welfare agencies. *Administration in Social Work, 1*(1), 548.

Patti, R. (1985, Fall). In search of purpose for social welfare administration. *Administration in Social Work, 9*(3), 1–14.

Perlmutter, F. D. (1984). *Human services at risk*. Lexington, MA: Lexington Books.

Perlmutter, F. D. (1985–86, Winter). The politics of social administration. *Administration in Social Work, 9*(4), 1–12.

Perrow, C. (1978). Demystifying organizations. In R. C. Sarri & Y. Hasenfeld, (Eds.), *The Management of Human Services* (pp. 105–120). New York: Columbia University Press.

Peters, T., & Austin, N. (1985). *A passion for excellence*. New York: Random House.

Peters, T. J., & Waterman, R. H., Jr. (1982). *In search of excellence*. Harper & Row.

Rapp, C. A. (in press). The strengths perspective of care management with persons suffering from serious mental illnesses. In D. Saleebey, (Ed.), *The Strength Model of Social Work: Power in the People*. New York: Longman.

Rapp, C. A., Hardcastle, D., Rosenzweig, J., & Poertner, J. (1982, Fall/Winter). The status of research in social service management. *Administration in Social Work, 7*(3/4), 89–100.

Richan, W. C. (1980). The administrator as advocate. In F. D. Perlmutter & S. Slavin, (Eds.), *Leadership in Social Administration* (pp. 72–85). Philadelphia: Temple University Press.

Rosenthal, R., & Jacobson, L. (1968). *Pygmalion in the classroom: Teacher expectations and pupil's intellectual development.* New York: Holt, Rinehart & Winston.

Scott, R. A. (1967). The factory as a social service organization: Goal displacement in workshops for the blind. *Social Problems, 15,* 160–175.

Shulman, L., Robinson, E., & Lucky, A. (1981). *A study of the content context and skills of supervision.* Vancouver, Canada: University of British Columbia.

Slavin, S. (1980). A theoretical framework for social administration. In F. D. Perlmutter & S. Slavin, (Eds.), *Leadership in Social Administration* (pp. 3–21). Philadelphia: Temple University Press.

Stuart, R. B. (1977). *Trick or treatment.* Champaign, IL: Research Press.

Taber, M. (1980). *The social context of helping.* (DHHS Publication No. 80–842). Washington, DC: U.S. Government Printing Office.

Taber, M., & Finnegan, D. (1980). *A theory of accountability for social work programs.* Unpublished paper, University of Illinois School of Social Work, Urbana, IL.

Trecker, H. B. (1946). *Group process in administration.* New York: The Woman's Press.

Turem, J. (1974). The call for a management stance. *Social Work, 19,* 615–623.

Wager, L. W. (1972). Organizational "linking pins": Hierarchical status and communicative roles in interlevel conferences. *Human Relations, 25*(4), 307–326.

Weick, A., Rapp, C. A., Sullivan, W. P., & Kisthardt, W. (1989). Strength perspective in social work practice. *Social Work, 34*(4), 350–354.

Wiehe, V. R. (1980, Fall). Current practices in performance appraisal. *Administration in Social Work, 4*(3), 1–12.

Zald, M. N. (1970). Political economy: A framework for comparative analysis. In M. N. Zald, (Ed.), *Power in Organizations* (pp. 221–261). Nashville, TN: Vanderbilt University Press.

# CHAPTER 2

# Social Program Design

One of the most important—and most frequently ignored—responsibilities of social administrators is program design. Too often programs are initiated simply because they are "hot" or because certain resources are readily available. Without carefully thought out design, social programs are almost inevitably unable to effectively meet client needs. In this chapter, we present a model of program design that identifies the elements of social programs and ways to develop each component. This process, however, is not linear. In keeping with the "learning for a living" principle that we introduced in the last chapter, you need to view the process as iterative—perhaps a spiral rather than a circle, always looping back on itself but always moving forward as well.

We begin by defining our basic terms—program and program design—and exploring why program design is important to successful management. We then look at preprogram design considerations and program design components—a series of eight steps that constitute a design model for client-centered programs. Finally, we provide specific suggestions for putting the program design to work and diagnosing inadequate program design, including a program analysis checklist to guide managers in designing or evaluating program proposals. The chapter ends with an extended case study demonstrating the model.

## DEFINING TERMS

### Program

A program is an aggregate of actions directed toward accomplishing a single goal. The social program is *how* people are helped. Social programs attempt to find workers satisfying and fulfilling work. Social programs manifest society's desire to assist some of its members.

An agency or organization can operate one or more programs. In fact a single team or unit could be responsible for several programs. For example, many state child welfare organizations have frontline teams responsible for achieving both child protection and permanency planning. Although these purposes are closely related, achievement of each requires very different sets of behaviors that may be contradictory. Abused children can be protected by removing them from their home and placing them in foster care. But placement in foster care makes it more difficult to insure a permanent home. Consequently, clarity and reconciliation of competing or seemingly contradictory goals begins with an analysis of the actions directed at accomplishing a single goal.

This definition of program allows several independent or semi-independent units to be viewed as part of a single program. In many mental health centers, for example, the outpatient program is separate from the day treatment program. If the goal of both programs is to increase community tenure of people suffering from severe mental illness, then both would be considered as one program.

## Program Design

Program design is both a product and a method. As a product, program design is a written document that prescribes the minimum sets of behavior of multiple players required for the program to achieve its goals. The product is viewed as a working document to be adhered to and to be altered rather than a statement that is submitted for funding and only pulled out when preparing next year's budget request.

The design of a program is analogous to the design of a product such as a television, automobile, or a house. When an automobile manufacturer decides to design a new model, a large number of resources are devoted to the design effort. Engineers of various types as well as marketing experts are involved in the design phase. Much of the design effort is aimed at examining the many design components and how they will be assembled to produce a new product. The same is true of social programs, yet seldom are social programs designed with the same attention to detail. Like the automobile, an inadequate design will lead to a weak product. A poorly designed or inadequately designed human service program will make program operations and optimum program performance difficult if not impossible.

As a product, the program design should be precise, logical, coherent, and squarely focused on producing benefits for clients if it in fact is to assist clients and if it is to gain political support. Patti (1983) states:

> Organizational elites are likely to be hesitant to commit the resources and support the program needs to buffer its initial vulnerability. A board or agency executive may endorse the general purpose and thrust of a new program, but the support will usually be provisional until there is clarity regarding such matters as the objectives to be sought, the clientele to be served, the services provided, and so on. (p. 70)

The desirability of preciseness is opposed by some who believe vagueness is more likely to gain political support. (Gruber, 1986) As a method, program design is a framework by which critical management decisions are made. Design is a process that makes explicit worker and management decisions and provides analytical tools for making these decisions. Program design must allow for the systematic blending of agendas among society, individual clients, and program personnel. In fact, the program design process can be a mechanism for rallying staff and getting the commitment of key external forces. (Patti, 1983) The design framework allows managers to use it as a diagnostic tool to locate obstacles to better performance. As a former student said, "It's like a roadmap in a strange city."

## WHY IS PROGRAM DESIGN IMPORTANT?

One way to address this question is to look at the common problems caused by poor program design:

- Staff and managers are asked to do too much with too little.
- Staff and clients are not clear as to what is expected of them and for what purpose.
- Other agencies, professionals, clients, and public are not clear as to the purpose of your program leading to conflicts and failure to support the program.
- Funders do not know what it takes to do the job producing unrealistic expectations.
- Meetings and paperwork proliferate and could be prevented by clearer sets of expectations.
- Crisis orientation or other modes of organizational behavior in which much energy is expended but performance does not improve.
- The latest "hot idea" is selected for program interventions avoiding a careful exploration of potentially more powerful alternatives.

For example, purchase of service arrangements from public agencies is now a common form of service delivery. (Benton, Field, & Millar, 1978) One common problem is holding programs accountable, or to put it another way getting them to deliver, when services are contracted or agencies share an affiliation agreement. A major obstacle has been the vagueness of the program goals, the unspecified nature of the intervention, and the lack of performance standards directly related to the program's mission.

Another related problem is indiscriminate use of community services by frontline professionals. Some mental health case managers will arrange individual psychotherapy for virtually all cases while others will recommend day hospital attendance for the same cases. In child welfare, some workers will arrange counseling for virtually all cases while others have a predilection to use homemakers in the same type of care. "Knee-jerk" decisions may be permissible if these services had empirically supported track records. In lieu of such comparison information, it is not possible to consider these decisions as reflective of good mental health or child welfare practice. Often these decisions are based on convenience rather than careful analysis of the case and of the service.

A third problem has been the dearth of resources for the most troublesome cases. In part, many agencies cream off the most desirable and easiest clients. These agencies seek to increase the number of client referrals by keeping eligibility criteria vague and widening the resources for referrals. This allows them to take the best clients available. Clients deemed inappropriate are left with few options. In fact, creaming has been a major criticism of urban renewal and housing programs (Palumbo & Harder, 1981), community mental health centers, and employment programs such as the U.S. Employment Service. While underfunding and street-level bureaucrats have received much of the blame, we believe that the central cause has been inadequate program design rather than problems of policy or implementation.

A fourth prevalent problem is the lack of supportive behavior by external constituencies like the court system and hospitals. For community mental health programs to be successful, a variety of key players must consistently perform in certain ways. Maintaining chronically mentally ill clients in the community is virtually impossible with a judge who refuses to consider community alternatives for treatment of commitment cases. Similarly, in child welfare, permanency planning cannot be done with a juvenile court judge who refuses to return children home or will not terminate parental rights.

The lack of job satisfaction of so many employees is another recurring problem. Staff are asked daily to intervene in the most difficult and complex human situations with too few supports and resources, and sometimes with too little guidance. Few mechanisms are in place to systematically show them the results of their efforts nor to celebrate their successes.

The following case highlights the consequences of incorrect program design. The program on first blush was solid. But, in fact, the program devoted virtually all of its efforts and resources to teaching skills that the clients already knew how to do. The program needed outreach, case management, and *in vivo* support but had no such capacity at the time. The design flaws could be in selecting the wrong goals, the wrong target population, or the wrong sets of service technologies.

> The Northeast Mental Health and Guidance Center operates a modest partial hospitalization program for about thirty chronically mentally ill clients. The program operates from nine to five, five days a week, and includes activities focused on recreation and socialization, health, daily living skills, prevocational skills, arts and crafts, stress management, meal planning, cooking, music, and interpersonal relations. Counseling services and medication clinic are a part of the program. The staff is also concerned with the degree to which clients are satisfied with the program and how well the clients are doing when not at the center. The staff is warm, caring and works diligently. The only data collected is on rehospitalization and symptomatology.
>
> Program staff were asked to evaluate the vocational and daily living skills of a sample

of clients in terms of whether they had the ability to use, and to what degree they used the skills when in the community. Each client was assessed as being able to perform at least 90 percent of the fifty-two skills included in the inventory. However, fewer than half of the clients performed these same skills in the community although the skills were in their repertoire.

Each of these flaws are complex but many can be attenuated, if not solved, by thoughtful design. A carefully designed program offers the promise of improving effectiveness, increasing efficiency, producing higher levels of job satisfaction, reducing conflict, and eliciting more support from constituencies. Program design is one set of management strategies that can improve the performance of the organization.

## PREPROGRAM DESIGN CONSIDERATIONS

As we pointed out at the beginning of this chapter, program design is not linear but iterative; it is a process in constant revision. As you learn more about your clients, their problems, and your intervention, you will want to revise certain elements of your program. As you consider new design elements you will want to reconsider elements previously specified. The social administrator must keep the nature of the process in mind. Similarly there are three considerations that comprise the preprogram phase. In the preprogram design phase social administrators must consider: (a) the blending of social programs with social work values, (b) the continuous need for information, and (c) the use of multiple levels of intervention.

### Social Programs and Social Work Values

Social work theories come from social problem analysis. The problem analysis necessarily includes the harmful factors that contribute to the social problem. Once it is completed, the analysis usually includes a host of individual and environmental toxins. In the words of William Ryan (1971):

> The formula for action becomes extraordinarily simple: Change the victim. All of this happens so smoothly that it seems downright rational. First, identify a social problem. Second, study those affected by the problem and discover in what ways they are different from the rest of us as a consequence of deprivation and injustice. Third, define the differences as the cause of the social problem itself. Finally, of course assign a government bureaucrat to invent a humanitarian action program to correct the differences. (p. 9)

The tendency for human services to employ rehabilitative and social control purposes and strategies comes directly from this "blame-the-victim" way of thinking. (Neugeboren, 1985) In this way, the person with chronic mental illness needs daily living skills training or psychotherapy; the unemployed welfare mother needs vocational training; the abused child who is demanding and disruptive in a series of foster homes is emotionally disturbed and requires psychiatric care. It is relatively easy to gather support and sanction for these kinds of interventions. As Fairweather (1972) states, "Thus it appears to be axiomatic that an intervention is acceptable to a society in direct proportion to the degree that the innovation does not require a change in the roles or social organization of that society." (p. 7)

Others choose to blame the environment. Poverty, lack of intellectual stimuli, hostile community attitudes, depressed local economies, poor housing, and lack of recreational, and socialization opportunities have been thought to be the cause of social problems. The "blaming-the-environments" ideology is derived from a similar thought process as blaming-the-victim: Find differences in the living circumstances of two groups or two individuals and identify the differences as the cause of a problem.

These blaming perspectives are both right and wrong at the same time. By the time a person reaches a human service agency both sets of factors have contributed to the client's situation. Cause becomes less relevant than what is going on now and how do we obtain the desired positive outcome. In addition, both lines of thought view differences as bad and lead to attempts to make people the same:

> There are demonstrable differences among many groups in this society. Given any two groups of sufficient size, there will be differences in a multitude of individual and environmental variables. These differences [should be] viewed as being among the assets of a pluralistic society. The magnitude of such differences, although statistically reliable, are of questionable social significance. More importantly, they provide a basis for unwarranted negative expectations . . . and erect stumbling blocks to confound effective intervention. (Davidson & Rapp, 1976, pp. 226–227)

In short, the blaming theories prohibit us from seeing client and environmental strengths that may be a more powerful tool for fashioning our interventions. Although social work has traditionally given rhetorical support to client strengths, there remains no model of social work practice that is based on client or environmental strengths. (Cowger, in press; Sullivan, in press)

*Community integration* is also a highly regarded social work value. Many programs are based on principles such as promoting the most normal and family-like environment, maintaining vulnerable populations in their own home, or returning them to their community. Clearly the design of the partial hospitalization program mentioned earlier did not recognize the underlying program value prior to embarking on the design process. The values recognized by the social administrator prior to the design phase do make a difference. When recognized and addressed they help frame the problem, and the solutions that arise become coherent and consistent responses to the problem.

## Information Needs of Program Design

The information needed to design effective social programs is considerable. It includes information and data on the social problem, description and extent of people confronting the social problem, and the past performance of alternative interventions. Sources of information range from census data and government statistical publications to the professional literature and the collective practice wisdom of agency personnel.

The selection of an intervention is particularly demanding in terms of information. The designer confronts four obstacles. First, social work helping theories need to be based on the latest available knowledge, but the research is not always adequate to make informed decisions. Sometimes it is a lack of relevant research; sometimes it is that the research reports contain precious little information on the intervention being evaluated so that replication is impossible; and sometimes the research is based on pilot programs that have had considerably more resources available to it than your organization will have access to.

Second, there is a tendency to select an intervention on the basis of popular trends or ideas, or the unspecified reputation of a particular program rather than on evidence of its efficacy. This predilection is unsound because popularity is a poor surrogate for evidence of effectiveness.

Third, there is a natural inclination to apply current agency methods to new problems or new target groups. For example, in many places psychotherapy remains as the principal intervention for chronically mentally ill individuals seeking a richer community life. It may be packaged as case management, day treatment, or even as a vocational program, but the basic intervention is the same with consistently poor results. (Stuart, 1977; Morrison & Bellack, 1984; Dion & Anthony, 1987; Bond & Boyer, in press)

But the central constraint confronting the manager is access to what is known. Few managers have the time to be familiar with the most recent research. Many managers do not have working relationships with university faculty who are often abreast of the latest innovations.

With these constraints notwithstanding, the quality and quantity of research available to inform our intervention selection has increased dramatically in just the last ten years. A decade ago the reviews of intervention research were quite sobering suggesting that few interventions were effective. (Fischer, 1973; Prather & Gibson, 1977; Stuart, 1977; Wood, 1978) More recent reviews have painted a brighter picture. Reid and Hanrahan (1982) reviewed experimental studies of clinical social work that found "structured approaches addressed to specific problems, behaviors, or social skills appear able to effect constructive change." (p. 338) In child welfare there is a critical mass of rather consistent findings identifying the critical factors influencing permanency planning for children. (Costin & Rapp, 1984; Emlen, Lahti, Downs, McKay, & Downs, 1977; Fanshel & Shinn, 1978; Rapp & Poertner, 1978) And a variety of effective interventions have taken these factors into account. (Chappell, 1975; Claburn, Magura, & Resnick, 1976; Emlen et al., 1977;

Festinger, 1975; Stein & Gambrill, 1977; Stein, Gambrill, & Wiltse, 1974; Watson, 1982) A similarly substantial body of intelligence concerning community-based interventions for the chronically mentally ill is available. (Gowdy, Rapp, & Poertner, 1987; Rappaport, 1977; Rubin, 1984).

## Levels of Intervention

An ecological perspective of social work suggests that clients should be assisted through interventions directed from a variety of levels of the social organization: individual, group, organizational, institutional, community, and societal. (Davidson & Rapp, 1976; Germain & Gitterman, 1980) The relationships within and between levels can comprise a given social work theory at any moment in time. (Rappaport, 1977) A sample of interventions organized by level for three human service fields is shown in Table 2–1. It should be noted that an intervention directed at any single level can have impact on other levels that are not the direct target of intervention or what Kelly (1971) terms "radiating impact."

At each level, several strategies will be available. Unfortunately, many of our past efforts have been narrowly focused on the level of the individual and usually have involved only one strategy. The complexity of the problems we face (see problem analysis section) usually demands multiple level interventions in order to have a reasonable chance of success. For example, a psychosocial program that wants to achieve and maintain employment for clients must have prevocational training, contracted job slots with businesses, on-the-job training with job coaches, a method for creating demand-skill matches, a trained worker pool, and long-term support and advocacy resources (case management staff and/or volunteers). In fact, employment will probably not be maintained unless there are socialization and housing resources associated with the program. As a general rule, interventions focused on multiple levels are more likely to produce client benefits and achieve program goals.

We suggest the following principles for intervention selection:

- The social work perspective (ecological or person in environment) is a useful way of viewing a social problem and stimulating interventions.
- Care must be exercised in avoiding blaming interventions.
- Consideration of individual and environmental strengths must be included.
- Interventions need to blend client and societal desires.
- Multiple-level interventions are more promising.

## PROGRAM DESIGN COMPONENTS

Taber and Finnegan (1980) designed the basic program framework. It includes the following components:

- Analyze the social problems.
- Determine who is the direct beneficiary of the program.
- Determine the social work theory of helping.
- Specify the service providers.
- Identify the key persons required to produce client benefits.
- Specify the helping environment.
- Describe actual helping behaviors.
- Identify emotions and responses.

In the remainder of this chapter, we describe each of these components and provide specific guidelines for making critical program design decisions. We present these components in the order listed above, which is a logical one, but we emphasize that in real life, information and decisions made in subsequent steps may suggest alterations in previous steps. Taken together, however, what follows will provide a specific analytic framework for social program design.

## PROGRAM DESIGN STEP 1: ANALYZE THE SOCIAL PROBLEM

The first step in program design is an analysis of the social problem that the program will address. The social problem analysis becomes the basis for establishing the program goal. Inadequate goal setting, as we saw in Chapter 1, is a major flaw in our social programs and acts as a wedge between clients and managers, and clients and the organization.

Social program goals are usually vague (e.g., stimulating social interaction, improving the quality of life) or overly ambitious (e.g., prevent child abuse, reduce poverty). Goals most often describe the helping process rather than the client outcomes to be produced (e.g., to provide services, to develop a program, to teach). One of our favorites is: "Develop and establish a system for identifying and referring technical and professional resources to coordinate and enhance staff expertise of organizations assisting persons make informed career decisions, develop new careers, or successfully achieve mid-life career changes."

Inadequate goal setting makes it difficult, if not impossible, to manage a program and keep it on course. Inadequate goal setting opens us up to criticism and attack for being ineffective, self-serving, and wasteful. Inadequate goal setting frustrates employees who do not see their efforts pay off. This leads to the "activity trap": work expands to fill the time available for its completion. In short, we cannot get where we want to go if we don't know where we want to go. To gain acceptance and yield the desired outcomes, a program design must come from an analysis of the particular social problem.

**TABLE 2–1. SAMPLE INTERVENTIONS**

| Level of Organization | Community Mental Health | Child Welfare | Elderly |
|---|---|---|---|
| Individual | Case Management<br>Psychotherapy<br>Pharmacological treatment<br>One-to-one volunteer match with client<br>Individual vocational rehabilitation | Counseling for child<br>Counseling for mother/father<br>Individual parent education<br>Parent education material<br>Parent advocate/ child advocate | Case management<br>Consumer education<br>Advocacy |
| Family | Family therapy<br>Family support group<br>Respite care<br>Psychoeducational workshops | Family therapy<br>Family contracting<br>Homemaker services<br>Home visitors | Caregiver support programs<br>Family problem-solving meetings<br>Consumer education |
| Group | Group therapy<br>Medication monitoring groups<br>Support groups<br>Skills development classes/groups | Parents Anonymous<br>Parent education classes<br>Batterer groups<br>Parent support groups<br>Sexual abuse victim groups | Caregivers support<br>Adult day care<br>Community advocacy<br>Silver-haired legislator |
| Community/ neighborhood | Drop-in center<br>Mobile crisis unit<br>Emergency shelter | Child care exchanges<br>Juvenile court case planning case review systems<br>Parent center | Mutual help<br>Neighborhood organizations<br>Older citizens centers |
| Institutional | Change criteria for rehospitalization<br>Change criteria for discharge<br>Change criteria for involuntary hospitalization<br>Make the client be director of the service received<br>Create client advocate/ ombudsman position | Change criteria for placement decisions<br>Ban corporal punishment in schools<br>Institute life skills programs in schools | Reform guardianship program<br>Create ombudsman program<br>Consumer protection legislation |
| Societal | Increase funding for community support services and defund state hospitals | Increase funding for family support services and defund foster care<br>Universal provision of parenting education | Division of assets legislation<br>Elder abuse legislation<br>Increasing funding of community long-term care option |

## Defining the Problem

A social problem exists when a cultural group or some segment of it identifies a deviation from a social standard that is believed necessary for the maintenance of cultural life. (Chambers, 1986) As Blumer (1971) states: "Social problems are not the result of an intrinsic malfunctioning of a society but are the result of a process of definition in which a given condition is picked out and identified as a social problem. (p. 301) The importance or severity of the social problem is based on the degree of perceived threat to the integrity of cultural life and the size or status of those people who are labeling it as a social problem. Human service managers do not create social problems but begin their program design work once the society or community has identified a social problem.

Since human service programs are seen as a solution or part of a solution to an identified social problem, the first step in program design is a careful yet pragmatic analysis of the social problem being addressed. As Taber and Finnegan (1980) state: "A clear description of the problem for society and for individuals lays the groundwork for establishing goals and justifying the need for the problem's amelioration." (p. 6) Incomplete problem analysis inevitably leads to vague or overly ambitious goals, misguided intervention strategies, and imprecise targeting of services. One rather well publicized example was the 1962 amendments to the Social Security Act.

> Increased funding was provided for social services and at the same time goals for the recipients of social services of "self care," "self support" and "strengthening family life" were adopted. For twenty-five years the profession of social work has been trying to convince Congress that "trained social workers" should staff the direct service positions in Public Aid. In the early 1960s a Congress which was alarmed by rising AFDC rolls was ready to buy the NASW argument. President Kennedy proclaimed the amendments as a shift toward rehabilitation, rather than relief. A few short years later, as AFDC rolls rose even more steeply, social workers hastened to revise their policy position on public aid. Social casework clearly was not enough. Social and structural reforms were needed. Furthermore, public aid agencies were not administering social services properly. Well-qualified social workers were not given professional recognition and were not provided incentives for performing well. Clearly these second thoughts were valid. The unfortunate thing is that they should have been obvious with a bit of objective analysis before 1962. The embryonic social work profession should have never hinted so strongly that it could solve the problem of poverty which has escaped the best efforts of political and intellectual leaders for centuries. (Taber & Finnegan, 1980, p. 3)

Another example of inadequate social problem analysis occurred in the early years of the deinstitutionalization movement in mental health:

> The Mental Health Centers Construction Act of 1963 and related guidelines from the Department of Health, Education and Welfare called for the establishment of a new kind of community-based center. The concept of "community mental health"

implied a dual promise: treatment and rehabilitation of the severely mentally ill within the community and the promotion of mental health generally. The first promise was to be fulfilled by the development of an extensive support system of coordinated services for the mentally ill. These "least restrictive" services were to replace the traditional function of large custodial institutions. 50% reductions in patient populations at state institutions were to be achieved in 20 years. The second aim of the program, the broad improvement of the nation's mental health status, was to be achieved by preventive programs originating in the mental health centers. There was a mood of enthusiastic optimism, which in retrospect bordered on blind faith. The shortcomings of the initial legislation, the lack of an adequate system of follow-up care, the hard realities of insufficient funding, the probable impact of patients on communities, and even the uncertainties as to effective therapy—all of these were largely ignored in the rush to implement the new goals. For thousands of hospitalized patients released haphazardly to a nonsystem of community aftercare, this oversight meant real hardship and even tragedy. (Bassuk & Gerson, 1978, p. 48)

In both these examples, the social problem was not clearly analyzed leading to promises that could not be kept, public and professional criticism, wasted resources, and, at least in the case of mental health, a great deal of human suffering.

In Chapter 1, we introduced the notion that human service managers are responsible for blending the agendas of a variety of groups such as clients and the larger society. Social problem analysis provides one opportunity for doing this because such an analysis requires the dual obligation to individuals (e.g., clients, their families) and to the larger society. Each program must be justified along both dimensions for the program to have a reasonable chance for adequate support (e.g., funding and community goodwill) and success.

## Frameworks for Analysis

The complexity of social problems has led to a variety of complex frameworks for analysis. For the busy human service manager, however, the problem analysis task must be more modest. Minimally, it needs to identify and organize the key factors that will guide the critical decisions involved in the program design. The following typology (Taber & Finnegan, 1980; Taber, 1987) identifies the three elements of a social problem analysis and the relevant dimensions under each:

I. Problem for society
   A. A resource cost to society
   B. A threat to the health and safety of members of society
   C. A threat to societal values such as social integration

II. Problem for individuals
   A. A deprivation of a minimal standard of health and decency
   B. A threat of abuse or exploitation
   C. A barrier to full social participation

III. Factors contributing to the problem's existence or prevalence
   A. biological/physical    or    individual
   B. behavioral                    family
   C. social                        community
   D. psychological            societal
   E. economic                  historical
                                        political

The typology is not important in itself but is intended to assist managers in specifying why a given situation is a problem and what needs to be changed.

## Analyzing the Problem

First, in the center of a large blackboard or piece of paper, write the phrase that captures the problem. Here are some examples:

- multiple rehospitalizations (recidivism)
- social isolation
- unemployment
- transience
- inconsistent use of community services
- inappropriate use of community services

This first step is not trivial. The phrase that goes into the center makes a difference. Different starting points generate different analysis and different programs.

There is no formula directing you where to start. But we have found that the more specific you can be the more useful the product. For example, sexual abuse of young girls is more useful than child abuse. We have also found that a certain amount of trial and error is useful. If the initial framing of the problem doesn't seem to work, try reframing it.

Second, on the top right side of the phrase, list how the situation is a problem for society. Use the three dimensions under this category to help provoke thinking. Society is a broad term that can refer to any grouping or subgrouping of people who experience the problem but who are not the individuals of concern. For example, inappropriate use of community programs wastes precious societal resources devoted to the client group.

Third, on the bottom right side of the phrase, list how the situation is a problem for the individual, again refer to the above typology. The individual is almost always the client and sometimes may include the client's family.

Fourth, on the left side of the phrase, list the factors that contribute to the problem's existence or prevalence. The main sources of such information come from practice experience and the relevant research literature. The goal here is to generate as many factors as possible. It is not unusual to produce lists of ten to twenty-five factors. For clarity, you should group them in some fashion.

Table 2–2 contains a completed problem analysis using the problem of social isolation.

Translation of Table 2–2 into a narrative problem statement becomes a powerful means of communication with a variety of constituents. The description of social isolation and its consequences for the individual and society is a vivid portrayal of the problem. The lengthy list of contributing factors clearly communicates the complexity of the problem. This demonstrates that no simple solutions exist for complex social problems.

At this point you generally have a good idea of your goal for the program. Write it down in draft form, focusing on the benefit(s) that a client would accrue. More specific direction and criteria for goal statements will follow consideration of who will be the client.

### TABLE 2–2. PROBLEM ANALYSIS: SOCIAL ISOLATION AMONG THE CHRONICALLY MENTALLY ILL (CMI)

**Factors Related to Community Services:**

1. Community programs are competitive instead of cooperative.
2. Services do not teach daily living skills in natural settings.
3. Vocational programs are inappropriate for CMI.
4. No outreach programs.
5. Programs offer no opportunity for client input or leadership.
6. Housing is inadequate.
7. Programs foster passive behavior.

**Factors Related to Community Participation:**

1. CMI lack opportunity to develop friendships with community members.
2. Concerned community members lack knowledge of and access to CMI.
3. CMI lack advocates when problems arise in the community.
4. CMI lack transportation.
5. CMI live near or at the poverty level.

**Factors Related to Mental Illness:**

1. Symptoms of mental illness fluctuate even when treated.
2. Mental illness can cause problems with social adaptation.
3. Mental illness creates diverse needs demanding a wide variety of services.

**Problem for Society:**

1. Isolated CMI are often rehospitalized and cause more financial cost.
2. Isolated CMI misuse services resulting in resource waste.
3. Isolated CMI use valued emergency and law enforcement resources.
4. Isolated CMI who are in substandard conditions are perceived as a health threat to society.
5. Isolated CMI are perceived as dangerous.
6. Treatment of CMI threatens freedoms valued by society.

**Problem for Individual:**

1. Isolated CMI lack opportunity for positive, consistent relationships.
2. Isolation reduces motivation for self-improvement.
3. Isolated CMI don't access services.
4. Isolated CMI are targets of crime.
5. Isolated CMI have no defense against unethical practices or conditions.
6. Isolated CMI lack alternatives for social interaction.
7. Isolated CMI lack role models who demonstrate coping/living skills.

# PROGRAM DESIGN STEP 2: IDENTIFY THE DIRECT BENEFICIARY OF THE PROGRAM

A critical question in designing social programs is "who benefits?" Yet many human service managers abrogate their responsibility and authority by only vaguely answering this question and implying that all people who can be thus described can be served and helped by the program. The result is that critical decisions are made by frontline professionals often in highly idiosyncratic ways, and creaming becomes more of a likelihood. Imprecise definition of the people to be served is, in addition, a major source of interagency and agency-public conflict. People are denied service and often view the decision as arbitrary and capricious. Referral sources, for example, a juvenile court or hospital, sometimes requests service for "inappropriate" clients—those that the program is not designed to serve. In some agencies these referrals consume a great deal of time to process before a decision "not to accept" is made. This is a waste of precious resources that could be devoted to serving appropriate clients. These problems would be avoidable if clear specifications were formulated. Here is a case in point, a residential treatment program for children received 296 referrals in a 27-month period and accepted 61 youth or 20 percent of the referrals. The paperwork, the meetings, and the travel costs associated with the 236 children who were not accepted is unconscionable. These valuable resources could have been used to benefit clients. As the National Conference on Social Welfare reported: "Sixty percent of the people who seek social services are turned away from agencies; only 17 percent of the remaining applicants seen by agencies are actually served; and only one of five people referred from one service to another ever reach the agency to which they were referred." (Quoted in Patti, 1983, p. 117)

In 1985, a state child welfare agency opened only about 50 percent of the abuse and neglect reports that had been investigated and referred for service. There were no criteria established for making these decisions. Consequently there was great variation in criteria used between area offices, teams, and individual workers. Idiosyncratic judgments weaken the service given clients, in this case protecting children, and makes workers and the organization vulnerable to litigation.

Another problem caused by inadequate definition of the target population is reduced client benefits. Deciding who will and will not be served must be done thoughtfully and analytically, and with consideration given to clients' needs, program theory, and critical constituents, such as legislators and governing boards. Identification of who will benefit and who will not cannot be an area of wide discretion and arbitrariness. The case study of the Mental Health and Guidance Center cited earlier is a good example. One view of the story is that the program had the correct goals and was employing a strong intervention technology but that it was just serving the wrong clientele. In other words, the partial hospitalization program would be justified and offer considerable promise for helping if it served only individuals with chronic mental illness who did not have vocational and daily living skills in their repertoire.

Both managers and frontline professionals must answer the question, "Who benefits?" A casework program for teenage parents had established its target population as those youth in their first or second trimester. A pregnant teen in her third trimester was denied service because "good" casework practice cannot be performed so late in the pregnancy. This decision was made despite the fact that there were no other services available. Is this a decision for the caseworker, the manager, or both? Identification of who will and will not benefit cannot be an area of wide discretion and arbitrariness.

## The Population

Analyzing a population group is a way to identify who will be served. This method narrows the eligible group through a series of management and program decisions. The following procedures should help managers in making program decisions. The general process is represented in a population funnel in Figure 2–1.

One difficulty of determining who the population is to be at this stage of the analysis is a lack of specificity of other program elements. The program theory, service procedures, and helping environment are just three design elements that influence client selection. Experience has found that most people involved in program design have some ideas of these features at this stage even though they have not been specified. This preliminary knowledge is usually sufficient to proceed. The designer also needs to return and refine the population funnel as additional design elements are specified.

*General Population.* The general population most frequently includes all people in a catchment area or political jurisdiction. Some characteristics that might be

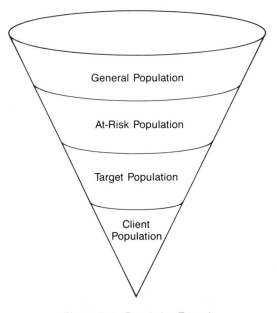

**Figure 2–1.** Population Funnel

relevant in determining the need for the program include the following. The general population for a child welfare program would probably include information on children and families in a given area. An employment program would describe labor force participation and industry data. A program for the chronically mentally ill may focus discussion on the prevalence of mental illness and chronic mental illness in particular.

*At-Risk Population.* From the general population, there is a subgroup who is particularly vulnerable to the described social problem. A description of the at-risk population typically includes characteristics of people who are the most vulnerable and estimates of the number of people who possess these characteristics. For example, a program to maintain youth within the community needs to consider what puts youth at risk of being removed from the community by schools, courts, mental health systems, and families.

*Target Population.* The target population is that subset of the at-risk population that is *eligible* for the program. It is probable that not all of the youth who are at risk of removal from the community will be the focus of a particular intervention. The characteristics of youth and the complexity of factors that place youth at risk make it unlikely that a single program in a single agency could do it all. The program theory and the agency auspice are the two primary sets of factors that establish limits for the target population.

A prevention program necessarily casts a wider target population net than a treatment program. It may, therefore, exclude individuals who are already experiencing problems. On the other hand a treatment program may require the problem to be in evidence. Alcohol abuse prevention and treatment programs are good examples. A particular helping theory may limit the at-risk population because it requires a relatively homogeneous client population. Certainly parenting an infant versus an adolescent requires very different parenting education and consequently a very different target population even though both parents may be at risk of abusing their child. The helping theory contains expectations of clients that also limit the target population. It is not reasonable to include at-risk individuals within the target population if they clearly cannot meet client expectations. A parent education program requiring an eighth grade reading ability probably cannot be targeted to mothers who do not read at this level.

Program auspice, or who is running the program, may also limit the targeted population. Courts, schools, or mental health centers have very different constraints placed on them. In the case of maintaining youth within the community, each of these entities would have a slightly different population. Legal mandates included in state or national legislation may also limit the target population, as will funding policies.

*Client Population.* The client population is that subgroup of the target population who will become clients. We know that only a portion of people eligible for a program will in fact receive service. The key question for the manager is who from the target population will receive services and who will not. Three sets of limiting factors usually come into play:

*1. Pragmatic.* The most common pragmatic consideration is program capacity. That is, at any one point in time program resources are available to serve X amount of eligible people. Too often programs have been rendered impotent because these tough decisions have not been made, consequently case loads have ballooned, workers have been unable to do their jobs, and clients and the public are frustrated by the results. If limits must be set, the manager must decide which cases will take priority. Will individuals be served on a first come first served basis with a waiting list? Once an opening occurs how will it be filled? The point is that these decisions can and should be made in the design stage by the manager, not during operations by frontline workers at an affiliated service location or by other decision makers such as judges and influential community members.

*2. Ethical.* A person may be eligible for a program but may not want to receive services. For many programs, the clients must be voluntary, at least in the sense that they make themselves available to receive services. An example of how this factor alone may radically reduce the number of people who will be served can be seen across the nation in the emergence of a new subgroup of young chronically mentally ill individuals. (Bachrach, 1982; Pepper, Ryglewicz, & Kirshner, 1982)

> This group is characterized as being between the ages of 18 [and] 35, transient in nature, having shorter but multiple hospitalizations, and known to act out in various ways. Generally this population is relatively crisis oriented and has not responded to traditional forms of aftercare programs. This group of "new chronics" or "young chronics" are not docile. They demand services at times and reject them at others, often defining their problems related to poverty, isolation, and alienation rather than mental illness. (Modrcin, Rapp, & Chamberlain, 1985)

The poor performance of traditional aftercare programs is related to an inability to engage and maintain voluntary participation among younger chronic patients.

*3. Client capabilities.* To benefit from the programs, clients must exhibit certain abilities or possess certain resources. Alternatively the program must be designed to take these into account. Individuals in the target population may need transportation to participate; they may need to be available at certain times of the day; they may need to be willing and able to participate in a group. The question for the manager is what minimum capabilities must a client possess to have a reasonable chance of benefiting from the program.

The following case provides an example of a target population analysis done in designing a parent education program. Expectations of clients must be examined at both the target population and client population levels.

### General Population

This program will focus on largely rural Axis County, whose 1980 population totaled 11,483. Of this number, 30 percent are aged 18 or less, 24 percent are aged 60 and older. The county's primary industry is agriculture-related, but in the last ten years the county experienced a net migration increase of 13 percent as persons moved into Axis County to work in adjacent Brown County's light manufacturing business. With a per capita income of $5,780, Axis County is one of Kansas' less affluent areas and fully 14 percent of the county's population subsist on poverty level incomes, of which one-fourth are families with women as head of household and at least one child age 18 or under.

Various socioeconomic factors are placing stress on Axis County resources; the county population is growing older, reducing its tax base and placing more demand on existing health and social services. The recent influx of new residents who live in Axis County but work in Brown County is altering traditional small "farm towns" into "bedroom communities" in which new residents increase demands on available housing, schools, and public and social services, as well as on informal social and cultural groups such as churches and recreational programs.

Approximately 1,725 people living in Axis County experience problems with alcohol and drug dependence. Over one-half of those divorcing in the county in 1981 did so prior to their sixth year of marriage, and in over 65 percent of these divorces at least one minor child was involved. About 8 percent of the county's labor force is unemployed, and the average education level is eighth grade. Last year there were 100 instances of child abuse and neglect reported with forty of these confirmed.

### At-Risk Population

Since this is a prevention program, it is important to note its inclusive focus. Current technology does not allow for accurate prediction of parents who will or will not abuse. The concern is clearly with directing preventive strategies toward those with certain characteristics or circumstances that increase the likelihood of potential abuse and neglect. While little data is available to quantify these factors for Axis County, the following elements tend to define those families more at risk of child abuse and neglect than others.

Several socioeconomic stresses are affecting Axis County families, which increases the potential risk for child abuse and neglect to occur. The vast majority of Axis County's 2,000 families subsist on low incomes as farm-related work becomes increasingly unprofitable and utility, taxes, and living costs rise. Social isolation is a reality for many families. Social isolation is increased for those recently arrived residents who came to Axis County to work in nearby Brown County factories, as they lack the informal/financial support once provided by family and friends.

Social isolation, a reality in rural counties like Axis, is exacerbated by a lack of county resources to provide public social services taken for granted in urban regions. Services are centered in the county seat, making such programs as health care, counseling, self-help programs, education, emergency assistance, etc., practically inaccessible for many. Formal child care is virtually nonexistent for Axis County families; public housing is available for elderly and disabled persons almost exclusively.

Concerning psychological stresses on Axis County families that identify them as at-risk, it is estimated that about 250 families struggle with alcohol/drug abuse, and 25 percent of parents experienced abuse or neglect as children. In 1984, 93 families and 796 individuals used county mental health services one or more times to address personal concerns such as marital problems, depression, and inadequate coping skills.

Other at-risk factors for families include single parents, families with children a year apart in age or less, families with a child under three years of age or with physical/emotional developmental problems. It is estimated that at least 50 percent of county families experience one or more of these factors.

### Target Population

This parent education program will focus on parents with children aged 5 to 12 years of age. This group numbers approximately 1,000 families. An interest and willingness to participate in parent education is estimated to reduce the target group to 300 families. Other factors that will further limit parent participation include: parents must have basic reading, writing, and communication skills; parents who have previously been confirmed as having abused or neglected their children will be excluded; families in which either child or parent has severe emotional or behavioral disorders will be excluded (these restrictions are necessary to insure the program's focus on a preventive and participatory education process inclusive of the majority of families' experiences). Taking these factors into consideration, the target population is estimated to include 200 families in Axis County.

### Client Population

Several program design considerations further define the program's client population. On the part of the client, these requirements include: stated commitment to participate in the group discussion, individual assessment, and "homework" components of the program; stated commitment to complete the entire educational program; and a schedule that permits parents to attend evening sessions. Due to these guidelines and to agency limitations of financial and staff resources, the program will serve a total client population of 80 to 96 parents in its first year of operation.

## PROGRAM DESIGN STEP 3—DETERMINE THE SOCIAL WORK THEORY OF HELPING

The use of theory to guide practice is a time-honored tradition in social work. Yet the specifics of how theory guides practice tend to be vague. Still more ill defined is the identification and use of social work theory by the social administrator. A quick review of the current management texts in social work reveals scant attention to social work theory. In contrast, Munson (1983) devotes a whole chapter to theory but only gives the definition of types and functions of theory. The use of theory in management is given little attention.

This lack of practice application of theory exists despite the experience of those who have been on the front line of social work. The frontline person who operates from an illness theory makes certain assumptions, behaves in certain ways, attempts to produce specific types of outcomes with clients. The person whose theory of helping involves focusing on the client's behavior makes different assumptions, behaves differently and attempts to produce other types of outcome with clients. The worker who identifies client strengths and builds upon these to satisfy client desires behaves still differently. Given that theory influences or directs practice, the social administrator needs to have the skills to define an intervention theory and to assist workers in the use of that theory.

Social work theories are derived from multiple sources including the complex relationship between our clients, our profession, and society. Social work theory development as a scholarly activity has also grown enormously over the last fifteen years. This includes the framework for developing theory (Thomas, 1984) and the increased empirical verification of the efficacy of interventions. (Reid & Hanrahan, 1982) Knowledge and use of *intervention research* and *program evaluation* is now a requirement of professional social work education (CSWE standards).

## Intervention Theory

From a social administrator's point of view, the social work theory of helping is the heart of program design. It is the social administrator's responsibility to select the most powerful ingredients to produce desired client outcomes. The program design elements that constitute the core of the intervention theory are as follows:

- The client outcome goal
- The client outcome objectives
- Expectations of the client
- Expectations of the worker

The connections between the elements unify them and form them into a useful framework for theory and administrative practice. The helping transaction is driven by a mutually agreed upon goal that specifies the positive outcome for the client. Attainment of this goal is predicated on accomplishing certain objectives. The attainment of the objectives is based on the client and worker fulfilling certain expectations. In a more classical sense, if worker and client exhibit the specified behavior, then the objectives will be met. If the objectives are met, then the goal will be attained.

Social work theories range in complexity with the client outcomes falling into the categories of changes in affect, knowledge, behavior, status, and environment. Intervention theory links the outcomes. Frequently our theories posit that one set of changes or outcomes leads to a second set and ultimately to a third. It is not difficult to find programs that hypothesize that specific changes in affect, knowledge, and environment precede changes in behavior that ultimately result in a change in status.

For example, a parent education program serving a client population of parents who were identified as having abused or neglected a child has, as a goal, moving the children through the public child welfare system which would return them to safe homes and end state intervention. The goal of this parent education program is reached if the following is accomplished. (1) Parents are pleased with their interaction with the teacher and feel that they are learning. (2) Parents also demonstrate increased parenting knowledge then they will. (3) They exhibit positive changes in parenting behavior and provide a safe home so that. (4) State intervention can cease. This is demonstrated diagrammatically in Figure 2–2.

## Goals

A program theory comes directly from a problem analysis. Goals address the desirable outcome for the client, and the objectives and expectations relate to a

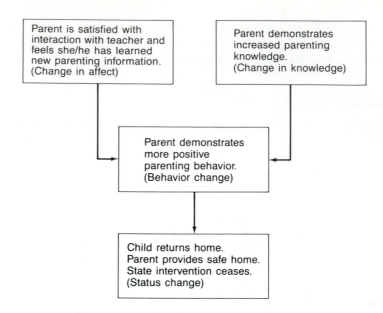

**Figure 2–2.** Parent Education Theory of Helping

selection of contributory factors for which technologies exist to produce positive change.

***Standards for Goal Statements.*** Most programs have but one goal, although (as will be seen later) they usually have multiple objectives. Every goal should meet all of the following criteria:

*The goal must be related to the social problem analysis.* The goal statement should be directly derived from the problem statement. Since most social problems are complex, involving a host of contributing factors, any single program usually seeks to influence but a few. In fact, many factors are well beyond the ability of current social work interventions to produce positive change. To insure the problem-goal relationship, the manager should return to the list of factors contributing to the existence or maintenance of the social problem, and circle those factors his or her program seeks to influence or change. It is these factors that provide the substance for the program goals. The goal derived from the problem analysis described in Figure 2–2 is for the chronically mentally ill to increase the number of consistent relationships that promote community living.

*The goal must be outcome oriented.* The goal statement should be written for clients and not for the agency. For example, program goals *should never* be phrased in terms of "the program will provide." This is what the agency is going to do, but it does not reflect the desired outcome. Rather than stating "the agency will provide prevocational training and job placement," the goal should be "clients will complete prevocational training and obtain employment."

*The goal must be realistic.* The goals must be fiscally, technologically, ethically, and legally possible. Perhaps the earlier deinstitutionalization example can highlight this issue best.

1. *Fiscal realism.* A nationwide discharge of hospital patients required an extensive community network of services. Hospital reductions took place before an intact community system was fiscally possible. Expectations for quality community care were not met despite the fact that millions of federal and local dollars were allocated for services. Currently, there are over 2,000 community agencies, but the goal of "least restrictive" treatment is still beyond current standards of care. The dual promise of community mental health is at the root of this problem. Many believe the fiscal expenditures for community services were spent helping "the worried well" resulting in large populations of underserved chronic patients.
2. *Technological realism.* At the time deinstitutionalization was initiated, little was known about community reintegration of pyschiatric patients. Goals were unrealistic based on a lack of proven methodologies for goal attainment. Much of what is currently known about effective community management of chronic patients comes from community support program pilot projects that occurred long after hospitals were emptied.
3. *Ethical and legal realism.* Legal action based on past and current community treatment of psychiatric patients has increased. Ex-patients and advocates maintain that the wholesale release of patients without appropriate community support resulted in a breach of legislative intent and unethical professional practice. Another example might be goals that require aversive conditioning strategies or research-driven programs where control group subjects may be denied service.

*The goal must be clearly stated.* The goal statements should be understandable to most people. They should be devoid of agency or professional jargon, adjectives, and adverbs (e.g., "appropriate," "ego capacities"). The goal *should* capture the central reason for the program's existence.

*The goal must refer to the client population.* The goal statement should have some mention or reference to the target population (e.g., chronically mentally ill, pregnant teenagers). The goal need only mention the client population. This population has been explicitly defined in the first program design step.

*The goal must be precise.* The goal statement should be observable and measurable or at least it strongly implies such. For example, the goal of improving quality of life is vague and probably overly ambitious. In mental health, however, a specific instrument, the Oregon Quality of Life Instrument (Bigelow, Brodsky, Stewart, & Olson, 1982) has been designed and tested for use with the chronically mentally ill. To the degree that the manager has confidence in this instrument and that it relates to the program's central purpose, the use of the term "quality of life" would meet this standard. However, in most other fields such instruments are not available in which case the use of the term would be too imprecise.

*The goal must be positive.* Goal statements should be written in terms of what will be accomplished rather than in terms of the absence of something (e.g., increase employment versus reduce unemployment). At times, attempts to make a goal statement positive will do injustice to precision and clarity. In these cases let it be negative. Some would argue that "to reduce hospitalizations" is more precise than "to increase tenure in the community." In most cases, beginning a goal with "to increase . . . " will propel the program designer in the right direction.

## Objectives

Objectives are a series of statements that split the goal into specific benefits to be received by clients. These client-outcome objectives are not the only ones required. Programs also need to acquire resources and produce service events. But in terms of the theory of intervention, only the client-outcome objectives are required. Objectives require problem analyses and information about the client population, key players, and other components of program design. This is an interactive process; requiring the administrator to consider many design aspects simultaneously.

There are eight criteria for an adequate objectives statement. Four of these are identical to those discussed for goal setting: Objectives must be *client-outcome oriented, clear, positive,* and *realistic.* The four additional criteria for objectives are

1. *The objective must set a single standard.* Each objective should have a number or percentage or rate that defines *adequate* performance. Rarely will any objective be reached for all clients, nor does the manager ever want to be in the position of implying such. For example, an objective may state that 75 percent of all clients will be employed for a minimum of ten hours a week. The figure set should be based on the manager's assessment that anything below that figure the manager will be disappointed with an appraisal of what is possible. The single standard is a powerful way of building realism into the program. (Carter, 1987; Carter, 1983)
2. *The objective is measurable.* Every objective should be directly measurable and observable; it should be unambiguous.
3. *The objective has time parameters.* Time limitations should be stated. Common time parameters are fiscal year, program year, calendar year, quarterly, and so on.
4. *The objective is related to the goal.* The objectives decompose the program goal into statements of specific benefits.

# Expectations of Client and Provider

Specifying the reciprocal obligations of clients and social worker rounds out the theory of helping. In our society certain role behaviors are widely known and accepted. One learns how to be a patient, how to be a parent, how to be a student. We all master these roles and have a keen understanding of what we can expect from the people in the opposite role—the doctor, the child, the teacher. Without precise knowledge of legitimate expectations there will be breakdowns of communication and strong feelings of resentment at being "let down." Here is an example. A friend says her psychiatrist didn't help her. Discussion of the visit with the psychiatrist revealed that my friend was passive and uncommunicative. I explained that the intervention was predicated on her active verbal involvement. Several months later, she reported the psychiatrist as being much more helpful.

The role of social work clients is not at all well understood. There is the unfortunate stereotype of "welfare chiseler" or "dependent person," which, sad to say, is perpetuated by social workers as well as by the general public. The client-psychotherapist relationship is becoming better understood, especially in upper-middle class circles. Several sociologists have analyzed this role. More to the point, literary portrayals have popularized the therapist-patient role. Many literary allusions to social worker-client relations, on the other hand, portray the reciprocal roles as dominant-submissive, manipulative-helpless. Since the social worker-client role is so little understood, it is not surprising that many cases used for teaching social work involve many minutes and many hours spent in clarifying acceptable behaviors and mutual obligations.

Identification of legitimate reciprocal obligations recognizes the mutual, interacting, and reciprocal nature of social work. The "powers and duties" that each person carries when acting toward the other becomes clear. It is important here to specify the minimum expectations the client can hold towards the worker and those

**TABLE 2-3. CLIENT AND WORKER EXPECTATIONS**

| Factor | Possible Expectation |
|---|---|
| 1. Professional or agency ethics | 1. Confidentiality. |
| 2. Client needs<br>3. Nature of intervention | 2. & 3. Sessions will be held only when all family members are in attendance. |
| 4. Agency policy | 4. Failure to attend activities for a one-month period will result in inactive status and required reapplication for membership. |
| 5. Professional commitments | 5. No action will be taken on behalf of the client without client's explicit approval. |
| 6. State statutes | 6. A written plan will be completed within three weeks. |
| 7. Custom | 7. Client and worker will review their contract every three months. |

the worker can hold towards the client. Neither the client nor the worker should be set up for failure due to unreasonable expectations. At the same time both must be challenged to learn and grow.

In the example of the friend and the psychiatrist, I established the expectation of verbal involvement. When the friend asked what she should talk about I suggested she leave directing the conversation to the professional but that she start talking about anything that came to mind. These minimum expectations were sufficient to significantly alter the helping transaction. As Table 2–3 suggests, expectations may emanate from a variety of factors.

Another set of decisions is the consequence of an expectation not being met. Can a client appeal, and if so, how? Will service be terminated? Will certain reports of records be made? Will failure to meet expectations automatically lead to certain decisions?

In most social work programs, a program description cannot list all possible sets of expectations. As is true of so many management areas, the goal is to identify those behaviors that, if left unspecified, are less likely to occur and are critical for client success. This implies a continual process of learning and revision. Clearly language is also a problem. The difficulties and importance of language will be addressed more completely in the personnel management chapter. For now it is important to state expectations as behaviorly as possible.

Goal: To move children through the public child welfare systems by returning them to safe homes and ending state intervention.
Change objectives: At the end of the ten weeks.

1. Each parenting education class will obtain a minimum parent satisfaction score of 75 on the parent-satisfaction scale.
2. Each parenting education class will obtain a minimum parenting-knowledge-gained score of 63 on the parenting-knowledge-gained instrument.
3. Each parenting education class will obtain a parenting skills score of 61 on the parenting skills inventory.

**Parents will do the following:**

• Parents will talk with their caseworker about the following parenting skills:

1. Communicating with their child
2. Building self-esteem
3. Handling stress and anger
4. Managing their child's behavior

• Parents will complete and sign the three party agreement specifying which parenting skills they seek to learn.
• Parents will attend all parenting sessions.
• Parents will telephone the worker before a session if they cannot attend.
• Parents will be home for scheduled home visits.
• Parents will complete homework assignments.
• Parents will practice skills with their children.
• Talk with the caseworker at the conclusion of the service about the skills they acquired.

**Caseworker will do the following:**

- Assess with the parent their parenting skills and circle the parenting skills to be acquired using the three party agreement.
- Call the parent twice a month and ask about their satisfaction with the service and barriers to full participation.
- Visit the parent twice a month to discuss their progress toward acquiring the specified parenting skills and observe their interaction with their children.

**The teacher will do the following:**

- Visit the parents before the agency begins parent assessment of parenting skills and circle those to be acquired using the three party agreement.
- Arrange the room before each session as specified in the parent education manual.
- Greet the parents individually by name, help them relax and participate in the session.
- Include parents' ideas in class discussion.
- Tell parents when they did something well.
- Tell the parents the agenda for each session.
- Help participants clarify what they are trying to express by feeding back their ideas.
- Encourage each participant to talk in class about things important to him or her.
- Ask each participant to identify the parenting problems on which he or she are working.
- Ask each participant to identify the outcome for what he or she is trying to change.
- Tell each participant the choices he or she has, so that the participant can make his or her own parenting decisions.
- Conduct each class session according to the parenting curriculum unit's goals, objectives.
- Select exercises from the curriculum that meet the needs of the group.
- Specify homework assignments.
- Discuss homework results each week.
- Make a home visit at least every second week to discuss progress toward acquisition of parenting skills and observe parenting behavior.
- Discuss with parents the acquisition of skills at the conclusion of the service and identify those acquired using the three party contract.

## Other Objectives

From a total program design or management point of view additional objectives are required. The program cannot operate without resources, service events, a minimum of staff morale, and attention to efficiency. The operation of the enterprise hinges on reaching all performance area objectives. This then constitutes a complete set of objectives.

When establishing objectives in the remaining performance areas, it is important to be selective. Although a host of resources are required for a program, not all of them need to be objectives. Pens and pencils may be an essential resource, but they can be lumped in with office supplies. On the other hand, the need for 500 hours of service a month to bring in reimbursement dollars and produce client benefits must be an objective. The objectives that need to be written for each performance area are those that the manager needs to attend to for the program to succeed.

## PROGRAM DESIGN STEP 4: SPECIFY THE SERVICE PROCEDURES

The service procedures are the typical stages of the helping transaction. Every helping transaction has a beginning, middle, and end. While much of the real world is not linear, this process assists managers, workers, and clients to stay focused on their goal. A description of a service procedure usually includes each helping phase, the length of the phases, the outcome of each phase, and key decision points. The most common and generic formulation is assessment, case or intervention planning or contracting (including goal settings), intervention, and evaluation. Unfortunately, this breakdown is not very descriptive of any specific service, and the categories, especially intervention, are probably too broad. The manager should use labels that are tailored to his or her service. Examples of other breakdowns of service procedure phases are outlined below:

### *Case Management* (Modrcin, Rapp, & Chamberlain, 1985)
1. Assessment
2. Development of Comprehensive Plan
3. Procurement of Services
4. Monitoring and Advocacy
5. Tracking and Evaluation

### *Compeer*
1. Referral Solicitation—Volunteer Recruitment
2. Client Intake—Volunteer Screening
3. Professional Orientation—Volunteer Training
4. Volunteer Contract
5. Beginning, Middle, and Ending Phase Intervention
6. Evaluation

### *Psychosocial Prevocational Program* (Rapp, Poertner, & Bomhoff, 1986)
1. Work Skills Training Phase
2. Application Phase
3. Work Initiation and Assessment Phase
4. Contract Phase
5. Work Phase

It is important to define an outcome so that both worker and client will know when they are ready to move on. Outcomes could be a signed contract, a decision (e.g., a psychosocial club member takes an in-house work position), a completed assessment report, a client's satisfactory performance level, or a time limit (e.g., after three months, contract renegotiation will occur).

## PROGRAM DESIGN STEP 5: IDENTIFY KEY PERSONS REQUIRED TO PRODUCE CLIENT BENEFITS

The effectiveness of virtually all social services is determined not only by the worker and the client but by a secondary cast of players. This factor is rarely addressed in program descriptions or design activities. Yet it is unusual when a program, for example, serving the chronically mentally ill succeeds without the partnership and cooperation of all the players involved. Hospital discharge staff, officials and workers at affiliated agencies, group home managers, employers, referral sources, administrators, volunteer board of directors all influence the outcome of service.

In this area, the manager must answer three questions:

1. Who are the key players?
2. What minimum set of specific behaviors must the key person consistently perform for the program to reach its objectives?
3. What will be done to elicit and maintain the behavior?

Crucial to the first question is: Is the program likely to achieve its objectives without the cooperation of this person or group? The second decision should be answered behaviorally and should only include minimum, *critical* behaviors not all the behaviors you would like to see. On occasion, the manager may want to specify the amount or frequency of behavior required. Table 2–4 portrays an analysis of key players for an employment training program for the blind.

## PROGRAM DESIGN STEP 6: SPECIFY THE HELPING ENVIRONMENT

One social work strength is the recognition of the importance of the environment to the functioning of people. The description of the setting specifies those characteristics that will enhance the client/worker transaction and ultimately the client outcome. A *service setting* is the typical situation, both physical and social, in which interactions take place. The physical situation may be the counselor's office, a street corner or the client's apartment for case management, a work site for job training, or the offices of a community agency for an advocacy service. Particular space requirements or requirements of privacy or comfort for disabled persons should be indicated clearly. For recreational/socialization programs, it is considered important to have an environment that offers many materials to stimulate participation and interaction. Privacy is essential for some programs but openness and accessibility may be equally essential for some services, such as organizing tenants in a low-income neighborhood or a social activity program for the chronically mentally ill.

**TABLE 2-4. KEY PLAYERS**

| Description | Behavior Required | How to Elicit Behavior |
|---|---|---|
| *Internal* | | |
| A. Vocational Rehabilitation Counseling (VRC) throughout the state of Kansas | A. 1. Refer clients to the program<br>2. Encourage and counsel clients | A. Educate counselors about the program and the equipment used (VIA seminar and update literature) |
| B. Other program area teachers at the Rehabilitation Center for the Blind | B. Refer clients to the computer assisted learning phase and use the computers | B. Educate teachers on the various uses of the equipment with their individual programs |
| C. Department of Administration—Purchasing | C. Acquire IBM compatible computer system, software, and supplies. *Note:* State contract for Zenith | C. Submit request for purchase of computer system, software, and supplies |
| *External* | | |
| D. Computer suppliers | D. Maintain equipment within 24-hours of service call | D. Request bids from local computer service representatives |
| E. Suppliers (hardware and software) | E. Furnish up-to-date product literature and technology developments | E. Subscribe to various catalogues and computer magazines |
| F. Parents and family | F. Encouragement of client during difficult times in the training process | F. Maintain contact with parents and family and report progress and difficulties the client may be experiencing. Also, encourage their involvement (if possible) |

| G. | Business community | G. | Accept clients on trial basis employment opportunity | G. | Offering tax credit incentives and payment of two (2) weeks wages |
| H. | Employment agencies | H. | Accept referrals of clients from program and solicit employment opportunities for the clients | H. | Demonstrate the capabilities blind individuals possess with the aid of adaptive devices on computers |
| I. | Projects with Industry (PWI) (specific agency that works with assisting handicapped in finding employment) | I. | Help clients to find employment opportunities and assist in actual search and transportation | I. | Contact PWI via the Vocational Rehabilitation Counselor (VRC) |
| J. | Media | J. | Periodic news coverage of the activities at the Rehabilitation Center with particular attention to the client's progress with the CRT program | J. | Invite media personnel to the center to observe and participate in computer learning activities |
| K. | Washburn University | K. | Demonstrate acceptance of blind students from the CRT program by establishing computer classes that provide computers with adaptive devices for the blind. Demonstrate acceptance of blind students from the CRT program by computerizing the library in order to make materials more independently accessible for the blind | K. | Approach the school with the idea of a pilot project and work with the university in developing a grant proposal |

The social aspects of the service setting are equally as important as the physical aspects. How many people are usually present? What is the symbolic value of the location or the situation for different participants? Is it desirable that the setting be the client's homeground or the worker's homeground? Setting the stage for client-worker interaction may include defining values, goals, or purposes as much as adjusting the lights or closing the door.

Special features of the program that facilitate access should also be described. Will transportation be provided when necessary? What times and days will the service be available? Will child care arrangements be offered? Access is influenced by these physical factors and by social factors. (Gillespie & Marten, 1978) Will the workers be of the same racial or ethnic group? How will clients in a waiting room be made comfortable? In small rural areas, people may be embarrassed to be seen entering a mental health clinic. Could there be an entrance that is not visible to the street? Could the service be offered through a nonstigmatizing setting—a library or school?

## PROGRAM DESIGN STEP 7: DESCRIBE ACTUAL HELPING BEHAVIORS

Complete description of any complex phenomenon is impossible. But we can examine a phenomenon from a variety of perspectives, thus increasing our insight and understanding. Imagine a large Victorian house sitting in the middle of a city block, obscured by a tall fence. The grandure and intricacy of the house cannot be seen from any one perspective. By approaching the fence and viewing the house from each available knot hole or break in the fence, however, one obtains a variety of views of the house. A rather complete description is obtained from the totality of the perspectives. A social work transaction is equally complex. While we specified behaviors when we identified expectations, this was a minimal list of behaviors. This component of program design takes a different look at the helping transaction and attempts to describe in more detail the richness of the endeavor. This normally includes representative and observable behaviors of both workers and clients.

Although a behavioral description is difficult, certain patterns of communication, of conduct, and typical actions can be identified. Examples are perhaps the most efficient means of indicating typical behavior. The worker in a day treatment facility may physically restrain a client who is violent so that neither may be injured. The client in a sheltered workship will become better groomed, will report promptly for work, and will perform assigned tasks. The group therapist may shout and show anger in repudiating antisocial activities. The caseworker with a rape victim will listen closely to her; will exhibit warm, supportive behavior; will be factual; and will not destroy evidence. A staff member working with a mental hospital resident who is preparing to go into the community will sit next to the resident at lunch and provide prompts and feedback when the person habitually rearranges food on the plate before eating.

A few more examples may help to further explain patterns of behavior. Some service programs specify observable behavior outside as well as inside the service situation. The college student who is so anxious that she cannot take examinations may have the behavioral goal of completing a written examination without leaving the room. The adolescent in family counseling may be working toward the ability to disagree with parents without having a shouting match.

Just as in the case of identifying key players, the program developer must think through which behaviors are essential to the success of the program. Those behaviors should be summarized, outlined, or illustrated by an example.

## PROGRAM DESIGN STEP 8: IDENTIFY EMOTIONAL RESPONSES

Every social worker has experienced emotions while helping a client. Specific emotional responses occur normally in certain situations. Both workers and clients experience emotional reactions. Most workers have experienced responding emotionally in ways that help the client and in ways that do not. In other words, most of us make mistakes. Yet this emotional component of the helping transaction is seldom considered by program designers.

The helping process, whether focused on change or simply on maintenance and delivery of concrete services, stimulates strong emotions. Furthermore, just as the instrumental steps taken in helping are a joint enterprise of client and worker, so are emotional involvements. Today most helping professionals are keenly aware of the fact that helping is not affectively neutral. This fact needs to be recognized in program descriptions, as well as in professional training.

The emotions of client and of worker may be crucial to the success of a service program and should be clearly articulated. Community support program work requires intensive personal involvement on the part of both client and worker. Clients can become frustrated in their efforts to survive in a complex social and work environment with limited adaptive skills. Workers often face the disappointment of slow progress or regression. Recurrence of a client's delusional state may jeopardize recent accomplishments, causing a worker to become anxious about the outcome. Explosive confrontations can occur.

The tasks in this section of the design are, first, to identify the emotions likely to be experienced by *clients* and to specify the most helpful response to these emotions; and second, to identify these emotions likely to be experienced by the *worker* and the accompanying response. How will the worker respond to the identified emotions? What provisions will be made to help workers—supervision, team interventions, support groups, training?

A few examples from actual program descriptions should make the point clear.

In socialization training for severely physically handicapped children workers need to be hopeful and firm with reasonable expectations. Feelings of pity should not play a part in helping these children. Handicapped children, it would seem, cannot possibly incorporate acceptable performance standards unless they experience the existence of these standards, and their own experience in meeting them again and again. In family counseling where social workers are seeing several family members together and there is severe family conflict, it is not reasonable to expect that a series of stormy and emotional sessions could be held without affecting the worker. On the other hand, it might be very important that workers, in order to avoid being conscripted, so to speak, by dominant family members, should make clear both before the session begins and during it, the nature of their emotional reaction. In this case, the program description could simply note that it is normal for workers to feel repugnance, anger, affection, and to feel more sympathy with one family member than another. These emotions, however, will be managed by verbalizing them during therapy sessions. A third example is from a program for severely disabled or terminally ill clients. Social workers, especially those who have not had to come to terms with their own mortality and frailty, find it very threatening and disabling to talk frankly with their clients about death. Elderly terminally ill clients often talk in detail about the arrangements for their funeral or how their personal goods should be distributed among children. The worker may find this discussion very sad and feel that the clients should not discuss their own impending death in such fashion because it is "giving up." In this case, the program description indicates that such emotional pitfalls are common, but workers must be able to match the objectivity and courage of clients to be helpful.

## The Need for Good Descriptions

In the final analysis, the importance of being clear about affective involvements is not to improve professional skill or to improve practice, although these goals are vitally important in other contexts, but to improve management and accountability. The description of affective involvements tells the manager what qualifications of workers are needed, how to adjust the service process to accommodate emotional factors, and what particular physical arrangements and facilities may be necessary. Since some service programs are particularly emotionally threatening or demanding it is important for a program description to provide for adequate relief time, consultation, or other means to support professional workers in this difficult role.

## Putting the Steps to Work

To summarize the components of program design, it might be most helpful to think in terms of a recipe book. A minimum requirement for a recipe is to list the ingredients for a particular dish and show how these ingredients are put together. A good recipe book guides the preparation process, yet encourages creativity by the cook. Some recipe books are extremely terse on these procedures, and where that is the case a kitchen planner really might not know how much space, what pans, cooking utensils, and special facilities or equipment and skill are necessary to cook a particular dish. Fine cuisine requires a clear process that not only shows the cook the steps but also the *method* for carrying out these steps. It will be helpful, even to the experienced chef, if there are little discussions of such matters as selecting fresh vegetables, the variations in preparation that are possible, and some intimation of the particular arts, the aesthetics, and emotional factors that go into the preparation of really fine dishes. In like manner, it is essential for the program developer to give to the audience a lively appreciation of the client-worker interaction in its full and vital reality including ingredients, necessary steps, typical ways to carry out the service, and even the moral and emotional nature of the interaction.

## The Program Design Document

The program design document should be a working, dynamic product. It should be referred to when program issues are raised. It should be revised as program decisions are reformulated and adjustments made. It should be used with program staff and external constituencies. At any point in time the document should be complete and up-to-date, which would prevent a manager from saying, "Well, we changed a few things that are not included here." As a working document, the design can help keep the program focused on performance.

## Getting the Program Design Off the Shelf

We stated earlier that the model of program design proffered here is based on an assumption that, once designed, the product would be used as an ongoing management tool. This means that the product can be useful for *managing* the program as well as for submitting grants to *fund* the program. Design products can be used in three specific ways: (1) as a basis for developing other organizational requisites; (2) for program monitoring; and (3) for diagnostic purposes.

The analytical processes used, the critical management decisions made, and the wealth of description developed provide a rich source of direction for carrying out a variety of important management tasks. In managing people, for example, the design can help guide the development of job descriptions, determine caseload size, establish qualifications of prospective staff, and partially dictate the nature of supervision and staff meetings.

In managing information, the design is a principal tool for developing the management information system. It also helps determine the substance of feedback, which is required by various organizational levels.

In terms of managing resources, the design is the principal product upon which to develop a budget. It should also be used to focus the interactions between organizational members and key players. The design suggests information that should be shared with prospective and accepted clients. In addition, the design can be used to develop brochures, to provide information to the media, and as a basis for developing speeches and other educational efforts.

*For Program Monitoring.* The process of implementation is "frequently marked by trial, error, instability and change." (Patti, 1983, p. 52) Many common problems generally considered implementation problems have been addressed in the discussion of the program design process. For example, what clients out of the total pool of people should be accepted? What should I do about some key players? What process should I follow to reach what goals? The design is a prescription that will need constant monitoring and alteration especially in the early stages of program operations.

The program design is the principle source of key variables that the organization needs to monitor. As such it acts as a problem-finding tool. (Livingston, 1975; Mackworth, 1969) Are the clients members of the target population? Are direct service workers following the protocols described in the service plan? Are key players performing the behaviors necessary for success? A sample of such a checklist can be found at the end of this chapter.

*For Program Diagnosis.* As a monitoring tool, the design is the basis for proactive surveillance of the program. Preestablished dimensions are used to search for congruence between the design and implementation. The program design can also be used to help locate sources of problems and thereby better guide their remediation. Problems that occur during the operation of a program are often viewed as implementation problems when in fact they may be a function of inadequate or incorrect design. For example, if a client complains about some facet of service, it may be that mutual expectations are unclear or ambiguous or incomplete (design) or it could be that workers are not meeting the expectations of the service plan (implementation). Even if it is the latter situation, there may be specific obstacles workers are confronting that could serve to further develop and specify the service plan.

The use of the program design as a management tool presupposes that the design is a dynamic one. It should be regularly changed and added to as subsequent program decisions are made.

## DIAGNOSING INADEQUATE PROGRAM DESIGN

Table 2–5 (pp. 66–67) was developed to help community support program managers locate indicators of inadequate program design for programs already under operation. It includes three categories:

1. *Event.* These are occurrences that may be attributable to poor program design. They are descriptions of single cases that often have problems associated with them. Each event could, however, also reflect a pattern rather than an isolated case. This listing of events should be viewed as a sampler to which others could be added.

2. *Diagnosis.* These questions reflect specific program design elements that

could be contributing to the event. An affirmative answer would suggest that improvements in the program design may be warranted.
3. *Relevant design elements*. These design elements relate to the event and diagnosis. The manager should turn to the section in the text that describes the element of concern.

In general, each event can be caused by multiple factors, program design being only one set. Clients, staff, central office, or a judge are often blamed for events, when in fact there are systemic factors contributing to it. This table should help managers identify these systemic factors.

## PROGRAM ANALYSIS CHECKLIST

The following checklist/questionnaire has been designed to guide managers in designing new programs or in evaluating proposals for new programs. It is a reference document that helps summarize the principles of adequate program design. The checklist can easily be used to guide human service agencies in describing the programs for which they are requesting public or private funds. Managers should be able to affirmatively answer each question.

    I. Performance
        A. Are there clear program statements and standards for client outcomes, productivity, efficiency, and resource acquisition?
        B. Do the staff know them and feel comfortable with them?
        C. Does each staff member get reports on these performance areas for themselves and the program or unit?
        D. Is program performance a regular topic of conversation (informal and formal)?
    II. Is it clear what social problem the program is designed to address?
        A. How does the client experience the problem?
        B. How does the larger community or society experience the problem?
        C. What are the factors that contribute to the problem's existence or maintenance?
    III. Does the goal reflect the benefits clients will receive (outcome oriented), and does it meet the other standards?
        A. Measurable/observable
        B. Relatedness to the problem analysis
        C. Realistic
        D. Clear (e.g., lack of jargon, adjectives, adverbs)
        E. Positive
        F. Some mention of the client population
    IV. Are the target and client populations unambiguously defined?
        A. How are you recruiting clients?

**TABLE 2-5. DIAGNOSING INADEQUATE PROGRAM DESIGN**

| Event | Diagnosis | Relevant Design Elements |
|---|---|---|
| 1. Client does not follow through on service plan (e.g., does not participate in psychosocial club activities, drops out of work program) | Are there programmatic obstacles to compliance? Are the consequences for compliance and noncompliance clear? Was the client prepared for the current program phase? Is the client angry, scared, or distraught to the point that compliance is difficult? | • Mutual expectations<br>• Setting<br>• Affective<br>• Natural history |
| 2. Service is not effective when client completes it (i.e., client outcomes are not accomplished even though clients complete program) | Is the intervention too weak? Is the intervention directed at only one level? Is there a subgroup of clients for whom it is effective? Can the service be further targeted? Is the service plan not explicit enough? | • Selecting the intervention<br>• Target population<br>• Service plan |
| 3. Can't tell if client(s) is making satisfactory progress<br>  a. Service agency claims success but funding group disagrees<br>  b. Client claims success but staff is unsure<br>  c. Staff claims success but client is not satisfied | Do the program goals and objectives meet standards? Are measures unambiguous? | • Goals<br>• Objectives |
| 4. Client(s) complains about some facet of service | Are expectations unclear or ambiguous? Are workers not meeting the expectations of the service plan? | • Service plan (mutual expectations in particular) |
| 5. The volunteer or staff contacts occur but they are disruptive to the client | Are expectations unclear or ambiguous? Are there adequate provisions for volunteer or staff involvement? | • Mutual expectations<br>• Key players<br>• Affective involvements |
| 6. Case decisions are not made in a timely manner<br>  a. Worker does not know when to process a change in program status | Are time lines for decisions explicit and written in the service plan? Are criteria for making decisions explicit? | • Natural history |

| | | |
|---|---|---|
| b. Worker does not know when to close a case<br>c. Volunteer does not know which program is occurring | | |
| 7. Access to service is cumbersome or not timely<br>a. Referrals to agencies are rejected<br>b. Referrals are placed on waiting lists<br>c. The needed service does not exist | Is the client/target population unambiguously defined?<br>Does the client population need to be further limited?<br>Should program expansion or a new program be considered? | • Target population<br>• Key players |
| 8. Affiliated agencies in the community support program network don't cooperate with program decisions | Are the reciprocal expectations behaviorally explicit?<br>Are efforts ongoing to monitor feedback and enforce these expectations?<br>Are decision-making criteria unambiguous and agreed to? | • Key players<br>• Natural history |
| 9. Relationship with referral sources and community support program network agencies marked by conflict and acrimony<br>a. Agencies blame other agencies<br>b. Clients blame agencies<br>c. Agencies blame clients | Are the reciprocal expectations behaviorally explicit?<br>Are efforts ongoing to monitor feedback, and enforce these expectations?<br>Are decision-making criteria unambiguous and agreed to? | • Key players<br>• Goals<br>• Objectives |
| 10. Clients don't become fully engaged in services | Are emotional issues not being addressed or addressed poorly?<br>Do the minimum expectations of workers include treating the client with respect, courtesy, etc.?<br>Are mutual expectations explicit and agreed to? | • Affective involvements<br>• Mutual expectations |
| 11. | | |
| 12. | | |

    B. Are you serving the clients you should be serving or desire to serve?

    C. How much worker discretion is allowed in selecting clients?

V. Do the objectives reflect measurable client benefits and meet the other standards?

    A. Sets a single performance standard

    B. Sets a time parameter

    C. Relatedness to the goal

    D. Measurable/observable

    E. Realistic

    F. Clear

VI. Are the interventions employed by the program the most powerful? Are they directed at multiple levels (e.g., individual, family, group, institutional, etc.)?

    A. Is there research support for the intervention?

    B. Is it based on the best available knowledge in the field?

    C. Is there an adequate environmental intervention effort?

VII. Is the program adequately specified?

    A. Setting

        1. Is the setting accessible to clients (physically, socially/psychologically, geographically)?

        2. Does the setting provide the necessary accouterments needed to help?

        3. Is it the best possible setting for clients? Would another setting be better for clients?

    B. Natural History

        1. Are the phases (stages) of the program clearly described?

        2. Are decision points in the life of the client's involvement with the program reflected?

        3. Are the outcomes for each phase unambiguously defined?

        4. Would a client be able to read the natural history and understand it?

        5. Are these phases adhered to by staff?

    C. Key Players

        1. Are all the key players identified?

        2. Are the specific behaviors required of each player defined?

        3. Are the key players and behavior *required* for the program's success?

        4. Does each key player know what your expectations are?

        5. Does each key player meet the program's behavioral expectations?

        6. Are there provisions for key player involvement and feedback?

    D. Mutual Expectations

        1. Is there a list of what all clients can expect from the program and its staff?

    2. Does the program staff agree on these expectations? Can they independently construct the same list?

    3. Is there an easy client complaint/appeal procedure in place?

    4. Is there a list of minimum expectations for clients?

    5. Does your staff agree on these?

    6. Is it clear how failure to meet these expectations will be handled by program personnel?

    7. Does your staff enforce and adhere to these expectations?

E.  Affective Involvements

    1. Are there program provisions on how to handle emotional reactions of clients?

    2. Is there agreement on how emotional reactions of clients will be handled?

    3. Are there program provisions for how emotional reactions of staff will be addressed?

    4. Do all staff know and use these provisions?

F.  Actual Behavior

    1. Does the staff consistently implement the program of service as designed?

G.  Miscellaneous

    1. Do all staff see the positive client results of their efforts?

    2. When a characteristic does not succeed, is the program analyzed to see if it was a problem with the design or implementation of the design?

    3. Where did the program go wrong? What could have been done differently?

# SUMMARY

In this chapter, we described a set of tasks and procedures for systematically designing social programs in which client benefits are the centerpiece. After defining terms and discussing values and information needs, the chapter instructs the reader in the eight step process including basic management tasks as setting goals and objectives, deciding on the program's target population, and selecting the interventions. We conclude the chapter by describing how the client-centered performance manager can use the program design as an ongoing management tool for identifying other organizational requisites, program monitoring and as an aid to diagnosing program inadequacies. Specification of the program through design is essential to designing an information system that keeps the program performing as intended. Designing such an information system is the next set of management tasks.

## REFERENCES

Bachrach, L. L. (1982). Young adult chronic patients: An analytical review of the literature. *Hospital and Community Psychiatry, 33*(3), 189–197.

Bassuk, E. L., & Gerson, S. (1978). Deinstitutionalization and mental health services. *Scientific American, 238*(2), 46–53.

Benton, B., Field, T., & Millar, R. (1978). Social services: Federal legislation vs. state implementation. Washington, DC: Urban Institute.

Bigelow, D. A., Brodsky, D., Stewart, Z., & Olson, M. M. (1982). The concept and measurement of quality of life as a dependent variable in evaluation of mental health services. In W. R. Tash & G. L. Stohler, (Eds.), *Innovative Approaches to Mental Health Evaluation*. New York: Academic.

Blumer, H. (1971, Winter). Social problems collective behavior. *Social Problems, 18,* 298–306.

Bond, G. R., & Boyer, S. L. (in press). The evaluation of vocational programs for the mentally ill: A review. In J. A. Ciardiello & M. D. Bell, (Eds.), *Vocational Rehabilitation of Persons with Prolonged Mental Illness*. Baltimore: Johns Hopkins University Press.

Carter, R. K. (1983). *The accountable agency*. Beverly Hills: Sage.

Carter, R. K. (1987, Fall/Winter). Measuring client outcomes: The experience of the states. *Administration in Social Work, 11*(3/4), 73–88.

Chambers, D. E. (1986). *Social policy and social programs*. New York: Macmillan.

Chappell, B. (1975). One agency's periodic review in foster care: The South Carolina story. *Child Welfare, 54*(7), 477–486.

Chu, F. D., & Trotter, S. (1974). The MADNESS establishment: Ralph Nader's group report on the National Institute of Mental Health. New York: Grossman.

Claburn, W. E., Magura, S., & Resnick, W. (1976). Periodic review of foster care: A brief national assessment. *Child Welfare, 55*(6), 395–405.

Costin, L. B., & Rapp, C. A. (1984). *Child welfare: policies and practice*. New York: McGraw-Hill.

Council on Social Work Education (1984). Handbook of accreditation standards and procedures. New York: Council on Social Work Education.

Cowger, C. (in press). Assessment of client strengths. In D. Saleebey, (Ed.), *The Strengths Perspective in Social Work Practice: Power in the People*. White Plains, NY: Longman.

Davidson, W. S., II, & Rapp, C. A. (1976, May). Child advocacy in the justice system. *Social Work Journal, 21*(3), 225–232.

Dion, G. L., & Anthony, W. A. (1987). Research in psychiatric rehabilitation: A review of experimental and quasi-experimental studies. *Rehabilitation Counseling Bulletin,* 177–203.

Emlen, A. C., Lahti, J., Downs, G., McKay, A., & Downs, S. (1977). *Overcoming barriers to planning for children in foster care*. Portland, OR: Regional Research Institute for Human Services.

Fairweather, G. W. (1972). Social change: The challenge to survival. Morristown, NJ: General Learning Press.

Fanshel, D., & Shinn, E. B. (1978). *Children in foster care: A longitudinal investigation*. New York: Columbia University Press.

Festinger, T. (1975, April). The New York Court review of children in foster care. *Child Welfare, 54*(4), 211–245.

Fischer, J. (1973). Is casework effective? A review. *Social Work Journal, 18*(1), 5–20.

Germain, C. B., & Gitterman, A. (1980). *The life model of social work practice*. New York: Columbia University Press.

Gillespie, D. F., & Marten, S. E. (1978). Assessing service accessibility. *Administration in Social Work, 2*(2), 183–197.

Gowdy, E., Rapp, C. A., & Poertner, J. (1987). Managing for performance: Using information to enhance community integration of the chronically mentally ill. Lawrence, KS: University of Kansas School of Social Welfare.

Gruber, B. (1986). A three-factor model of administrative effectiveness. *Administration in Social Work, 10*(3), 1–14.

Kelly, J. G. (1971). The quest for valid preventive interventions. In G. Rosenblum, (Ed.), *Issues in Community Psychology and Preventive Mental Health*. New York: Behavioral Publications.

Livingston, J. S. (1975, January/February). The myth of the well-educated manager. *Harvard Business Review, 53*(1), 96–106.

Mackworth, N. H. (1969). Originality. In D. Wolfle, (Ed.), *The Discovery of Talent*. Cambridge, MA: Harvard University Press.

Modrcin, M., Rapp, C. A., & Chamberlain, R. (1985). Case management with psychiatrically disabled individuals: Curriculum and training program. Lawrence, KS: University of Kansas School of Social Welfare.

Morrison, R. L., & Bellack, A. S. (1984). Social skills training. In A. S. Bellock, (Ed.), *Schizophrenia: Treatment, Management, and Rehabilitation*. Orlando, FL: Grune & Stratton.

Munson, C. E. (1983). *An introduction to clinical social work supervision*. New York: Haworth.

Neugeboren, B. (1985). *Organization, policy, and practice in the human services*. New York: Longman.

Palumbo, D. J., & Harder, M. A. (Ed.). (1981). *Implementing public policy*. Lexington, MA: Lexington Books.

Patti, R. (1983). *Social welfare administration*. Englewood Cliffs, NJ: Prentice-Hall.

Pepper, B., Ryglewicz, H., & Kirshner, M. C. (1982). The uninstitutionalized generation: A new breed of psychiatric patient. *New Directions for Mental Health Services, 14,* 3–14.

Prather, J. E., & Gibson, F. K. (1977, September/October). The failure of social programs. *Public Administration Review, 38*(5), 556–564.

Rapp, C. A., & Poertner, J. (1978, Fall). Reducing foster care: Critical factors and administrative strategies. *Administration in Social Work, 2*(3), 335–346.

Rapp, C. A., Poertner, J., & Bomhoff, K. (1986). *Designing community programs that work for the chronically mentally ill*. Lawrence, KS: The University of Kansas School of Social Welfare.

Rappaport, J. (1977). *Community psychology: Values, research and action*. New York: Holt, Rinehart & Winston.

Reid, W. J., & Hanrahan, P. (1982). Recent evaluations of social work: Grounds for optimism. *Social Work Journal, 27*(4), 328–340.

Rubin, A. (1984). Community based care of the mentally ill: A research review. *Health and Social Work, 9*(3), 165–177.

Ryan, W. (1971). *Blaming the victim*. New York: Vintage Books.

Stein, T. J., & Gambrill, E. D. (1977, December). The Alameda Project: Two year report. *Social Service Review, 51,* 502–513.

Stein, T. J., Gambrill, E. D., & Wiltse, K. T. (1974, Fall). Foster care: The use of contracts. *Public Welfare, 32*(4), 20–25.

Stuart, R. B. (1977). *Trick or treatment: How and when psychology fails*. Champaign, IL: Research Press.

Sullivan, W. P. (in press). Reconsidering the environment as a helping resource. In D. Saleebey, (Ed.), *The Strengths Perspective in Social Work Practice: Power in the People*. White Plains, NY: Longman.

Taber, M. (1980). *The social context of helping* (DHHS Publication No. 80–842). Washington, DC: U.S. Government Printing Office.

Taber, M. (1987). A theory of accountability for the human services and the implications for social program design. *Administration in Social Work, 11*(3/4), 115–126.

Taber, M., & Finnegan, D. (1980). *A theory of accountability for social work programs*. Unpublished paper, University of Illinois School of Social Work, Urbana, Illinois.

Thomas, E. J. (1984). *Designing interventions for the helping professions*. Beverly Hills: Sage.

Watson, K. W. (1982, Spring). A bold new model for foster family care. *Public Welfare, 40*(2), 14–21.

Weick, A., Rapp, C. A., Sullivan, W. P., & Kisthardt, W. (1989). A strengths perspective for social work practice. *Social Work, 34*(4), 350–354.

Wood, K. M. (1978). Casework effectiveness: A new look at the research evidence. *Social Work, 23*(4), 437–458.

# Appendix
## *Model Program Design: A Parent Education Program for Mothers in the Early Stages of Recovery from Alcohol and Drug Abuse*

Theresa Early

## THE PROBLEM

Physical punishment of children—specifically, disciplining children by hitting—is widespread in schools and homes in the United States. In a 1989 survey of a random sample of 901 parents in Texas, 49 percent of parents interviewed said that they had spanked one of their children within the past few months. (Hill Research Consultants, 1989) In the same survey, 70 percent of parents sanctioned the use of corporal punishment in the schools, and 27 percent of parents reported that their children had been spanked in school. (Hill Research Consultants, 1989) Other studies have revealed even higher levels of parents disciplining children by hitting. (Straus & Gelles, 1988; Alvy, 1987)

Even though almost half of parents surveyed in the Texas study sanctioned the use of corporal punishment by the schools, a percentage of parents interviewed said that they felt one of their children had been seriously abused when disciplined at school: 3 percent of all parents, 6 percent of low socioeconomic status parents, 4 percent of black parents, and 5 percent of Hispanic parents. (Hill Research Consultants, 1989)

The use of physical punishment has many consequences for children, for parents, and for society. A recent human development text cites research studies that report that children show high levels of aggression when their parents frequently use power-assertive techniques (including physical punishment, shouting, attempts to physically move a child, or threatening any of these). (Newman & Newman, 1987) Further, children who are frequently disciplined through physical control fail to learn to control their own behavior, resulting in "minimal internalizations of moral prohibitions." (Newman & Newman, 1987) When children learn to act aggressively, they don't learn appropriate social skills or how to solve problems. These deficits in children's skills lead to poor peer relations, poor school performance, and feelings of guilt, anger, shame, and confusion.

Additionally, since such a fine line separates physical punishment from outright child abuse, child abuse must be considered to be one of the consequences of the use of physical punishment—a consequence for children, for parents, and for society. Daro reports the following consequences of child abuse for children younger than thirteen years of age, as revealed in the National Clinical Evaluation Study:

- About 30 percent of abused children had chronic health problems.
- About 30 percent of abused children had cognitive or language disorders.
- More than 50 percent of abused children had socioemotional problems including low self-esteem, lack of trust, low frustration tolerance, and poor relationships with parents.
- More than 50 percent of abused children had difficulty in school, including poor attendance and misconduct.
- More than 22 percent of abused children had learning disorders requiring special education services. (Daro, 1988, p. 154)

As the American Association for Protecting Children (AAPC) conservatively estimated the 1983 national incidence rate of child abuse at 11.8 per 1,000 children under age 18, it is estimated that 739,000 children were maltreated by their parents during that year. (Daro, 1988)

Daro's work estimates the monetary costs involved in providing services to maltreated children through public child welfare, public health, criminal justice, and rehabilitation systems, based on 23,648 children reported with serious physical injury resulting from maltreatment in 1983. (Daro, 1988) Using very conservative estimates of the number of these children who required health and remedial services, Daro estimates that the immediate inpatient medical costs for these children would exceed $20 million; special education costs would be more than $7 million in the one year following maltreatment; developmental disabilities services costs would exceed $1.1 million; and foster care costs would be around $460 million in the year following maltreatment. (Daro, 1988) These figures represent estimates of only the most immediate of interventions; the actual fiscal impact over these children's lifetimes is far greater.

The long-term consequences for children who are maltreated are not as well documented, but evidence exists that adolescents and adults who were maltreated as children continue to have problems that are related to maltreatment, including an increased prevalence of chemical dependency, increased rates of delinquent behavior and adult criminal behavior, and recurring physical and mental health problems. (Daro, 1988)

## Problem Causation/Maintenance

In a recent movie, *Raising Arizona,* a couple kidnap an infant and also steal a copy of Dr. Spock's baby book as an "instruction manual." In reality, babies don't come with instruction manuals, and many parents lack necessary knowledge and are unprepared for the demands placed upon them by their child's care. When parents lack knowledge of child development and behavior management, theirs and their child's, it is easy for them to be overwhelmed by the twenty-four-hour demands of caregiving. In an effort to gain control of their children, many parents resort to the use of physical punishment.

In the study of parents in Texas cited earlier, 73 percent of parents interviewed agreed with a statement that physical punishment should be used in schools only when all other kinds of discipline have failed. (Hill Research Associates, 1989) Thus, for many parents, physical punishment, while acceptable, is a method of last resort. In Alvy's (1987) study with black parents of Head Start children, white low-income parents of preschool aged children, and white high-income parents of preschool aged children, at least 20 percent of parents who used physical discipline stated they used hitting as a last resort.

The reasons that parents cited for hitting their children differed somewhat in the racial groups studied by Alvy. More black parents used hitting as a teaching method, largely to improve behavior, and to teach obedience. They believe it is necessary because of their young children's limitations in reasoning and language. White parents in the study, on the other hand, "tend to hit when their children have angered them and nothing else seems to work, and they want to let their children know that they mean business." (Alvy, 1987, p. 89)

Giovannoni (1985) states that "the acceptance of corporal punishment throughout society, without any clear sanctions against its excessive use, or even any clear distinctions between how much is acceptable and how much is excessive, can be seen as a source of potential child abuse rooted in societal values." (p. 195) As Giovannoni clearly has indicated, societal attitudes about corporal punishment contribute to the continuation of its use, as well as contribute to the potential for child abuse. The "place" of children in the society also contributes to the use of physical punishment; because children still are seen as property of parents, parents have great latitude in disciplining their children.

Interestingly, while it has been known for many years that horses, dogs, and other animals are not effectively trained through physical punishment, the notion persists that nothing but physical punishment will work with young children. It seems that if parents were able to better control their own anger and impatience for children to learn appropriate behavior, they might be able to effectively use more humane techniques to teach their children.

Finally, the presence in families of chemical abuse or spouse abuse creates an environment in which physical punishment is more likely to occur. Alcohol and drugs often lower the user's frustration tolerance and self-control. When chemical-abusing parents are confronted with misbehavior, it is likely that they will use physical punishment for these reasons and because their own reasoning is impaired. Similarly, when mothers are themselves being abused, their efforts to control their children are more likely to be through asserting power over the children through physical punishment.

## POPULATION TO BE SERVED

### General Population

The catchment area for this program is the State of Kansas, which had an estimated 2.476 million residents in 1987. Of these, 1.043 million were aged 18 years old through 45 years old, and approximately 51 percent of the total population was female, based on figures from the 1980 census. An estimated 532,000 women ages 18 to 45 resided in Kansas in 1987. (Kansas Statistical Abstract, 1987–1988) The 1980 census of the United States revealed that 66.7 percent of the Kansas population lived in urban areas, although one-fourth of Kansas counties have a population density of less than five persons per square mile.

Nationwide figures for 1985 reveal that of all family households, 49.6 percent had children in them and 59.3 percent of female-headed households had children. In 1985, it was estimated that Kansas contained 925,800 households and that the average Kansas household was comprised of 2.56 persons. (U.S. Bureau of the Census, 1987) Assuming that Kansas figures are near the national averages would mean that in 1985 between 460,000 and 549,000 Kansas households had children living in them and that at least 400,000 Kansas women were mothers of at least one child younger than 18 years of age.

In 1987, an estimated 651,000 children lived in Kansas. (Kansas Department of Health and Environment, 1988) Nationally, 41 percent of children live with both parents and slightly more than 50 percent live with their mothers only, so fully 91 percent of children live with their mothers. (Rosen, Fanshel & Lutz, 1987) Again applying the national statistic to Kansas figures for number of children younger than 18 years of age indicates that more than 590,000 Kansas children live with their mothers, and about 326,000 of them with only their mothers.

It is estimated that about 4 percent of United States females abuse alcohol. If this rate holds true for Kansas, more than 21,000 Kansas women experience problems with alcohol abuse. Women abuse many other drugs as well, so the numbers of women who are substance abusers is likely to be considerably more than 21,000.

In 1987, the per capita income in Kansas was $15,126, which is very close to the national average. (Kansas Department of Health and Environment, 1988) A great deal of variability in income among Kansans exists, however. In 1986, per capita income in individual Kansas counties ranged from a low of $10,000 to $11,900 to a high of $18,000 to $20,400. Of 105 counties, seven had per capita incomes in the highest range and twelve had per capita incomes in the lowest range. (Kansas Department of Health and Environment, 1988)

Registered live births in Kansas in 1986 numbered 39,177; marriages numbered 22,667, divorces/annulments numbered 12,364; and deaths numbered 22,133. In 1987, Kansas recorded 353 deaths of infants younger than one year old. At least one minor child was involved in 57.1 percent of all dissolutions of marriage in 1987; 13,281 minor children in all were involved in dissolutions. (Kansas Department of Health and Environment, 1988)

## At-Risk Population

A program to prevent child abuse through reducing the use of physical punishment must examine those factors in the general population that increase the likelihood that physical punishment will be used. Factors that are thought to be associated with increased physical punishment of children include spouse abuse in the family, poverty and related stresses on the family, unemployment, and substance abuse by parents.

It is difficult to quantify the numbers of people affected by these factors that contribute to the incidence of physical punishment of children. A 1985 National Family Violence Survey estimated that spouse abuse was experienced by 34 of 1,000 women in the United States. (Straus & Gelles, 1988) Researchers in this field tend to agree that this estimate is lower than the actual rate of spouse abuse. If this rate is an underestimate, more than 18,088 Kansas women experienced spouse abuse in 1985.

One measure of poverty is the number of people who receive Aid to Families with Dependent Children (AFDC) benefits since eligibility for the program is determined by comparing a family's income to the government's official poverty level. In 1987, a monthly average of 73,171 Kansans received AFDC benefits, 48,069 of them children. (World Almanac, 1987)

Kansas Department of Human Resources figures indicate Kansas had a labor force of 1.267 million in 1987, with an unemployment rate of 4.9 percent. This means that in 1987, some 62,000 workers were unemployed.

## Target Population

This program is targeted to women in early recovery from substance abuse. The portion of the substance-abusing women it will serve are those who have completed a substance abuse treatment program. According to Kansas Alcohol and Drug Abuse Services, in 1987, 8,460 women were admitted to chemical-dependency treatment programs in Kansas. Most treatment programs have dropout rates of 20 percent or less, so we are estimating that almost 7,000 Kansas women complete a substance abuse treatment program per year.

## Client Population

The population for this program is further limited by the auspice of the program agency. The program primarily will be for residents of First Step House in Lawrence, a women's residential reintegration facility. Clients in this program will be women who are pregnant, parenting, step-parenting, or considering pregnancy/adoption; about 80 percent of the residents meet these criteria. First Step House has capacity for sixteen women at a time, who stay an average of three months. It yearly serves around seventy-seven women. Approximately sixty-two First Step House residents per year will be eligible for the program. Additionally, women from Douglas County who are in early recovery from substance abuse and who are pregnant or parenting may be referred to the program on an out-client basis when there is space available. In all, the program will serve sixty-eight women per year, in four, twelve-week cycles of classes.

## EXISTING SERVICES

In Kansas, the program at First Step House is unique—there are no other programs in the state that target women in early recovery from substance abuse for any services. Women who complete substance abuse treatment programs and do not go to First Step House have access to a variety of community services, depending upon their community. In almost any area of the state, women would have access to Alcoholics Anonymous or some other mutual support group geared to substance abuse issues. These groups, beneficial as they may be, tend to have greater attendance by men than by women. Women who are substance abusers carry a greater stigma than men substance abusers do. Women in these groups may hesitate to seek help with parenting since the societal standards for the behavior of mothers is even higher than for other women. Additionally, since the group is concerned primarily with the substance abuse experiences of the members, parenting concerns are seldom likely to be addressed.

Women who are in a metropolitan area may have access to parent information or "helplines," or to parenting classes and support groups. But no existing parenting classes or support groups in the state of Kansas target the needs of mothers in the early recovery stage of substance abuse, or in any other stage of recovery. The early recovery stage is a stage in which those recovering must restructure their lives to prevent relapsing into further substance abuse. Mothers in this stage have many issues to resolve around what their parenting may have been like during the active stages of their substance abuse and how they are going to parent differently in recovery.

Parent education programs exist in many areas of Kansas, from the isolated rural areas to the major metropolitan areas. Most of these programs are targeted to particular parents: parents of infants, teenage parents, mothers who have been battered, parents of teenagers, parents of elementary school-aged children. The mothers who are recovering from substance abuse may be eligible for one or more of these community programs, but the primary need they have is to examine the role that substance abuse plays in their parenting. No other known parent education program purports to do this.

## THEORY OF INTERVENTION

### Intervention Goal

Mothers who are in early recovery from substance abuse will increase their use of positive behavior management of their children.

### Intervention Objectives

At the end of the ten-week session:

1. Eighty percent of participants will learn positive behavior management skills, as evidenced by scores of 85 percent on Nurturing Quiz.
2. Eighty percent of participants will report scores of 4 for their use of two of six behavior management techniques on question 25 of the Nurturing Quiz.

3. Ninety percent of participants will report improvement in two parenting skills.
4. Ninety percent of participants will gain increased confidence in their parenting, as indicated by lower scores on the Parenting Stress Index following the last session.

## Expectations of Participants and Client-Service Staff

First Step House counselors will have the following responsibilities for prospective participants in their caseloads or those people referred from an outside source:

- Interview each participant to fill out parenting strengths assessment form.
- Give directions for Nurturing Quiz each time participant fills it out.
- Have participant fill out Nurturing Quiz.
- Talk with participant about her parenting strengths revealed by the Nurturing Quiz.
- Ask each participant which three parenting skills the participant wishes to improve.
- List skills participant desires to improve on parent education contract.
- Sign parent education contract.
- Give written strengths assessment and parent education contract to parent educator.

Each participant will do the following:

- Fill out Nurturing Quiz before first parent education session and following last parent education session.
- Fill out Parenting Stress Index before first parent education session and following last parent education session.
- Tell counselor three parenting skills participant wishes to improve.
- Sign parent education contract.
- Attend weekly parent education/support group.
- Do homework assignments each week.
- Talk about homework with Parent Educator and other mothers.
- During the parent education group, talk about the topic for each session as it relates to them and their children.
- Following last parent education session, report to counselor whether she has improved in the three skill areas listed in contract.

Parent Educator will do the following:

- Give directions for Parenting Stress Index each time participant fills it out.
- Talk with each participant about her parenting strengths assessment.
- Explain parent education contract to participant.
- Sign parent education contract.
- Arrange the meeting room prior to each session.
- Schedule trained child care volunteers for each session.

At each session, Parent Educator will do the following:

- Greet participants by name.
- Ask participants what parenting concerns they have had during the week.
- Ask participants about their experiences in doing the homework.
- Present information relevant to the topic of each session, personally or through the use of guest speakers, films, or other methods.
- Blend discussion of participants' concerns and questions into presentation of new material.
- Explain homework for the coming week to participants.

# PROGRAM OBJECTIVES

## Resource Acquisition

1. Each quarter Parent Educator will schedule eight trained volunteers in teams of two to care for participants' children during parent education sessions.
2. Parent Educator will call DCCCA for referrals every week for three weeks prior to beginning each quarter's parent education sessions.
3. Parent Educator will review parent education materials and select curriculum to be used prior to first quarter's parent education session.
4. Parent Educator will order parent workbooks or manuals prior to each quarter's parent education session.
5. Executive Director will prepare FCTF grant renewal request by March 1990.
6. Executive Director will secure additional matching funding equal to 20 percent of FCTF grant by March 1991.

## Service Events

1. Seventeen women per quarter will participate in parent education classes.
2. Fourteen participants will attend at least eight of ten weekly parent education/support group sessions.

## Efficiency

1. Parent Educator will spend 15 percent of her time each week in connection with parent education classes.

## Staff Morale

1. Each quarter, Parent Educator will report to Executive Director three things she likes about her job.
2. Each quarter, child care volunteers will report on volunteer survey knowing what to do and getting help they need in caring for participants' children.

# SERVICE PROCEDURES

## Planning Phase

During the planning phase of the program, several tasks must be accomplished. It is during this phase that resources must be acquired to carry out the program: money, volunteers, curriculum and materials, community support, and staff training. The executive director has major responsibility for securing funding, through writing grants and other fund raising activities.

Volunteers will be needed during the parent education sessions to come and care for participants' children. The Clinical Director, who also is the Parent Educator, will contact child development and social welfare instructors at the university whose classes regularly volunteer time to First Step House. The Parent Educator will interview prospective volunteers and conduct a one-day orientation and training session prior to the beginning of parent education classes. Each quarter, eight volunteers will be needed for child care, working in teams of two.

Another task during this phase will be the selection of curriculum and materials. The Parent Educator will review several packaged parenting programs. Since the packaged programs are in general fairly comprehensive, it is preferable that one be used as the primary resource to teach the classes. After selecting a curriculum, the parent educator will order the parent workbooks, if any are needed, and assemble any supplemental information she feels is necessary for this population.

During the planning phase, the Executive Director and the Parent Educator will meet with staff from DCCCA, another local substance abuse agency, to discuss the parent education program. This meeting will have several purposes. First, DCCCA staff are experienced in the substance abuse field, as are First Step House staff, and they may have ideas or information that would be helpful in implementing the parent education program. Second, it is important to build on the positive working relationship the two agencies share by informing DCCCA of the addition to First Step House's program offerings, both because DCCCA is a referral source and because the agency is influential among drug and alcohol services at the local and state levels. DCCCA's endorsement of the program will be important for program success. A final purpose of the meeting between First Step House and DCCCA staff will be to discuss the possibility of DCCCA referring women in the community who are not residents of First Step House to the parent education program and establishing a procedure for such referrals.

Once per week in the three weeks before the first class session, the Parent Educator will call the DCCCA contact person to ask whether there are any community referrals from DCCCA. If there are referrals and there are slots available in the classes, the Parent Educator will assign a counselor to complete the intake process.

A final task for the Parent Educator in preparation for the intake and class phases of the program is the training of counselors in intake procedures, including giving the Nurturing Quiz and assessing parenting strengths and the parent education contract. Additionally, a full staff meeting will focus on the parent education program, to let the staff know what the program procedures will be, what material will be covered, what the expectations of clients will be, what emotional responses staff may expect from clients, and suggestions of ways for staff to respond to clients in regard to feelings and behavior resulting from the parent education classes. (See "Affective Involvement" section for a more complete discussion of this point.)

## Intake Phase

During the intake phase, First Step House counselors will interview prospective participants in their caseloads or from DCCCA to complete the parenting strengths assessment. First, the counselor will explain the parent education program and the assessment process. The parenting strengths assessment will consist of the Nurturing Quiz, completed by the participant, a listing of strengths revealed by the Nurturing Quiz, and the participant's self-report of parenting strengths. The next step in the intake process is for the participant to list on the parent education contract three parenting skills she wishes to improve through the parent education classes. Finally, the counselor and the client sign the parent education contract, as an agreement between the two of them that the client wishes to improve three parenting skills, that she is willing to work on improving the skills, and that the counselor will help the client in this work. The counselor then will give the Parent Educator the parenting strengths assessment and the parent education contract.

Prior to the beginning of classes, the Parent Educator will meet with each participant individually to talk with her about the parenting strengths assessment, sign the parent education contract, explain the Parenting Stress Index, and have the participant fill out the Parenting Stress Index. The Parent Educator will ask the participant if she has any questions about the parent education classes, and answer questions the participant may have.

## Class Phase

Classes will be two hours weekly in the evening for ten consecutive weeks. Each class session will be both educational and supportive in nature. Prior to the beginning of classes, the Parent Educator will plan sessions taking into account the individual learning goals set by participants. Each session will begin with the Parent Educator asking participants how parenting has gone for them during the previous week. The Parent Educator will listen to issues the participants bring up in this informal sharing time so that she can relate her presentation of material to participants' immediate concerns. Additionally, since the Parent Educator is also a staff member of the residential facility in which many of the participants and their children live, she will have observed the parenting of some of the participants. During the class sessions, the Parent Educator will use positive examples from her observations of participants' parenting to point out participants' strengths and praise them for handling situations well.

Homework will be assigned to participants each week so that they may try out some of the skills and ideas discussed. Each week, the Parent Educator will ask participants to talk about their experiences with the homework.

The curriculum will cover areas such as behavior management, child development, managing angry feelings, and communication. The Parent Educator will have the primary responsibility for presenting information in the educational portion of the sessions, but she also will draw upon the ideas of the participants in discussing how to handle difficult parenting situations. Since one of the objectives is for the participants to feel better about their parenting, the Parent Educator will help participants to recognize parenting strengths in themselves and other participants.

Because of the nature of the residential program, a few participants may begin the parent education classes at some point other than the first session. The Parent Educator will need to repeat concepts and material from earlier sessions as they are necessary for later presentations, both because some participants may not have attended earlier sessions and also as review for everyone else.

At the last class session, participants will again fill out the Parenting Stress Index and the Nurturing Quiz. Participants also will be asked to evaluate the class, listing three things they liked about the classes and three things that need to be done differently.

## Evaluation/Planning Phase

Following the class phase, the Parent Educator will compare scores on the Parenting Stress Index from before the classes and after the classes. If the objectives of the program are being met, scores on the Parenting Stress Index should be lower following the classes. The Parent Educator also will compare scores on the Nurturing Quiz from before and after the classes to determine areas in which the program should be modified.

Information on participant outcomes (changes in Parenting Stress scores and Nurturing Quiz scores) will be reported in the quarterly report. Planning for the next quarter's classes will consist of making revisions to presentations suggested by participants and by participants' scores on the outcome measures, measuring volunteers' morale, making sure volunteers are trained and available for child care for the next quarter, and again contacting DCCCA for out-client referrals.

## KEY INDIVIDUALS REQUIRED FOR PROGRAM SUCCESS AND THEIR BEHAVIOR

Several individuals' cooperation will be necessary for this parent education program to be successful. It will be important that First Step House counselors complete their duties in the intake process with prospective participants. The information that the counselor gives the mother will have an effect on the mother's perception of the parent education program, so it will be important for the counselor to be trained to explain the program and complete the intake process in a way that helps the participant to understand the objectives of the program, the expectations of participants, and what she may expect from the Parent Educator and counselor. The strengths assessment completed by the counselor and the parent education contract, which is guided by the counselor, will be used in planning the parent education sessions, so it is important that this information be gathered. Minimum expectations for the counselor will be to interview each participant to fill out the strengths assessment; to give directions for and have participants fill out the Nurturing Quiz; to talk with each participant about her parenting strengths revealed by the Nurturing Quiz; to ask each participant which three parenting skills the participant wishes to improve and list those skills on the parent education contract; to sign the parent education contract; and to give the written strengths assessment and parent education contract to the Parent Educator.

Although the program will not be dependent upon outside referrals for the majority of participants, the cooperation of the DCCCA referral coordinator in making appropriate referrals will be necessary. For the program to meet the service events objectives, a few participants from the community who are not residents of First Step House will be accepted in the parent education program. Referrals will come from the DCCCA referral coordinator. The minimum expectations for the DCCCA referral coordinator are that he or she at least once per quarter will inform other DCCCA staff of the availability and eligibility requirements of the parent education program and ask them to provide the names of women on their caseloads who are potential participants. This will happen on an ongoing basis. The referral coordinator then will contact potential participants by telephone to explain the parent education program and determine whether the mother is interested in the program. The referral coordinator will then contact the Parent Educator with names and phone numbers of potential participants. To facilitate the referral process, the Parent Educator will call the referral coordinator once per week for each of the three weeks prior to beginning a new cycle of parent education classes.

Finally, it will be important that there be cooperation from volunteers who will provide child care during the parent education classes. Volunteers for this service primarily will be obtained through two Kansas University instructors who require volunteer service of their students. Expectations of the instructors are that they will contact the Parent Educator at the beginning of each semester with the names of students who are prospective volunteers. Expectations of the volunteers are that they will attend an interview with the Parent Educator; that they will attend a one-day orientation and training session on a Saturday; that they will sign up to care for children during two or three parent education class sessions during a ten-week period; and that once per quarter they will report to the Parent Educator whether they know what to do and get the help they need in caring for the children.

## THE HELPING ENVIRONMENT

The weekly, two-hour long parent education classes will take place in the dining room of the facility, which is able to be closed off from other areas of the building, enabling the participants and the Parent Educator to be free from distractions. Since the room is used for other purposes by many of the same people, and since these classes are only one of several common activities for many of the participants, symbols will be necessary to establish the uniqueness of the gathering. The dining tables will be taken down or moved against one wall and the room will be arranged as a circle of chairs to emphasize the open, participatory nature of the classes, with space for a flip-chart, video equipment, or other audio/visual aids. The Parent Educator will post the topic for the session on the flip-chart so that participants are reminded of the topic as they arrive.

During the classes, participants' children will be involved in activities supervised by at least two trained volunteers, in the playroom of the facility. The volunteers will lead group games or other active play with the children for about one and one-half hours, then will read stories and engage in other calming activities for the last half hour so that the children will be winding down to prepare for bedtime when their mothers get out of class. Mothers will be able to give their attention to the parent education classes since volunteers will be caring for their children.

## ACTUAL BEHAVIORS

### Intake Phase

To illustrate what actually happens in the parent education program, we will consider the fictitious participant Shelly who has a three-year-old daughter and a seven-year-old son. When Shelly entered in-patient treatment for substance abuse, it was necessary for her to leave her children in the care of her ex-husband's parents, the children's grandparents. Now that Shelly and her children are at First Step House, Shelly feels guilty that she had to leave her children and that she didn't care for them as well as she would have liked to during the time she was actively using alcohol and drugs.

When her counselor at First Step House first told her about the parent education program that was going to be starting, Shelly had mixed feelings about it. She already had to attend so many meetings that she felt like that was all she did. Besides, she already knew she was a lousy mother and didn't need somebody else to tell her that she was. On the other hand, she really could use some help figuring out what to do when Joey refused to do something because "Grandma said I don't have to."

The counselor asked Shelly to name three things she likes about being a mother, then she asked her to answer some multiple-choice questions on a Nurturing Quiz. After Shelly finished answering the questions, the counselor read over her answers and praised Shelly for understanding how to use time-out. The counselor pointed out other strengths to Shelly: that she provided a safe place for her children to live while she was in treatment, that she wants her kids with her now, and that she enjoys seeing her kids' schoolwork. Some of what the counselor identifies as strengths are the things Shelly listed as what she likes about being a mother and some are observations the counselor makes from knowing Shelly and her situation. It is the counselor's job during this assessment to help Shelly identify her parenting strengths, to praise Shelly for her strengths, and to help her use her strengths to improve her parenting.

Now the counselor asks Shelly if there are any areas of bringing up her children that she feels she needs some help with, that she would like to change. After having talked about things that are going well with her kids, it is easy for Shelly to admit that there are things she would like to do differently: she would like not to yell so much; she feels guilty when she punishes her children; and she wishes she knew what to do when Joey uses what Grandma said as an excuse. The counselor checks to make sure she understands and reframes Shelly's concerns as wanting to talk to her children instead of yell at them; wanting to provide discipline and structure without feeling guilty; and wanting to avoid power struggles. Then the counselor asks Shelly is she is interested in working on these three areas. Shelly says that she is, so the counselor lists them on a parent education contract and asks Shelly to sign it to indicate that she wants to work on those skill areas. The counselor signs her name to the contract, telling Shelly that by signing the contract, the counselor is agreeing to help Shelly work on these aspects of her parenting; although the work will primarily be through the parent education classes, the counselor will be checking with her on her progress and will be available for support and assistance at Shelly's request. Shelly asks what happens next, so the counselor explains that she will give the contract, quiz, and list of Shelly's strengths that they identified to the Parent Educator, who then will meet with Shelly before the classes begin.

## Class Phase

Now let's jump ahead in time to the fifth week of the parent education class. The fifth session focuses on communication issues of exploring alternatives, problem ownership, and I-messages—all of which are important skills for parents to master in order to use positive behavior management. By this point in the series of classes, the participants will be accustomed to the routine of the classes, and they should be seeing some changes in their own and their children's behavior.

Dinner is over and the two child care volunteers for the evening have arrived. The Parent Educator, with the help of one of the mothers and her eleven-year-old daughter, move the dining tables out of the way and arrange fifteen chairs in a circle with the flip-chart placed just outside the circle. The participants begin to arrive in the dining room, bringing their workbooks, pads, and pens. Several of the participants carry coffee cups, which they fill on their way to take seats. The Parent Educator greets each participant by name and chats informally with various members of the class. By 7:00 PM, all of the participants have taken seats.

The format for the class will be a few minutes of checking in with participants to see if there are pressing parenting concerns that the Parent Educator needs to incorporate into the presentation and discussion; a discussion of the previous week's homework to reinforce the concepts learned last time; presentation of new material through discussion and role play; discussion of the practice exercises for the coming week; and a summary of the content presented.

The Parent Educator begins the session by greeting the group and referring to the flip-chart on which are listed the main topic and objectives for the evening. She opens the discussion by asking participants how parenting has gone for them since the last class. Since all of the participants have experience with the self-disclosure that is demanded by treatment for substance abuse, participants are open to participating in the group by sharing their personal experiences. Several participants briefly describe problems they encountered with their children and one participant tells of a positive experience she had with trying something discussed the week before. The Parent Educator listens reflectively to the participants' concerns and describes how each of them illustrates a concept from an earlier class or may be related to the topics for the evening. It is important that the Parent Educator blend participants' immediate parenting needs with the material she plans to present and that she let participants know their concerns will be addressed further. Participants who share during this time receive positive feedback from the Parent Educator for their efforts and for contributing to the group.

Next the Parent Educator asks what experiences participants had with the homework assignment from the week before, which was to practice reflective listening. Again, several participants discuss their experiences and the Parent Educator praises them for their efforts. When participants ask questions during this portion of the class especially, the Parent Educator refrains from putting herself in the position of expert but instead asks the group for solutions. This has the effect of lessening the pressure on the Parent Educator to be prepared for every question and have every answer and also reinforces that the members of the group have a great deal of knowledge and experience in parenting themselves. When solutions to problems come from the group itself, participants see their peers and themselves as more capable.

In introducing the new material for the evening, the Parent Educator uses a variety of techniques. First she asks the group what they think exploring alternatives might mean. Some of the participants may have read the material in their workbooks prior to the class, although there is no expectation that they will have, and they may volunteer what is meant by exploring alternatives. The Parent Educator develops the idea of exploring alternatives, explains how to use the method, and offers examples. To stimulate discussion, she asks the group questions such as why a parent would want to use exploring alternatives.

After having explained the concepts the session focuses on, the teacher leads the group through exercises in exploring alternatives, using I-messages and determining who owns a problem. The Parent Educator structures activities taking into account that individuals in the group have different learning styles, so chooses exercises that involve participants in hearing, speaking, reading, and writing. The Parent Educator role plays several situations with different participants, each time asking the other participants to watch for certain behaviors. Following each role play, the Parent Educator asks those who had roles to describe what it felt like to be that person in that situation. Frequently throughout the presentation, the Parent Educator invites participants to ask questions.

When all new material has been presented, the Parent Educator summarizes the major points of the material, then turns the group's attention to the homework exercise. The Parent Educator reads aloud and explains the instructions for the exercise and asks participants to think about a particular time they will try the exercise with their children.

The session ends on time, and the Parent Educator thanks all participants for their participation and hard work. Some of the mothers linger and talk for a few minutes, while others go get their children from the playroom. By 9:15, all of the mothers have taken their children from the playroom. The Parent Educator thanks the child care volunteers and asks them how the evening went for them. It is important that the Parent Educator give the volunteers positive feedback for their work with the children and that she make sure the volunteers feel they can handle the children. If there are situations the volunteers feel they are unable to handle, the Parent Educator will schedule a training session to improve the volunteers' skills and confidence.

## AFFECTIVE INVOLVEMENTS OF CLIENTS AND CLIENT-SERVICE STAFF

All parties in a helping transaction experience emotional responses to the transaction. It is helpful in program implementation and management if some attention is paid to determining what the likely emotional responses of all persons may be, so that the worker may be prepared with effective ways to handle predictable client responses. Additionally, it is helpful for workers to consider what their own emotional responses may be so that they are prepared to deal with their effective response in appropriate ways and settings. Some emotions that come up for workers may demand a particular type of response with the client and a different response later on to get rid of the feeling.

Anticipated affective responses of participants and suggested worker strategies include:

| *Participant Response* | *Worker Strategy* |
| --- | --- |
| Anger | Listen reflectively. Empathize. Remain calm and keep voice even and matter-of-fact. |
| Defensiveness | Explain the program fully. Explain mutual expectations. Point out participant strengths. Avoid blaming. |
| Guilt | Emphasize that no one is a perfect parent. Focus on future of past. Praise participants for efforts at gaining knowledge and changing behavior. |

The helping transaction will elicit affective responses on the part of the worker as well. Some anticipated emotions for the worker and appropriate ways to deal with the feelings include:

| *Worker Emotion* | *Appropriate Response* |
| --- | --- |
| Frustration | Be realistic about expectations of yourself and clients. Look for small changes in behavior. Celebrate mistakes. |

Anger | Take a few seconds to tell yourself you needn't get angry. Breathe in and out slowly before responding. Talk about feelings with other staff.

Insecurity | Draw on participants' strengths to answer questions. Arrange for training. Practice role plays and presentation with staff. Ask for feedback from supervisor or other staff.

## REFERENCES

Alvy, K. T. (1987). *Black parenting: Strategies for training*. New York: Irvington.

Daro, D. (1988). *Confronting child abuse: Research for effective program design*. New York: The Free Press.

Dinkmeyer, D., & McKay, G. D. (1982). *The parent's handbook: Systematic training for effective parenting*. Circle Pines, MN: American Guidance Service.

Family Development Resources, Inc. (1986). *The nurturing quiz*. Park City, UT.

Giovannoni, J. M. (1985). Child abuse and neglect: An overview. In J. Laird & A. Hartman, (Eds.), *A Handbook of Child Welfare* (pp. 193–212) New York: The Free Press.

Grotevant, H. D. (1987). *Final report: Evaluation of the recovering parents program 1987*. Austin, TX: Corporate Child Development Fund.

Helyar, T. (Ed.). (1988). *Kansas statistical abstract 1987–88* (23rd ed.). University of Kansas: Institute for Public Policy and Business Research.

Hill Research Consultants (1989). *Texas parents study: Discipline in homes and schools*. The Woodlands, TX.

Kansas Department of Health and Environment (1988). *Annual summary of vital statistics, 1987*. Topeka: Division of Information Systems.

Newman, B. M., & Newman, P. R. (1987). *Development through life: A psychosocial approach*. Chicago, IL: Dorsey.

O'Brien, R., & Chafety, M., M.D. (1982). *The encyclopedia of alcoholism*. New York: Facts on File.

O'Brien, R., & Cohen, S., M.D. (1982). *The encyclopedia of drug abuse*. New York: Facts on File.

Rosen, S., Fanshel, D., & Lutz, M. E., (Eds.). (1987). *Face of the nation, 1987: Statistical supplement to the 18th edition of the Encyclopedia of social work*. Silver Spring, MD: National Association of Social Workers.

Straus, M. A., & Gelles, R. J. (1988). How violent are American families? Estimates from the national family violence resurvey and other studies. In G. Hotaling, D. Finkelhor, J. T. Kirkpatrick, & M. A. Straus, (Eds.), *Family Abuse and Its Consequences* (pp. 14–36). Newbury Park, CA: Sage.

U.S. Bureau of the Census (1987). *Statistical abstract of the United States: 1987* (107th ed.). Washington, DC.

World Almanac (1987). *The World Almanac and Book of Facts 1988*. New York: Pharos Books.

# CHAPTER 3

# Managing Information

A manager designs programs and manages information, personnel, and resources. Chapter 3 focuses on information. Description and case examples will show how powerfully information can affect the performance of social programs. We also highlight the most prevalent mistakes managers make in terms of gathering and disseminating information. One of the core principles described in Chapter 1 is "learning for a living." In this chapter, we sketch the outlines of a learning organization and place the role of information within it. The bulk of the chapter is devoted to the concepts and tasks needed to develop a client-centered information system that enhances performance and serves the learning organization. Topics include the purposes of information systems and alternative ways of measuring client outcomes, productivity, resource acquisition, efficiency, and staff morale. The chapter concludes with a set of guidelines for designing performance oriented data reports.

## PERFORMANCE REQUIRES INFORMATION

To listen to human service managers, one would conclude that the largest obstacle to better performance is some combination of better people and more resources. In large part, this may be true. Since social services are labor intensive, organizational performance is largely dependent on the individual and collective competence of the personnel. Likewise, additional funds to employ more staff and create more programs would, indeed, help. This is particularly true now, when social workers are being asked to serve more clients with increased effectiveness with static or reduced dollars. More resources and better staff, however, are not necessarily guarantees of better performance nor is better performance dependent on these.

The dilemma, of course, is that these two elements are the most difficult to influence. Administrators already try to hire the best available candidates given the constraints of salary, civil service, geographic location, and the quality of education candidates receive from universities. Some agencies provide staff development programs for their employees, but funds for these have always been and will continue to be rather meager. Similarly, organizations are always chasing dollars through appropriations and grants. The chances of huge increases in social service budgets are slight, and even if budgets were to increase, they would still not satisfactorily serve clients.

Without negating the need for competent staff and more resources, organizational performance can be improved, and improved radically in some cases, by exploiting the power of information. Few would quarrel with the premise that information can be influential. But maybe a few real life examples of how information has improved organizational performance would help make this proposition come alive. The next several pages contain such examples.

### CASE 1

The first visible sign of the Boeing Company's presence in the de Havilland aircraft plant in Toronto, Canada, is highly visible indeed. Bar charts keeping track of each worker's progress are posted at every stop on the assembly line.

Once a light fixture, or a row of interior-wall panels is installed, the job is checked off.

The bar charts are one example of how Boeing is starting to make its mark on the former government-owned aircraft company. It purchased de Havilland in January for $110 million.

"At first, workers feared the charts would expose them to too much Big Brother scrutiny," said David Mathewson, director of manufacturing engineering.

But for now at least, it appears suspicion has turned to acceptance while productivity has increased. The charts make the workers more accountable and are improving the flow of parts into the Dash 8 commuter planes.

"Workers are proud to be recognized for their accomplishments and are taking the charts as a challenge," says Ted Onarheim, assistant superintendent of the assembly line.

### CASE 2

The statistics office of a state public welfare agency was experimenting with several new computer programs and wanted reaction from the field. A report providing an office-by-office breakdown of the percentage of child welfare cases that had a service plan was distributed to the sixteen regional offices. The cover memo requested feedback on the usefulness of the data and its presentation. The response was quite a bit more than they had hoped. Not only did the area managers indicate their interest in the report but within three months the number of cases without a service plan was reduced to less than a hundred for the state. The worst area performance, which was 24 percent on December 16, 1981, was 11 percent on January 16, 1982. Please note: There was no hint of rewards or sanctions in the memo nor was one given by phone or during meetings.

### CASE 3

A supervisor of case managers working in a Kansas community mental health center received reports that his staff was consistently avoiding goal setting with their chronically mentally ill clients. As a result, much of the work seemed directionless, emphasizing maintenance and crisis intervention over growth and developmental activities. He wanted an increase in the number of goals set and an increase in the amount of goal-directed work. He began posting a summary graph showing the total number of goals each case manager set with their clients per month. This report was posted on an easily seen bulletin board in the case managers' work area. Within two weeks, goal setting with clients increased 25 percent.

### CASE 4

Participants in a partial hospitalization program sponsored by a community mental health center were consistently showing very little vocational interest or activity. Program staff began gathering data monthly on clients' vocational status and reporting this to their program consultant. He returned this data to program staff using a simple bar graph every three months. The result of gathering and feeding back information on clients' vocational interest and activity was evident almost immediately. Three months after instituting this strategy, the percentage of the program's clients showing no interest or activity in vocational areas declined from an original 64 percent to 34 percent; three months later this percentage decreased an additional 6 percent, so that 72 percent of program participants were now involved in some form of vocational activity. This same strategy was used in three other mental health centers. The results for all four centers were seventy-four clients who moved to a higher level of vocational activity and only thirty-one clients who regressed.

Look at a university class if you remain skeptical. A student's grade in a course is probably the most powerful determinant of that student's behavior. Class sessions that cover material needed to complete an assignment are always well attended. Readings are read if a student knows they may be called on to summarize an article and some grade is assigned to that activity. Inquiries like, "Will this be on the test?" and "How long should this paper be?" are all indicative of a concern if not preoccupation with grades over learning. The power of that one letter!

These short vignettes support what the organization theorist Mason Haire said, "What gets measured gets done." (Quoted in Peters & Waterman, 1982, p. 268) When information is made available, people respond to it.

Peters and Waterman (1982) in their study of successful companies observed:

> We are struck by the importance of available information as the basis for peer comparison. Surprisingly, this is the basic control mechanism in the excellent companies. It is not the military model at all. It is not a chain of command wherein nothing happens until the boss tells somebody to do something. General objectives and values are set forward and information is shared so widely that people know quickly whether or not the job is getting done—and who's doing it well or poorly. (p. 266)

They also observed that the data was never used to "browbeat people with numbers." (p. 267) The data alone seemed to motivate people.

What is clear from all of these examples is this: *The collection and feedback of information influences behavior.* (Nadler, 1977; Taylor, Fisher, & Ilgen, 1984; Taylor, 1987) Current research suggests several principles involving the use of information by human service managers to improve organizational effectiveness. The outline below briefly states these principles.

*Principles for Using Information to Enhance Performance\**

1. The role of information in an organization is to initiate action and influence behavior.
2. The act of collecting information (measurement) generates human energy around the activity being measured.
3. To increase the expenditure of energy for performance, the collection and feedback of information must be systematically linked to explicit goals, standards for performance, and rewards.
4. To insure that information directs human energy toward enhanced performance, data collection, and feedback must be used to: (1) foster and reinforce desired behaviors; (2) identify barriers to performance and problem-solve; and (3) set goals for future performance.
5. Feedback directs behavior toward performance when it provides "cues" to workers to identify clear methods for correction, and when it helps workers learn from their performance.
6. Feedback motivates behavior toward performance when it is used to create expectations for external and internal rewards, is linked to realistic standards for performance, and is directed toward the future versus used punitively to evaluate past performance.

Managers who are committed to increasing performance have at hand a powerful tool. By proactively and systematically collecting and feeding back information, managers can enhance the goal-directed performance of program staff, as well as increase their motivation, professional learning, and sense of reward. Subsequent sections will outline in greater detail the methods program managers can use to design information systems based on these principles.

## CURRENT USE OF INFORMATION BY MANAGERS

A study, conducted with a large, state, public welfare agency, assessed the use of computer-generated reports by personnel in seventeen decentralized area offices. (Rapp, 1982) Questionnaires were administered to administrators, managers, and supervisors. Of the 152 questionnaires mailed, 124 or 82 percent were returned. The subjects were asked to specify how often they based fourteen management actions upon six separate data-based reports that they received monthly or quarterly.

The findings suggest that about 50 percent of the time respondents distributed reports to subordinates, discussed them with subordinates, and engaged in problem-solving activities with subordinates or superiors. Respondents used the reports less than 50 percent of the time for evaluating and rewarding employees, requesting more resources, reallocating resources, revising methods, procedures and policies,

---

*These findings are summarized from the work of David A. Nadler (1977), M. Susan Taylor, Cynthia D. Fisher, and Daniel R. Ilgen (1984), and M. Susan Taylor (1987).

or improving the accuracy of the information. The findings suggested a pattern: When data-based reports are used, they are likely to be used passively (e.g., distributed or discussed). Rarely are the reports used for more aggressive management action (e.g., to acquire and allocate resources, to reward employees, to revise procedures).

Considering the costs to this agency of collecting information and feeding it back to managers, one wonders if it is worth the cost. Frontline staff spend a disproportionate amount of time filling out data forms. This data is sent to a central processing unit made up of twelve to fifteen full-time technical staff including data entry, computer programmers, systems analysts, and unit management. Expensive computers and computer programs store and manipulate the data generating reams of reports to be mailed out to managers who spend an average twenty-five minutes on each report. The costs are enormous. One study estimates that 30 percent of patient stay costs in a hospital could be attributed to information system demands. (Richart, 1970; Jydstrup & Gross, 1966)

Despite the fact that it is the frontline worker who most often supplies the data, some managers see information systems to be for managers only. In a recent social agency staff meeting the executive director in responding to an example of measuring client satisfaction, said, "We routinely measure the satisfaction of our clients." Two staff responded, "We do?" Several more looked puzzled—a few nodded affirmatively. This little scenario illustrates that measurements can generate attention and energy, but only if people are made aware of them.

Despite the costs and general lack of use, the majority of managers also want more information. Case studies of information system design efforts report that managers always ask that the system generate more information than can be justified. (King & Clelland, 1981; Poertner & Rapp, 1980) System designers continue to believe that the more comprehensive the system the better. (Ackoff, 1967) For managers, information and print-outs seem to be a "security blanket." A regional director of a large state child welfare agency once commented that every month she received three boxes of computer reports that she placed unopened in the storeroom closet. When asked "Why do you keep them?" she replied, "Just in case central office ever asked me for some data." Central office never did. Only recently have system designers begun to appreciate the debilitating consequences of information overload and to establish procedures for filtration and condensation of information. (DeBlasis, 1976) As Herzlinger (1977) states:

> Nonprofit organizations do not lack data; if anything they enjoy an overabundance of numbers and statistics. Rather, they lack systematically provided information to help management do its job. Without *good* information, it is obviously difficult for managers to make reasoned and informed decisions, evaluate performance, motivate their employees, and protect the institution against fraud." (p. 81)

The penchant for more and more information diffuses the energy and attention that measurement is suppose to generate. If the goal is to maintain children safely within the community and this is measured and attended to in a variety of ways, then child welfare workers will generate energy and attention to that end. If what is measured and attended to is a diffuse list like the following, little attention is paid to anything:

- What workers do with every minute of their work day
- How many court reports are in on time
- The agency's foster care allocation
- The newspaper article critical of the agency
- The central office memo on workers' political activities
- The computerized case records with missing data
- The four children dumped in the waiting room with no identification
- Who is going to be the next agency director
- The worker who is having trouble with alcohol
- The goals set with families
- The report from the local state representative for justification for not placing Mary Jones

Besides being too general, information is all too frequently used in detrimental ways. A recent exchange between a worker and his supervisor about a report on client satisfaction went something like this:

> Here is the client satisfaction report on your caseload. It looks pretty good. As you can see your average satisfaction score dropped this quarter. You were five points below the agency standard. I looked at the responses to the items and see that a lot of your clients don't agree that they know what the goals are for counseling. I think you need to work on this for next quarter.

Personal experience and the work of David Nadler (1977) indicates that the worker is likely to be defensive, angry, feel a decrease in competence, and possibly sabotage the information next quarter. None of these consequences are intended or desired, but they occur all too frequently.

Here are lessons drawn from discussion on the use of information in social agencies:

- Information is expensive—social administrators need to minimize the cost and maximize the use.
- What gets attended to gets done—social administrators need to attend to what is important.
- When everything is important nothing is important—social administrators need to attend to the few important elements of performance.
- Information can be used in detrimental ways—social administrators need to use data in ways consistent with the principles identified earlier in this chapter.

# THE LEARNING ORGANIZATION

If funds are the lifeblood of an organization, then information is its intelligence. A provocative, yet little realized, promise of information systems is that they become a tool for the "learning organization" to improve its performance. (Taber, Anderson, & Rapp, 1975) A learning organization takes periodic readings on its performance and makes adjustments so that performance is improved.

For an organization to take periodic readings on its performance and use these readings to adjust and improve performance three things are required:

- There must be an organizational culture that supports learning and that includes contingencies for enhanced learning. Within the organizational culture, performance enhancing strategies require a supportive environment. This is not to say that if the support environment does not exist, social administrators should throw up their hands and say it is hopeless. The importance of the culture is emphasized to remind administrators that they have an important role in constructing the environment in which management technologies can succeed.
- A manager must have the knowledge and skill in the learning organization to use information to enhance performance. The manager can either sense what is important and bring it to everyone's attention or diffuse attention by focusing on trivial elements.
- There must be an information system, an ongoing system, to measure, store, retrieve, and report performance enhancing information.

## Organizational Culture and Contingencies

Organizational members in a learning organization believe people are capable of learning and desire to learn. There is no social program that is so successful that there is nothing left to learn. Yet many organizations block learning by excusing poor performance or blaming others for mistakes. Common excuses include that the caseloads are different and more difficult, lack of resources, lack of staff or time. Blame often is directed at key players such as families, courts, other agencies, or the clients themselves. Excuses and blame block learning by assuming a protective or defensive stance.

The learning posture assumes that staff are doing their best and that they confront myriad obstacles and constraints. These need to be identified and addressed, not tolerated or assumed to be unchangeable. It also assumes that the organization has much to learn from the higher performers within the agency. The responsibility for these cultural mores is the performance manager, and it is the information system that provides all staff with that valued feedback indicating success, suggesting the possibility for improvement, and directing the staff to the important areas for learning.

Organizational culture not only establishes the desire to learn but it also dictates whether data are interpreted and action taken. For example, a manager of a community program for the chronically mentally ill receives data on the movement of clients into and from independent living situations. Managers will devote time to interpreting the data if they know their superiors are going to question their performance—whether it is inadequate or outstanding. Managers will probably take some action if their evaluations are partially based on the movement of clients. In many agencies, the match between the data and the organizational contingencies is discrepant except for financial reports. For example, many personnel evaluation systems still measure such things as punctuality, responsibility, and cooperation, rather than performance. (Wiehe, 1980) It is the rare organization where

- the desired outcome for clients is clearly stated and regularly communicated,
- client outcomes are a regular and explicit item on staff meeting agenda,
- client outcome data are featured in agency public relations material,
- client outcomes are the subject of agency memos,
- the program's "batting average" on client outcomes is posted, and
- successful staff are featured in board meetings.

The point is, when data is reflective of the organizational contingencies, the likelihood of organizational personnel spending time interpreting data and acting upon it is increased.

This dilemma is often characteristic of the entire system of human services and contributes to the slow rise in concern about performance information within a specific organization or unit. Unlike business, human services do not get rewarded for effectiveness in terms of client satisfaction, client behavior change, or client status change. (Rapp & Poertner, 1983) Administrators are rarely reprimanded or even questioned as to how many clients "improved." Staying within the budget, staying out of the press, and continuing to serve an adequate number of clients seems to suffice. Reports for federal and state governments are dominated by numbers concerning number of clients served in various categories, dollars spent, and amount of service activity. Rarely do they reflect whether these produced any benefits to clients. Businesses, on the other hand, need to take careful periodic readings on production, quality control, and share of the market and profits if they are to survive.

Social administrators are responsible for their organization's culture and contingencies. Of the five performance areas, the acquisition of resources and tracking the number of units of service produced are the most frequently attended to and culturally supported areas. The social administrator needs to take responsibility for the organization's culture and goals as they relate to client outcome, staff morale, and efficiency. Many of the cultural elements required to support these performance areas are included in other chapters. In the realm of information, the key is to find a variety of ways to have data become important symbols for communicating organizational priorities and accomplishments.

## Skills, Knowledge, and Attributes of the Manager

The social administrator is the crucial element in how staff performs. It is largely through the manager's efforts, behaviors, and actions, that an organization transforms its resources into performance. In the learning organization, the manager's attitude is that information and data enhance learning. Along with this, the manager needs to know what performance is and how it can be measured. And finally the manager needs the skills to provide information to staff in ways that will enhance their learning and make them act upon the information to enhance their performance.

Several studies have shown that specific professional groups (i.e., social workers and nurses) eschew the use of data. (Friel, Reznikoff, & Rosenberg, 1969; Reznikoff, Holland, & Stroebel, 1967; Rosenberg, Reznikoff, Stroebel, & Ericson, 1967) "Indeed, some managers of nonprofits view their lack of quantitative skills as a rather endearing imperfection—like having freckles." (Herzlinger, 1977, p. 84) In this situation, even if all other elements of the learning organization are addressed, resistance would still be found. Training programs, within agencies and as a part of administrative curriculum, have not addressed the design and use of data-based reports to improve performance. Such skills, therefore, are based on a given manager's self-taught, on-the-job training. The literature has few sources that speak directly to techniques for interpreting or using data. The previously mentioned study (Rapp, 1982) further verifies this situation. The respondents in the study rarely used the six reports as performance tools. This was true for the four reports rated useful and the two reports rated useless. The current use of reports seems to reflect a particular manager's style and is less affected by the type of report or its substance. For managers to realize the power of information, they must view the data as an important element of the learning organization.

## Skills in Designing Performance Measures

Managers must know what constitutes performance. It is very difficult to improve performance if you don't know what that performance is. This involves the identification of units and areas of operation that perform adequately, as well as problem areas. The literature and curricula on management are replete with content on problem solving, but relatively little attention has been devoted to problem finding. Yet a number of people have argued that problem-finding skills are a more potent predictor of successful managers than problem-solving skills. (Mackworth, 1969; Livingston, 1971) Problem-finding information is necessary to prevent organizational crises, evaluate staff and keep the program on course. Data-based management reports focused on performance are in part problem finders. The reports never tell the manager what to do, only where to do it.

Managers must also know how to measure performance. Measurement frequently conjures up images of problem evaluation with the technical expert who comes into an agency and interviews clients, staff, and files. Another inadequate image is the psychometrician who develops measurement instruments for such concepts as self-esteem or locus of control, obsesses about validity and reliability, and is never satisfied with the result.

Measurement of performance has been a neglected area in social work. Finances are the most prevalently measured in most organizations today. Data reflecting overexpenditure is often quickly reported, interpreted, and acted upon. Measurement frequently stops here. Positive examples like counting the number of children safely maintained in their own home seldom occurs.

Furthermore, a manager must be able to judge the relationship between the instrument and what it purports to measure—in this case performance. A manager may judge that a potential measure does not reflect performance or that the results will not be the best indicator of the desired performance. For example, a report on the level of psychiatric hospitalizations may stimulate a reconsideration of the measure itself. Perhaps length of stay or number of hospital days consumed would be a more accurate reflection of a program's intent. Interpretation is enhanced when the measure says something very directly about the purpose and performance of the agency.

Although measurement is a technical area, there are only a few measurement concepts that managers need and can readily learn. There is a wealth of measurement technologies currently being used from which managers can borrow and learn. Since what gets measured gets attended to, managers must develop the knowledge to measure performance.

## Skills in Using Information

Next, managers must have the skills to use information as part of the learning organization's feedback system. Action is unlikely, if not impossible unless the manager can bring meaning to the numbers. Have the results say something about organizational performance. Minimally, this means the manager needs to assign a value to the number. Does the number reflect adequate performance, inadequate performance, or outstanding performance?

Managers should use information to instigate actions, to influence behavior. *Datum* becomes *information* only when it can be interpreted and acted upon. Perhaps the most effective information system is the greasy spoon restaurant.

> Upon entering the greasy spoon, you read or scan the menu and a waitress comes to take your order for a bacon, lettuce, and tomato sandwich without mayonnaise. On a 3″ × 5″ pad of green paper, the waitress writes: "BLTHM," which she places on the revolving wheel by the cook's window. The cook reads "BLTHM" and prepares the sandwich. The waitress delivers the meal to your table and records the price on the 3″ × 5″ paper. You take the piece of paper to the cashier who enters the information on the register, takes your money, and gives you change.

The greasy spoon is the perfect information system in that this little 3″ × 5″ piece of paper contains all the symbols necessary for the various greasy spoon employees to do their job. And there is no waste. Every symbol or piece of data influences the behavior of the staff and is therefore information.

In the human services field, data-based performance information can instigate managers to do the following:

- share information widely
- reward employees or units for outstanding performance
- identify factors contributing to high performance
- identify barriers to adequate performance
- request a plan of action by which improved performance will be pursued
- engage in problem-solving with subordinates
- provide training or consultation
- change policies, procedures, or methods
- request additional resources or reallocate resources (dollars, effort, etc.)
- review selected cases
- enforce current procedures or policies

This list should be merely viewed as a sampler.

An information system like the 3″ × 5″ piece of paper in the greasy spoon is nothing more than the mechanism for measuring, collecting the data, storing it, and formatting the data to communicate meaning. The next several sections will discuss these various components. But before we discuss the purely technical aspects of measuring performance, we will look at a few general ideas about developing an information system.

## The Information System

All the components of an information system need not be complex, formal, nor computerized. When the specifics of how to measure performance, how to format reports, how to set standards, and what management actions should be taken are presented, there is an implication that all of this is part of a formal computerized MIS. In reality the degree of mechanization will vary widely depending on factors such as size and resources of the agency. The manager of an organizational unit of seven to ten people is very likely to measure, report, and act on staff morale with a less formal and noncomputerized information system. Surely the director of a state agency with 2,000 employees requires the use of the computer, but the essential point is that the skills, knowledge, abilities, and methods required are the same with or without a computer. The following describes some of the types of systems that exist.

*Housekeeping Systems.* Organizational "housekeeping" and reporting demands have largely spurred the development of information systems. Using large, main frame computers, systems have been developed to increase the efficiency and accuracy of "getting out the checks" to clients, staff, and other agencies. Other well-established housekeeping functions include maintaining budget records, maintaining lists of provider agencies, and maintaining records of clients. (Taber, Anderson, & Rapp, 1975) The large computer systems have also allowed top level administrators to more efficiently marshal information needed by legislators, federal agencies, and other constituent groups. After twenty years, the housekeeping and reporting functions of these systems are well established and well developed.

These computerized systems, however, have been a burden to lower level personnel within the human service organization. It is these personnel who shoulder most of the responsibility for inputting, updating, and correcting the data yet the systems have not produced many benefits for them. The paperwork demands have now reached crisis proportions. The needless collection of information diverts precious service time, lowers job satisfaction, reduces the likelihood of any information being used (information overload), reduces the accuracy of the information, and through it all, decreases performance. Lower level personnel have often vented their frustration into sabotaging a system. (Taber, Anderson, & Rapp, 1975)

These systems have been expensive and cumbersome and have placed redundant demands on organizational personnel. A typical pattern of development in large, state human service organizations was to begin with computerized budgets including payroll, expenditures, and income. Stimulated in part by the trend towards purchase of service, a second system was developed to reimburse other agencies for services. A third system to capture client records was added. The federal government then required states to document the amount of time workers devoted to specific activities resulting in a fourth system. This process continued so that within fifteen years, a state agency would have six to ten separate computer systems that could rarely produce integrated reports and that required frontline workers to record identifying characteristics of cases six or seven times for each transaction. A similar if less obvious pattern has occurred in community programs, such as mental health centers. Despite the costs, the largest payoff from computer and information systems has come from the replacement of clerical operations—the use of computers for "housekeeping." (Kean & Morton, 1978; Rapp, 1984)

*Decision Support Systems.* Another management information system helps managers make better decisions. (Ackoff, 1967; Mintzberg, 1975; Vogel, 1985) In its current form, a decision support system (DSS) involves analyzing decisions and decision makers, developing mathematical and psychological models, and presenting these models to managers for their use. Yet one DSS advocate states:

> The literature on the application of computers in government and business indicate very little use of DSS. . . . In general, the main problem seems to be a mismatch between DSS design or performance and the requirements of decision makers or decision making. . . . Because of the mismatch, many systems which are developed cease to be used or are used for routine report generation rather than for direct support of decision makers. (Bennett, 1983, p. 24)

Thirty years of research and development have not produced systems that managers use to make decisions and enhance organizational performance. Feldman and March (1981) give some insight into this dilemma.

> Organizations, as well as individuals, collect gossip. They gather information that has no apparent immediate decision consequence. As a result, the information seems substantially worthless within a decision-theory perspective. The perspective is misleading. Instead of seeing an organization as seeking information in order to choose among given alternatives in terms of prior preference, we can see an organization as monitoring its environment for surprises. . . . The surveillance metaphor suggests either a prior calculation of needed information or a kind of thermostatic linkage between observations and actions. (p. 176)

This suggests that the emphasis on developing a management information system (MIS) to help managers make decisions or solve problems has been based on a primarily false premise. Managers need information for problem solving, but MIS may be the most effective in meeting managers' performance guidance or problem-finding requirements.

*Performance Guidance Systems.*  This new type of information system is a tool for the learning organization. It operates like a thermostat in that it takes readings on performance, compares these readings to a standard, and acts based on the comparison. A brief comparison of the guidance system to the decision support and housekeeping systems may highlight the thrust of this type of information system.

First, the goal of a housekeeping system is to improve the efficiency and accuracy of routine clerical operations. Housekeeping systems may be thought of as labor-saving and problem-preventing systems. By automating a routine process, they reduce errors and the number of staff required to maintain the process. The goal of a decision support system is to help solve problems or make decisions. Once a decision is made action steps need to be formulated, assignments made, and follow-up monitoring agreed to. Implementation of the decision follows and a series of meetings and memos initiated before anything gets done. The goal of a guidance system is to instigate action. The data produced by the system leads directly to action. The guidance system monitors performance, senses problems, and informs staff where to act.

Second, the design of each of the three systems is very different. Housekeeping systems are designed by identifying a well-structured operation, routinizing the process, and writing computer programs and procedures for operation of the system. Decision support systems are designed by identifying the decision, identifying the decision maker, creating a decision-making process, and implementing the model. The design of the performance guidance system begins at the heart of the human service enterprise. It begins with a clear definition of organizational purpose from which performance measures are developed. There is nothing amorphous about the relationship between guidance systems and organizational performance.

Third, the level of complexity of both housekeeping and guidance systems is low while decision support systems tend to be complex. Decision making is a complex psychological phenomenon that is not well understood. The decision models developed are often mathematical and intricate. Consequently decision support systems are frequently dismissed as not including the correct data or sufficient data or are too complex. This complexity makes implementation of decision support systems difficult. Performance guidance systems, on the other hand, filter and condense information rather than require more. The relative simplicity of housekeeping and guidance systems supports implementation.

A fourth characteristic of information systems is the level of involvement of direct service staff. Housekeeping systems frequently seek to free frontline staff from routine clerical functions so they can spend more time in direct service. Management information systems when designed as decision support systems serve the manager and consequently do not involve frontline staff until after the decision is made. Guidance systems systematically and automatically involve all relevant staff. The clear focus on performance and involvement of all levels of the organization can unify the organizational agenda. This is one of the guidance system's greatest strengths. The design and use of the performance guidance system is the topic of the remainder of this chapter.

## MEASURING PERFORMANCE

The first chapter described five management and organizational performance areas: client outcomes, productivity, resource acquisition, efficiency, and staff morale. For a social program (or manager) to succeed, staff and clients must perform in each of these areas. Resources need to be acquired and used efficiently, events that result in benefits to clients must be produced, staff morale must be maintained, and ultimately the desired outcome for clients must be exhibited. Each of these performance areas requires systematic monitoring, but it is the measurement of client outcomes that is the centerpiece of the client-centered manager.

There are five reasons why client outcomes have been difficult to measure.

First, service decisions have been viewed as idiosyncratic to each case. The services provided are highly individualized and not precisely described. Intervention is often less a social technology than a collection of rather vague methods. Service delivery is done in private, in an office or home. Rarely can a manager or supervisor monitor performance by watching. In large urban agencies with huge caseloads, observing the service event would not be feasible even if it were not done in private. This differs from other organizations, like auto manufacturers, where the supervisor or foreman can personally view worker performance.

Second, defining performance measures as they relate to client outcomes is difficult due to the human service organization's multiple constituencies. Constituencies include legislators, citizens, clients, staff members, courts, boards, media, and other agencies and other professionals. Each group has interests, agendas, and claims upon the organization that are not only different but oftentimes incompatible.

(Martin, 1980) Within this context, defining performance measures that are meaningful to all constituencies is problematic at best. For example, reducing the number of chronically mentally ill persons entering nursing home care as a performance measure would be resisted by the nursing home lobby and a portion of the medical community yet would likely be supported by legislators, policy makers, and advocacy groups.

Third, although performance measures are often derived from the goals of an organization, the goals are often vague or overly ambitious. In mental health, for example, it is not uncommon to find agency goals statements such as "to reduce mental illness" or "to reduce the incidence of chronic mental disability" or "to reduce the impairment caused by the illness." Mental health agencies have neither the resources nor the technologies to accomplish these. We can increase the number of chronically mentally ill who participate in employment, recreation, education, and independent living. We can increase the number of chronically mentally ill remaining out of hospitals who are in our care.

Fourth, measuring performance is difficult because of the complexity of the delivery system. A multitude of public and private agencies are involved in human service delivery, necessitating a maze of coordination agreements, referral networks, and intra-agency connections where goals are often in conflict. The service system itself is less a system than an amalgam of loosely knit agencies where performance is partly determined by others not under the direct control of one particular agency.

Fifth, and most importantly, performance has not been measured in terms of client outcomes. Most professionals and organizations have resisted doing this. It has been seen as impossible, threatening, and useless: "You cannot measure client benefits," or "The service is delivered by well-educated, competent professionals who don't require monitoring." In terms of the "useless" perspective, Carter (1987) comments, "Why should I risk knowing how successful my program is? The legislators already know day care is a good service. Why should I risk finding out if the parent is satisfied with the care provided to their child. If it's lower than expected or assumed, then I lose." (p. 74) Carter (1984) in an earlier work stated that, "public administrators often consider the measurement of program success irrelevant to their ongoing survival or their expansion." (p. 6) He goes on to argue that the perception is not only that client outcomes are irrelevant but that many managers consider such data as harmful in attracting public support.

All of these characteristics make it difficult to develop and use performance guidance systems. But the benefits to the manager in enhanced client outcomes and staff morale—and the possibility of using this information to acquire myriad required resources—are worth the struggle.

## SOME BASIC MEASUREMENT CONCEPTS

Measuring performance is a technical skill with which many social workers are uncomfortable. While it is true that some scientists devote their careers to measurement, there are only a few easily accessible measurement concepts that social administrators must understand. In developing performance measures, six concepts guide the selection of what information will be collected, stored, and reported.

## Measures Need to Be Valid

The performance measure needs to be a valid reflection of what is intended; does it measure what it is supposed to measure? While this seems straightforward, an example may demonstrate how mistakes can be made:

> In 1971, the New York Policy Department announced changes in the operations of its narcotics squad. Before, the squad had worked under a quota system with each officer being put under pressure to make at least four arrests a month. The result was that the squad began arresting street corner peddlers, ignoring the complicated and time-consuming cases involving major dealers. The actual amount of drugs confiscated decreased. (Berkley, 1978)

The moral of this story is that there are several ways of measuring a given phenomenon and that the selection of a particular measure cannot be a mechanical exercise. The poor selection of measures can lead to a waste of precious time, or can actually cause reduced performance. It is validity that the psychometrician obsesses over with little satisfaction. It is validity of the measure that people question. It is important to consider validity without letting it become the major obsession or a hindrance to action. It is seldom true that a measure is or is not valid. It is much more likely that a measure is more or less valid. For the social administrator the important questions are:

- Are we measuring the right performance?
- Is this the most valid way of measuring that performance?
- How can we improve the measures we are using?

This kind of thinking results in social administrators using measures even if "total" validity has not been proven. At the same time it dictates that managers "audit" the results of the use of a measure and are open to changing and refining it.

## Measures Need to Be Observable, Replicable, and Uniform

The bottom line is that everyone counts the same thing in the same way. For example, in some agencies reports of client contacts are unreliable because one worker will count telephone contacts while another counts only in-person contacts. Another illustration is counting caseloads. Some workers complete intakes for clients during their first contact while other workers provide several contact episodes prior to completing a formal intake.

## Measures Need to Be Understandable

The performance measure needs to be expressed in terms everyone can understand. Often managers receive reports in which the data is unclear. Percentages are reported, but how they were computed is not described. Tables are presented in which the labels (columns, rows, title) are not explained or abbreviations used that are not universally known. At times innovative formats are used (e.g., movement tables) without instruction in how to read them. Measures derived from complicated formulas can lead a manager to not understand what is being reported. Occasionally, the time period given may be unclear.

## Measures Need to Be Susceptible to Change

The performance measure should be susceptible or sensitive to change within the time period reported. For example, the percentage of clients moving from pre-vocational training to competitive employment situations is a change that occurs over months or years for many disabled client groups. Concerted worker efforts to locate and place clients in jobs will influence this indicator, but the influence would not be felt next week. A monthly or quarterly report would be more likely to reflect meaningful change.

## Develop Few Measures

There are two reasons to limit the number of performance measures. First, people can only handle a few pieces of information at a time. Too much information confuses and leads to lack of use. Second, the presence of many measures will disperse organizational effort rather than focus it. As Peters and Waterman (1982) state: "The organization gets paralyzed because the structure not only does not make priorities clear, *it automatically dilutes priorities*. In effect, it says to people down the line: 'Everything is important; pay equal attention to everything.' The message is paralyzing." (p. 307) As was discussed in Chapter 1, organizational focus is one of the dimensions—and perhaps the most important dimension—in getting anything done.

## Measures Need to Be Efficient

A performance measure should make as few demands on personnel as possible. The burden of collecting information is felt by everyone and particularly by frontline professionals. No one wants to divert more worker time from direct service. Therefore, performance measures when possible should be derived from existing data. If new data are needed, then, the instruments and procedures should be as simple as possible. Managers should find opportunities to eliminate the need for more forms.

In some cases even worthwhile data should not be collected because it is just too demanding. For example, mental health research suggests that one powerful determinant of integrating a psychiatrically disabled person into his or her community is the extent of social support building. Few community psychosocial programs, however, systematically collect this information and for good reason. Social support remains a conceptual quagmire (Barrera, 1986) for which no adequate or economical measures have been developed. The ideal community integration information system would regularly collect data regarding clients' social supports: clients' perceptions of support in current relationships, frequency of social contacts, number of social supports used, and need for additional supports. But at the present time the resource costs to develop an information system to include documentation and tracking of social supports are just too great.

This example offers some important lessons: (1) No information system will ever be able to do it all. Particularly in large complex organizations, information systems are vital but not a panacea. (2) There is no substitute for good client-worker teamwork. The training and expertise of frontline workers is the critical determinant of client outcomes, and this needs to be supported and enhanced whenever possible. (3) The supervisor, through regular systematic case review, is the primary location for tracking important elements of performance that are not efficiently tracked by the information system.

The point is simply that all outcomes and worker functions that contribute to organizational performance must be systematically monitored. The information system is only one management tool. Managers need to use a variety of tools to enhance organizational performance.

## SOME MANAGEMENT DECISIONS ABOUT MEASUREMENT

Building an information system around client outcomes will require the human service manager to make some important decisions. Managers should consider the following: the vantage point from which measurement occurs, the use of existing measures versus developing new measures, the blending of client and societal goals, the timing of data collection, and the marshaling of resources to assess client outcomes.

### Vantage Point

The vantage point refers to the source of ratings or evaluations. For client outcomes the most common choices are clients, the intervenor (usually the direct service worker), or a significant other such as a parent, teacher, or spouse. With some measures, no decision is necessary. Client satisfaction by definition is to be from the client's vantage point. Most measures of status change are unambiguous and are usually completed by agency staff. Most attitude questionnaires and learning measures are completed by the client.

The vantage point decision becomes critical when using other measures such as behavior change. Different people view these phenomena differently and different people have access to different information. Maluccio (1979) and Beck and Jones (1974) both found significant discrepancies between how workers and clients view case progress and what factors contribute to progress. Modrcin (1985) found large differences in the ratings of workers and significant others regarding socialization and leisure time behavior of a group of chronically mentally ill clients. In all three studies, the workers viewed client performance lower than did the other raters. Maluccio (1979) hypothesizes that the lower ratings by workers are a function of a pathology orientation and limited information concerning client's behavior when not in direct contact with the worker. A common finding is lack of agreement among clients, practitioners, and independent observers on effectiveness measures. (Bergin & Lambert, 1978; Lambert, 1983) The disparity is as much conceptual and value based as it is measurement. (Reid, 1987)

The client-centered manager always places a premium on the client vantage point and that view should be included whenever possible. But the best solution is to gather data from multiple vantage points. When multiple perspectives and indicators converge, confidence in the results increases. The drawback is that such a strategy adds complexity and cost, which may limit feasibility in some situations.

## Existing Measures versus Develop New Measures

In general, the human service manager should use existing measures that have been tested for validity and reliability. This is true only if measures can be found that directly capture the outcomes desired by the program. For instance, one can easily miss the mark if a measure of depression is used to assess the outcome of a service designed to teach a disciplinary alternative to spanking. While this example may seem far-fetched, many such examples can be found. Finding existing measures is difficult. One excellent source is reviews of the research published in the professional literature. Examples include the recent work of Rubin (1984); Rubin and Gibelman (1984) and Gowdy, Rapp, and Poertner (1987) concerning the chronically mentally ill; and Reid and Hanrahan (1982) concerning social work intervention. These research reviews often include a description of the dependent variables used and provide references to locate more detailed information.

Research or resource centers within universities or an individual faculty member with ongoing interest and expertise in your service area are other sources of measures. For example, Carter (1986) has developed an inventory of measures for a variety of child welfare programs under the auspice of the National Child Welfare Resource Center at the University of Southern Maine. The Urban Institute has published collections of outcome measures used for human services operated by state governments. (Miller, Hatry, & Koss, 1977) Oftentimes a phone call to a national expert or a national office (e.g., Child Welfare League of America, National Institute of Mental Health, Family Service Association of America) can provide the necessary information or needed leads.

If the search for existing measures is not fruitful, the manager needs to develop new ones. Client satisfaction can serve as a case example. (Later in this chapter the steps in developing a client satisfaction measure are identified.) The steps in developing other measures are very similar. When in doubt the social administrator can consult with faculty in schools of social work who have experience in measurement development.

## Blending Client and Societal Goals

Social administrators, like direct-service colleagues, are frequently faced with an important conflict of values. The profession espouses client self-determination as an important value. Yet society provides resources to attain specific societal values. Child protective services are to protect children, not to allow parents self-determination in parenting. Case management for the chronically mentally ill aims to reduce dependency on society, not to allow the person to "hang out" downtown. Examples are numerous. Social workers face them daily. The social administrator too is not immune to these value choices and must struggle with them. Social workers can address these value conflicts in at least two ways. They may consciously choose a position based on ethical analysis, or they may blend societal goals and client goals.

Ethical analysis involves identifying competing values, specifying accompanying obligations, recognizing the consequences of the obligations, weighing the relative effects of the consequences, and making a considered judgment. (Ruggiero, 1973) While this appears complex, social workers do it every day when they decide that the safety of the child outweighs the parent's right to self-determination.

Blending of apparent conflicting goals is a social work skill applicable in a variety of contexts. Frequently the abusive parent also values the safety of the child. The abuse may arise out of a belief that violence corrects behavior. The desire to correct the behavior can be blended with the goal of protecting the child by teaching the parent nonviolent ways of correcting behavior. Blending societal and client goals is as important a consideration for the social administration selecting measurements as it is for the frontline worker making case decisions. If the social administrator selects employment status as an outcome measure for chronically mentally ill individuals, the administrator is going to have to continually interpret for frontline staff the value basis for its selection and how this blends with apparently competing values such as client self-determination.

## Data Collection Choices

The human service manager has a range of choices concerning methods and timing of data collection. There are four major methods: self-administered questionnaires, interviews, observation (often structured by checklists), and agency record-keeping. When you combine the four methods with the perspective of clients, workers, significant others, and volunteers, the number of choices is large. Existing measures will usually prescribe both the method and vantage point.

Data collection can be made at several points. At intake, or at the onset of a particular service (pre), can be combined with at termination, or completion of a particular service (post). This is a common schedule, which is appropriate for most outcomes. Under this schema, managers can make defensible claims that a service is demonstrably effective even if strict scientific criteria cannot be met.

Carter (1984, 1987) argues that follow-up data should be collected as well. Follow-up data is that which is collected after termination or completion of service (three months, six months, year). The notion is that human service interventions should make an impact beyond the duration of the intervention. There is evidence that gains made by clients in human service programs are not sustained. (Davidson & Wolfred, 1977; Maluccio & Marlow, 1972; Prather & Gibson, 1977) Follow-up data are powerful when reporting to external constituencies and for programmatic development. The drawback concerns the additional costs involved and difficulties in tracking ex-clients.

## Marshaling Resources

The design, collection, storage, and retrieval of client-outcome data can be an expensive enterprise. Data collection in particular can consume large portions of precious personnel time. The human service manager needs to always keep economy of time in mind when designing the information system, with particular attention to direct-service workers' time. In this regard, the manager should explore the use of clerical staff and volunteers for as many data collection tasks as possible. For example, client satisfaction and other forms of questionnaires can be designed for administration by trained clerical staff. A small cadre of well-trained and well-supervised volunteers can be used to conduct interviews. In residential agencies employing night staff, these personnel could have responsibility for entering data into the computer or manually collating the data. Simply put, data collection is often mishandled by an unrealistic view of the staff resources available to perform selected tasks.

## MEASURING CLIENT OUTCOMES

The goals and objectives established during the program design phase drive client-outcome measurement. This statement, however, camouflages myriad critical decisions the human service manager is required to make. The most central decision concerns how to measure the desired outcomes. Before jumping to the conclusion that the agency has to develop their own, a manager should consider employing the host of techniques and instruments that have already been developed. Social work interventions are designed to work with clients to produce outcomes in one or more of these categories: changes in affect, knowledge, behavior, status, or environment. This section will review these categories of change, with existing measurement approaches for each type.

## Changes in Affect

Changes in the way people feel about something or their emotional response to a situation is a frequent target of human service programs. Sometimes this change stands by itself. For example, having clients who feel good about the counseling they receive may be an end by itself. But frequently, a change in affect is seen as accompanying other important changes. It is commonly recognized that helping parents change parenting behavior also requires a change in attitudes or feelings about parenting, as well as knowledge of parenting techniques.

## Problems in Measuring Attitude

There are two common problems that confront the measurement of attitudes. The first problem concerns the tendency of clients to respond to items in socially desirable ways rather than as an accurate reflection of their beliefs. The tendency of clients to rate their satisfaction with services highly is in part a function of "trying to please." The best protection against this bias is to generate and test a large number of items that reflect variance or differences among people, thereby making the test less susceptible to socially desirable responses. When possible, anonymity of responses may also encourage truthfulness.

The second problem in attitude measurement is when people appear to change their attitudes in a negative direction when they have really just become more sensitive to the feelings and attitudes in question. Howard (1980) identified this phenomenon as "response shift bias." This is seen when one responds at one time to "How I feel" and then through the service process one realizes that "I really do not feel that positive or comfortable so I now respond more negatively." The change appears to be negative when what has occurred is increased awareness. This is a particular problem for pre/post assessment or repeated measures. Howard suggests careful attention when writing items and pairing items with retrospective questions. The retrospective question asked participants to respond to the same item in reference to how they perceived themselves before the intervention. When this is carefully designed into the instrument, it is possible to more accurately determine attitudes and attitude shifts.

## Rapid Assessment Instruments

The measurement of affective changes has been the subject of much of the work in developing rapid assessment instruments for clinical practice. These instruments are characterized as a standard set of questions designed to evaluate the degree of a client's particular affective problem or state. They are short (no more than two pages), easy to administer by the client (less than fifteen minutes), easy to score (less than five minutes), and can be incorporated into the usual client interview process. Examples of several different types of scales that social administrators might select to assess change in affect include rapid assessment approaches identified by Levitt & Reid (1981), Hudson's (1982) clinical measurement package, self-reporting symptom checklists, and client satisfaction scales.

## Client Satisfaction

The measurement of client satisfaction with services is an important tool of the client-centered human service manager. (Patti, 1985; Rapp & Poertner, 1983) The process of developing a measure for other types of affective changes is very similar to the process suggested here for developing a measure for assessing client satisfaction. The development of a client satisfaction instrument is provided as an example that the social administrator can use by analogy to develop measures for other changes in affect.

Client satisfaction is the feelings clients possess about the help offered by the organization. Despite the attention the measurement of client satisfaction has garnered, in many ways it remains a "definitional muddle." (Lebow, 1983) It is clear that client satisfaction is a multidimensional concept involving perceptions of goal attainment, service provider facilitative behavior, and agency characteristics such as ease of access. (Poertner, 1985; Poertner & Wintersteen, n.d.) Client satisfaction instruments are sufficiently important to warrant systematic attention and development rather than the casual way many agencies develop such measures.

Managers sometimes view client satisfaction with skepticism. To their credit they say that to know that a client is satisfied is not sufficient. Managers want to know if the person received the intended benefits. This gets to the heart of what is meant by client satisfaction. There are those approaches to client satisfaction that simply ask the person if they were satisfied with the service they received. If this is the approach to client satisfaction, the skeptical manager is correct. There is, however, a growing body of literature suggesting that assessment of client satisfaction is the clients' reporting on critical elements of service delivery. The program design technology of Chapter 2 clearly identifies critical elements of the service transaction. It is these elements that constitute the items of a client satisfaction instrument. For example, if a central design element of a counseling program is that the client and worker develop goals for counseling, then an item such as "the counselor helped me identify goals for counseling" is indicated. Clearly the client's perspective on the important element of the service transaction is valuable to workers and managers alike.

The development of a client satisfaction assessment instrument begins by identifying those critical elements of the service transaction for which client feedback is valued. Identification of these elements or dimensions comes primarily from four sources: (1) the specifications of the service transaction from the program design; (2) clients; (3) frontline service staff; and (4) the client satisfaction literature.

Program design specifications identify critical elements of the service setting, client and worker behavior, the service process, and the service episode. Scale items can be identified from each of these design elements. Client feedback on these elements can be a powerful mechanism for assuring that the transaction mirrors the intended design. The use of clients in generating and testing questions should be of primary concern. Few existing scales have involved clients in constructing items. This suggests the need for mechanisms to facilitate this process. One of the most promising approaches has been reported by Fawcett, Seekins, Whang, Muiu, and Debalcaz (1982), whereby clients are involved members of an interagency task force. The issues generated by this approach tend to cover many specific service delivery concerns, which can be translated into scale items, as well as increase the possibility that the instrument will tap client dissatisfaction. Service delivery staff are another source of items that measure satisfaction. Staff members who provide direct service to clients have access to information on client concerns.

The pool of items to be field tested needs to be drawn from a variety of sources to have the best chance of adding to previously untapped facets of satisfaction. Following a carefully developed plan, selecting items from a range of sources, and involving persons most closely aligned with the issue to be measured are all steps designed to increase validity. Additional steps to insure validity are important but may be costly.

The client satisfaction literature, when it takes the approach of identifying critical elements of the service transaction, is very helpful. This approach is characterized by someone or some group writing potential client satisfaction items, having clients respond to them, and then using statistical techniques to identify items and clusters of items important to clients. The investigator's approach, the service, and the client population all contribute to different groupings of items. A common theme across these studies, however, is that clients view goal attainment and the helping relationship as very important. Any client satisfaction scale needs to include these two service dimensions.

## Formatting Items

Once elements of the service transaction for which client feedback is desired are identified, the items for the scale can be written. The collection of client satisfaction scales are a rich source of possible items. All of these scales appear in the client satisfaction literature and have been subjected to some empirical verification. The authors have found two additional guides helpful in client satisfaction scale development.

First, items worded negatively are very difficult to answer. The evaluation of a statement such as "Did the counselor seem to dislike you?" on a six-point scale, from "strongly agree" to "strongly disagree" puts people in the position of evaluating a double negative—a difficult task for anyone.

Secondly, although the choice of response dimensions is seldom the focus of study, they are likely to make a difference in how people respond. Research seems to show there are at least two important factors in selecting a response dimension: the number of points on the scale and the labels used. Several of the scales included in the appendix used four- or five-point responses. There is some evidence that six-point responses result in more reliable scales. (Braskamp, Brandenburg, & Ory, 1984)

Carefully considering the wording of the response dimension is also important although little is known about this factor. Those response dimensions that use a form of satisfaction (extremely satisfied to extremely dissatisfied) may result in inflated responses. Gutek (1978) has found a tendency in our culture for people to inflate their responses when asked about their level of satisfaction, which may not occur if different wording is used. Two alternatives that have worked reasonably well for the authors are an agree-disagree dimension or a frequency of occurrence dimension, such as "never" to "all of the time."

Now that the critical elements of the service transaction have been translated into scale items using a six-point response dimension, it is time to consider the unique perspective of each individual client. Every client satisfaction scale needs to include at least one open-ended question. At a minimum the last question ought to be something like: "Please use this space to tell us anything else you want to about receiving service here." Some shorter client satisfaction instruments pair open-ended and closed-ended questions so that for each element of the service transaction assessed by a scale item there is also an open-ended question such as "Are there any improvements you would suggest?" Responses to these open-ended questions are important for identifying the unique perspectives of individual clients. It is also a valuable source of positive feedback for staff (Poertner, 1985), as well as a valuable source of ideas for the client-centered manager to make services more responsive to clients' needs.

Once a pool of items has been identified together with a response dimension, the scale needs to be tested and refined. This testing primarily involves using statistical tests, such as Cronbach's Alpha, a measure of reliability and examining clusters of items through factor analysis. Although there are a variety of computer programs available that may even reside on the agency's computer, the manager will probably want to obtain consultation from someone with more psychometric experience at this stage. The intent here is to identify items that "are not working" and need to be rewritten or eliminated.

## The Acquisition of Knowledge

Many human service programs have a knowledge acquisition purpose or component: parent education, self-help groups, health promotion programs, crime prevention programs. Even many psychotherapeutic or counseling approaches are focused on learning "insight" or "self-awareness." Fortunately measuring knowledge gained is a generally more straightforward task than other client-outcome areas.

If you have decided that a main component of your program is educational, then you will want to measure for this outcome. Suppose that you want to find out if your clients increased their knowledge of self-protective behaviors. You have already decided what you will teach and what the concepts are that you want your clients to learn. The next step in this process is to determine the most appropriate way to identify what your clients learned.

The assessment of knowledge acquired through a particular intervention is reasonably straightforward. Perhaps one of the best known knowledge outcome assessment technologies is the pre-test/post-test technique. Most of the time, it is reasonable to attribute improvements in post-test scores to the educational intervention. Pre- and post-tests can be developed using true/false, multiple-choice, or open-ended questions. The type of questions used is determined by several factors like the verbal skills of the client and the level of learning to be assessed.

***True/False Questions.*** This type of assessment is designed to measure for simple recognition or recall of the material. It is also useful to use with clients who do not exhibit a high level of verbal skills, for example, children or adults reading at a lower-than-average level.

***Multiple-Choice Questions.*** Multiple-choice questions can be written to evaluate higher levels of learning such as application (problem-solving or applying ideas in new situations) or comprehension (restating or reorganizing material to show understanding). Multiple-choice items are most useful when the person being assessed possesses adequate reading and writing skills.

Multiple-choice item tests require that clients select the correct answer from an array of possible answers. Typically, the multiple-choice question presents the problem in one of two formats: the complete question (e.g., "What should you do *first* if you suspected a child has been abused?") or the incomplete statement (e.g., "The first thing you should do if you suspect a child is being abused is to . . ."). With these two formats, the client selects either the correct answer or the best answer from the list of options provided. "In the correct answer form, the answer is correct beyond question or doubt while the others are definitely incorrect. In the best answer version, more than one option may be appropriate in varying degrees; however, it is essential that the best response be the one that competent experts agree upon." (Clegg & Cashin, 1986, p. 2) The multiple-choice format is simple; it is constructing a meaningful and worthwhile item that is so difficult and time-consuming.

***Open-Ended Questions.*** Open-ended questions can be written in much the same way as multiple-choice questions; only the client must supply the answer(s). An open-ended item requires that a client know material well enough to either solve a problem or recall the material, instead of merely recognizing an answer provided in a correct-answer form question. While it is often appealing to use open-ended questions, they should be written and used with great care. If clients are not highly articulate, it is simply unfair to expect them to respond to open-ended questions. Every social administrator can easily recall writing volumes on essay questions in college in the hope that the correct response is included. The best open-ended question is the one for which the correct answer can be identified clearly and unambiguously. For example, "Identify the three rules of anti-victimization presented in the film."

Writing test questions or items is no easy task. They need to be written and refined over time. Only in using the items can you determine if they are measuring the knowledge you intend for clients to learn. The instruments that you use need not be limited to only one type of item. For instance, you may want to use multiple-choice and true/false items on the tests in order to get at varying levels of cognitive changes.

After you have decided on what items to use to measure knowledge acquisition, the instrument is ready to administer. The pre-test should be given to clients before the intervention begins. This will allow you to see how much knowledge clients have about the subject before they become involved in the learning of the material you are going to present. The time that the post-test is administered will vary depending on the service. For example, the post-test can be given at the end of the last session of a parent education program, or it can be given weeks or months after the last session. Once the assessment is complete, tests are scored. A comparison of the pre- and post-test scores determines the improvements that clients have made.

## Behavior Change

Measures of behavior change fall into two categories: skills and performance. Skills refer to a client's ability to do some behavior and the program's ability to teach these behaviors. The test for this is usually whether clients have the behavior in their repertoire. In other words, if I gave this person a million dollars (or some other equally grand reward) would this person be able to do the requested behavior. This is of a higher order than the cognitive mastery of a subject. For example, an individual with severe mental illness enrolled in a prevocational program may be able to list the specific tasks needed to find a job (learning) but may not be able to do the actual tasks of finding a job (e.g., search want ads or engage a prospective employer). Another example is the parent who can describe three techniques for nonphysical discipline, but when asked to demonstrate the techniques, the parent cannot do it. Skill training is a major element of a wide variety of social programs including vocational programs, day treatment and partial hospitalization programs, programs for people with developmental disabilities and so on.

Measuring skills always requires observation of the client either through role-playing or in the natural environment. Behavioral checklists guide the observer. To test discrimination and generalization, observations in a variety of settings would be necessary.

A second category of behavior change is actual behavioral performance. Performance asks an even higher order question, Do the clients use the knowledge and/or skill in their lives? Does the mother use time-out or privilege restrictions instead of paddling a child? Does the person who knows how to ride the bus system, do so? How often? Behavior change measures seeking to capture behavioral performance can be designed for client self-reports, and professional or significant other evaluations.

The most common forms of behavior change measurement are based on individual case plans developed between client and direct-service worker. A simple method is illustrated in Figure 3–1. Rates of goal attainment can easily be computed by client, by worker, by team, or by agency.

A slightly more sophisticated method is Goal Attainment Scaling. (Kiresuk & Sherman, 1968; Baxter, 1973; Jones & Garwick, 1973) The technique assesses the degree of achievement of specific, individualized client goals as negotiated between workers and clients. The procedure involves

1. identifying goal areas,
2. weighting the goal areas in terms of importance,
3. forming a scale of possible outcomes,
4. scoring the outcomes after intervention, and
5. computing the goal-attainment score.

Figure 3–2 presents an example of a completed Follow-Up Guide. It takes about forty minutes to construct such a guide (i.e., identify the goal areas, select weights, and scale predicted outcomes) and another twenty minutes to complete a follow-up interview, score the scales, and calculate the scores. Goal Attainment Scaling, like other goal achievement methods of capturing behavior change, are most useful when the agency wants to allow the client and worker to negotiate individual client changes and is best used as part of the treatment process. In fact, there is some evidence that the actual setting of goals by clients helps the therapeutic process. (Seaburg, 1976) Please note that Goal Attainment Scaling can include goals about feelings or knowledge but most often the focus is on behavior. Individualized goal-attainment outcome measures are usually not sufficient for all audiences. As Calsyn and Davidson (1978) stated:

> Since program success is measured in goals achieved rather than specific criteria such as days of hospitalization, recidivism, or employment, two programs can have the same mean GAS score and have accomplished radically different objectives . . . goals achieved may not be a satisfactory criterion of success for most publicly funded programs which are accountable to public officials and the general public as well as to clients and service providers. (p. 306)

Under these prevalent conditions, the human service manager is best advised to use measures of individualized goal attainment that speak directly to the client and measures that have more universal meaning. The parent education program discussed earlier is a good example. Both individual goal attainment data and abuse reports data were gathered. Other examples include Stein and Gambrill (1977)

**LIFE DOMAIN:** Leisure Time Activities
**LONG-TERM GOAL:** Engage in one activity outside of the home six days per week.

| Goal and Steps Toward Achievement | Responsibility for Activity C or CM | Date Accomplished | Comments |
|---|---|---|---|
| **Short-term goal: Plant a garden.** | | | |
| 1. Ask parents for permission and agree on a location. | John | 11-6 | |
| 2. Decide on contents of the garden. | John | 11-7 | |
| 3. Ask neighbor to borrow rototiller. | John | 11-8 | |
| 4. Dig up garden. | John | 11-8 | |
| 5. Go to library and get book on home gardening. | John and case manager | 11-12 | |
| 6. Buy seeds and plant. | John | 11-16 | |
| 7. Write up schedule for garden maintenance. | John and father | 11-16 | |
| 8. Follow schedule. | John | | |
| **Short-term goal: Go swimming three times per week.** | | | |
| 1. Call YMCA and find out: | | | |
| a. When is open swimming scheduled? | John | 11-20 | |
| b. How much does a membership cost? | | | |
| 2. If cost is excessive, approach swimming instructor concerning John's situation: | Case manager | 11-25 | |
| a. Ask for suggestions (neutral strategy). | | | |
| b. Suggest John act as assistant in return for access to the pool. | | | |

_____
Client Signature

_____
Case Manager Signature

**Figure 3–1.** Agenda

115

## SAMPLE CLINICAL GUIDE: CRISIS INTERVENTION CENTER

### PROGRAM EVALUATION PROJECT

Level at Intake: /

Level at Follow-up: *

Level at intake: 29.4
Goal Attainment Score
(Level at Follow-up): 62.2
Goal Attainment Change Score: +32.8

SCALE HEADINGS AND SCALE WEIGHTS

| Check whether or not the scale has been mutually negotiated between patient and CIC interviewer. | SCALE 1: Education ($w_1 = 20$) Yes x No | SCALE 2: Suicide ($w_2 = 30$) Yes x No | SCALE 3: Manipulation ($w_3 = 25$) Yes x No | SCALE 4: Drug Abuse ($w_4 = 30$) Yes x No | SCALE 5: Dependency on CIC ($w_5 = 10$) Yes x No |
|---|---|---|---|---|---|
| **SCALE ATTAINMENT LEVELS** | | | | | |
| a. most unfavorable treatment outcome thought likely. (−2) | Patient has made no attempt to enroll in high school. / | Patient has committed suicide. | Patient makes rounds of community service agencies demanding medication, and refuses other forms of treatment. / | Patient reports addiction to hard narcotics (heroin, morphine). | Patient has contacted CIC by telephone or in person at least seven times since first visit. |
| b. less than expected success with treatment. (−1) | Patient has enrolled in high school, but at time of follow-up has dropped out. | Patient has acted on at least one suicidal impulse since first contact with the CIC, but has not succeeded. / | Patient no longer visits CIC with demands for medication but continues with other community agencies and still refuses other forms of treatment. | Patient has used hard narcotics, but is not addicted and/or uses hallucinogens (LSD, Pot) more than four times a month. / | Patient has contacted CIC 5-6 times since intake. / |

| | School | Suicidal impulses | Treatment | Drug use | CIC contact |
|---|---|---|---|---|---|
| c. expected level of treatment success. (0) | Patient has enrolled and is in school at follow-up, but is attending sporadically (misses an average of more than a third of her classes during a week). | Patient reports she has had at least four suicidal impulses since her first contact with the CIC but has not acted on any of them. | Patient no longer attempts to manipulate for drugs at community service agencies, but will not accept another form of treatment. | Patient has not used hard narcotics during follow-up period, and uses hallucinogens between 1 and 4 times a month. * | Patient has contacted CIC 3-4 times since intake. |
| d. more than expected success with treatment. (+1) | Patient has enrolled, is in school at follow-up, and is attending classes consistently, but has no vocational goals. * | * | Patient accepts nonmedication treatment at some community agency. * | Patient uses hallucinogens less than once a month. | |
| e. best anticipated success with treatment (+2) | Patient has enrolled, is in school at follow-up, is attending classes consistently, and has some vocational goal. | Patient reports she has had no suicidal impulses since her first contact with the CIC. | Patient accepts nonmedication treatment, and by own report shows signs of improvement. | At time of follow-up, patient is not using any illegal drugs. | Patient has not contacted CIC since intake. * |

**Figure 3-2.** Goal Attainment Follow-Up Guide (Source: Hargreaves, W.A., et al., *Resource Materials for Community Mental Health Program Evaluation; Volume IV—Evaluating the Effectiveness of Services*, p. 128.)

concerning permanency planning in child welfare, Rapp and Chamberlain (1985) concerning case management for the chronically mentally ill, and Seidman and Rappaport (1974) concerning such populations as children who have behavior and learning problems or adolescents on probation.

## Status Changes

Movement of people between statuses is a characteristic of social systems. Contributions to social theory have come, for example, from applications in changing voter intentions (Anderson, 1954), industrial mobility (Goodman, 1962), and upward mobility in organizations (White, 1970). As a method of evaluation, status change has been used for affirmative action (Churchill & Shank, 1975), employment programs (Durbin, 1968), living arrangements for the elderly (S. Fanshel, 1975), functional status of the elderly (Burton, Dellinger, & Damon, 1980), mental health (Bass & Windle, 1973; Miley, Lively, & McDonald, 1978; Rapp, Gowdy, Sullivan, & Wintersteen, 1988), and child welfare (Taber & Poertner, 1981).

The central idea common to these applications is that the goal of the social or service system is to move a person to a more desirable status or to maintain the person in a "most desirable" status. The permanency planning movement in child welfare, recidivism in corrections, and in-home care of the elderly are inherently concerned with status change. In mental health, deinstitutionalization and such concepts as "least restrictive environment" reflect a model of status change as a goal.

The development of status measures must meet four criteria. First, the list of possible statuses needs to be exhaustive. Second, each specific status needs to be mutually exclusive. A person should not be able to be in two statuses at the same time. Third, the statuses must be able to be hierarchically ordered from least desirable to more desirable and a reasonable degree of consensus achieved for this ordering. Fourth, the measures need to be sensitive to change. In large part this means determining the time interval within which to observe client transitions. If the interval between reporting periods is too short, little change would be seen and the paperwork burden increased. If the interval is too long, there may be multiple transitions, and thereby actually camouflaging patterns of movement. In addition, long intervals between reporting do not allow a reasonable degree of immediate feedback and prevent timely corrective actions. Two examples of status hierarchies for the chronically mentally ill in two life domains are shown below.

*Living Arrangement Status*
1. Psychiatric hospital ward
2. General hospital psychiatric ward
3. Nursing home or IC-MH
4. Emergency shelter
5. Adult foster care
6. Lives with relatives (Heavily dependent for personal care and control)

*Vocational Status*
1. No vocational activity
2. Prevocational classes
3. Screening and evaluation of vocational interests and abilities
4. Working on GED or basic academic skills
5. Attending college (six credit hours or less)

7. Group home
8. Half-way house
9. Boarding house
10. Lives with relatives, but is largely independent
11. Supervised apartment program
12. Shares apartment and capable of self-care
13. Lives alone or with spouse and capable of self-care
14. Other (specify): _____

6. Attending vocational school or training
7. Active job search
8. Participating in work program at MHC
9. Employed at sheltered employment outside of MHC
10. Participating in ongoing volunteer activity
11. Attending college (seven credit hours or more)
12. Remains home to take care of children or others
13. Any job or set of jobs requiring less than 30 hours per week
14. Any job or set of jobs requiring more than 30 hours per week
15. Other (specify):_____
16. Retired

The use of statuses has a number of appealing qualities. First, it has the ability to unify the agendas and performance expectations of the agency's multiple constituencies. Frequently status maintenance or change is the avowed goal of public policy—for example, maintaining children in the least restrictive, most family-like environment. In addition, statuses in any social service program are finite. In contrast, models of behavior change and goal attainment are often formulated through the interaction between the client and the worker, and can be highly idiosyncratic. The finite property of status change can enhance organizational control and the process of supervision and allow for increased focus at multiple organizational levels.

A major drawback of status change is the possibility of being subject to administrative manipulation, rather than based on the client's progress or needs. For example, it is possible that children could be "dumped" out of foster care due to budget constraints, not due to improved families. Such administrative actions tend to be rare, however, and when they occur they are usually accompanied by a public outcry. When focus on change is subject to organizational, programmatic, and managerial efforts, then such measures are realistic and helpful. Status change also poses fewer dangers to validity and reliability, and the data are often already available in case files or data bases.

## Environmental Changes

Measurement of environmental changes is the least developed client-outcome area. This is not surprising since much of the impetus for measurement comes from psychology, which has historically paid little attention to a client's environment.

(Rappaport, 1977) Nevertheless, items that assess the adequacy of a person's residence, food, and finances are included in some scales such as the Oregon Quality of Life Scale (Bigelow, Brodsky, Stewart, & Olsen, 1982) and are good examples of assessment of environmental changes. Kane and Kane (1984) have identified a set of scales focused on the "person-environment fit," which have been developed for long-term care clients. Those scales attempt to assess such dimensions as

- the degree of perceived control, freedom, choice, autonomy, or individuality permitted by the environment (to the individual);
- structure, rules, and expected behavior imposed by the environment on the individual;
- relationships between individuals and caregivers in the environment;
- perceptions of activity and stimulation levels; and
- expressed satisfaction with various aspects of the environment. (p. 192)

These two scales are far from adequate and demonstrate the lack of development in this area. Students, scholars, and managers alike need to assist in the development of useful measures of environmental change.

It is clear from the preceding pages that technologies do exist to measure client outcomes. They not only exist, but the scholarly journals are increasingly including new measures. Assuring that clients are receiving intended benefits is such an important management concern that social administrators need to select measures, monitor the results of their use, continue to refine the measures, and use them as a basis for being responsive to clients.

## MEASURING PRODUCTIVITY

Productivity is the amount of service provided or those key helping processes that produce the desired client outcome. A variety of constituencies requires every human service organization to make a given level of effort. Along with financial accounting, virtually all agencies collect productivity data in at least one of these forms: client count, service episodes, service events, or elapsed time. Each measure has particular strengths and weaknesses, and therefore care must be used in selection.

First, productivity can be measured by counting the number of persons who are participating in the program. *Client counts* are the most prevalent measure of productivity because they are easily understood and convey meaningful information to lay persons, workers, administrators, and funders. They can be used as an indication of target population coverage and as a means of assigning caseloads. But client count is rarely sufficient as a measure of productivity. It assumes all clients are receiving the same amount of service or that the clients are homogeneous and that situations are of equal intensity or severity. Program repeaters can also inflate client counts. For example, in manpower programs, the same client may receive placement services and be placed two, three, four times yet only one client is served.

Second, productivity can be measured by counting *service episodes*. A service episode is the complete period in which a service is provided. One service episode could include recognition of the problem by the client, the effort to find help, a period of working with one or more professional helpers, and termination. A service episode encompasses more than one particular service event. This method avoids the problem of repeaters included in client counts because each separate placement, in the example above, would be a service episode. Counting service episodes is particularly well suited for short-term or emergency services like crisis hot-lines or emergency room service. These services are quick and rather uniform and the possibility of contact with clients more than once is high. The chief disadvantage is that service episodes are not applicable to services that are long term or could vary considerably from client to client.

Measuring productivity through *service events* requires the counting of specific actions on the part of the worker. These specific actions are derived directly from the program design and could include such events as a group session, an interview, a home visit, a class session, a home delivered meal, a physical examination, a case review, or a telephone call. The primary strength of this unit of measurement is its ability to represent the implementation of the program design. A major disadvantage is that counting worker actions, or service events, tends to camouflage the radical differences between events. Some events are more crucial to producing client outcomes than others, and some events require more time or intensity than others. It follows then, that a measure that counts all events equally can be very misleading.

*Elapsed time* is another method for measuring units of service. In this case, the units are time oriented like days of nursing home care, hours of counseling, hours spent delivering home health services to the elderly. The great advantage of elapsed time as a measure is its precision with respect to the use of resources. It is possible to show the hours of worker's time and therefore resources allocated to different types of cases and to one particular client, or to the caseload as a whole. The measure also has a special utility when making budget presentations since there is a direct correspondence between elapsed time of the worker and cost factors in the program. The great disadvantage of elapsed time is that it is focused on the expenditure of time by the worker without any attention to the number of clients served, their characteristics, the amount of help received, or even the service activity performed in the program. But, if the activity of the worker over time is in some sense constant then this unit might be useful.

## LINKING PRODUCTIVITY AND CLIENT OUTCOME

Although every human service organization needs a set of productivity measures that captures overall program effort, the client-centered performance manager can also use productivity measures to directly improve client outcomes and organizational focus. This requires the manager to select those productivity measures that represent a programmatic subset of worker behavior that is the most influential in producing desired client outcomes. Selecting these behaviors or service events can be based on the relevant research, practice wisdom, and the underlying program theory. In some fields, the practice research is capable of providing strong relationships between behavior and outcomes. For example, an increasing body of research is suggesting that the following program behaviors are influential in maintaining chronically mentally ill people in the community (preventing hospitalization) and enhancing their quality of life:

- Client attending regular medication clinic appointments (Hogarty, 1979; Linn, Caffey, Klett, Hogarty, & Lamb, 1979)
- Early appointment with mental health clinic following discharge from the hospital (Nuehring & Ladner, 1980; Altman, 1982)
- Linkage of client to community resources (Test & Stein, 1980; Rapp & Chamberlain, 1985)
- Support to the family (Anderson, Hogarty, & Reiss, 1980; Hatfield, 1978; Boyd, McGill, & Falloon, 1981; Shenoy, Shires, & White, 1980)
- Outreach mode of service delivery (Test & Stein, 1980; Rapp & Chamberlain, 1985)

In child welfare, there is a similarly credible list of factors that influences permanency planning:

- Worker's ability to assess parental adequacy (Shapiro, 1976; Costin & Rapp, 1984)
- Setting permanency goals in a timely fashion (Emlen, 1976; Fanshel, 1976)
- Frequency of caseworker contact with the natural family (D. Fanshel, 1975; Arizona Social Service Bureau, 1974; Shapiro, 1976)
- Frequency of parental visiting of their child in foster care (Maas & Engler, 1959; Fanshel & Shinn, 1978; D. Fanshel, 1975)
- The use of in-home services focused on the parents (Gruber, 1973; Jenkins & Norman, 1975; Jenkins & Sauber, 1966)
- Regular and systematic case reviews (Jones, 1978; Festinger, 1975; Emlen, 1976; Chappell, 1975; Claburn & Magura, 1978)
- Service contracting between family and worker/agency (Wiltse & Gambrill, 1974; Stein, Gambrill, & Wiltse, 1974; Stein & Gambrill, 1977)

The lists can be extended based on the practice wisdom of agency personnel. Their experience often contains implicit or explicit linkages between their behavior and successful client outcomes. In addition, as identified in the chapter on program design, every program is built on an underlying theory that states if we do this then this benefit will accrue to the client. Interviews with a variety of organizational personnel will often uncover these implicit connections.

From these three sources, the manager or guidance system designer creates a list of key service events that, if increased in frequency or quality, would increase the percentage of successful client outcomes and therefore improve attainment of the organization's purpose. The information system is designed to report the frequency of these critical events throughout the organization (Gowdy, Rapp, & Poertner, 1987; Rapp & Poertner, 1984). The collection and reporting of the data will help focus the efforts of organizational personnel and provide feedback on their performance. (Nadler, 1977; Taylor, 1987).

## Resource Acquisition

*Funds.* All human service organizations need funds, personnel, technology, clients, and public support and influence to produce client benefits. All social administrators must spend time acquiring these resources. The systematic measurement of these resources may or may not be needed depending on the nature and size of the organization. For example, a large mental health center may receive funds from Medicaid, state grants, private insurance carriers, endowment funds, corporate and private gifts, contracts with schools and industries, local tax levies, and client fees for service. The manager usually knows how much money is needed for agency services to be maintained or for needed expansion of services to occur. Based on the estimate of need, the manager would want to systematically monitor how much money is being received from what source. The danger in not doing so is that the "books" will not balance at the end of the fiscal year. In contrast, a small community-based volunteer program, which receives its modest funding from only one source like the United Way, does not need formal systems of monitoring the acquisition of funds.

*Personnel.* A large complex organization may want to systematically measure the particular qualifications and talents of its staff. These same organizations may want to systematically measure the number of women and minorities at various organizational levels to help insure their presence in higher level positions. A small agency would not need to. Some organizations benefit greatly from the use of volunteers and others. These agencies would want to measure the number of volunteers, the number of hours of service, and the length of tenure the volunteers have with the agency.

*Clients.* All agencies need to acquire clients whose characteristics are consonant with the agency's target population. It is also true that the capacity of virtually all programs is less than the number of people who could benefit from the service. In many cases, people can meet the target population criteria but still not be the "most in need." For example, a program designed to provide education to families with chronically mentally ill members would typically include content on medications, the etiology of mental illness, coping strategies, and community resources. These psycho-educational approaches have demonstrated consistently good results in terms of decreasing patient symptoms and hospital admissions, increasing knowledge gained, and satisfying family participants. What is also clear is that these increasingly prevalent programs tend to reach middle- and upper-class families. Poorer families with less resources tend not to participate and have resisted becoming involved. In such a situation, the manager would want to carefully monitor client characteristics even within the target population.

Acquiring appropriate clients often requires multiple referral sources. Depending on the program, referral sources could include the police and courts, family and friends, other agencies, self-referrals, schools and corporations, and in large agencies, staff from other programs or divisions. In many cases, the manager needs to monitor the number of clients being referred from various sources. In some cases, monitoring the number of people referred who meet the target population criteria from each source is important. No agency wants to devote time to processing inappropriate clients nor contributing to the discomfort of people who get "turned down" because they do not meet the criteria.

*Technology.* The human service manager also needs to acquire the technology that will produce the client benefit. This could include equipment (computers, cars), the intervention knowledge incorporated into the program design, supplies (paper, desks, forms), training experiences, agency libraries, and so on. Although the need for systematic measurement will vary by agency, it is nonetheless important that the manager attend to these resources. In particular, the number of hours of training in what content areas for what personnel applies to most agencies.

*Public Support.* Public support and influence is critical to all agencies. This is the most amorphous of resources, the measurement of which could include surveys of the general public or key informants, awards and other forms of recognition (e.g., complementary letters), scrapbooks of newspaper articles, number of requests to take part in professional, community, or state planning or work groups. A more powerful measure of public support and influence would be based on the behavior of the key players specified in the program design. Under this approach, the manager would systematically measure the degree to which each key player behaved as desired by the program. For example, the permanency planning supervisor may want to keep score on the frequency with which a judge has verified the "reasonable" efforts made by frontline staff to prevent placement of children. An influential agency would be the one where key players garner high levels of consistent compliance. It could be in terms of such actions as making funding decisions, setting policy, or making referrals and getting them accepted. This approach has the added benefit of being focused on the primary reason for public support—the improvement of client outcomes.

## Efficiency

Efficiency is the ratio between program inputs and outputs. Since the client-centered manager is always trying to deliver the most effective service to as many clients as possible, measures of efficiency are one means of monitoring how well the agency is doing. The most common measure of efficiency is the cost per unit of service: the cost of an hour of counseling or a day of nursing home care. The computation is merely total program funds divided by the total units of service. Funders often use such calculations to compare the performance of similar programs. Efficiency, however, is seldom considered beyond these examples.

There are several measures of efficiency that are particularly useful to the client-centered manager. One measure is the percentage of available direct-service time that is spend in direct-client (or collateral) contact. Total direct-service time (per week) is the number of direct-service workers (full-time equivalents) times thirty-six hours (forty hours minus 10 percent for vacation time, sick leave, personal days, holiday). This figure is divided into the number of hours spent in client contact. This will provide an approximation of the amount of time consumed by paperwork, meetings, travel, and so on. If clients get helped primarily through contact with staff, then the manager should want a higher level of time spent with clients.

Another potentially powerful efficiency measure is the percentage of direct-service time devoted to key events. For example, an outreach/incommunity mode of service delivery is a critical factor in producing client benefits for case management with the chronically mentally ill. The manager of such a program would want to monitor the percentage of client contact that occurs in the community.

The selection of the most *useful* efficiency measures is a difficult task, which in large part is derived from the program design and the client-centered management principles contained in this book. Table 3–1 contains a sample of efficiency measures, the client-centered principle it relates to, and qualifications on its use. For example, the principle of serving as many people in the target population as possible needs to be weighed against possible harmful effects to effectiveness and staff morale.

## Staff Morale

Staff morale as a performance area refers to the attitude or feelings of staff about their work environment and the degree to which this environment satisfies their needs. The chapter on personnel management contains a more detailed discussion of job satisfaction, its meaning and common elements. In this section, we will briefly review several of the current technologies for measuring job satisfaction.

Assessment of job satisfaction is analogous to assessing client satisfaction. It is the perspective of the staff person that is important just as the perspective of the client is required in client satisfaction. Job satisfaction is an attitude or feeling, as is client satisfaction. There are features of the workplace that contribute to job satisfaction just as there are features of the service transaction that contribute to client satisfaction.

*Informal Approach.* For the social administrator with a small staff and with frequent contact there really is no better way to assess staff morale than on a

**TABLE 3-1. EFFICIENCY MEASURES**

| Computation<br># of clients served | Indicator | Client-Centered<br>Management Principle |
|---|---|---|
| # of people in target population | % of target population | Program should serve as many of the target population as possible. (Possible tradeoffs: effectiveness, morale) |
| $\dfrac{\text{\$'s expended in direct service}}{\text{total program \$'s}}$ | % of $'s going to direct service | As many $'s as possible should be used in the trenches. Corollary—keep administrative costs low as possible |
| $\dfrac{\text{\$'s in direct service}}{\text{\$'s in administration}}$ | amount of dollars for direct service per $1 of administration | As many $'s as possible should be used in the trenches. Corollary—keep administrative costs low as possible |
| $\dfrac{\text{\# of hours of key events}}{\substack{\text{\# of direct-service time,}\\ \text{available}}}$ <br> or <br> $\dfrac{\text{\# of hours of key events}}{\substack{\text{\# of direct-service hours}\\ \text{provided}}}$ | % of available direct-service time devoted to key events <br><br> % of actual direct-service time devoted to key events | As much direct service time should be devoted to key events. (Possible tradeoff: morale) |

one-to-one basis and through small group conversations. A personal relationship that includes mutual respect and openness will elicit useful and honest responses to questions about job satisfaction. Management-by-walking-around (MBWA) has been suggested as an important way to attend to job satisfaction. (Peters & Waterman, 1982) MBWA accompanied by the type of personal relationship mentioned above is an excellent way to determine levels of job satisfaction. Noticing the interaction of people in the work unit, their apparent pleasures and frustrations derived from the work, is a genuine way to assess job satisfaction.

While this personal and informal approach to measuring job satisfaction may be ideal, there are several problems that threaten its reliability and validity. The first and most obvious hindrance to this approach is the possibility of inflated or inaccurate feedback because of the perception that the manager controls rewards and resources. Many people within organizations have difficulty openly showing success or frustration with a person who is "their boss." Second, the informal approach can easily get pushed off the manager's agenda. The demands of the agency or the program's multiple constituents requiring immediate attention frequently results in a delay of attending to staff needs. It is the rare staff member who demands attention to job satisfaction. Third, it difficult for the administrator to remember the job values and needs of several staff. Locke (1976) has identified more than a dozen job values important to most people. Individuals value these dimensions differently and may have additional values not shared by others in the workplace. For a manager to keep in mind the top six job values of seven different staff is difficult.

*More Structured Approaches.* Given these drawbacks, we suggest that every social administrator use some more formal method to structure assessment of job satisfaction while attempting to retain the personal relationship with each staff person. Four methods of structuring assessment of job satisfaction will be reviewed.

The first, and perhaps the easiest, way to keep staff morale on the agenda within a small work group is to develop one to five open-ended questions to which staff respond in writing or within a staff meeting.

At specified intervals staff can be asked to respond to questions such as:

- What are some of the ways I can help you do a better job?
- What are some of the things around here that I can help change to make this a better place to work?
- What are some things I could do to help you feel better about your work?

Those questions are only suggestions; managers need to develop questions that fit their style and that will tell them how their staff value their jobs. The preceding questions do have two features that we have found useful. First, they ask what the manager can do rather than how the staff person feels. Second, the questions reflect important, commonly held job values: the work itself, working conditions, and rewards and feedback. As is true with all measurement, there is great value in just keeping staff morale on the agency agenda. Use of the questions and acting on staff responses will communicate to staff that these are important questions to which they can respond openly and honestly.

A second method of measuring staff morale is really just a variation on the use of open-ended questions. Each staff person receives six note cards. Staff are requested to use three cards to list: "What on the job has gone well in the last month?" One incident or item is written on each card. The other three cards are used to list: "What would you like to see done differently?" The administrator can collect all of the cards in two piles and even shuffle the cards in each pile to preserve anonymity if necessary. The cards that list what has gone well are a rich source of data on the critical incidents contributing to staff morale. Managers can use these to reward themselves for their efforts and construct situations so staff can continue to have the same types of experiences. The cards that identify what staff would like to see done differently can be used to improve the working environment.

There are two formal job satisfaction scales that we have found to be useful. The first of these is the Quality of Work Life Indicator. This scale consists of twenty-eight items that include the usual dimensions of job satisfaction but also include items that reflect organizational norms or culture. This scale has been used in a variety of settings from small units to large agencies and has shown to be useful in diagnosing job satisfaction and suggesting areas for improvement. (Poertner, Gowdy, & Harbert, n.d.) This scale has been most effective when the focus of the results is on two sets of items.

The first set of items should show a clear consensus that things are going well. Answers to the items should reveal that at least 75 percent of the staff responded favorably. For example, if at least 75 percent of the staff agree that it is the norm for people to take pride in their own work and the work of the organization, then this is cause for celebrating staff pride and thanking everyone for their efforts. This set of items is used to reward staff for those elements of the workplace that are positive.

The second set of items are those for which there is no consensus at either end of the scale. These items are used to brainstorm management strategies that may reasonably result in a consensus in the positive direction. For example, if no more than 33 percent of staff can agree or disagree that it is the norm for the goals of the organization to be clear and well communicated, then work on defining organization goals is indicated.

The Job Description Index (JDI) is included as the last instrument for measuring job satisfaction. This instrument was developed through an exhaustive literature review and testing process. (Smith, Kendall, & Hulin, 1969) The JDI includes five dimensions: work, pay, promotion, co-workers, and supervision. The respondent simply responds yes or no to each item under each element. Scores are obtained for each dimension or for global job satisfaction. This scale is an efficient way of assessing job satisfaction in a large agency.

## PRINCIPLES OF PERFORMANCE REPORT DESIGN*

Once the social administrator has determined what to measure and how to measure it, the goal is to provide performance information to organizational personnel in such a way as to facilitate its use for improving program performance. How the report is presented, organized, and formatted is critical to how the information will ultimately be used. In this regard, there are six design principles that managers need to consider.

### Principle #1: Every Report Needs a Standard

Numbers reflecting performance are meaningless if there is nothing to compare them to. What does the figure forty-five clients in partial hospitalization in December 1986 mean? Is it adequate performance? Inadequate? Outstanding? From

---

*This section is based on: "The Design of Data-Based Reports," John Poertner and Charles A. Rapp, *Administration in Social Work,* Vol. 10(4), Winter 1986, Haworth Press, pp. 53–64.

January to December 1986, 523 persons were in partial hospitalization; is this worthy of commendation or castigation? If a standard is not present in the report, the reader must locate the standards on an annual goal sheet or some interdepartmental memo and incorporate the information into the report. This can be a time-consuming process and does not facilitate the use of the reports.

Frequently numbers are reported for which no standard has been established. Such situations result in the report being discarded because it is not interpretable or readers apply their own idiosyncratic standards. One person may view the number as reflective of good performance while another would see the same number as poor. In any case, a lack of standards does not help an organization attain its goal.

Establishing performance standards is usually based on historical patterns of the program, of other programs, or practice wisdom. A fourth method of standard setting avoids the use of historical information through the use of ranks.

*Past Experience of the Program.*  Most social programs are manifestations of ideas that have a history, and it is from that history that an estimate of a sensible numerical target can be derived. One should be cautious, however, in using prior program history for this purpose. Generalizing from past experience is only safe to the extent that the conditions and the people concerned are the same or at least plausibly similar. For example, prior experience could show that a program reduced commitments of the mentally impaired to state hospitals by fifteen people per month. That program experience can be safely used to project a standard for a new program only if the client population and the level of program effort (staffing, funding, etc.) is similar. Of course, if those differences can be clearly specified, then some creative arithmetic can shade expectations in the appropriate direction.

It may seem reasonable to expect that where programs are replications of past experience, better outcomes can be expected. The principle is that improved program management and outcomes should be expected in repeat performances. A 10 percent improvement over past efforts may be a reasonable expectation, absent any other basis. Here is where "guesstimates" are appropriate. Note that they are carefully constrained to an estimate of *improvement* and an "add-on" to the basic expectation derived from concrete experience.

*Past Experience: The Experience of Other Program Efforts.*  While no two social programs are exactly the same, there are many that are very similar and where that similarity is strong, the experience of another program can be used as a figure for modeling outcome and implementation targets. (Carter, 1986) Our caution above also applies here. Other programs fielded in other places and at other times can be expected to differ. Thus, it pays to take extra care in being clear about program similarities and differences.

Either direct communication or a careful reading of the research literature can yield information about the outcome and implementation experience of other programs. It is now reasonably common to find the results of program effort in a wide variety of academic and professional journals. For example, reports of program experience that would be useful in constructing numerical targets can be found regularly in such journals as *Evaluation Quarterly, Policy Studies Review,* the *Community Mental Health Journal, Social Work, Child Welfare,* and the *Social Service Review,* among others. Authors of these reports are usually quite responsive to requests for further detail if it is needed.

***Practice Wisdom.*** Where none of the foregoing sources are available, one often overlooked source is the practice wisdom of those who have experience with activities and/or clients of concern. A good case can be made for the notion that practice wisdom is seriously underused. Most program designs come from the practical, empirical experience of practitioners who first saw the basic elements of the design operate in a small set of instances. For example, a permanency planning program that intends to free children from what is called "foster care drift" surely originated in the observations of practitioners who saw such things as (1) children in need of care could occasionally be removed permanently from inadequate parents even by the most intransigent and uninterested juvenile judge, (2) even older, or very debilitated, severely multiply handicapped children could sometimes be placed in adoption, and (3) some foster children who were required to be released to what was thought to be inadequate parents turned out all right. Eventually, research was done that more firmly documented these observations, but the point is that some program designs based on these ideas were implemented even before that research was complete. The research later justified the funding for more extensive national programs along the same lines. A fieldworker's practice wisdom is a legitimate source for report standards. For example, many practitioners and administrators had, very early on, fairly clear ideas about how many children were in a condition that was later called "foster-care drift," what characteristics they had, and how much and what kind of program effort it would take to impact the problem.

***Ranks.*** Ranking organizational units can serve as a useful method for setting standards. Many people and organizations, in fact, are competitive and motivated towards being "number one" or at least above average. It is important when using ranks as standards to consider the performance area and the measurement involved in assessing that performance. For people to consider their rank as important, they need to consider the performance behaviors themselves to be important. The key is for staff members to be clear about how performance behaviors are explicitly related to the goals for service.

The use of ranks has its weaknesses, however. It is possible that the performance of every unit would be considered inadequate, yet there will always be a number one rank. Similarly, the opposite phenomenon where everyone is performing in outstanding fashion, but someone still had to be ranked last could occur. This in turn could actually reduce motivation and performance.

The selection of a standard (the actual number reflecting desired performance and the type of standard) is based on two factors: achievability (but not too easy) and importance.

Achievability involves setting a standard that *can* be attained for the vast majority (75 to 100 percent) of people or organizational units. This is not to say that everyone will attain it nor that it will be equally easy for all the parties. An exaggerated example might be to increase the number of chronically mentally ill individuals in independent living arrangements from 48 percent to 90 percent within three months. There is no way a team could do this without hurting some clients and staff in the process. On the other hand, the standard cannot be too easy to attain. More specifically, if the person or unit need not do anything more to achieve the norm, there is little satisfaction in getting it done.

Importance relates to how necessary a given level of performance is. Some outcome indicators may be judged more reflective of organizational mission than others. Perhaps the number of persons being discharged from the hospital within one week versus the number living at the highest level of independence may be seen as more central. The importance of productivity measures often leaves room for discretion. For example, the research indicates that the frequency of worker contact with clients *in vivo,* on-going service plan/goal setting, and frequency of contact with clients' significant others/collaterals are all critical to maintaining people in the community. Which is most critical is not known. The manager can make some judgments, however, of which one should receive primary attention during the year. He or she should also reinforce the priority by setting a higher standard on that dimension.

There is as yet no neat formula for setting standards. It requires the knowledge and judgment of the manager. While much time has been spent discussing the types of standards, the critical element for performance report design is that the standard is present in the report.

## Principle #2: Too Much Information Reduces the Ability to Perform

Performance reports are more likely to be used to improve performance if they are simple. That is, they contain only the numbers needed by the manager. If a manager has to sort through hundreds of numbers to locate the critical few, they are not likely to spend the time reading it. Several rules of thumb can be proposed:

1. Put one concept, theme, or dimension per page.
2. Data should be distributed only if relevant to the receiver. (If a program manager does not need to know of the performance of other programs such information should not be routinely provided. The notion is that reports should be tailored to the receiver.)
3. Too much data diffuses efforts by implying a broad range of purposes, goals, and performance indicators. A few key performance indicators can help focus the efforts of semi-autonomous staff, units, and agencies.
4. In tables, keep rows and columns to 7 plus or minus 2. A $9 \times 9$ table contains 81 pieces of information, which is a lot for any normal human mind to read, understand, and analyze.

## Principle #3: Aesthetics Are Important (Pictures Are Worth 1,000 Numbers)

Aesthetics go well beyond the "numbers of numbers" previously mentioned. A performance report should allow the reader to easily read it and evaluate whether the data reflects adequate, inadequate, or outstanding performance. Only when this condition has been met, can emphasis be placed on managerial action based on the data.

Graphs are more likely to be read and understood than data presented in tabular form. Graphic displays are more visual and conclusions are more likely to "leap off the page." Variations are extensive and care must be exercised that the graphic portrait fits the performance information. Variations include many familiar methods such as bar graphs, pie graphs, line graphs, and the use of maps. There are others less familiar like box plots, window plots, and stem and leaf graphs.

Graphs can illuminate or lie. There are three points to keep in mind when constructing graphs. First, establish the increments for an axis by incorporating the range of the data. Frequently you can simply divide the range by the space available to set the increments. Occasionally there are one or two data points that are very different from the remaining data. In these rare cases a break can be made in the graph. See Tukey (1977) for some helpful examples. Second, it is important to keep the increments along the axis uniform. If a space is to represent 100 units, every space needs to represent 100 units. Third, frequently there is a large gap between zero and the first data point. In these cases the axis can be broken. Again it is important to show this on the graph.*

## Principle #4: Labels Should Be in English

Each table or graph should have a title describing it so that a person not familiar with the agency can understand what is being reported. The same principle holds for column and row headings. Abbreviations may have to be used on occasion due to space, but a glossary should be included at the bottom of the page, on the back, or in a cover memo. This principle is particularly important for newly issued reports. When percentages or index numbers are used, a description of how the number was obtained is useful. For a percent, the question, "Percent of what?" should be answered on the table or graph.

## Principle #5: The Rule of Aggregation

The level of data aggregation included in a report should match the recipient's place in the organization. If serious about providing information to help a person do their job better, then the data must say very clearly something about the person's job. For

---

*Some good resources for graphs include *Exploratory Data Analysis* by John Tukey, Reading, MA, Addison-Wesley, 1977; "Graphical Methods in Statistics," by Stephen Fienberg, *The American Statistician,* Vol. 33, No. 4, November 1979, pp. 165–178; "How to Display Data Badly," by Howard Wainer, *The American Statistician,* Vol. 38, No. 2, May 1984, pp. 137–147.

example, statewide data on the allocation of staff time has little import for a team supervisor because it says nothing about his or her domain. Similarly, providing a regional administrator with lists of clients is inappropriate. In general, the direct-service worker domain is the client; the program and the agency administrator's domain is the entire agency or the state.

In a small organization with two or three layers it may be possible for audiences at all levels to share the same information. In large multilayered organizations attending to level of aggregation is more important. For example, frontline workers need data on their cases and data aggregating their caseloads for their supervisor. Similarly area managers of a statewide organization need data aggregated to report on the performance of their supervisors or program managers and data aggregated for the area.

## MOVEMENT TABLES: AN INNOVATIVE AND POWERFUL REPORT DESIGN

Movement tables are a relatively new innovation designed to show client status changes. Deinstitutionalization in mental health and child welfare, recidivism in corrections, and in-home care for the elderly are all focused on the movement of clients through the service system. The movement table application, as a method for monitoring and appraising client transitions, has been applied in affirmative action (Churchill & Shank, 1975), manpower (Durbin, 1968), living arrangements for the elderly (S. Fanshel, 1975), functional status of the elderly (Burton, Dellinger, & Damon, 1980), mental health (Bass & Windle, 1973; Miley, Lively, & McDonald, 1978), and child welfare (Taber & Poertner, 1981).

The traditional method used to report client status change and program performance is to compare, for example, vocational/educational situations by month:

| Vocational Status | Month 1 | Month 2 |
|---|---|---|
| No Activity | 14 | 17 |
| Moderate Activity | 10 | 14 |
| Substantial Activity | 27 | 31 |
| Competitive Activity | 12 | 12 |
| | 63 | 64 |

While the distribution and totals are similar, this data tells the manager very little how clients have moved from one status to another. For instance, is the "17" showing "No Vocational Activity" in month 2 comprised entirely of new people in the program or did clients who were employed drop to this status in month 2? If the latter is true, it means very different management action needs to occur than if the former is true.

The first step in constructing a movement table is usually to group the list of discrete statuses into a maximum of five meaningful categories. Movement tables with more than five categories are difficult to read and interpret. The list below provides an example of grouping fourteen vocational/educational statuses relevant to the chronically mentally ill into five categories or levels.

### *Status Levels for Vocational/Educational Outcomes*
- **Level A:** A client with no activity in this area
- **Level B:** Prevocational activity
    1. Prevocational classes
    2. Screening and evaluation
- **Level C:** Moderate vocational activity
    3. Working on GED or basic skills
    4. Attending college (six hours or less)
    5. Vocational school or training
    6. Active job search
- **Level D:** Substantial vocational activity
    7. Participating in work program at MHC
    8. Employed in sheltered employment outside MHC
    9. Participating in ongoing volunteer activity
- **Level E:** Competitive vocational/educational activity
    10. Any person who remains home to take care of the house and/or children while a spouse/partner is employed
    11. Attending college (seven hours or more)
    12. Any job requiring less than thirty hours/week
    13. Any job (or set of jobs) requiring more than thirty hours/ week

Once the categories have been established, a movement table can be constructed. Table 3–2 is an example of a movement table for vocational/educational statuses. The columns represent the number of clients who moved *to* a given level and the rows represent the number of clients who moved *from* a given level. For example, the second row of Table 3–2 that is labeled "Prevocational Activity" includes the numbers 6, 14, 5, 3, 2.

6     represents the number of clients who moved from prevocational activities to no vocational activity.

14     represents the number of clients who moved from prevocational activity to prevocational activity, in other words, remained at the same level.

5     represents the number of clients who moved from prevocational activity to moderate activity.

3     represents the number of clients who moved from prevocational activity to substantial activity.

2     represents the number of clients who moved from prevocational activity to competitive activity.

**TABLE 3-2. OUTCOME MEASURE #2: VOCATIONAL/EDUCATIONAL STATUS**

**Community Support Program**
**Vocational Movement Table for**

**August**
(month)

| FROM \ TO | No Activity | Prevocational Activity | Moderate Activity | Substantial Activity | Competitive Activity |
|---|---|---|---|---|---|
| No Vocational Activity | 12 | 9 | 4 | 5 | 1 |
| Prevocational Activity | 6 | 14 | 5 | 3 | 2 |
| Moderate Vocational Activity | 1 | 2 | 8 | 7 | 6 |
| Substantial Vocational Activity | 4 | 5 | 3 | 11 | 9 |
| Competitive Vocational Activity | 0 | 3 | 0 | 4 | 10 |
| Total at end of month: | 23 | 33 | 20 | 30 | 28 |

$$\text{Movement Index} = \frac{\text{Improved Vocational Status}}{\text{Declined Vocational Status}} = \frac{51}{28} = 1.8$$

Caseload: 134

Action taken:

Movement tables, if designed properly, can provide extensive information in an economical fashion. The levels of statuses are in hierarchical order in terms of desirability. For example, moving psychiatrically disabled persons from no vocational activity to moderate activity is viewed as progress. Movement tables are also a way of capturing client outcomes in a more sensitive manner and thereby allowing the program to receive credit for small but significant progress. For example, due to the severity of the illness and the state of the local economy, not all chronically mentally ill clients can or desire to hold a full-time competitive job. For others, this goal may take several years of rehabilitation. The movement tables capture increments of progress. The client who has not worked for fifteen years who is now volunteering in a meals program for the elderly has made a significant improvement for which the program should receive credit.

A second use of movement tables for measuring vocational outcomes is that an index of movement can be computed for comparison to a standard. Using the data in Table 3–2, the index is computed by ignoring the numbers on the diagonal (top left cell to bottom right cell—12, 14, 8, 11, 10) and then dividing the number of persons who moved "up" in vocational status by the number who moved "down."

$$\frac{\text{Movement}}{\text{Index}} = \frac{\text{Number of Clients with Improved Vocational Status: Above Diagonal}}{\text{Number of Clients with Declined Vocational Status: Below Diagonal}}$$

The number of persons moving toward improved vocational status can be found by adding the numbers above the diagonal. The number of persons declining in vocational status can be computed by adding the numbers below the diagonal. If the index is above 1.0, performance is in the desired direction, with more persons moving "up" than "down." In contrast, performance below 1.0 indicates a program that is not moving clients toward improved vocational status. At 1.0, program performance is unchanged. In the Table 3–2 example then:

$$\frac{\text{Movement}}{\text{Index}} = \frac{\overset{\text{Row 1}}{(9+4+5+1)} + \overset{\text{Row 2}}{(5+3+2)} + \overset{\text{Row 3}}{(7+6)} + \overset{\text{Row 4}}{9}}{\underset{\text{Row 2}}{6} + \underset{\text{Row 3}}{(1+2)} + \underset{\text{Row 4}}{(4+5+3)} + \underset{\text{Row 5}}{(0+3+0+4)}} = \frac{51}{28} = 1.8$$

This table indicates that the ratio of clients progressing to regressing is almost 2 to 1, which is certainly solid performance for that month.

A second way of summarizing a movement table into a single performance measure is to assign weights to each "cell" of the movement table. This weighting system is illustrated in Table 3–3. Each "cell" of the table is weighted to reflect positive, neutral, or negative values for client movement. The number of people in each cell is multiplied by the weight assigned to that cell and then summed. To standardize the resulting table across programs of varying caseload sizes, the sum is divided by the total number of cases. To illustrate this measure, the numbers in Table 3–2 and the weighting in Table 3–3 are multiplied to produce the following:

| | | | | |
|---|---|---|---|---|
| −12 | +9 | +8 | +15 | +4 |
| −6 | 0 | +5 | +6 | +6 |
| −2 | −2 | 0 | +7 | +12 |
| −12 | −10 | −3 | 0 | +9 |
| 0 | −9 | 0 | −4 | +10 |
| −32 | + −12 | + +10 | + +24 | + +41 = *31* |

This figure (31) is then divided by caseload size (134) resulting in the number .23, which can then be used to compare the performance of teams or programs.

The strength of this method over the movement index is three-fold. First, this method includes more client data in its computation by giving assigned values to the upper-left and lower-right cells. Second, this measure distinguishes client movement

**TABLE 3–3. WEIGHTING SYSTEM APPROACH TO VOCATIONAL MOVEMENT TABLE**

|  | No Activity | Prevocational Activity | Moderate Activity | Substantial Activity | Competitive Activity |
|---|---|---|---|---|---|
| No Vocational Activity | −1 | +1 | +2 | +3 | +4 |
| Prevocational Activity | −1 | 0 | +1 | +2 | +3 |
| Moderate Vocational Activity | −2 | −1 | 0 | +1 | +2 |
| Substantial Vocational Activity | −3 | −2 | −1 | 0 | +1 |
| Competitive Vocational Activity | −4 | −3 | −2 | −1 | +1 |

involving two or more levels from clients who move only one level. Third, this measure clearly explicates the differential value placed on certain statuses. The main drawbacks are the summary figure only has meaning when compared to similarly derived figures (in itself, this measure has no intuitive meaning, and the calculations are complex).

## Creating Report Packages

Up until this time, the discussion has focused on the design of a single data-based report. It was suggested earlier that each report should be limited to a single theme. Look at this in terms of a package, not a collection of single reports. A report package should tell a story of program performance and should be organized, perhaps like an essay. It should have a flow that helps convey the performance story and is reflective of how the manager will use the data.

The first page should list the key performance indicators (the agency report card), then each subsequent table provides more detailed information on the indicators. For example:

    page 1   Key performance indicators
    page 2   Vocational/educational movement table
    page 3   Number of clients in each of the 14 discrete vocational statuses
    page 4   Living arrangements movement table
    page 5   Number of clients in each of the discrete living statuses

Another way to organize the package would be like this:

    page 1     Key performance indicators for the agency
    page 2–5  Key performance indicators for four teams

Two other ways would be to have the client-outcome data reported followed by data on key-service events or similarly, the client-outcome data, productivity data, resource data, efficiency data.

The report package should facilitate management interpretation and action, and therefore it needs to be readable and as brief as possible. The use of color coding in particular sections is helpful in allowing a manager to find the particular topic of intererst.

## MANAGER USE OF INFORMATION

This chapter has demonstrated the importance of information to the client-centered social administrator. It has shown the manager what to measure, how to measure it, and how to format the information. In one sense, the manager's job is complete. An effective performance guidance system has been designed. In another sense the manager's job is just beginning—with completion of the information system design, the manager's use of the system begins. The client-centered manager uses the performance guidance system as a tool to create and maintain an environment or culture which is

- client-centered,
- performance-oriented,
- rewarding to staff,
- problem-sensing, and
- learning oriented.

The system helps establish a series of symbols in the organization that creates and maintains a client-centered performance environment.

### Hierarchy of Information Use

This chapter has also sought to describe myriad information and information systems that are relevant to human service organizations. For the performance manager, however, the most important subset of information concerns that which can improve organizational performance with particular emphasis on enhancing client outcomes. The power of information to influence performance can be seen in terms of levels.

In level one, the mere collection of information tends to generate human energy around the activity being measured. This effect occurs if a limited amount of information is collected. If a lot of information is reported, and in many human service agencies this is true, the effect will be minimal and activity will be suppressed, not provoked. Therefore, the performance manager must design a lean data collection system.

In level two, energy devoted to performance can be further enhanced when the information collected relates directly to performance and is systematically fed back to personnel. Performance feedback alone seems to add an increment of power that collection procedures alone does not.

At level three, the maximum power of information occurs when the manager intelligently uses the data. In particular, the performance manager uses the information to instigate rewards for staff, to locate the high achievers and help locate successful practices that may warrant dissemination, and to locate inadequate performers such that obstacles can be identified and addressed. In a sense, every number reflecting performance can and probably should be used to provoke some form of management action. If the data does not provoke action, one must carefully review the data itself (it may not be important) and/or the manager's performance.

Management use of information can be aided by constructing cues. One type of cue is to have a section on each report entitled, "Action Taken." The requirement is that the manager would record what action was planned to be taken based on the report and once taken, the action would be checked off. This has a salutary effect of making the reports into working management tools rather than pieces of paper to file away.

A second form that cues can take are "action menus." In this form, the manager would develop a list of possible actions that could be taken based on the information contained in the report. Depending on the level of performance reflected in the report, the manager would select the actions from the menu. Action menus can be joined with the first method of cuing. This second form of cuing has the added advantage of not only reminding the manager to do something but it also helps remind the manager of the range of actions available.

## SUMMARY

In the hands of the skillful manager, information is a powerful tool for increasing program performance and client outcomes. This chapter was devoted to providing the framework by which client-centered managers design, implement, and use performance guidance information systems to create a learning organization. Information is a primary tool for assisting people to understand their jobs, know how they are doing, and satisfy their job values. These are essential elements of personnel management, which is the focus of the next chapter.

## REFERENCES

Ackoff, R. (1967, December). Management misinformation systems. *Management Science, 14*(4), 147–156.

Altman, H. (1982, September). Collaborative discharge planning for the deinstitutionalized. *Social Work, 27*(5), 422–427.

Anderson, T. (1954). Probability models for analyzing time changes in attitudes. In P. F.

Lazarfeld, (Ed.), *Mathematical Thinking in the Social Sciences* (pp. 17–66). Chicago: Free Press.

Anderson, C. M., Hogarty, G. E., & Reiss, D. J. (1980). Family treatment of adult schizophrenic patients: A psycho-educational approach. *Schizophrenia Bulletin, 6*(3), 490–502.

Arizona Social Service Bureau. (1974). *Foster care evaluation program*. Phoenix: Department of Economic Security.

Barrera, M. (1986). Distinctions between social support concepts, measures and models. *American Journal of Community Psychology, 14*(4), 415–445.

Bass, R. D., & Windle, C. (1973, Spring). A preliminary attempt to measure continuity of care in a community mental health clinic. *Community Mental Health Journal, 19*(1), 53–62.

Baxter, J. (1973). *Combination validity/reliability study*. Unpublished data report from the Program Evaluation Project Report.

Beck, D. F., & Jones, M. A. (1974). A new look at clientele and services of family agencies. *Social Casework, 55*(10), 589–599.

Bennett, J. L., (Ed.) (1983). *Building decision support systems*. Reading, MA: Addison-Wesley.

Bergin, A. E., & Lambert, M. J. (1978). The evaluation of therapeutic outcomes. In S. L. Garfield & A. E. Bergin, (Eds.), *Handbook of Psychotherapy and Behavior Change: An Empirical Analysis* (pp. 139–191). New York: John Wiley.

Berkley, G. E. (1978). *The craft of public administration* (2nd ed.). Boston: Allyn & Bacon.

Bigelow, D. A., Brodsky, G., Stewart, L., & Olsen, M. (1982). The concept and measurement of quality of life as a dependent variable in evaluation of mental health services. In G. J. Stahler & W. R. Rash, (Eds.), *Innovative Approaches to Mental Health Education* (pp. 345–366). New York: Academic.

Boyd, J. L., McGill, C. W., & Falloon, J. R. (1981). Family participation in the community rehabilitation of schizophrenics. *Hospital and Community Psychiatry, 32*(9), 629–632.

Bradley Festinger, T. (1976, September/October). The impact of the New York court review of children in foster care: A follow-up report. *Child Welfare, 55*(8), 515–544.

Braskamp, L. A., Brandenburg, D. L., & Ory, J. C. (1984). *Evaluating teaching effectiveness: A practical guide*. Beverly Hills, CA: Sage.

Burton, R., Dellinger, D., & Damon, W. (1980). Making the area agencies on aging work: The role of information. *Socio Economic Planning Science, 14,* 1–11.

Calsyn, R. J., & Davidson, W. S. (1978). Do we really want a program evaluation strategy based solely on individualized goals? A critique of goal attainment scaling. *Community Mental Health Journal, 14*(4), 300–308.

Carter, R. (1984, Fall). Measuring up. *Public Welfare, 42*(4), 6–13.

Carter, R. (1986, October 28). Success measurement in child welfare services. Paper presented at the National Child Welfare Resource Center, University of Southern Maine, Portland, ME.

Carter, R. (1987, Fall/Winter). Measuring client outcomes: The experience of the states. *Administration in Social Work, 11*(3/4), 73–88.

Chappell, B. (1975, July). One agency's periodic review in foster care—The South Carolina story. *Child Welfare, 54*(7), 477–486.

Churchill, N. C., & Shank, J. (1975). Accounting for affirmative action programs: A stochastic flow approach. *Accounting Review, 50*(4), 643–656.

Claburn, W. E., & Magura, S. (1978, Winter). Administrative case review for foster children. *Social Work Research and Abstracts, 14*(1), 34–40.

Clegg, V. L., & Cashin, W. E. (1986). *Improving multiple-choice tests: Idea paper No. 16.* Manhattan, KS: Center for Faculty Evaluation and Development, Kansas State University.

Costin, L., & Rapp, C. (1984). *Child welfare: Policies and practice* (3rd ed.). New York: McGraw-Hill.

Davidson, W. S., & Wolfred, T. R. (1977, Winter). Evaluation of a community-based behavior modification program for prevention of delinquency: The failure of success. *Community Mental Health Journal, 13*(4), 296–306.

DeBlasis, J. P. (1976). *Management information systems: A current appraisal.* Philadelphia: University of Pennsylvania, The Wharton School, Department of Decision Science.

Durbin, E. P. (1968). Manpower programs as Markov chains. Memorandum RM 5741-OEO. Santa Monica, CA: The Rand Corporation.

Emlen, A. (1976). *Barriers to planning for children in foster care: A summary.* Portland, OR: Portland State University.

Fanshel, D. (1975, December). Parental visiting of children in foster care: Key to discharge. *Social Service Review, 49*(4), 493–514.

Fanshel, D. (1976, May 15). *The impact of research on social policy: Foster care of children as a case example.* Paper presented on the 40th Anniversary Celebration of the School of Social Work, University of Hawaii, Honolulu.

Fanshel, D., & Shinn, E. B. (1978). *Children in foster care.* New York: Columbia University Press.

Fanshel, S. (1975). The welfare of the elderly: A system analysis viewpoint. *Policy Science, 6,* 343–357.

Fawcett, S. B., Seekins, T., Whang, P. L., Muiu, C., & Debalcaz, Y. S. (1982). Involving consumers in decision-making. *Social Policy, 13*(2), 36–41.

Feldman, M. S., & March, J. G. (1981). Information in organizations as signal and symbol. *Administrative Science Quarterly, 26,* 171–186.

Festinger, T. (1975, April). The New York court review of children in foster care. *Child Welfare, 54*(4), 211–245.

Friel, P. B., Reznikoff, M., & Rosenberg, M. (1969, May). Attitudes toward computers among nursing personnel in a general hospital. *Connecticut Medicine, 33*(5), 307–308.

Goodman, L. (1962). Statistical methods for the mover-stayer model. *Journal of the American Statistical Association, 56*(296), 841–868.

Gowdy, E., Rapp, C. A., & Poertner, J. (1987). *Managing for performance: Using information to enhance community integration of the chronically mentally ill.* Lawrence, KS: The University of Kansas School of Social Welfare.

Gruber, A. R. (1973). *Foster home care in Massachusetts.* Boston: Governor's Commission on Adoption and Foster Care.

Gutek, B. (1978, Fall). Strategies for studying client satisfaction. *Journal of Social Issues, 2,* 44–55.

Hatfield, A. G. (1978, September). Psychological costs of schizophrenia to the family. *Social Work, 23*(5), 355–359.

Herzlinger, R. (1977, January/February). Why data systems in nonprofit organizations fail. *Harvard Business Review, 55*(1), 81–86.

Hogarty, G. E. (1979). After-care treatment of schizophrenia: Current status and future direction. In H. M. van Praag, (Ed.), *Management of Schizophrenia.* The Netherlands: Van Gorcum.

Howard, G. (1980). Response-shift bias: A problem in evaluating interventions with pre/post self reports. *Evaluation Review, 4*(1), 93–106.

Jenkins, S., & Norman, E. (1975). *Beyond placement: Mothers view foster care*. New York: Columbia University Press.

Jenkins, S., & Sauber, M. (1966). New York: *Paths to child placement: Family situations prior to foster care*. New York: Department of Welfare and the Community Council of Greater New York.

Jones, M. A. (1978, November). Stopping foster care drift: A review of legislation and special programs. *Child Welfare, LVII*(9), 571–580.

Jones, S., & Garwick, G. (1973). Guide to goals study: Goal attainment scaling as a therapy adjunct? *Program Evaluation Project Newsletter, 4,* 1–3.

Jydstrup, R. A., & Gross, M. J. (1966). Cost of information handling in hospitals. *Health Services Research, 1,* 235–271.

Kane, R. A., & Kane, R. L. (1984). *Assessing the elderly*. Lexington, MA: Lexington Books.

Kean, P. G. W., & Morton, M. S. S. (1978). *Decision support systems: An organizational perspective*. Reading, MA: Addison-Wesley.

King, W. R., & Clelland, D. J. (1981). The design of management information systems: An information analysis approach. In M. L. Gruber, (Ed.), *Management Systems in the Human Services* (pp. 276–286). Philadelphia: Temple University Press.

Kiresuk, T., & Sherman, R. (1968, Winter). Goal attainment scaling: A general method for evaluating comprehensive community mental health programs. *Community Mental Health Journal, 4,* 443–453.

Lambert, M. J. (1983). Introduction to assessment of therapeutic outcome: Historical perspective and current issues. In M. J. Lambert et al., (Eds.), *The Assessment of Psychotherapy Outcomes*. New York: John Wiley.

Lebow, J. L. (1983). Client satisfaction with mental health treatment: Methodological considerations in assessment. *Evaluation Review, 7*(6), 729–752.

Levitt, J. L., & Reid, W. J. (1981). Rapid assessment instruments for practice. *Social Work Research and Abstracts, 17*(1), 13–19.

Linn, M. W., Caffey, E. M., Klett, C. S., Hogarty, G. E., & Lamb, H. R. (1979). Day treatment and psychotropic drugs in the aftercare of schizophrenic patients. *Archives of General Psychiatry, 36*(10), 1055–1066.

Livingston, J. S. (1971, January/February). The myth of the well-educated manager. *Harvard Business Review, 49*(1), 79–89.

Locke, E. A. (1976). The Nature and causes of job satisfaction. In M. D. Dunnette, (Ed.), *Handbook of Industrial and Organizational Psychology* (pp. 1297–1349). Chicago: Rand McNally.

Maas, H., & Engler, R. (1959). *Children in need of parents*. New York: Columbia University Press.

Mackworth, N. H. (1969). Originality. In D. Wolfe, (Ed.), *The Discovery of Talent*. Cambridge, MA: Harvard University Press.

Maluccio, A. M. (1979, September). Perspectives of social workers and clients on treatment outcomes. *Social Casework, 61*(7), 394–401.

Maluccio, A. M., & Marlow, W. D. (1972, June). Residential treatment of emotionally disturbed children: A review of the literature. *Social Service Review, 46*(2), 230–251.

Martin, P. Y. (1980, Summer). Multiple constituencies, dominant social values, and the human services administration. *Administration in Social Work, 4*(2), 15–27.

Miley, A. D., Lively, B. L., & McDonald, R. D. (1978). An index of mental health system performance. *Evaluation Quarterly, 2*(1), 119–126.

Miller, A., Hatry, H., & Koss, M. (1977). *Monitoring the outcomes of social services.* Washington, DC: Urban Institute.

Mintzberg, H. (1975). *Impediments to the use of management information.* New York: National Association of Accountants.

Modrcin, M. J. (1985). *The comparative effectiveness of two models of case management services to the chronically mentally ill.* Unpublished doctoral dissertation, The University of Kansas, School of Social Welfare, Lawrence, KS.

Nadler, D. A. (1977). *Feedback and organization development. Using data based methods.* Reading, MA: Addison-Wesley.

Neuhring, E. M., & Ladner, R. A. (1980, Spring). Use of aftercare programs in community mental health clinics. *Social Work Research and Abstracts, 16*(1), 34–40.

Patti, R. (1985, Fall). In search of purpose for social administration. *Administration in Social Work, 9*(3), 1–14.

Peters, T., & Waterman, R. H., Jr. (1982). *In search of excellence: Lessons from America's best run companies.* New York: Harper & Row.

Poertner, J. (1985). A scale for measuring clients' satisfaction with parent education. *Social Work Research and Abstracts, 21*(3), 23–28.

Poertner, J., Gowdy, E. H., & Harbert, T. (n.d.). *Quality of work life: It's not just job satisfaction.* Lawrence, KS: The University of Kansas, School of Social Welfare.

Poertner, J., & Rapp, C. A. (1980, March). Information system design in foster care. *Social Work, 25*(2), 114–119.

Poertner, J., & Wintersteen, R. (n.d.). *Measurement of client satisfaction with social work services.* Unpublished manuscript, The University of Kansas, School of Social Welfare, Lawrence, KS.

Prather, J. E., & Gibson, F. K. (1977, September/October). The failure of social programs. *Public Administration Review, 37*(5), 556–564.

Rapp, C. A. (1982). *The evaluation and use of information services to area offices.* Lawrence, KS: The University of Kansas School of Social Welfare.

Rapp, C. A. (1984, Summer). Information, performance and the human service manager of the 1980s: Beyond housekeeping. *Administration in Social Work, 8*(2), 69–80.

Rapp, C. A., & Chamberlain, R. (1985, September/October). Case management services to the chronically mentally ill. *Social Work, 30*(5), 417–422.

Rapp, C. A., Gowdy, E., Sullivan, W. P., & Wintersteen, R. (1988, Summer). Client outcome reporting: The status method. *Community Mental Health Journal, 24*(2), 118–133.

Rapp, C. A., & Poertner, J. (1983). Organizational learning and problem finding. In M. Dinerman, (Ed.), *Social Work in a Turbulent World* (pp. 76–88). Silver Spring, MD: National Association of Social Workers.

Rapp, C. A., & Poertner, J. (1984). *Beyond housekeeping: Information, permanency planning performance and the child welfare manager.* Lawrence, KS: The University of Kansas School of Social Welfare.

Rappaport, J. (1977). *Community psychology: Values, research and action.* New York: Holt, Rinehart & Winston.

Reid, W. J. (1987). Service effectiveness and the social agency. *Administration in Social Work, 11*(3/4), 41–58.

Reid, W. J., & Hanrahan, P. (1982). Recent evaluations of social work: Grounds for optimism. *Social Work, 27*(4), 328–340.

Reznikoff, M., Holland, C. H., & Stroebel, C. F. (1967, July). Attitudes toward computers among employees of a psychiatric hospital. *Mental Hygiene, 51*(3), 419–425.

Richart, R. H. (1970). Evaluation of a medical data system. *Computer and Biomedical Research, 3,* 415–425.

Rosenberg, M., Reznikoff, M., Stroebel, C. S., & Ericson, P. R. (1967, July). Attitudes of nursing students toward computers. *Nursing Outlook, 15*(3), 44–46.

Rubin, A. (1984). Community based care of the mentally ill: A research review. *Health and Social Work, 9*(3), 165–177.

Rubin, A., & Gibelman, M. (1984). *Social work research in mental health: The state of the art.* Rockville, MD: National Institute of Mental Health.

Ruggiero, V. R. (1973). *The moral imperative.* Port Washington, NY: Alfred.

Seaburg, B. A. (1976, January). The contract: Uses, abuses, and limitations. *Social Work, 21*(1), 16–21.

Seidman, E., & Rappaport, J. (1974, Summer). The educational pyramid: A paradigm for training, research, and manpower utilization in community psychology. *American Journal of Community Psychology, 2*(2), 119–130.

Shapiro, D. (1976). *Agencies and foster care.* New York: Columbia University Press.

Shenoy, R. S., Shires, B. W., & White, W. S. (1980). A schiz-anon group in the treatment of chronic ambulatory schizophrenics. *Hospital and Community Psychiatry, 31*(6), 421–422.

Smith, P. C., Kendall, L. M., & Hulin, C. L. (1969). *The measurement of satisfaction in work and retirement: A strategy for the study of attitudes.* Chicago, IL: Rand McNally.

Stein, T. J., & Gambrill, E. D. (1977, September). Facilitating decision making in foster care: The Alameda Project. *Social Service Review, 51*(3), 502–513.

Stein, T. J., Gambrill, E. D., & Wiltse, K. T. (1974, Fall). Foster care: The use of contracts. *Public Welfare, 32*(4), 20–25.

Taber, M., Anderson, S., & Rapp, C. A. (1975). *Child welfare information systems.* Urbana, IL: University of Illinois.

Taber, M., & Poertner, J. (1981, August). Modeling service delivery as a system of transitions. *Evaluation Review, 5*(4), 549–566.

Taylor, M. S. (1987, Fall/Winter). The effects of feedback on the behavior of organizational personnel. *Administration in Social Work, 11*(3/4), 191–203.

Taylor, M. S., Fisher, C. D., & Ilgen, D. R. (1984). Individuals' reactions to performance feedback in organizations: Control theory perspective. In K. M. Rowland & G. R. Ferris, (Eds.), *Research in Personnel and Human Resource Management* (Vol. 2) (pp. 81–124). Greenwich, CT: JAI.

Test, M. A., & Stein, L. I. (1980). Alternative to mental hospital treatment. *Archives of General Psychiatry, 37*(10), 409–412.

Tukey, J. (1977). *Exploratory data analysis.* Reading, MA: Addison-Wesley.

Vogel, L. H. (1985, Spring). Decision support systems in the human services: Discovering limits to a promising technology. *Computers in Human Services, 1*(1), 67–80.

Wainer, H. (1984, May). How to display data badly. *The American Statistician, 38*(2), 137–147.

White, H. (1970). *Chains of opportunity.* Cambridge: Harvard University Press.

Wiehe, V. R. (1980, Fall). Current practices in performance appraisal. *Administration in Social Work, 4*(3), 1–112.

Wiltse, K. T., & Gambrill, E. D. (1974, Winter). Foster care, 1973: A reappraisal. *Public Welfare, 32*(1), 7–15.

# CHAPTER 4

# Managing Personnel

Personnel comprises about 85 percent of human service expenditures and thereby places a premium on the client-centered manager's personnel management skills. Part of a manager's job and performance is centered on the job satisfaction of employees. People satisfied with their jobs, we assume, will be more effective. This chapter devotes attention to job values, job design, and redesign (task analysis, job descriptions), staff recruitment and hiring, performance appraisal, training and staff development, and creating a reward-based environment. The features and strategies of organizational culture are discussed including organizational values, symbols, rites and rituals, stories and language. Finally, group supervision is discussed as a powerful method of establishing and using organizational culture to enhance performance.

No performance area has received more attention and still creates more problems for social administrators than personnel management. The goal(s), the setting, and behavior of staff are a few program design factors that need consideration to assure beneficial outcomes for clients. The manager collects information and carefully brings it to the attention of staff to keep the program operating as intended for clients. Critical resources needed by staff are obtained and used judiciously to benefit as many clients as possible. The direct-practice social worker is the second most important person in the social work transaction. Clients are the first.

From this perspective, staff are not mere instruments to be used by managers. The *inverted organization* places frontline staff and clients at the pinnacle of the organization. Managers are as concerned about the needs, growth, and development of their staff members as they are about clients. People come to work in programs to meet a variety of their own needs. When few of these needs are met or when they are ignored, staff can become cynical, angry, or depressed. The management literature has never been able to establish a positive relationship between staff morale and productivity, nor has the relationship between meeting the needs of social workers and their meeting clients' needs been explored. It is difficult to imagine that there would be any instance where a depressed and cynical worker would be as effective in producing positive client outcomes as an energized social worker whose work needs are satisfied. The overly burdened spouse caring for a victim of Alzheimer's disease, the mother crying and remorseful because she went too far and hurt her child when she could no longer tolerate the child's crying, and the battered wife fearful of returning home yet fearful of making it on her own all require helpers who are equipped to respond to these emotionally laden situations in positive ways.

Clients are at the pinnacle of the social work organization. They should benefit from working with social workers whose jobs are within the context of a socially sanctioned organization. Workers come to their profession, their jobs, and their organizations with a variety of work values that they are attempting to satisfy. Social workers' jobs should be, therefore, carefully designed to assure that clients obtain the intended benefit, that the work itself satisfies the worker, and that organizations continue to provide opportunities for both clients and workers. Social administrators have a variety of mechanisms available to them that will blend client, worker, and organizational needs in ways that increase the likelihood that everyone involved will receive the maximum benefit.

The basic principles that guide the social administrator were presented in Chapter 1 and permeate this and every other part of the model. The design of a program is a carefully conducted analytic process that determines a host of program features including expectations of workers. The design and operation of an information system is essential. This system enables agencies and workers to learn from their efforts, receive rewards, and satisfy many job values. It is the job of social administrators to mesh workers' and organizational needs. Consequently, this chapter begins with a discussion of job values and the idea that a job is a set of tasks. Workers' job values make their needs explicit. Identification of the tasks required to produce performance make the organizations' needs explicit.

In this chapter, we offer seven strategies for meshing organizational and worker needs:

- job descriptions
- staff recruitment and hiring
- job redesign
- performance appraisal
- training
- staff development
- the reward-based environment

Administrators need to be aware that these strategies take place within an organizational culture. They also need to consciously shape and change the culture in positive ways. Therefore, this chapter explicitly considers the concept and components of organizational culture and the ways managers can shape it. At the end of the chapter is a group supervisors model that demonstrates how many of the personnel management concepts can be blended together.

One caveat is in order. Personnel management is not only a difficult set of management tasks, it is also the subject of frequent litigation. No attempt is made here to provide the legal advice for staying out of court. It is our belief that the social administrator using the approach of this text will seldom be the target of suits and appeals. However, it does happen. Even the best manager is human and makes mistakes. We suggest that the social administrator in a small agency that does not have a specialized personnel department consult with an attorney who specializes in personnel matters. In the large agencies with personnel departments, social administrators should avail themselves of this expertise, attend personnel department workshops, and follow established procedures. It is important to keep in mind the difference between procedures that "keep you out of court" and those that get the work of the program done with satisfied staff. The social administrator must attend to both sets of procedures even when they may appear to conflict.

## WORKERS' JOB VALUES

In *Work in America* (Special Task Force to the Secretary of Health, Education and Welfare, 1973), the definition of work is "an activity that produces something of value for other people." (p. 3) This clearly places the emphasis on what the client or organization is getting from staff. One page later, however, the task force comments: "Far less attention has been paid to the personal meaning of work, yet it is clear from recent research that work plays a crucial and perhaps unparalleled psychological role in the formation of self-esteem, identity, and a sense of order." (p. 4) This certainly reflects the status of work in the social agency. Many social workers are confronted with organizational units that emphasize producing something of value for someone else with little or no attention to the individual social workers' needs. This may be attributed to external pressures on the organization, lack of clarity about what workers need, or lack of useful definitions of job satisfaction and approaches for its measurement and enhancement.

### Unique and Shared Job Values

Locke (1976) defines job satisfaction as the "results from the attainment of values which are compatible with one's needs." (p. 1307) This definition has two crucial implications. First, job satisfaction is not the answer to the question, "How satisfied are you with your job?" Job satisfaction results from attainment of key work values. Too often people will respond to the "How satisfied" question with "Very satisfied," while listing their unattained job values such as frustrating tasks, coworkers, pay, and so on. Gutek (1978) demonstrates that in this society we tend to inflate our response to how satisfied we are about our jobs, the services we receive, or the communities in which we live. In addition, it is just not helpful to know that a person is somewhat satisfied with his or her job. What the social administrator needs are the specific job values that are being attained and those which are not.

The second implication of Locke's definition is that job satisfaction, or a worker's set of job values, is unique to the worker. Social workers can easily embrace the idea of individual uniqueness. But how does one manage a large staff when job satisfaction is unique to each individual? It may be helpful to think about the job values of three workers, Joe, Mary, and John. Figure 4–1 shows how job values, while unique, also overlap, are shared collectively.

Joe, Mary, and John share many job values. Besides their individual values, they each share values with one other person, and in some cases all three share the same value. The social administrator who attends to the job values of these three staff attends both to the common and to the unique aspects of job satisfaction.

The relative importance of job values also varies between individuals. While Joe, Mary, and John may all include autonomy as a job value this may be John's most important value, preferring to complete tasks his own way within his own time frame. Autonomy may be much less important to Joe, who wants to do a task himself but wants a deadline imposed by someone else.

How aware a worker is of his or her job values adds yet another layer of complexity. The staff person who is asked, "What are your job values?" is likely to offer an incoherent response. The person may not be fully aware of his or her job values. Similarly, a person's job values evolve and change over time. Social administrators must be sensitive to staff job values, assisting staff in defining their job values, and recognizing that some values or the relative importance of job values may change over time.

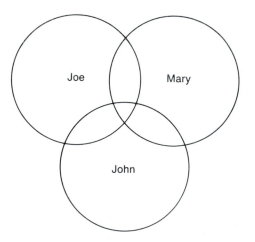

**Figure 4–1.** Joe, Mary, John's Job Satisfaction

## Identifying Job Values

Locke (1976) lists the most common and important job values that are well documented in the job satisfaction literature. These values cluster around the work itself, rewards, working conditions, agents in the workplace, and self-esteem. People tend to want work that

- is mentally challenging,
- they can successfully accomplish,
- is of personal interest, and
- is not too physically tiring.

People tend to want rewards that are

- just,
- informative, and
- consonant with aspirations.

People tend to want working conditions that

- are compatible with individual physical needs and
- facilitate task completion.

People tend to want agents in the workplace who

- help attain job values such as interesting work, pay, promotion;
- have values similar to their own; and
- minimize role conflict and ambiguity.

People tend to want high self-esteem.

Self-esteem as a job value deserves added explanation. It is easy to take this dimension, consider it a personality trait, and begin screening people on self-esteem as part of the job selection process. Even if this were possible there is another way to view self-esteem. Self-esteem can be viewed as the result of a person's feelings of competence and acceptance. Consequently the social administrator, by demonstrating to staff that they are valued people and pointing out their strengths, will shape and enhance self-esteem.

This set of job values was used as a starting point with a group of administrators from a range of agencies receiving United Way funds in a middle-sized community. This group uniformly reported that their staff were highly satisfied and that they attended to job satisfaction informally but regularly. These administrators were asked to take this list of job values, select one staff person and discuss these values with that person. The results were startling. All of the staff were delighted that someone was paying attention to what they wanted from their jobs. Some staff reported that this was the first time anyone in the agency paid attention to these job values. Some staff who were not selected for the exercise asked when they would have their turn. Some staff identified values not included in Locke's list. The lessons were clear. Staff preferred systematic over informal attention to job satisfaction. Locke's list was not inclusive but provided a useful starting point. The importance of individual job values varied widely between people, jobs, and agencies.

The individual interview was an effective but costly way for these administrators to determine job satisfaction. The information management chapter provides several other methods for measuring the job satisfaction of staff. These methods are useful for uncovering the job values common to staff in an agency or unit. Attending to their collective job values will enhance staff morale. At the same time the social administrator needs to attend to each individual's job values.

Once job values are known, enhancement of individual and collective attainment of these values is relatively straightforward. Table 4–1 provides a brief overview of major job values and related strategies that can improve job satisfaction. Task analysis, job redesign, program design, and elements of the organizational culture such as communicating, defining roles, and enhancing self-esteem are all covered elsewhere in this text.

## THE JOB AS A SET OF TASKS

Locke (1976) defines a job as "a complex interrelationship of tasks, roles, responsibilities, interactions, incentives, and rewards." (p. 1301) This statement is one reason personnel management is so difficult. Given the complexity, how does a social administrator keep from getting mired in the relationships between the various elements? The answer, in part, is to consciously oversimplify the situation by focusing on the constituent elements. The first element we will examine is the job as a set of tasks.

### Benefits of Task Analysis

The danger of viewing a job as a set of tasks is forgetting Locke's admonition that it is not that simple. If a social administrator forgets that rewards and work environment elements like job values are as important as the tasks, there is little benefit to focusing on tasks. With this in mind, there are many advantages to developing a clear list of tasks for each job in the social program. Austin (1981) identifies eight advantages:

- clarifies job expectations
- facilitates performance review
- provides continuity during staff turnover
- serves as an information base for completing agency accountability reports
- is a tool for monitoring the relationship between the work and goals and objectives of the agency

**TABLE 4-1. STRATEGIES TO ENHANCE ATTAINMENT OF JOB VALUES**

| Common Job Values | Enhancement Strategies |
|---|---|
| Work that<br>• is mentally challenging,<br>• they can successfully accomplish,<br>• is of personal interest, and<br>• is not too physically tiring. | • task analysis<br>• job redesign |
| Rewards that are<br>• just,<br>• informative, and<br>• in line with aspirations. | • the reward-based environment |
| Working conditions that<br>• are compatible with individual physical needs and<br>• facilitate task completion. | • attention to the physical environment of the agency |
| Role clarity | • program design<br>• persistent and consistent communication of role definitions |
| Self-esteem | • communication to each person of their inherent value<br>• rewards for successful task accomplishment |

- helps identify training needs
- helps assure equity for all workers in a unit
- when used in the developmental stage it can save time in clarifying job expectations

Clarification of job expectations may be one of the most important results of specifying tasks. It is clarity of expectations that is a major mechanism for blending organizational and worker goals. It is the task that is the basic unit for accomplishing agency goals. When each person in the social program accomplishes his or her task, the program objectives and goals are met. When social administrators know the tasks required to accomplish program goals, they will be clear on what is needed to produce success. Similarly most workers place role clarity as a high job value. (Locke, 1976) A recent survey of three hundred social workers in hospitals and mental health agencies found "for people to know exactly what their job requires" to be an important component of job satisfaction and a quality work environment. (Poertner, Gowdy, & Harbert, n.d.) When a worker can identify the tasks required, role clarity is assured. The task then serves as a unifying element, helping the agency and the worker to accomplish their respective goals.

The performance model posits that the manager's job is to produce positive outcomes for clients, acquire resources, produce products, enhance staff morale, and do this as efficiently as possible. The task is the basic element that results in performance. When the frontline worker develops a goal with a client, one critical element towards a positive outcome for the client is accomplished. When an administrator compares client goals against the goal criteria and praises the worker for good clear goals, both staff morale and client outcomes are enhanced.

The task is the basic unit through which workers attain their job values. The task that is so difficult that it can never be satisfactorily accomplished results in anger and frustration. The task that becomes so routine that there is nothing left to learn results in boredom. Social administrators who can recognize the importance of these job values and the tasks to be accomplished can match people with tasks and enhance staff morale.

## Writing Task Statements

The writing of task statements is hard to do, time-consuming, frustrating, and often results in a product that is never used. The writing of task statements can also be a clarifying and unifying process that results in a tool that promotes organizational and personal goals. To avoid the former and accomplish the latter, social administrators need to be guided by three principles:

1. Tasks are written in "English" (clear, jargon-free, understandable language).
2. Identifying tasks is a collective process.
3. Tasks produce performance.

Writing tasks clearly is easy to say and hard to do. "Coordinating the activities of the treatment team" appears to be in English but can probably only be understood by the person who wrote the statement. A couple of principles from general semantics are useful in writing task statements. Semantists talk about verifiable referents that represent the meaning of a term. "Chair" is a useful word for communication because it is a thing that we can point to and agree to call a chair. "Walking" is a useful word because there is an activity that we have all learned and agreed to call walking. A word like "coordinating," however, is another matter. Our experience is that there is no verifiable referent for coordinating. A task description that uses ambiguous or vague words that have different meanings to different people does not clarify expectations nor accomplish any of the other potential benefits of task statements. Task statements must be written using a vocabulary for which there are consensually agreed-upon referents.

Writing task statements is not just a matter of identifying fuzzy or abstract terms and replacing them with behaviors or objects. A vocabulary with no abstractions or generalizations becomes verbose and tedious. Abstraction and generalization also assist communication by making it more efficient. Imagine writing a detailed definition of "chair" that encompasses all of the concrete items as we would all agree are chairs. Similarly, imagine writing a task statement for every behavior that a work unit might agree constitutes coordination. Job descriptions that attempt this level of specificity produce frustration, are filed, and forgotten. One answer to this apparent dilemma is to write or edit task statements as a group exercise. Fine and Wiley (1971) in their original work on writing task statements emphasize the importance of group editing of the task statements. To produce task statements that communicate and reliably reflect activities of a job across worker categories, all of the members of the work unit must edit the statements and agree upon the verifiable referents for the vocabulary.

Another solution to the dilemma of vocabulary and level of abstraction is to remember that tasks produce performance. There must be a direct link between the action of the task statement and

- producing a client outcome,
- acquiring a resource,
- maintaining staff morale, and
- producing service events.
- enhancing efficiency

The litmus test for inclusion of a task statement in a job description is performance. This not only helps identify the most useful level of abstraction but also helps sort out useful from unproductive tasks. Viewing the task analysis job description as a detailed list of all of the behavior exhibited by the worker while on the job results in the same type of lengthy, trivial, and useless job description as obsessing about all the behaviors that constitute what people agree to call coordinating. The performance oriented job description includes only those tasks that contribute to client outcome, resource acquisition, productivity, efficiency, or staff morale.

Fine and Wiley (1971) developed several aids that can be useful for writing task statements. The worksheet in Figure 4–2 is one of these aids. The questions at the top of each column determine if a statement contains all the information required.

The following example of a task statement about staff morale contains the necessary information and communicates clearly to the workers: "Case managers verbally praise fellow case managers for accomplishing goals with clients to enhance staff morale."

This statement answers Fine and Wiley's (1971) six questions:

1. Who: Case manager (subject)
2. Performs what action? Gives praise (action verb)
3. To Whom? Fellow case managers (direct object)
4. Upon what cue? When another worker accomplishes a goal with a client
5. Using what tools, work aids, or skills? Verbal praise (language is the tool)
6. To produce what performance goal? Enhance staff morale

## ADMINISTRATIVE STRATEGIES TO BLEND AGENDAS

The social administrator now knows his or her staff's job values and what the tasks are that benefit clients. Personnel management must now blend these two agendas in ways that maximize client, worker, and organizational benefits. The following

| Who? | Performs what action? | To whom or what? | Upon what cues? | Using what tools, work aids, skills? | To produce what performance? |
|---|---|---|---|---|---|
| Subject | Verb | Object of verb | | | |

**Figure 4–2.** Model Sentence Worksheet for Task Statements

mechanisms for blending agendas are included in nearly any discussion of personnel management. But these mechanisms are used differently in the client-centered organization. Personnel management by its very name suggests control. The focus here is mutual satisfaction, not control.

## JOB DESCRIPTIONS

When a work unit has produced job descriptions that comprise performance oriented task statements, expectations are clarified and both workers and administrators have valuable tools for accomplishing individual and organizational goals. There are at least four other uses for these job descriptions that deserve attention:

- job design/redesign
- staff selection and hiring
- performance appraisal
- training

Before going on to these uses, it is useful to stop and briefly discuss the idea of the job as a set of tasks and the usual job descriptions that exist in an agency. Ideally a formal job description should be a collection of performance oriented tasks. This, however, is not always possible to accomplish, particularly in large agencies with established personnel systems that may require something different in a job description. In addition, resources may not exist for a manager to take time out to have the work unit develop the task statements. What should the administrator do who takes a job as a protective service supervisor and finds relatively meaningless job descriptions and overworked staff? Here are some suggestions:

- Use the task and job framework as one of the ways to think about what the workers and unit need to accomplish.
- Use every opportunity to help others in the unit think about his or her job as a set of performance related tasks.
- Use every opportunity to formalize this way of thinking.
- Write out task statements as time allows.

For example, meetings with frontline staff could be used to reinforce the tasks required by staff to protect children, acquire resources, and maintain staff morale. Meetings with supervisors and others in the agency could focus how job descriptions could reflect current practice or how to obtain the resources to formalize training and task specifications. A file could be started of task statements drafted as time allows.

## STAFF RECRUITMENT AND HIRING

Peter Drucker (1967), when studying effective executives, observed that "there have been people who make decisions fast, and people who make them rather slowly. But without exception, they make personnel decisions slowly. . . ." (p. 33) Decisions about staff selection as one subset of personnel decisions need to be made carefully. It is the person you select for the job who will perform well or be an obstacle. It is the person you select for the job whose job values you need to blend with the organization's. It is the person you select for the job who likely will be with you for a very long time. In staff selection, like spouse selection, major immediate changes are unlikely and divorce is painful and costly.

For the purposes of this chapter, staff selection encompasses five major points. When selecting staff, a social administrator must

- know what is needed,
- know and communicate the organizational context,
- locate as many people as possible who meet the need,
- collect evidence that the person can do the job, and
- remove barriers to saying yes.

### Know What You Need

This is the first, and perhaps the most straightforward, part of the selection process. The task analysis-based job description is the most important part of knowing what you need. Even if a personnel management system requires a somewhat fuzzy job description, the list of performance-producing tasks is the clearest way to know and communicate job expectations. Knowing what you need in terms of worker characteristics is also important. Social work values and principles of affirmative action suggest the need to think about how your staff reflects client and community characteristics. A staff that reflects the diversity of many American communities in terms of race, sex, age, and disabilities not only manifests the agency's adherence to the values of the profession but can provide tangible benefits to service delivery. For example, sex, race, and age seem to affect service utilization. (Weiss, Greenlick, & Jones, 1970) Accessibility can be enhanced if the agency and its personnel are of the same culture or have the same characteristics as a client group. (Gillespie & Marten, 1978)

## Know the Organizational Context

Three aspects of knowing the organizational context are of special interest here. The first is the formal set of personnel policies and procedures that exist for the organization. No attempt will be made to discuss the variety of possible policies and procedures. There are federal laws (Title VII of the Civil Rights Act of 1964), federal executive orders (No. 11246), and case laws that are relevant to staff selection decisions. State laws vary as to how they affect personnel policies and procedures. In addition, since personnel decisions are frequent targets of litigation, court decisions quickly alter policies and procedures. The social administrator must know the existing personnel policies and procedures for the agency. Depending on the size and sophistication of the personnel function within the agency, the social administrator may also need to find ways to stay updated on federal laws, rules and regulations; state laws, rules and regulations; and current case law. In a large agency it is likely that a specialized personnel officer will stay abreast of the latest information and keep everyone informed. In the smaller agency, the administrator may need to consult with a reliable personnel consultant or an attorney.

The second aspect of knowing the organizational context is to be aware of and take responsibility for knowing and communicating organizational values, norms, and goals to people you are considering hiring. By and large, people want to work in organizations whose basic values are similar to their own. People will frequently eliminate themselves from the job pool if they see that the work unit's values are very different from theirs. Too often, we have seen staff selected whose values are very different from the organization's or department's. The result has frequently been isolation and staff turnover.

Organizational values, norms, and goals can be communicated in at least three ways: written material, symbols, and people. The social administrator needs to make certain that what is communicated reflects what is desired. In this era of increased attention to public relations and marketing, materials with a strong, polished public image are being promoted. These materials can also accurately reflect the organizational context or culture. In *Theory Z*, Ouchi (1982) places great emphasis on corporate philosophies. He even includes examples from corporations such as Hewlett-Packard, Dayton-Hudson, and Eli Lilly. The idea is to capture the client-centered philosophy of the organization and communicate organizational values, norms, and goals. This is needed for people within the organization and for those who may become a part of it.

Organizational norms are also communicated through signs and symbols that exist in the environment. Bulletin boards, display cases, posters are just a few of the messages that communicate organizational norms. Waiting rooms, individual office decor, and coffee or break rooms all say something about the organization. Social administrators need to consciously manipulate these symbols both to shape organizational culture and to communicate to those who are potential members of the culture.

Thirdly, people communicate organizational norms. Structuring opportunities for staff to interact with potential employees outside the formal job interview can be a potent way of communicating organizational norms. The candidates can then determine if there are people in the environment who share their basic views and will help them attain job satisfaction.

## Locate as Many People as Possible Who Meet the Need

Even in a time when a job announcement may generate many times more applicants than you want to screen, there are real advantages to reaching out to obtain the best collection of applicants. Left to chance there may be one or two stars in a group of fifty applicants, or there may be none. Even if there are one or two, they can easily get lost. Doing whatever is required to assure there are several high performing candidates in the pool increases the chances of selecting the person who will make a real contribution. While the "old boy network" and corporate "head hunters" have perpetuated dominance by white males, they have also assured many organizations of having high performing staff. The challenge for the social administrator is to use many networks to assure a diverse and highly qualified pool of applicants. This is where affirmative action principles can be helpful. You want diversity in your pool of applicants so this is reflected in your staff. Consultation with affirmative action specialists is essential. This person could be from a specialized office within your agency or an outside personnel expert.

## Collect Evidence That the Person Can Do the Job

The person you want to hire has demonstrated a consistently high level of performance of the required tasks, enthusiastically wishes to continue these efforts, and has basic job values consistent with the work unit. The mental health center director wants a case management supervisor who has a proven record as a successful supervisor with proven performance in producing client outcomes, a productive work unit, and a satisfied staff. Of course the person who fits that description is not likely to want your job. They probably want a different, more challenging job. In which case, the social administrator is left in the position of selecting a person who has demonstrated performance in the greatest number of tasks and has clear ideas as to how to go about acquiring the skills to perform the new challenges.

Given this reality, the screening phase is a major element in the hiring process. In this phase, the administrator collects evidence of the required task the candidate has performed, of the quality of task accomplishment, and of the job values the candidate holds and whether they are consonant with the organization. This evidence can usually be found in products, references, and the employment interview. Some tasks naturally produce products that can be requested and judged. For example, a case plan (which has been altered to protect confidentiality) can demonstrate a case manager's case planning skills. Similarly a management report or a supervisor's feedback about a client-outcome can be evidence of task performance and the quality with which it was performed.

The checking of references may be as misused as the employment interview as a method of collecting evidence of task performance. Many people now rely on telephone interviews rather than letters of references to obtain more valid and reliable information, but the mistakes made in the employment interview are also likely to be made in the interview of references. Lopez (1975) lists common errors in the employment interview that we have also observed in interviewing references:

- Content is covered haphazardly.
- Questions vary between interviews.
- A decision is made before complete information is obtained.
- The interviewer looks solely for evidence that will support a prior decision such as eliminating the person as a candidate.

The social administrator who was once a direct practitioner will recognize this list as similar to many errors made in the client interview. Direct practitioners know that changing the wording of a question easily changes the response, or that a quick decision frequently leads to looking for evidence that the decision is correct while ignoring evidence to the contrary. The lesson is to carefully approach the interview and collect evidence of what and how tasks were performed.

The same cautions apply to the interview of the candidate. The employment interview has been so misused that a body of case law and regulations has yielded lists of unacceptable interview questions. (Pecora & Austin, 1987). These lists change frequently based on legal decisions and new legislation. Social administrators need to consult with their personnel department or attorney on the current status of case law, statutes, and policies related to the agency and job openings. As a general rule, if you use the interview to find evidence of completion of tasks required of the job you will be within legal limits. Table 4–2 is a summary of Lopez's recommendations for the employment interview process, along with the goals of each section.

Good communication skills are necessary for a productive interview. The ability to listen, ask various kinds of questions, direct the flow of information from general to specific, and use reflection, restatement, summarization, and silence are

**TABLE 4–2. THE EMPLOYMENT INTERVIEW**

| Process | Goals |
|---|---|
| *Warm-up: 15% of time* | |
| Discuss a nonthreatening piece of information provided by interviewee. | Help interviewee relax, open up, build trust. |
| *Main interview sequence: 70% of time* | |
| Restate mutual understandings. | Clarify expectations of job, |
| Interviewer presents job. | agency, unit. |
| Interviewee presents self. | Obtain evidence that interviewee |
| Review work history. | has done tasks. |
| | Obtain evidence of quality of task completion. |
| *Closing stage: 15% of time* | |
| Restate mutual understandings. | Clarify mutual understandings, |
| Summarize interview. | expectations of selection |
| Next steps. | process. |

generic communication skills required of direct practitioners and administrators alike. These same skills are required in the reference interview or the employment interview.

## Removing Barriers to Saying Yes

The social administrator who obsesses about using a variety of strategies to clearly communicate organizational values and job expectations will expend valuable time and energy getting highly qualified people to apply for the job and will carefully collect evidence of performance of required tasks only to have the person say no. There is no simple list of why people say no. It ranges from "My children don't want to move" to pay being too low. In any given agency, organizational, or community context, the degree of control over the barriers to the person saying yes varies greatly. While in reality there are some things over which the social administrator has little or no control, the most productive approach is for the administrator to be sensitive to potential barriers throughout the process and to view all barriers as removable. For example, if the person volunteers that they have a spouse that will need a certain type of job then job hunting may be necessary. If the person says they are concerned about the quality of available day care, then assisting the person in finding quality care is part of the hiring process.

## JOB DESIGN/REDESIGN

Workers' job needs may and frequently do change. So do the needs of the organization. Therefore, job redesign becomes an important management tool for blending the ongoing and changing needs of workers and agencies. This requires viewing any set of job tasks as fluid and changing. *Work Redesign* (Hackman & Oldham, 1980) is an indepth examination of the topic. Stripped to the basics, the job redesign literature includes four concepts:

1. Organizations accomplish goals through people, jobs, and tasks.
2. People attain a variety of job values through their job and its task.
3. Job redesign includes swapping tasks so that both 1 and 2 are accomplished.
4. Swapping of tasks has implications for all other parts of the organization.

For the social administrator who already has the first two points well in mind the challenge is to balance the last two. As Hackman and Oldham (1980) note, job redesign can take many forms from simple job enrichment (adding new and interesting tasks to a person's job) to quality circles and other types of total reorganization of the work within an organization. More often than not the social administrator is involved in smaller efforts where there is a set of tasks to be accomplished to produce performance and a group of people with varying interests and abilities to do the tasks. The administrator's job is to put the tasks together in ways that will most effectively produce performance while recognizing the interests and skills of people and using the tasks to help people satisfy their job values. For example, the protective service worker who has done her set of job tasks well for a long period of time might be feeling the need for new and challenging tasks. Discussion of all the possible activities, for which there is never enough staff, will likely yield a set of tasks for which the worker would like to assume responsibility. It could be community education, influencing key players such as judges or attorneys, or training new staff.

The following example illustrates the fourth element of job redesign. A large number of child abuse reports are not being investigated. The worker who is supposed to investigate reports of child abuse has his hands full with cases that have been reported and verified. Although there is no easy solution, the administrator must find the resources to be able to investigate the reports the agency receives. A brainstorming session with the staff at this point is crucial. Such a session might yield the following: A foster care worker might be able to give up some foster care cases and conduct some child abuse investigations. Or perhaps volunteers could take on some of the staff worker's routine paperwork, which would free up his time for investigation. Of course, if the amount of work outstrips available staff the first responsibility of the manager is to advocate for additional staff.

## PERFORMANCE APPRAISAL

Another major strategy for helping workers meet their needs is performance appraisal. Performance appraisal is normally thought of as a mechanism to review a person's work and make judgments about their performance from the organization's point of view. But this approach to performance appraisal has resulted in frustration, low staff morale, and the never-ending search for the right way. When the emphasis is turned toward meeting individual needs and blending these with organizational needs, the real intent of performance appraisal is attained.

Lawler, Mohrman, and Resnick's (1986) study supports the contention that emphasis on the worker brings benefits to the organization. In this study of performance appraisal within General Electric they found the following:

- Eighty-two percent of appraisers said that things really important to them were discussed in the appraisal event.
- Forty-six percent of subordinates felt that things important to them were discussed.
- Subordinates (much more than appraisers) saw the most important decisions as being made previously by the appraiser.
- Appraisers saw the communication between appraiser and subordinates as balanced. Subordinates saw communication as coming mostly from the appraiser.

Not surprisingly, appraisers were generally more satisfied with the event than subordinates. Given the vastly different perspectives, it is difficult to see the performance appraisal as meeting either worker or organizational needs. While these findings are from General Electric, not a social agency, informal conversations with social workers, who work for a variety of agencies and who have experienced a variety of performance appraisal systems, suggest a similar study conducted in social work would produce similar results. Rarely do social workers affirm that they participated in a performance appraisal that helped them meet their needs.

## Why Have a Performance Appraisal System?

Faced with their first annual performance appraisal, either as reviewer or reviewee, many people wonder what they are doing and why. From an organizational perspective, the answers range from this determines your pay to evaluation is a good unto itself—there need not be another purpose. The explanation and the event are frustrating and punishing.

*Purposes of Performance Appraisal.* The literature identifies two sets of purposes for a performance appraisal system. One set identifies the organizational agenda:

- allocates merit pay
- provides documentation (e.g., discharge)
- determines promotion, transfer
- identifies training needs
- validates criteria in personnel research
- helps counseling and development (Carroll & Schneier, 1982, pp. 232–233)

The second set of purposes is to meet a worker's needs:

- identifies the person's goals:
- provides job-related feedback
- communicates performance expectations clearly

When the social administrator examines this variety of purposes and the formal performance appraisal systems that exist in his or her agency, there is frequently a mismatch between the formal systems and the purpose. If an administrator wants to foster individual learning, then the usual performance appraisal system that is identical for all staff, that evaluates past performance, and that happens once or twice a year is doomed. It simply violates too many principles of the use of information to enhance performance, principles of adult learning, and many people's job values. Given the disparity between formal performance appraisal systems, their purposes, and the conditions under which people learn, how is the social administrator to blend organizational and personal goals? The answer is best illustrated by that rare person who responded affirmatively to the question, "Has anyone experienced a helpful and positive performance appraisal as an appraisee?" When asked about the key to this success she responded "There were never any surprises—I knew every day how I was doing. I received regular, consistent, and helpful feedback on how I was doing." This is the key to using performance appraisal.

***Characteristics of Effective Performance Appraisal.*** The performance appraisal system that enhances personal and organizational learning is the one that is designed in full recognition of

- the person's job values,
- principles of using information to enhance performance, and
- principles of adult learning.

Integrating these three characteristics into one performance appraisal system may seem like a superhuman effort. But the performance oriented manager already has the skills to identify and attend to a person's job values as well as the ability to use information to enhance performance. Using principles of adult learning to help staff acquire new knowledge and skills is covered later in this chapter. For now the key questions that will combine these characteristics into an effective performance appraisal system are

- How well is the person completing his or her job tasks?
- How well does the information system give the person adequate feedback on task accomplishment?
- How well does the current reward-based environment meet the person's needs for encouragement and contribute to a feeling of competence?

- What tasks would the person like to learn to do differently?
- How would the person like to go about meeting these learning goals?
- How will we know when the person has met the learning goals?

## Types of Performance Appraisal Systems

In the ideal organization the culture, information systems, reward-based environment, and staff development functions adequately answer all of these questions. In this case a performance enhancing appraisal system is operating. Occasionally in an effort to answer the first question or to satisfy a different type of organizational need, such as allocating merit pay or documentation for discharge, a specific type of performance appraisal format is desired or required. Carroll and Schneier (1982) conducted a survey of personnel specialists and then rated eight different performance appraisal systems as they related to various purposes. The results are in Table 4–3. It is readily apparent that several of the performance appraisal formats do not work well for any purpose. The formats that appear to perform well are management by objectives, behaviorally anchored rating scales, critical incidents, and performance standards.

## EFFECTIVENESS OF VARIOUS APPRAISAL METHODS

A body of literature exists on each of these technologies so only a brief description and appropriate references will be given here.

## Management by Objectives (MBO)

A manager establishes goals with a person for a specified period of time and gives the person adequate feedback and rewards on goal attainment. Critical features of MBO systems include:

- The goals are consistent with the person's performance-based task analysis.
- The goals are outcome oriented, positive, realistic, and measurable.
- The goals are established with the person.
- A plan is necessary for how a goal is to be attained.
- A periodic review of the progress toward the goal is required.
- Feedback and rewards are necessary for goal attainment.

Defined in this way, MBO can be remarkably consistent with the ideal conditions for a performance enhancing appraisal system. Frequently, MBO systems exist in organizations that have been formalized in such a way as to destroy their effectiveness. In such a situation, the social administrator needs to bend the formal

**TABLE 4-3. EFFECTIVENESS OF VARIOUS APPRAISAL METHODS FOR DIFFERENT PURPOSES, REQUIREMENTS AND ORGANIZATIONAL SETTINGS, AS DETERMINED BY A GROUP OF EXPERTS***

Please rate the effectiveness of the following performance appraisal methods against the evaluation criteria as described in the following:

| PAR System Criteria | Traits | MBO | BARS | Checklists | Critical Incidents | Forced Choice | Ranking Technique | Performance Standards |
|---|---|---|---|---|---|---|---|---|
| *Economic Criteria* | | | | | | | | |
| 1. Cost of development | 7 | 3 | 1 | 3 | 3 | 2 | 7 | 2.5 |
| 2. Cost of administration | 7 | 3 | 3 | 5.5 | 4 | 5 | 6 | 5 |
| 3. Speed in filling out | 7 | 2 | 5 | 5 | 4 | 5 | 5 | 6 |
| 4. Ease of use by raters | 6 | 3 | 6 | 5 | 4 | 3 | 5 | 6.5 |
| *Personnel Criteria* | | | | | | | | |
| 1. Useful as validation criteria in personnel research | 2 | 5 | 5 | 4.5 | 4 | 5 | 5 | 5.5 |
| 2. Useful in allocating merit pay | 2 | 5 | 4 | 4.5 | 4 | 4 | 5 | 6 |
| 3. Provides documentation (e.g., for discharge) | 2 | 5 | 5 | 4.5 | 6 | 2 | 4 | 6 |
| 4. Useful in promotion, transfer | 2 | 5 | 4 | 4.5 | 5 | 4 | 5 | 5.5 |
| 5. Useful in identifying training needs | 2 | 6 | 5 | 5 | 5 | 2 | 2 | 4 |
| 6. Useful in counseling and development | 2 | 6 | 5 | 5 | 6 | 2 | 2 | 3 |

TYPES OF APPRAISAL FORMATS

*Counseling Criteria*

| | | | | | | | |
|---|---|---|---|---|---|---|---|
| 1. Provides job-related feedback | 2 | 6 | 5 | 5 | 6 | 2 | 1 | 5.5 |
| 2. Communicates performance expectations clearly | 1 | 6 | 6 | 5 | 3 | 1 | 1 | 6.5 |
| 3. Provides performance standards clearly | 1 | 6 | 7 | 4 | 3 | 1 | 1 | 7 |
| 4. Provides employees with useful guidance regarding *how* to improve future performance | 1 | 5 | 6 | 4 | 4 | 1 | 1 | 3.5 |

*Acceptance Criteria*

| | | | | | | | |
|---|---|---|---|---|---|---|---|
| 1. Acceptance to raters | 4.5 | 5 | 5 | 6 | 5 | 2 | 5 | 6 |
| 2. Acceptance to ratees | 3.5 | 5 | 5 | 4 | 4 | 2 | 2 | 5 |
| 3. Psychometric soundness | 3 | 4 | 6 | 4 | 3 | 5.5 | 3 | 5 |

*Usefulness in Different Types of Organizations*

| | | | | | | | |
|---|---|---|---|---|---|---|---|
| 1. Useful in dynamic, loosely structured organizations | 4 | 5 | 3 | 4 | 4 | 3 | 4 | 2 |
| 2. Useful in formalized, bureaucratic organizations | 3 | 6 | 6 | 4 | 4 | 4 | 4 | 6 |

*As rated by a group of personnel/human resource experts. Scale values are from 1 to 7 (highest). Table values represent the median score of the group. Values are meant merely as a general guide with small differences in values having little meaning. (*Source: Stephen J. Carroll and Craig E. Schneier. Performance appraisal and review systems: The identification, measurement and development of performance in organizations. Glenview, IL: Scott Foresman, 1982.*)

system as much as possible to incorporate the elements that will make the MBO system work. Albrecht (1978) and Carroll and Schneier (1982) are good references for implementing MBO systems.

## Behaviorally Anchored Rating Scales (BARS)

These are really sets of scales with one scale for each job dimension or task. For example, if one task is to write a case plan with a client then a behaviorally anchored scale could be created for this task. The points on the scale are brief descriptions of actual behaviors that are linked to a dimension such as excellent to average to poor. The difficulty with BARS is creating such a system if it doesn't exist. With a separate scale required for each task and the need for a behavioral description for each scale point, the resources required for the development of such a system are large.

*Managing Human Services Personnel* (Pecora & Austin, 1987) describes the development of BARS, as does *Performance Appraisal and Review Systems.* (Carroll & Schneier, 1982)

## Critical Incidents

The use of critical incidents has been advocated for a variety of purposes for many years. (Carroll & Schneier, 1982; Locke, 1976) Critical incidents are anecdotes or sets of behaviors which have been shown to be successful or unsuccessful in the job. For example, an effective permanency planning worker in the public child welfare arena would write behavioral descriptions of the important tasks that go into developing a case plan with a family. Critical incidents allow much richer behavioral descriptions of events. Like the BARS this approach clearly specifies the most desirable behavior thought to be effective in accomplishing a task. One can easily see the disadvantage given the complexity of behavior exhibited by social workers, many of which produce positive results. Also like the BARS the development and use of such a system is costly (Carroll & Schneier, 1982).

## Performance Standards

The use of performance standards requires measuring performance and comparing it to a standard. (See Chapter 3 on use of information to enhance performance.) The basic ingredients are

- using the information system to collect data on critical aspects of performance,
- formatting the data in ways that enhance the positive use of information,
- making certain that reports have standards, and
- using reports for giving feedback and reward, which enhances learning.

The social administrator in a learning organization has a performance appraisal system that will enhance learning. For the social administrator who is confronted with a formal performance appraisal system that doesn't work, we suggest blending worker and organizational needs and working to change the system to one that enhances learning.

# TRAINING

## Benefits of Training

The importance of staff training cannot be overemphasized. Training is another powerful mechanism for the social administrator to use to achieve both worker and organizational goals. It is through providing training opportunities that the organization can assure that

- the lastest helping technology is used,
- tasks are accomplished successfully and uniformly,
- staff morale is enhanced, and
- the most efficient methods are employed.

Similarly it is through training that workers can satisfy several of their job values. The previously mentioned job values of workers finding their jobs challenging and learning from their work are related to training. While workers want to be challenged, they also want to succeed. It is training that provides the knowledge and skills so that workers can succeed, while the practice of new skills in the work environment provides the challenge and learning. Clearly social administrators who attend to training needs have a greater chance to achieve organizational and personnel goals.

## When to Train

The social administrator must watch for the misuse of training. It can become a knee-jerk reaction to agency problems or a supposed panacea thrown at some organizational dilemmas. On the other hand, while formal training is not a substitute for lack of resources, technology, managerial direction or support, or defined outcomes, it can positively affect performance when these features are in place. Figure 4–3 shows that training should be considered only after appropriate organization contingencies are established, jobs are clarified, and resources are gained. Each level acts as a prerequisite to the levels above it if performance is to improve. There is little sense in designing jobs, policies, procedures, and methods if the desired performance has not been established and rewards are not in place. Why worry about adequate resources (e.g., time, services, cooperation of key players) if it's not clear what the job is? For training, why waste valuable resources (it's very expensive as well) if the organizational contingencies and policies have not been established, and if resources are inadequate to implement the skills even if they are learned?

For example, the training of mental health workers for the purpose of integrating more people with severe mental illness back into the community will not have much effect unless the following has already happened:

**Figure 4–3.** Organization Priorities

1. The community integration performance indicators and reward structure have been implemented, and the administrators and managers have acted upon them. *(organizational contingencies)*
2. The policies, procedures, and methods supportive of this performance have been put in place (and others discarded if possible) and personnel *view their jobs as enhancing community integration. (job and task clarity)*
3. The resources needed (e.g., reasonable caseloads, adequate supervision, a well-designed management report package) have been provided.

In other words, unless program managers reward staff for community integration performance; establish procedures for social support building and methods for assessing clients' strengths, needs, and resources; and insure that staff receive the needed performance reports in a timely fashion this training will have limited effect on community integration performance. In contrast, if such supports are in place then training can be effective. Even then, formal training sessions may not be as preferable as supervisors providing ongoing quality education. In any event, any formal training requires supervisors to consult and follow-up with the employee in applying the skills and concepts to his or her job. Any training should make it clear at the onset and throughout the training period that the goal is to increase community integration performance or some aspect of it.

Certain events or indicators strongly suggest when training is needed.

1. when a new employee is hired
2. when an employee assumes a new job
3. when performance has been below standards or stable for an extended period of time
4. when mounting a new initiative or adopting a new intervention methodology

Even in these situations, the performance manager should insure that the prerequisites for training are in place if maximum benefit is to accrue.

## Selection of Content and Format

The first category of training content focuses on organizational values. *All* training should be seen as an opportunity to reinforce the values, vision (see Chapter 7), client outcomes, and uniqueness of the organization. This should be made explicit.

The second category of training content is focused on skills, both analytic and behavioral. In other words, training should change the way things are thought about or the way things are done. Minimally, every agency should have an established core curriculum for all new, frontline employees based largely on a task analysis and job design. Workers need to know how to perform the action and use the tools, equipment, work aids, and instructions to complete a task. The task analysis can be used to design training for new workers who have little knowledge or experience. It can identify the knowledge and skills that the tasks require and help in the designing of a complete training package. Every agency should also have a core curriculum for supervisory management staff, which is driven by the task analysis. In addition, advanced training opportunities and modules need to be available. Information gathered from clients, key players, frontline staff, performance reports, the literature, and knowledge of innovations implemented in other agencies could all generate topics for the training.

Lack of knowledge is not seen as a sufficient condition for embarking on training. Although it is often warranted as a part of a staff development plan, training must focus on analytic and behavioral skills and values. The cognitive mastery of a subject alone is inadequate if it does not lead to improved skills and sharing of values.

All training should be line driven. (Peters, 1987) This means that all content should be directly related to making frontline staff more effective or efficient. Even management and supervisory training must be *explicitly* linked to how it will improve the performance of frontline workers (see Chapter 7). Line-driven training also means that people in the trenches should be involved in the design, implementation, and evaluation of training to the maximum degree possible. Frontline workers should have a stake in training activities.

The focus on skills and values means that effective training must include discussion, dialogue, practice, practice, practice, and feedback, feedback, feedback. It needs to be conducive to participants' active involvement. Didactic instruction and group size should be limited. There should be mechanisms for follow-up consultation, support, and technical assistance. Supervision is a most common way to do this, but prescheduled reviews and group instruction or discussion sessions can be used. Finally, the training should be fun and entertaining. Participants should have a good time while they are learning.

## Sources of Training

Social administrators seldom need to design and conduct a training session. If an administrator has to conduct his or her own training, the text by Austin, Brannon, and Pecora (1984) is an excellent source. A university is also a good source.

In addition to locating state-of-the-art training sources, the social administrator needs to take advantage of the naturally occurring opportunities to train staff. All normal interactions with staff are training opportunities. The principles of adult learning listed below suggest how normally occurring events can assist staff in acquiring desired knowledge and skills. A staff member who is confronted by a situation about which he or she is uncertain, can learn from the experience. The situation will give them experience on which to build. And it presents the person with a problem they must solve. These are just a few of the principles of adult learning that a work situation can satisfy.

### Principles of Adult Learning
1. Emphasizes immediate usefulness.
2. Responds to concerns of learner.
3. Bolsters self-esteem—feeling of competence.
4. Is simple.
5. Uses problem-solving form.
6. Is noncompulsory.
7. Lets learner go at own pace.
8. Builds on experience.
9. Learning media matches learner's style.
10. Employs a variety of learning modalities.
11. Physical environment enhances learning.
12. Organizational climate values learning.
13. Learner is provided with focused, immediate feedback.
14. Learning process encourages the individual to reflect on their learning experience and improve on it. (Brennan & Memmott, 1982)

## Client-Centered Supervision

Supervision is the usual rubric under which naturally occurring training is discussed. The educational function of supervision described by Kadushin (1985) and so widely accepted is what we have in mind.

All too frequently administrators do not take the time to teach or to structure a supervised event so that learning can take place. In an important study in this area, Harkness (1987) found that normal supervision primarily involved discussion of agency policies and procedures. When supervision involved asking questions from the following list, outcomes for clients improved by an average of 17 percent.

### Client-Centered Supervision
I. The Client
  A. What does the client want help with?
  B. How will you and the client know you are helping?
  C. How does the client describe a successful outcome?
II. Helping the Client
  A. Does the client say there has been a successful outcome?
  B. What are you doing to help the client?

C. Is it working?

D. Does the client say you are helping?

E. What else can you do to help the client?

F. How will that work?

G. Does the client say that will help?

A group supervision model described at the end of this chapter is another powerful mechanism to enhance staff learning.

## STAFF DEVELOPMENT

Staff development is generally thought of as attending to the growth and development needs of workers. It ranges from seeing that staff has adequate training to do their jobs to helping individuals meet their career goals. Certainly the art history graduate who is hired to do child protective services needs extensive child welfare training to do the job. Both the person and the organization obtain substantial benefits from providing the required training. The benefits that an organization accrues from an administrator attending to career needs might not be obvious. For example, a caseworker who wants to go into real estate should quit his or her job. Helping this person attain his or her career goal frees up the position for someone who is truly interested in contributing to the organization. It might be argued that the person should be fired instead of given career counseling, but it is our experience that firing is frequently much more difficult, painful, and costly. Staff development is concerned with helping staff meet their goals by

- building on strengths,
- identifying what they want to learn on the job,
- identifying career goals, and
- developing a staff development plan.

Begin staff development by asking yourself what each staff person wants to learn on the job, as well as where they would like to be professionally in the future. This must be done in the context of individual differences. Therefore while most people value learning and are currently engaged in learning from their jobs, an individual person may not be able to identify anything he or she would like to learn. From a staff development perspective this is acceptable. Likewise, many people have a career goal for one, five, or ten years in the future while others have no identifiable career goal. Staff development then is the identification of these two aspects of each person's work world and helping them attain the desired skills and goals.

When staff members identify the knowledge or skills they would like to learn in their jobs, the response is relatively easy. Job redesign, seminars, workshops, and university courses are all available to address this need. The major social administration task may be the acquisition of resources to take advantage of these opportunities.

## Career Development Plan

The performance oriented administrator also takes responsibility for career development of staff. Helping a staff member accomplish a career goal involves a bit more work. Let's say, for example, that a case manager wants to be a program director in three years. Four separate staff development activities must be completed:

1. The skills required of the desired position must be identified.
2. Any formal degree or certificate requirements must be identified.
3. The strengths of the case manager must be identified.
4. A plan for acquiring the required skills and degrees or certificate must be developed.

Determining the requirements for the position is straightforward and is a useful activity for the case manager. Identification of the case manager's strengths deserves careful consideration. After the knowledge and skills for the program director's position have been identified, the case manager needs to examine all of the director's previous experiences, which will identify the knowledge and skills that he or she has already acquired. A staff member frequently requires assistance with this step simply because he or she tends to ignore previous experiences where he or she may have learned concepts or demonstrated skills essential for the new position. Previous work experience, formal educational experience, and volunteer experiences are all rich sources of information. This step also requires skills in framing and reframing these experiences. For example, a case manager may have been a volunteer coordinator in a previous position. It is important to examine this experience in terms of the activities or tasks involved. It is also important to examine this experience in terms of the skills demonstrated. Consequently this experience might be broken down like this:

| *Experience* | *Activities* | *Skills* |
|---|---|---|
| Volunteer Coordinator | Recruiting | Supervising |
| | Training | Instructing |
| | Task Assignment | Negotiating |
| | Evaluating task accomplishment | Leading |

By systematically examining all previous experiences, it is unlikely that any important knowledge or skill will be omitted. By examining all of these experiences in terms of tasks, activities, and skills it is more likely that all of the relevant connections will be made between past activities and requirements of the new position.

The manager and the case manager are now ready to develop the career development plan. The knowledge and skills required by the new position must be linked with the means of acquiring them. The means of acquiring this knowledge and skills are the same identified previously. Job redesign, seminars, workshops, and courses are all available. In this case, since the person has identified the career goal in terms of a number of years in the future, it is essential to identify time lines for acquisition of the knowledge or skills.

## THE REWARD-BASED ENVIRONMENT

Social work provides an opportunity to "touch others"; to make a difference in people's lives. It provides rich opportunities for learning and collegiality. Work should be a source of satisfaction, esteem, achievement, and pride. Work should be enjoyable. Yet for too many human service personnel, work is frustrating, depressing, punishing, and joyless. The agency environments are often oppressive and management is often perceived to be part of the problem.

### Managers as Sources of Rewards

Clients and employee's *require* reward-based environments that contribute to a person feeling like a winner.

> The old adage is "nothing succeeds like success." It turns out to have a sound scientific base. Researchers studying motivation find that the prime factor is simply the self-perception among motivated subjects that they are in fact doing well. Whether they are or not by any absolute standard doesn't seem to matter much. In one experiment, adults were given puzzles to solve. All ten were exactly the same for all subjects. They worked on them, turned them in, and were given the results at the end. Now, in fact, the results they were given were fictitious. Half of the exam takers were told that they had done well, seven out of ten correct. The other half were told they had done poorly, seven out of ten wrong. Then all were given another ten puzzles (the same for each person). The half who had been *told* that they had done well in the first round really did do better in the second, and the other half really did do worse. Mere association with past personal success apparently leads to more persistence, higher motivation, or something that makes us do better. (Peters & Waterman, 1982, p. 58)

Positively reinforced behavior slowly comes to occupy a larger and larger share of time and attention and less desirable behavior begins to be dropped. Yet, most managers appear not to understand the power of this concept. The reward structure in many organizations is inadequate. There is very little of it and where there is some, it is poorly implemented. The first rule of reinforcement is that the rewards need to be valued by the person being rewarded. While it is true that each person has his or her own set of job values and unique reinforcement menus, there are probably more similarities between people than differences. For example, most of us respond positively to written and verbal praise, and formal recognition through awards. Based on the work of B. F. Skinner, Peters and Waterman (1982) observed that high-performing managers follow five rules:

1. The reinforcement should be for a specific behavior.
2. The reinforcement should have immediacy—close time proximity between the behavior and the reward.
3. Small achievements (e.g., one client got a part-time job) warrant rewards (try to make everyone a winner).
4. The reinforcement should be unpredictable or intermittent (this happens naturally in large organizations because no manager can be aware of all behavior that warrants reward).
5. A fair amount of the reinforcement comes from top management (not just from your immediate supervisor).

This portrays an environment where people are receiving many rewards for many different behaviors at different times from many different sources. This also suggests that those reward systems that are at set times (annual reviews or employee of the month) are based on general criteria (made the greatest contribution to the agency) are less potent for meeting personal or organizational needs.

What reward mechanisms are available to managers? The following is a partial list:

### Verbal Praise
"Super job on the Jones case; I know it took a lot of work to help that guy into an apartment."

1. Go to the person's work area.
2. Call the person to your office.
3. Call the person at their desk.
4. Call the person at home.
5. Talk with the person if you meet in the parking lot, in the hall, at the coffeepot, while talking to a coworker.
6. Mention it at a staff meeting.
7. Mention it while you or the person is talking to a superior.

### Written Praise
1. Write person a personal note.
2. Write a memo for their personal file.
3. Send a memo to their supervisor.
4. Send a memo to agency director.
5. Include a mention of it in a newsletter.
6. Post a congratulations on a bulletin board.
7. Post a note on a person's office door or wall of work area.
8. Include mention of it in a news release.

### Symbolic Rewards
1. Give the person a certificate of recognition.
2. Post the certificate within agency.
3. Give the person a plaque.
4. Award the person with a traveling trophy.

These three types of rewards, combined with various venues, offers the administrator an impressive array of possible positive reinforcement opportunities.

The most prevalent obstacle to the creation of reward-based environments is the manager's belief that money, promotions, and other tangible rewards are the only or most powerful rewards. These rewards are limited, delayed, and often not under the manager's control. The evidence, however, is that symbolic rewards and verbal and written praise are as powerful as tangible rewards that the manager controls. William Manchester, in describing his World War II experiences as a foot soldier, said, "A man wouldn't sell his life to you, but he will give it to you for a piece of colored ribbon." Not only are they powerful, but they have a nice effect on the giver as well.

## Other Sources of Rewards

The list above was generated by focusing on the social administrator and the direct use of rewards. In fact, sources of rewards for people include the work itself, coworkers, and other people within the agency in addition to the direct supervisor. The social administrator constructing the reward-based environment takes responsibility for orchestrating rewards from all of these sources.

Rewards can be orchestrated from the work itself. Information systems that provide frontline workers feedback on their successes is rewarding. The open-ended responses from a client satisfaction survey that ends with: "Is there anything else you would like to tell us about receiving service here?" tend to be disproportionately positive and enormously rewarding. Design work so that task completion is evident and seeing the results of one's efforts can be extremely rewarding.

Social administrators establish the expectation that coworkers reward each other. This expectation can be accomplished through modeling or direct request. "Joe, will you tell Jerry what a good job he did on that project with you." One of the authors dropped in on a basketball practice one day and heard the coach say, "Tell him that was a nice pass or a good block. Let's all have fun together and tell each other when we do something well." A similar expectation can be established within any work unit. In other cases, peers could nominate colleagues for awards. The manager should make a habit of saying good things about people's work "behind their backs."

Others in the agency, particularly "higher-ups," are potent sources and targets for rewards. Social administrators at one level seek out those above to reward other staff. They also identify behavior of "higher-ups" to be rewarded. A call to a frontline worker from the agency director can be a powerful reward. The board president can be asked to drop by and tell Mary about what a great job she did last month improving the status of her caseload. Each year, Pam Hyde, the Ohio Commissioner of Mental Health, arranges for Governor Richard Celeste to sign certificates awarded to exceptional case managers. The reward-based environment is that in which everyone can feel like a winner and where rewards are varied and frequent.

On the way home from work each evening, a manager may well want to ask the question: "What did I do today to make my people feel like winners?"

## ORGANIZATIONAL CULTURE

The client and worker engage in a set of tasks from which clients and workers gain benefits. Getting these mutual needs satisfied is the job of the social administrator who uses personnel management technologies to blend agendas. All of this occurs within an organizational culture. Administration and staff can be victims of this culture, or the manager can take responsibility for creating a positive client and worker-centered organization culture.

It is not unusual for a person to rise in the morning wondering about what he or she will wear to work. He or she may think about particularly rewarding or frustrating clients from yesterday, last week, or last year. Workers who are particularly good friends and even those who may have left the organization some time ago may come to mind. This person attends a meeting and plays a role that he or she has played many times. These are all everyday instances of the effect of culture upon people in work units. Yet textbooks in social administration seldom consider the concept of culture. Culture, which is stressed as such an important dimension of direct practice, tends to be ignored by the social administrator. Organizational culture is a management tool in much the same way that a client's culture is a tool for the direct-practice social worker.

The idea of corporate culture has emerged in the management literature in recent years, becoming one of the latest fads. Ouchi (1982) in *Theory Z* put forth the idea that organizational culture was a central feature of Japanese corporations that contributed to their success. He suggests that the basic mechanism of control in the successful Japanese company is a philosophy of management. This philosophy is communicated through a common culture shared by key managers.

> The organizational culture consists of a set of symbols, ceremonies, and myths that communicate the underlying values and beliefs of that organization to its employees. These rituals put flesh on what would otherwise be sparse and abstract ideas, bringing them to life in a way that has meaning and impact for a new employee. (p. 35)

The anthropologist would not be at all surprised at this language. While anthropologists agree on the importance and power of culture, there is much less consensus on its definition. Louis (1985) extracts three basic components of culture from several definitions:

> First, there is content: the totality of socially transmitted behavior patterns, a style of social and artistic expression, a set of common understandings. Second, there is a group: a community or population, a society or class, a unit. Third, there is a relationship between the content and the group: content characteristics of the group, content peculiar to the group, or content differing from that of other groups. (p. 74)

The common understandings that are so important to the group are embedded in a set of values that are expressed in symbols, rituals, stories, and language. (Enz,

1986) This particular conceptual framework suggests the dimensions of culture that social administrators can shape.


## Values

Communication of a set of values that a work group can use as a unifying philosophy is seldom thought of as management behavior. Yet, communicating values occurs in a variety of ways through a variety of mechanisms. Every time an administrator speaks, tells a story, engages in a ritual, or issues a memo or report he or she is communicating values.

Our collective philosophy as social workers, your particular philosophy, and the broader social context are all important sources of values. Compton and Galaway (1979) suggest that two core social work values are respect for the dignity and uniqueness of the individual and client self-determination. Hepworth and Larsen (1982) suggest four cardinal values:

- People should have access to resources.
- Every person is unique and has inherent worth.
- People have a right to freedom.
- Society and the individual citizen have mutual responsibility for the realization of these values.

The National Association of Social Workers' code of ethics can be seen as a set of values.

The social administrator, however, does not practice in a vacuum. The social policy or social sanction under which agency programs operate are additional sources of values that must be implemented. The value of least restrictive and most family-like setting for out-of-home placements of children is sanctioned under PL 96–272. Under PL 94–142 this same value means that to the maximum extent appropriate, handicapped children should be educated with children who are not handicapped. (Turnbull, Strickland, & Brantley, 1982) Although this value of least restrictive is not explicitly identified in most social work references to values, it certainly is consistent with the profession's historical values of social integration as exemplified by people such as Jane Addams.

Naturally there are situations when values conflict with each other. Professional values may conflict with personal values. Public policy values can easily conflict with professional and personal values. This is the realm of ethics, which this chapter will not attempt to treat. The social administrator managing a program is in an ideal position to anticipate these value conflicts and assist staff to arrive at sound ethical judgments. We will go one step further in suggesting that the social administrator explicitly identify the values that direct a program and communicate these values in as many ways as possible. Program design as described in this text with its explicit description of goals for clients is an opportunity for the social administrator to identify and communicate values to the variety of people necessary for program success. This chapter has emphasized that workers tend to want people in the workplace with similar values. The identification and communication of key values then becomes a critical element of the staff selection process as well as for maintenance of job satisfaction.

The explicit values of a case management model developed for working with families of children with emotional disabilities is listed below. These values are displayed on a poster in the workplace. They are the first ideas encountered in explaining the program to potential case managers. They are the first content covered in training. They become the basis of a variety of symbols, rituals, and stories. These values become a major part of the shared philosophy of all those who work in the program.

### *Strengths Principles*
1. An active role by the family caregiver is essential for enabling the child to live in a normal environment.
2. Society should accommodate the needs of families who care for children with emotional disabilities.
3. Caregivers themselves are the best informants regarding their own needs and the demands of caring for a child with emotional disability.
4. Family caregivers have strengths.

If values are considered ideal states for clients and workers, the social administrator who uses values in a reinforcing environment will

- identify the valued outcome for clients in the public policy that directs and supports the program;
- identify the valued outcomes for clients as described in the program design;
- identify other values important to producing the desired client outcomes;
- identify worker directed values required to maintain staff morale and produce client outcomes;
- anticipate value conflicts and assist staff to make decisions in light of these conflicts; and
- use as many vehicles as possible to communicate these values to clients, staff, and other constituents.

## Symbols

It is not unusual when walking into a colleague's office to notice pictures and posters on the wall, titles of books on the shelf, size and type of desk, floor coverings, and windows. All of these are symbols that communicate something about the person, the agency, and something about what might occur in the office. In social agencies many of the posters and pictures seem to be soothing scenes or positive motivational messages. Pleasant mountains, an ocean, and southwest desert scenes are common. Sayings and poems from Saint Francis to Emerson abound. All of these tell us something about the person who purchased and hung the poster. It is rare for such symbols to tell us something about the agency or service. A rehabilitation agency posted a sign in the reception area that said: "Last month we moved 8 people into the community." The agency clearly communicated an important agency value. Take a walk through your work environment and look only at what is on the walls. What do these symbols communicate?

One of the authors walked into the waiting room of a program for children with emotional disabilities. The door was plain and solid with only the name of the program visible. Upon opening the door one was greeted by a large rectangular room with another solid door directly across from the entrance. The walls were light colored with posters depicting children and lined with chairs. There was soft music coming from the ceiling. There was no one in sight and little idea of what to do. Then a frosted glass window which was not immediately visible started to slide open and a disembodied voice said: "Can I help you?" While the overall effect was in some way pleasant, this environment was unsettling. If I were a parent who was caring for a child with an emotional disability, and I was in need of assistance, would I receive the message that there were people here to help? Social workers need to understand that the environment has an effect on people. Social administrators need to help create that environment through symbols.

Take another walk through your environment and study the physical arrangements. Think of yourself as a troubled client. What does the environment communicate? Now repeat the exercise putting yourself in the place of a direct-service worker who has had a difficult encounter with a client.

It is easy to feel that the physical environment is something the social administrator has little control over. After all, there is never enough money to remodel. In large agencies the physical space is controlled or dictated by some other bureau. Both of these are real limitations to creating the desired environment. But even in these situations something can be done. It may be small and appear insignificant; small things can have very large symbolic value. One of the authors was discussing this with a group of child welfare supervisors. The environment in which their workers were housed was the fairly typical large room with little cubicles made up of half walls and entrances without doors. This environment clearly created problems for workers who wanted to have meaningful conversations with clients and uninterrupted time and space to complete the ever present paperwork. Since most client contact took place in the home, the conversation turned to attempts by workers to communicate the need to be uninterrupted for completion of paperwork. Largely by themselves workers had found a variety of ways of communicating to others the need for uninterrupted time. Their efforts centered on the open entrance to their space and ranged from signs to curtains to be put up on an as-needed basis to barriers such as chairs, screens, and dowel rods. The lesson here is that people create a variety of ways of sending messages that help them control their environment.

Another place symbols show up in nearly all agencies is the bulletin board.

This space is typically the site of required government notices about such things as nondiscrimination. There are frequent notices of professional meetings and changes in policy. All of these items are important. But in how many agencies is the bulletin board a conscious tool of symbolic communication of agency values? How often are clients featured in positive ways on the bulletin board? How often are staff successes featured?

Think for a moment about all of the symbols available to a social administrator. This list could include the entrance to your agency or program, all of the walls, the bulletin board, display cases, newsletters, memos, plaques, and the floor. These are all venues available to you as a social administrator to construct symbolic messages that communicate the values and norms you need to have as the center of attention for your staff. Perhaps the two most important values to communicate in these venues are the importance of clients and direct-service staff.

One especially important job value, is the common values people share with others. When every opportunity is taken to communicate common agency values, staff morale is reinforced. This will also reap benefits in the staff recruitment process. Clearly communicated agency values in regard to clients and staff can help those interested in working for your program decide if their job values are more or less likely to be satisfied in your setting. Similarly, recall the multiple demands on the time and attention of all agency staff. In that agency where the basic client outcome is continuously communicated through a variety of symbols, all staff have an increased chance of maintaining this essential focus.

## Rites and Rituals

Deal and Kennedy (1982) talk about rites and rituals as "the systematic and programmed routines of day-to-day life in the company. In their mundane manifestations (rituals) they show employees the kind of behavior that is expected of them. In their extravaganzas (ceremonies) they provide visible and potent examples of what the company stands for." (pp. 14–15)

If one thinks about both the mundane routines as well as the formal ceremonies, the universe of interactions within an organization are pretty well covered. In other words, all of the behavior exhibited by the social administrator has an effect. *There is no throw away behavior.* This is not said to paralyze an administrator by the enormity of his or her power and influence, for most administrators feel that they have little influence, but to add another administrative tool to his or her repertoire.

*Rituals as Everyday Events.* Every interaction is an opportunity to communicate the importance of clients and staff. There is a host of rites in every organization. Think about the normal patterns of human engagement within any work environment. It may begin in the parking lot, in the entrance hall, at or in the elevator, at the coffeepot, at the mailbox, in the hall. In every one of these places people establish patterns of interaction that communicate how people value each other and what they expect of each other. Most people who have experienced conflict with someone in the workplace have noticed the tendency to avoid the other person whether it be by changing walking patterns or by simply being distracted to avoid eye contact. Every interaction is an opportunity to reinforce workers and demonstrate the norms about how people interact within the office.

Most people have job values that involve getting rewards that are just, informative, and in line with aspirations. Any list of rewards available to the social administrator would show that most rewards are verbally delivered in a variety of environments with differing audiences. This certainly encompasses the idea of rituals. The social administrator who sees normal interchanges and rituals as venues for rewards is creating the reward-based environment necessary for workers. When these rewards are connected to client benefits it further communicates the value of clients, preferred outcomes for clients, and rewards available to staff.

Similarly, self-esteem is an important job value for most workers. One aspect of self-esteem is a feeling of competence that is enhanced through the reward-based environment. Another aspect of self-esteem is a feeling of being accepted and valued as a person. Normal interactions or rituals that communicate unconditional respect enhance this aspect of self-esteem. Rituals that unintentionally ignore a person decrease that person's feeling of acceptance as a person.

*Ceremonies.*  If ceremonies are the formal opportunities for social administrators to demonstrate what the unit stands for, then it is the administrator's job to orchestrate these ceremonies. Many organizations have an employee of the year. This award can clearly communicate the value of staff. The social administrator can easily expand the number and types of ceremonies. All that you need to do is think about what you want to convey symbolically. The following is a list of potential events for which a ceremony can be important.

- Exceptional client achievement
- Exceptional worker achievement
- Exceptional worker efforts that failed
- Exceptional client efforts that failed
- Worker efforts that resulted in influencing a particularly difficult key player
- Staff efforts that resulted in acquiring a valued resource
- A key player's efforts on behalf of a client
- A community's efforts on behalf of a client (or clients)

Clearly this list could continue with the administrator devoting a disproportionate amount of time to ceremonies. And that is the point. The social administrator needs to have a broad view of ceremonies and orchestrate ceremonies whenever it will assist valuing of people and communicating the values of the administrator and program. The ceremony need not be as formal as the usual worker-of-the-year, although some need to be. All types of stickers, plaques, and other objects can symbolize the ceremony. The object is less important than the meaning provided by linking the object to the value and behavior.

## Stories

Anthropologists listen to the stories that tell about a culture's history and values. Stories within social agencies provide the same function. Stories about clients, workers, and other constituents contain the collective experiences of the agency filtered through the dominate values of the environment. Consequently, some experiences are captured in agency stories and many are not. We do not pretend to understand the process that determines which experiences become stories and which do not. What is important is that stories do affect people's behavior and outlook.

*Debilitating Stories.* Recall some of the stories you have heard within social agencies. What does each story tell you about that agency? A large, urban child welfare agency had an entrance that consisted of two locked doors at each end of the waiting room, which also housed a security guard. When staff were asked if there was a story about the double locked entrance that involved a violent parent the answer was no. The story involved a worker who "became over involved with a young client." The worker believed that the young woman was a victim of sexual abuse, but he was unable to obtain sufficient evidence to intervene with the full power of the state. He was taken off the case but continued to have contact with the young woman. He was convinced that sexual abuse was continuing and one day entered the office with a gun and confronted his supervisor. He shot the supervisor, was later caught, tried, pleaded insanity, and placed in a mental hospital.

This is an extreme story but one that raises many questions about what "really happened" and who "should" have done what. From an organizational culture point of view, it is what the story itself communicates about the values and norms of this organization that is of interest. Rather than dissect the entire story we would like to draw on only one aspect to illustrate the power of stories. The worker who was the subject of the story was clearly viewed as mentally ill or "crazy." We continually heard about the craziness of the office and most of the staff. Somehow strange behavior became a norm within this office culture. Of all of the things that must have occurred in this case, it was important to that culture to highlight the worker's insanity plea and hospitalization. The norm about strange behavior became the filter through which the story was told. Thus the norm was reinforced and passed on to new staff. The story set up this norm or expectation for other staff. While most workers would not exhibit the extreme behavior of the worker in the story, it was clearly communicated that strange behavior on the part of workers was part of what this office allowed or expected.

*Uplifting Stories.* Contrast this with a story told by a child welfare supervisor in another office. A worker responded to a report of suspected child abuse. When she arrived at the house everything seemed neat and clean with parents who appeared to be positive and concerned. The worker talked with the parents and carefully looked at the young girl who was the subject of the report. She did not find bruises or other clear evidence of abuse except for a small spot on her arm that really did not appear suspicious except it was the size of a cigarette burn. Just to be on the safe side she explained to the parents that she needed to take the child for a medical examination. Subsequent X rays demonstrated several old and untreated fractures. The child was subsequently protected.

This positive story accomplishes several things. It clearly communicates the central mission of the agency: protecting children once they have been reported as possible victims of abuse. It communicates this value more powerfully than a statement. The worker is a hero. It was through her effort and skill that this young victim was ultimately protected. Heroes are an essential element of any culture. Hero stories provide us with ideal behavior. Behavior that we can strive for. This agency probably has the usual several hundred-page policy manual. Somewhere in this manual, it says that workers are to see the child who is the suspected victim of abuse. The manual also tells workers that if they have some reason to believe that the child might have been abused, they should have the child examined by a physician. But reading this manual or having a trainer or supervisor recite the policy is not nearly as effective as the story.

*Finding Stories.* From a social administration point of view these stories suggest that administrators need to be good listeners and good storytellers. Listening carefully to the stories that are a part of the culture uncovers the norms and expectations of that culture. Once an administrator knows the stories and norms he or she can decide which ones further the desired norms of the office and which do not. Stories that communicate positive and important features of the office need to be retold. Stories that demonstrate negative norms need to be ignored. The child protection story could be retold a thousand times and still communicate the desired norms and practices effectively.

Yet everyone gets tired of hearing all of the same old stories. Besides times change, practices change, and heroes change. Therefore, it is important for the social administrator to become a creator and teller of stories. The story about the troubled worker could be ignored by administrators yet the norm is likely to be so strong that the story will continue to be told. This story may die when the norm changes sufficiently that the story is no longer needed. One way to begin to change the norm is to create stories that illustrate positive and competing values.

*Effective Storytelling.* Becoming an effective storyteller is not really very difficult even though most of us live in a culture where storytelling has become a specialized function of certain people rather than a part of everyday life. Movies, television, and churches are now the officially designated venues for storytelling. If you can recall particularly effective storytellers you have heard, you may recognize some of the features that make for an effective story. Elements like surprise twists and minute detail seem to make storytelling effective. For the social administrator interested in using stories to create heroes and communicate effective practice and policy, the critical feature is detail. Specifics communicate. In the positive child protection story the detail about the small mark on the girl's arm that could have been in the shape of cigarette is a detail that is essential for the story. This detail communicates the type of evidence that triggers a medical examination. If you go back to that story and attempt to learn how to examine a small child for such evidence, you will not find that detail and consequently not know how to do it. How a worker examines a child does make a difference to the young child who is the victim as well as to others. That detail either needs to be included in this story, another story, or learned in another format. No single story can be long enough to cover all of the essential details. The social administrator needs to be clear on what he or she wants to communicate and make certain that these details are included in the story.

The social administrator finds the material for his or her stories in the day-to-day operation of the office. The power of the stories previously told comes from the fact that they actually happened. The social administrator should listen for stories in the office that illustrate the norms and practices that he or she wants to reinforce.

Folklore has a classification system for story types. Similarly, in the social agency the administrator needs stories of a variety of types to illustrate essential features of the agency. Social administrators should seek out and retell stories that illustrate

- the client-outcome mission of the program,
- clients as valued individuals,
- the difficult situations that clients live with,
- how much it is possible for clients to achieve,
- direct-service workers as highly valuable people,
- worker behavior that assists others to continue to do excellent,
- the practices of direct-service workers that produce client benefits,
- work despite difficult conditions, and
- worker behavior that is effective for influencing key players.

## LANGUAGE

### Language and Its Difficulties

The primary mechanism for communicating the philosophy of a work unit is language. Most of the symbols used to transmit values are words. Likewise, stories are communicated through words and rituals are conducted with language. Yet is is useful to consider language as a separate mechanism for the transmission of culture.

Language has a variety of functions. Hayakawa (1964) reminds us that language functions to inform as well as to affect. Language promotes social cohesion as well as social control. Language obscures as well as clarifies. Social work uses language as a primary tool, yet gives little attention to its vocabulary.

The social administrator who suggests to a worker that she "coordinate the treatment to deal with the family issues" is likely neither to inform nor affect. The basic building blocks of language are words. Words are symbols that represent something. Yet, how often have we forgotten or never known what the particular symbol represents? "Coordination" is a favorite term in social services. Many people believe that clients and communities would be much better off if services were coordinated. One would be hard pressed to disagree with this concept. But is this because it is such a powerful and true statement or is it because coordination lacks an agreed upon definition? The referent for the symbol may have been lost or never established. The first plea to social administrators is to define their terms—make sure that the language of the workplace is a language of shared meanings.

Establishing a vocabulary of shared meanings is difficult. The process of linking words to what they stand for is a process of abstraction. (Hayakawa, 1964) The particular machine that I am using to type this paragraph is unique. It is possible for me to describe it in such detail as to demonstrate its uniqueness. At the same time this machine has many features that make it similar to millions of others. This collection of similar features allows me to classify it as a computer. If you have never experienced a computer, the label would mean nothing to you, and the idea of typing a paragraph on a computer would be nonsense. The process of learning a language in the workplace is the process of learning words AND relating these words to things or happenings. Words are not enough. Shared meanings come from shared objects and experiences.

Earlier in this chapter, you were provided with a structure for writing task statements. Perhaps the two most difficult aspects of this activity are vocabulary and level of abstraction. For a tasks statement to be useful in a workplace it must use a vocabulary with shared meanings. To arrive at shared meanings, it is sometimes advisable to use words in a task statement that describe common objects in the workplace or to describe behavior. However, the statement can be trivialized. It is not useful to describe a task as: "To grasp a pencil between thumb and forefinger and apply it to paper." This task statement would lead to jobs being described by long lists of tasks that few people could remember and would unnecessarily limit a person's autonomy. A ball-point pen, for example, would be just as appropriate as a pencil. The challenge is to construct task statements with a vocabulary that is abstract enough to direct behavior productively. A consequence of this is that the language of tasks becomes limited to the unit and people within the unit. A task statement with an agreed upon vocabulary in one place may not be clear and specific in another. For example, in one unit it may be well understood that contact with clients means a face-to-face conversation. In another unit, however, contact may be face-to-face or phone contact. In a recent visit to an agency, a worker received a FAX from a client. Does this satisfy the definition of client contact? As technologies are developed and used, terms may need to be redefined. In addition, as language changes over time the original vocabulary of the task statement must also change. Little in an organization that requires words to conduct its affairs can be viewed as fixed. Everything changes including language.

The difficulty of relating words to shared objects and happenings and operating at the same level of abstraction is made more so when the word is confused with the thing it represents. Confusing the actor with the role is a time honored pitfall in movies and television. There is a danger that Hal Holbrook begins to be seen as Mark Twain or Sean Connery as James Bond. Many actors go to great lengths to avoid being "typecast." The same type of confusion occurs with language. "Did you make that referral?" "Yes, I referred Mrs. Jones to the county health department." But what is a referral? Even in an environment where there may be a set of behaviors that everyone has agreed constitutes a referral, the word can come to be confused with the activity. Over time this has the effect of destroying the common meaning of the term. Sensitivity to this error would lead the social administrator to ask a different question. Consistent with the client-outcome focus of our performance approach, the question becomes "Did Mrs. Jones get the immunizations for her children from the health department that she needed?"

## The Use of Metaphors

The process of using language to develop and maintain a shared culture in a work unit requires the use of a variety of devices. Metaphors can be particularly potent. A metaphor is an implied analogy. It ascribes the characteristics of one thing to another. Metaphors are useful because they permit the explanation of something new and unfamiliar in terms of something known or experienced. Metaphors are efficient because they facilitate the communication of a large number of characteristics without listing all of them. This efficiency also facilitates remembering this list of characteristics that might otherwise be too long to remember. (Kresting & Frost, 1985) Here is an example: A caseworker says going to court in a case of child abuse is like going to a baseball game; it is a highly competitive environment in which you spend a lot of time in anticipation of something happening. This metaphor may get the worker to be more competitive in court, learn the rules of the court game, and come to terms with the time apparently wasted in the courthouse waiting for something to happen. As this example demonstrates there are also many potential problems with any particular metaphor. If the metaphor is told to a new worker who has never been to a baseball game the metaphor would not work. If the new worker knew about baseball but did not really understand the characteristics of the game being used to communicate (rules, pace, and competition), the metaphor would not work. Certainly there are many ways in which the court and baseball are very different. The listener could easily be confused about the characteristics that the courtroom and a baseball game share, or he or she could ignore the characteristics.

While this is not the place for an extended discussion of social work metaphors, we would like to caution the social administrator to select or accept metaphors carefully. One can easily view a child who behaves in such a way that it causes disruption at home and school as

- behavior disordered
- emotionally disturbed

- mentally ill
- miscreant
- a child in need of care
- a child with an emotional disorder
- a child with an emotional disability

These seven different labels are seven very different metaphors. The consequence of selecting one of these deserves careful consideration. If the child is considered to be mentally ill, the entire medical model of mental health treatment comes into play. In a recent project in a state hospital for children a social worker observed: "You know, when children leave here they are not cured." The observation is not surprising. But for most people a hospital signifies a cure. If the worker had this expectation and was disappointed, can you imagine how the child and the parent feel?

In this same project, the team selected the disability metaphor. This selection made some people uncomfortable. What does it mean that a child has a disability? If the child is really mentally ill, does this create problems? The second question is easily addressed. Illness is a metaphor as is disability. We need to select useful metaphors not be subjects of them. The first question is the important one. What does the disability metaphor mean? In part it means that public policy regarding people with disabilities is available. It also means that key ideas and values that accompany this field may be used. Ideas like normalization, mainstreaming, and reasonable accommodation are part of the disability model. And it means the person is not the disability. These ideas are relied on in this project with great acceptance by families, teachers, and other professionals. There are certainly other ideas about disability that are part of the public mind that may be harmful. Some people see disabilities as life long. Some of these children may have life-long emotional difficulties. Some will not. Are there harmful consequences to the child with the use of this metaphor? Currently there seem to be more benefits with this metaphor than with others but the search needs to continue. No metaphor can ever be perfect.

## THE POWER OF GROUP SUPERVISION

Group supervision has the power to establish a positive work culture that centers on both the client and the worker. Learning takes place in this model when staff members present problems they are having with a case. This problem-sharing happens in a group setting. Norms concerning how to conduct the group have been carefully established and communicated. For example, when a staff member presents a barrier, the group must generate a minimum of three potential next steps that are acceptable to the person presenting the problem before the group can go on to another problem. Each staff member goes away from the meeting with increased options. And other group members have had the advantage of hearing a variety of options for situations that may occur in their practices. The supervisor does not have to play the role of having all the answers, an uncomfortable role that many supervisors accept but that is destined to fail. The supervisor has the knowledge of the options generated by others, as well as the pattern of barriers identified across cases so that interventions can be developed at program or policy levels.

This model of group supervision satisfies many of the conditions for adult learning and is an efficient means of conducting training. We suggest that learning through this type of supervision is often more effective than the normal workshop format. The following is a description of a group supervision session that has been greatly telescoped for the purposes here.

*Promptness and enthusiasm are essential.*

Kate checked her watch and thought, "I better get going. It's time for the group to meet. I always get kind of excited when we meet."

*The session has an explicit structure. Taking an opportunity to reward staff for an important client outcome.*

Kate cleared her desk, picked up her copies of the agendas and checklist and headed out of her office. As she walked down the hall she met John. "Good morning, John. I heard that you were able to get Charles moved home yesterday."

"Yes, I have been working with Charles and his mother for two months and we all think it is a good time," said John.

"That's just great. I remember how stuck you felt just a few weeks ago. You have done a great job on this case," Kate said as she headed to get a cup of coffee before the supervision session. As she entered the coffee room she said good morning to Mary and updated the chart that showed the number of moves of children. She put a sticker of the Family Guidance Center logo next to John's name to signify his latest success.

*Symbols in the environment that reinforce agency values.*

As she walked into the room that was used for group supervision she noticed the pleasant decor. She had been able to get a local carpet store to donate an attractive area rug in a lively Native American pattern. The walls were nicely painted with colorful pictures interspersed with the posters she had prepared. There was one that said "Reunifying and maintaining families is our business." A second listed the four principles of strength that direct the program. A third poster is a chart of the number of goals set and achieved. Another chart records the percent time spent with clients as a graph with the standard of 50 percent drawn as a straight line. Kate noticed that last week the percent time spent with clients had dropped to 40 percent. She made a mental note to ask the group what she could do to remove barriers and get it back to 50 percent.

*A pleasant environment is viewed as important to staff morale. The pleasant environment is interspersed with symbols important to the agency mission and essential work processes.*

*Failing to meet a target is viewed as supervisor's opportunity to help remove barriers.*

The case management team began to arrive as Kate placed the standard agenda listing the following goals by each chair:

1. Focus on strengths to identify goals.
2. Keep in mind the adolescent's eventual need to develop skills for independent living.

3. Always explore the potential for use of natural helpers and community resources when establishing goals.
4. For each client or goal or need area, brainstorm at least three alternatives to fulfill the need.
5. Make it your goal to leave the session with a plan of action for each of your cases—including specific steps to be taken by case manager.

*A printed copy of the group norms is used as an agenda to make the norms explicit.*

The agenda was rarely consulted because everyone knew the group norms. She thought it was still good to keep this in front of people. Besides it helped socialize new staff into the process without taking more of her valuable time to explain this to new people. The group was friendly and jovial as they gathered.

*Time is a valuable commodity and is treated that way. The supervisor rewards John and makes it explicit what the reward is for.*

Kate said, "Shall we begin?" as she noticed the time. "I would like to begin by having John share his success from yesterday. I think we have another wonderful example that we can all use to help us remember what we are about. We can also use the story to demonstrate to others what we do."

"Sure I will share the story," John said. "After all it is not my success. If it weren't for all the ideas generated by you folks I never would have known what to do next. I am sure you remember when I was ready to give this case to anyone who would take it. As you may remember the latest barrier keeping Charles' mother from caring for him at home was getting Charles to the after-school program and then home. As you know Mom works and doesn't have a car. It's at least a mile from school to the aftercare program and another 3/4 mile home. All of your wonderful ideas about volunteers providing transportation fell through. But, Mary, I think it was you who said you thought that Charles could learn to ride the city bus even though Charles is only 11 and his psychiatrist did not think it was a good idea. As you reminded me, Mary, we can't forget about these kids needing to develop independent living skills. Charles was excited about the idea. But I have to admit it scared me. Anyway, Charles has ridden the bus from school to the after-school program at the Y by himself for the last week without incident. So according to our agreement with Dr. Miller, Charles was able to go home yesterday. Of course, we have lots of backup plans in case Charles has an episode at school or at the Y."

*Failure is celebrated to encourage creativity.*

*Charles, a client, becomes a hero and demonstrates what is possible.*

The group interrupted the last sentence with a burst of applause and shouts of congratulations.

*Kate focuses the group on what they need using her agenda.*

Kate said, "Who is stuck with a situation and needs ideas?" Kate uses the following agenda:

What situations are people having difficulty with?

What ideas do people have that might work in this situation?

Does the youth have a caregiver?

What does the youth want?

What are the youth's strengths?

How can we think about that as a strength?

What independent living skills is the youth learning?

How is school going for the youth?

What does the caregiver say they need to continue to provide care?

What are the caregiver's strengths?

How can we build on these strengths to increase their ability to provide care?

What are you doing that could be done by someone else?

"I cannot figure out what to do with Marvin," said Nancy.

"Where do you seem to be stuck?" asked John.

"Well, all Marvin does is fight. I can't seem to get anywhere him. He wouldn't really talk with me so I can't figure out any strengths on which we could build. I am just really frustrated."

*Each group member is a leader—not just Kate.*

The group was thoughtfully quiet. Kate said, "Okay group, you know the rules. Build on strengths and generate ideas about what Nancy can do next until she has a minimum of three ideas that she feels she can try this week."

"Is there anything in his file that looks like a strength?" asked Harry.

"You know typical hospital and school records. All problems, not a hint of a positive," replied Nancy.

"How about school subjects? Does he like some subject more than others?" asked Bill.

Nancy responded, "I have asked him about school subjects and all he says is he can't stand the other kids. He isn't performing well in any subject and the school psychologist doesn't know if it's ability or his emotional disability."

"Now wait a minute," said John. "If all we have to go on is his fighting how can we think about fighting as a strength?"

"That's right," said Mary. "Where is fighting socially acceptable?"

"I've got it," said Nancy. "Boxing! Doesn't the Y have a Golden gloves program?"

"It sure does," replied Henry.

"That's it. I'll ask Marvin about boxing," Nancy said hopefully.

*Be consistent about agreed upon norms.*

"Don't forget the rule," reminded Kate. "You don't leave without at least three ideas."

"That should be easy," said Henry. "How about Karate as a second choice? I know this place that teaches Karate from a mental discipline point of view. Lots of eastern philosophy and an emphasis on nonaggression."

"Well, there is always the old standby of wrestling," John

chimed in. "Not as classy as karate but another alternative."

Nancy said, "That's great. I'll try this approach. Maybe something will come of this. This is great. It may not work but at least I have options."

"That's right," said Kate. "You know all the situations you folks are working with are very difficult. If there were easy answers someone else would have found them long ago. It takes lots of different ideas and approaches before we get a breakthrough. And besides, we all learn a great deal from what doesn't work. The boxing, karate, etc. are still pretty general ideas. What are the next steps, Nancy?"

*The supervisor insures that next steps are clear.*

*The worker is the person who determines if her needs are met.*

"Yes. I will try to talk with Marvin about these options and see if one is appealing to him. If he is reluctant or unsure I'll try to have us just visit one or more of them," replied Nancy.

*New policies can be communicated in a variety of ways.*

"Say, I heard that there was a new policy on reimbursement of case management services. Do you know anything about that, Kate?" asked Jim.

*Valuable group time may be better used to focus on difficult aspects of cases.*

*Performance deficits are not framed in terms of "blame" but as obstacles to be overcome. The issue was not framed in terms of "compliance" but in terms of the importance to clients.*

"Yes," replied Kate gently. "I will send out a memo as soon as I get all of the details. We all know that these kids and their families receive the benefits of our efforts when we spend time working with them. I noticed that last week some things got in your way of spending at least half your time with clients. What barriers are you encountering that keep you away from these kids and their families?"

"Well, I don't know about the rest of you, but I seem to be spending a lot of time in meetings with mental health center staff," said Henry.

Kate noticed several people nodding their heads affirmatively. "What kind of meetings?" she asked.

"Everyone wants to meet with us," replied Nancy. "The doctors, therapists, even the agency director is asking us to attend staff meetings. She says that we need to know about agency program and policy changes."

*The supervisor fulfills her role in providing tools and removing barriers.*

"I will discuss this with mental health center staff," said Kate. "I don't want to take any more of your valuable time for this right now. I am sure we can find some way to satisfy their needs without you spending lots of time in meetings. I may have to come back to you for your ideas about this but right now I will give it a shot."

"I think if you could cut down the number of Mental Health Center meetings that we would be back to 50 percent time with families and kids," said John.

*The supervisor uses group feedback to check her perception of the meeting.*

After several more case discussions, Kate noticed that everyone seemed to have participated and seemed to be energized so she said, "It seems like we are about done. Is that right?" Everyone nodded affirmatively. "Fine. Would each of you fill out your supervision evaluation checklist and hand it to me as you leave? (See Figure 4-4.) Don't forget the celebration for Judge Snyder this Friday afternoon. You know

This is used to reflect on the meeting that might suggest something different for next week.

she has been a big help in several of our very difficult cases." Kate spent a little time socializing with staff as they went off to their work.

She took the evaluations and returned to her office to complete her session evaluation form before she compiled the case managers evaluations. (See Figure 4–5.)

Group supervision is a promising mechanism for addressing a variety of personal management concerns. The helping profession is a lonely one. A single worker works with a single client whether in an office or increasingly in the community on the client's problem. The work itself is challenging and demanding. But employees need connection and support; they need to feel a part of a collective with the same mission. Opportunities for celebration and sharing frustrations, and for mutual learning are needed. Furthermore, the organization (e.g., an agency, team) requires occasions for reinforcing the desired elements of the culture and identifying systemic barriers to performance. Group supervision has the capacity for addressing each of these needs.

In the previous description, several desirable characteristics of group supervision were manifest and highlighted in the side bar. But most importantly, the work

| | **Circle Your Response** | |
|---|---|---|
| 1. The session started on time. | Yes | No |
| 2. The seating arrangement allowed each person to be clearly seen. | Yes | No |
| 3. Interruptions occurred during the session. | Yes | No |
| 4. Each group member was involved in the discussion. | Yes | No |
| 5. Everyone contributed ideas and suggestions. | Yes | No |
| 6. The atmosphere in the group was optimistic and positive. | Yes | No |
| 7. Each person laughed at some point during the session. | Yes | No |
| 8. Conscientious efforts that failed were celebrated. | Yes | No |
| 9. References were made to problems, illness, or diagnoses during the session. | Yes | No |
| 10. Common characteristics or patterns among cases were identified. | Yes | No |
| 11. I feel like I know what to do next. | Yes | No |
| 12. At the end of the group session I felt energized and hopeful. | Yes | No |

Additional comments:

**Figure 4–4.** Worker's Group Supervision Assessment

1. Which cases were reviewed?

2. Which workers were *not* involved in the group process?

3. Who appeared negative about clients or attempted to shoot down a creative idea or potential resource?

4. Who admitted a mistake?

5. How were "mistakes" celebrated?

6. What natural helpers and/or community resources were identified for each case?

7. How did the supervisor reframe problem statements or diagnostic labels into strengths or goal statements?

8. What patterns of worker behavior (frustrations/struggles/successes, etc.) can be identified from case specifics?

9. Who received positive feedback for:
   Recognition and/or use of adolescent/family strengths

   Identification and use of natural/community resources

   Client achievements and goal attainment.

10. What unmet family needs or unavailable community resources were identified? What can be done to meet these needs?

11. Which worker seemed defensive or frustrated? What attempts were made to establish more realistic expectations or to break down tasks into smaller steps?

**Figure 4–5.** Supervisor's Assessment of Group Supervision Session

was clients, clients, clients. Nothing was allowed to intrude on the business of the team. Even issues like mental health center meetings were framed in terms of their impact on clients. Lengthy discussions about the latest forms, policies, and procedures were avoided and other mechanisms for communicating them established. There was no complaining about the latest forms, policies, and procedures. The supervisor did not blame workers for spending less than half their time with clients, so defensiveness was replaced by creativity and problem solving. In turn, the workers did not blame clients for their lack of achievement.

Rather than "talk about" cases, the team worked together—generating specific alternatives to be implemented. The overall effect is one of empowerment, not continued frustration. The alternatives may not work, but the team will learn from it and other alternatives will be produced.

## SUMMARY

In this chapter, the major influences of the quality of work life of human service personnel and the management strategies for enhancing the job satisfaction and effectiveness of employees were described. Included here were the ideas of values and culture with discussion of specific methods like task analysis and performance appraisal. The chapter concludes with a detailed look at group supervision as a mechanism for integrating many of the ideas suggested in the chapter. The social administrator would not have staff to satisfy without funds, not have a program without a helping technology and would not have clients without community support. The management of these and other essential resources is taken up in the next chapter.

## REFERENCES

Albrecht, K. (1978). *Successful management by objectives*. Englewood Cliffs, NJ: Prentice-Hall.

Austin, M. J. (1981). *Supervisory management for the human services*. Englewood Cliffs, NJ: Prentice-Hall.

Austin, M. J., Brannon, D., & Pecora, P. (1984). *Managing staff development programs in human service agencies*. Chicago: Nelson-Hall.

Bashshur, R. L., Shannon, G. W., & Metzner, C. A. (1970). *Some ecological differences in use of medical services*. Paper presented at the Annual Meeting of the American Sociological Association, Washington, D.C. Mimeographed.

Brennan, E., & Memmott, J. (1982). The information user as adult learner. *The management of information transfer for the employment and training field*. Lawrence, KS: The University of Kansas.

Carroll, S. J., & Schneier, C. E. (1982). *Performance appraisal and review systems: The identification, measurement and development of performance in organizations*. Glenview, IL: Scott Foresman.

Compton, B. R., & Galaway, B. (1979). *Social work processes*. Dorsey.

Deal, T. E., & Kennedy, A. A. (1982). *Corporate cultures: The rites and rituals of corporate life*. Reading, MA: Addison-Wesley.

Drucker, P. (1967). *The effective executive*. London, England: Pan Books.

Enz, C. A. (1986). *Power and shared values in the corporate culture*. Ann Arbor, MI: UMI Research Press.

Fine, S. A., & Wiley, W. W. (1971). *An introduction to functional job analysis: A scaling of selected tasks from the social welfare field*. Kalamazoo, MI: Upjohn Institute for Employment Research.

Gillespie, D. F., & Martin, P. Y. (1978, Summer). Assessing service accessibility. *Administration in Social Work, 2*(2), 183–198.

Gutek, B. Strategies for studying client satisfaction. (1978, Fall). *Journal of Social Issues, 2*, 44–55.

Hackman, J. R., & Oldham, G. R. (1980). *Work redesign*. Reading, MA: Addison-Wesley.

Harkness, D. R. (1987). Social work supervision in community mental health: Effects of normal and client focused supervision on client satisfaction and generalized contentment. Unpublished dissertation, The University of Kansas School of Social Welfare.

Hayakawa, S. I. (1964). *Language in thought and action*. New York: Harcourt, Brace & World.

Hepworth, D. H., & Larsen, J. A. (1982). *Direct social work practice: Theory and skills*. Homewood, IL: Dorsey.

Kadushin, A. (1985). *Supervision in social work* (2nd ed.). New York: Columbia University Press.

Kresting, L. A., & Frost, P. J. (1985). Untangled webs, surfing waves and wildcatting: A multiple-metaphor perspective on managing organizational culture. In Frost, P. J.; Moore, L.; Louis, M. R.; Lundberg, C. C.; & Martin, J., (Eds.), *Organizational culture* (pp. 115–168). Beverly Hills, CA: Sage.

Lawler, E., Mohrman, A., & Resnick, S. (1986, Fall). Performance appraisal revisited. *Organizational Dynamics, 13*(1), 20–35.

Locke, E. A. (1976). The nature and causes of job satisfaction. In M. D. Dunnette, (Ed.), *The Handbook of Industrial and Organizational Psychology* (pp. 1297–1349). Chicago: Rand McNally College Publishing.

Lopez, F. (1975). *Personnel interviewing, theory and practice* (2nd ed.). New York: McGraw-Hill.

Louis, M. R. (1985). An investigator's guide to workplace culture. In Frost, P. J.; Moore, L.; Louis, M. R., Lundberg, C. C., & Martin, J., (Eds.), *Organizational culture* (pp. 73–94). Beverly Hills, CA: Sage.

Ouchi, W. G. (1982). *Theory Z: How American business can meet the Japanese challenge*. New York: Avon.

Pecora, P. J., & Austin, M. J. (1987). *Managing human services personnel*. Beverly Hills, CA: Sage.

Peters, T. (1987). Thriving on chaos: Handbook for a management revolution. New York: Knopf.

Peters, T. J., & Waterman, R. H. (1982). *In search of excellence: Lessons from America's best run companies*. New York: Harper & Row.

Poertner, J., Gowdy, E. H., & Harbert, T. (no date). *Quality of work life: It's not just job satisfaction*. Lawrence, KS: University of Kansas.

Ro, K. K. (1969, July–August). Patient characteristics, hospital characteristics and hospital use. *Medical Care, 7,* 295–312.

Special Task Force to the Secretary of Health, Education and Welfare. (1973). *Work in America.* Cambridge, MA: The MIT Press.

Turnbull, A. P.; Strickland, B. B.; & Brantley, J. C. (1982). *Developing and implementing individualized education programs* (2nd ed.). Columbus, OH: Merrill.

Weiss, J. E., Greenlick, M. R., & Jones, J. F. (1970, October). *Determinants of medical care utilization: The impact of ecological factors.* Paper presented at the 98th Annual Meeting of the American Public Health Association, Houston. Mimeographed.

# CHAPTER 5

# Resource Management

Resources are the raw materials a human service agency acquires from the environment and distributes throughout the organization. Resources include money, personnel, technology, clients, and community goodwill and influence. The specification, acquisition, and allocation of many aspects of these resources have been included in other chapters. For example, interpersonal influence is the subject of Chapter 6. The program design chapter includes content on selection of program interventions (technology), key player behavior (goodwill and influence), and target population (clients). The managing people chapter discusses hiring of staff and job design.

This chapter will cover the following resource areas: the acquisition and allocation of funds, managing time, the acquisition and use of volunteers, and the acquisition and application of ideas. The central challenge of client-centered performance managers is to acquire resources sufficient to produce the client benefits and to allocate these raw materials so that the greatest impact on performance can be realized.

## FUND ACQUISITION

There are three general principles that underlie the acquisition of funds. First, be clear on the mission of your organization and the client outcomes you desire. This will help keep the performance manager from going after any money that becomes

Sue Pearlmutter, M.S.W., research assistant at the University of Kansas School of Social Welfare, co-authored this chapter.

**197**

available. Seeking money as a goal unto itself can lead to an unfocused set of activities that directs all energies toward the next grant proposal rather than to learning to produce improved client outcomes. Focusing on the goal has a corollary benefit of directing the manager to hidden funds. For example, if your agency seeks to assist children with emotional disabilities in remaining in family situations, normal classrooms, and become productive community citizens, funding opportunities are not limited to mental health. Additional funding sources related to these outcomes include child welfare, education, rehabilitation, and employment and training funds. Second, fund acquisition requires frequent contact with potential sources of funds whether it be government officials, legislators, or private individuals. It means consistent and intense involvement with the organization's environment. Third, fund acquisition requires highly developed program design skills. It is the program which you are selling. It is the program design whether in the form of a grant proposal or brief prospectus which becomes the heart of many attempts to acquire funds.

### Case Study:* Ohio Department of Mental Health

We have been very successful in applying for national grant applications as a way of getting innovative programs started. We do a lot of state and local partnerships. This is a very successful approach with foundations and the federal government, especially when they know the state and the local community are moving in the same direction. It showcases local systems that are willing to change. We provide a lot of the match money for such partnerships. It gives those staff national exposure, allowing them to see what is going on in the rest of the country and to bring information back to their own community and the state.

It also serves as a laboratory for us at the state level because we can only make good policies if we know what we're doing that gets in the way of the people who are trying to do the job. When we have a state and local partnership, we commit to that local area. If we're doing something at the state level that is interfering with the goals we have all set, we change the rules. We figure out how to do it differently to support the local area.

National grants also bring new dollars to local communities and reward people who are willing to be creative. This has been very successful for us. We have a grant from the Social Security Administration to work with the Bureau of Disability Determination to try to cut down the amount of time it takes for people to get social security. We have moved from a period of 140 days to get social security to 40 days. We have a teleclaims process and do it all over the phone. We train the Bureau of Disability Determination staff and our staff. Our case managers gather all the paper work. They know how to do it, so there aren't many phone calls that need to go back and forth. Our doctors have already seen the people, so Disability doesn't have to hire a second doctor for assessments. They're saving money, and the clients are getting their checks faster. Social Security is thinking of using this as a national model.

We are funding a program in Cleveland called "Money In Mailboxes," which is the largest federal Community Support Program (CSP) demonstration grant for homeless

---

*This material was excerpted from a speech delivered by Linda Zelch, Deputy Director for Program Development for the Ohio Department of Mental Health, The University of Kansas Policy Conference: Mental Health Reform in Kansas–Possibilities and Descriptions, on November 17, 1989.

people in the country. The program works to put homeless people in permanent housing, takes the supports to them, and has case managers out on the streets. That program also employs consumers in a peer support role to work on the streets with the case managers.

"Chums and Choices" is a program in Dayton for elderly people. It works with elderly mentally ill people in setting up a network of volunteers who help elderly people achieve what they want in their lives. We have a CSP national demonstration project in Licking-Knox, which is a very rural county. They are looking at permanent housing and how to accomplish that. They have hired an econometrician from Wooster College to look at the economics of that sort of support.

We are most proud of our Robert Wood Johnson Foundation grants. We were awarded three of their nine national grants for systems change. Those have been our biggest laboratories for change in Columbus, Toledo, and Cincinnati. This year we were awarded one of the twelve Robert Wood Johnson Kid Systems Change Grants for Cleveland where we are working with the schools and with our children's clusters to do systems change. We were recently awarded a grant from the federal government to study the effects of the state's Mental Health Act.

We have been very successful in establishing permanent housing. We use our capital construction loans, which are forty-year, zero percent, nonamortized loans, as a match to attract other dollars. We have built and renovated additional housing using grant funds from the Robert Wood Johnson Foundation as a match, seed loan and development loan programs from the Ohio House Finance Agency, Section 8 housing funds, Community Development Block Grant funds, bank loans, McKinney Permanent Housing Funds, and HUD funds.

We began to develop jobs for people by taking $628,000 of our state subsidy line item and transferring it to the Rehabilitation Services Commission, which is responsible for vocational services. By transferring our money to the Commission, they are able to draw down 3.4 million dollars from the federal government for services that are earmarked specifically for severely mentally disabled people. Then we did a major cross-training effort between our staff and their staff, to teach them how to access those dollars on behalf of mentally ill people. We also used our matching dollars to establish grants with the Rehabilitation Services Commission for competitive and supportive employment programs and mental health centers.

Author's Note: There is probably no better example of maximizing federal dollars to improve client outcomes than the Ohio Department of Mental Health. For a fuller discussion of their financial strategies, please see Mental Health Reform in Kansas: Possibilities and Prescriptions, (Ed.) Ben Zimmerman, published by the University of Kansas School of Social Welfare.

## Laying the Foundation

*Whose Job Is It?* The acquisition of funds in human service agencies is most often the responsibility of the chief executive officer. In private organizations with budgets in excess of $500,000 there is often a resource development staff person or a development office. In public bureaucracies, there is usually a team of top-level administrators, under the direction of the chief executive officer, who have fund acquisition responsibilities. Some public agencies have specific positions designated to act as liaison to state legislatures and another to act as liaison to federal officials.

Although top-level management has the dominant responsibility for fund acquisition, lower-level managers can play varied and valuable roles. These could include uncovering possible sources of funds through their personal networks, identifying critical gaps in services, and suggesting new program ideas for which funds should be sought, organizing data and consumers to support arguments for funding, and working with advocacy organizations to insure consumer input into funding initiatives. All lower-level managers have the responsibility of obtaining sufficient funds for the operation of the domain (e.g., team, unit, program, or office) for which they are responsible. While the fund acquisition ideas and strategies included in this chapter are written from the perspective of the agency, many of them apply to lower-level managers seeking funds from their own agencies.

*The Resource Development Plan.* Along with designing the program and the development of a budget, it is important to create a plan for fund acquisition. The plan details what is to be done, who is responsible (volunteers and/or staff), and the date by which each fund raising task is to be accomplished. This plan may be prepared by development staff, if such people exist in the agency, or it may be done by the director. Table 5–1 is a sample fund raising plan.

Several decisions need to be made as a part of developing the fund raising plan:

1.  Will the organization fund-raise on an annual basis, or will it require only occasional fund raising efforts?
2.  Which fund raising components fit best with this agency's mission, program, volunteer abilities, and its presence in the community?
3.  Who in the organization has the contacts, the level of comfort, the commitment and the follow-through to work within the development effort?
4.  What amounts of money can this organization realistically raise, and still be able to do its work?

Once these questions are answered and expectations are clear, a development plan can be created for the organization. The plan needs to be flexible to take advantage of opportunities. For example, a health related organization developed a fund raising plan that included two special events, designed to produce a total of $20,000: a memorials program to which donors could give, to remember friends or family members, which would produce $3,000 during the year, and funding from foundations, corporations, and individuals that would produce $17,000. After this plan had been approved by the organization's board, the group was approached to be the recipient of a major holiday benefit in the community, which, in the previous year, had netted another organization $35,000. The fund raising committee reconsidered the organization's needs and its capacity to participate in this benefit—with volunteers, prospects, and other assistance—and reworked its plan.

The plan should also be realistic and give details about how and from who funds will be raised. An organization planned to raise $50,000 through a direct mail solicitation campaign. The plan was to target a list of well-known community givers and mail on expensive package to the prospective donor. The plan did not consider the small rate of return in the use of direct mail, nor the size of the list, or the interest

**TABLE 5-1. FUND RAISING PLAN—AIDS SERVICE ORGANIZATION**

Goal: To raise $225,000 in support of ASO

Strategies: ASO will seek funding from a variety of sources including: 1) at least fifteen local and three national foundations; 2) government funding from the Centers for Disease Control, the Department of Health and Human Services, the State, County and City; 3) a direct mail solicitation targeted at past and potential donors; and two special events.

| Activity | Responsible Person | Date |
|---|---|---|
| Preparation of foundation grant request—Community Foundation, Johnson, Block, Foyer, Ross | Exec. Director | 2/15/90 |
| Design letter for direct mail campaign, determine lists to use | Fund raising Committee | 3/01/90 |
| Submit request for state and city funding | Exec. Director | 3/15/90 |
| Direct mail to printer | Exec. Director | 4/01/90 |
| Contact volunteers for art auction | Fund Raising | 4/15/90 |
| Application for CDC funding | Exec. Director | 4/25/90 |
| Complete mailing of direct mail | Staff/volunteers | 5/01/90 |
| Art auction group meets | ED/volunteers | 5/02/90 |
| Plan for implementing auction | ED/Comm. Chr | 5/15/90 |
| Contacts with caterers/contracts for food completed | Staff/volunteers | 6/15/90 |
| Foundation requests—10 letters | ED/Board Chair | 6/15/90 |
| Dinner theatre tickets available | Teen staff/volunteers | 7/01/90 |
| Arrange reception for dinner theatre | Volunteers | 7/15/90 |
| Final arrangements/implement event | Staff/volunteers | 7/31/90 |
| Auction invitations to printer | Exec. Director | 9/15/90 |
| Address invitations | Volunteers | 10/15/90 |
| Invitations mailed | Staff | 11/10/90 |
| Final arrangements for Auction | Staff/volunteers | 11/25/90 |
| Implement Auction | Staff/volunteers | 12/10/90 |

of the giver. Although the plan indicated the campaign would be underwritten, it was begun without the underwriting. The result was that the campaign barely paid for itself. The plan was not realistic. The details of direct mail solicitation were not understood or attended to.

*Telling Your Story.* Once a plan is in place, the development of a case statement or proposal is the necessary next step to any fund raising process. In three to four pages, the case statement tells what the organization is, what it is doing (program), what it wants to do (its mission), and how it intends to do it (action plan). It presents the budget and fund raising goals and a written rationale for income and expense. This is provided to prospective donors along with an agency brochure, a determination letter from the Internal Revenue Service (showing your organization's tax exempt status), a recent news or feature article, and a list of the organization's board of directors. This packet is helpful for volunteers and agency staff, as well as for funders, and can be used in a variety of situations: training prospective volunteers and staff; seeking donated goods, services, and other resources in the community; soliciting gifts from foundations, corporations, or individual donors; and visiting with community or governmental leaders.

## Fund Sources and Mechanisms

There are four major mechanisms for funding human service organizations and programs: appropriations, grants and contracts, contributions, and fees.

*Appropriations.* Appropriations are the primary means for funding public organizations. A legislature allocates money from tax revenue. This money is then used to operate an organization and the services its provides. Since purchase of service contracts and grants between state agencies and community-based agencies, both public and private, are a principal source of funding, the nature and amount of appropriations to state agencies is of critical concern to these private human service organizations. The principal determinant of the amount of funding is a function of last year's budget. Most of the budget is a product of previous decisions. (Wildavsky, 1974) Beyond this, current economic climate, the presence of "headline" social issues and problems, the presence and activity of supportive coalitions and lobby groups, and the skill of the administrator can affect only the budget margins.

It is important for the social administrator to know the appropriate process and how to influence this process. The state level appropriations process varies between states but typically includes seven stages that are completed in -12 to -15 month cycles. The process begins in July with the governor submitting budgetary guidelines to each department. These guidelines are formulated based on state revenue projections (e.g., taxes, money in the state treasury, federal funds expected) and policies proffered by the governor. The guidelines require each state agency to submit a proposed budget within certain fiscal targets. These guidelines often require two or three alternative budgets to meet different scenarios: One budget requires the same amount of money as the current fiscal year; one budget with a 5 percent increase in expenditures and one with a 5 percent decrease in expenditures.

The second stage occurs in July and August when the state agencies design their budgets within the governor's guidelines. The agencies consider the cost of new policy initiatives, federal requirements, salary increments for employees, increased costs due to inflation, and so on. The third stage commences when these budgets are submitted to the governor. The governor devotes the next three months to modifying and selecting from these budgets and negotiating with each agency. As revenue projections become clearer, the budgets are modified accordingly. In December, the governor's proposed state budget is completed and printed.

The fourth stage typically begins when the governor presents the "state of the state" speech in January, which contains an outline of the budget recommendations and new policy initiatives. The budget then is assigned to the ways and means committee in the House of Representatives and the appropriations committee of the Senate. These committees, their various subcommittees, and other standing committees of the legislature study, debate, hear testimony, and revise the budgets. From the committees, it goes to the floor of the legislature for further debate and formal votes. Differences in the budgets passed by the two chambers are sent to conference committees to resolve differences. This stage usually lasts four months.

The budget that the legislature passes then gets forwarded to the governor. In many states the governor has a line-item veto power that allows the vetoing of specific lines in the budget. In other states, the governor can only approve or disapprove the entire document. Vetoes are returned to the legislature where a two-thirds majority is needed to override the governor. If overridden, the budget or line item becomes law. If not overridden, the line is changed to conform to the governor's wishes.

In May or June, the approved budget is sent to the state agencies for a July start date. Employee raises, hiring of staff or cutting back staff is planned for, and contracts and grants to private agencies occur.

The previous section is an abstract of a very complex, iterative process that varies in each state. The process does offer a host of decision points that can be influenced by the human service manager. This section will briefly describe several of these strategies and principles.

## Strategies for Political Influence

Personal and professional relationships with decision makers and influential people is often where influence begins. This includes legislators, members of the governor's staff, state agency officials, and legislative staffs. How frequently do you interact with them? Do they call on you for advice?

Special interest and advocacy groups are also part of this strategy. Are you a member of associations of similar programs? Do you play an active role? Are you a member or involved in client-based advocacy organizations? Do these associations and organizations have supportive relationships with each other and with other human service groups? Are coalitions who can speak with "one voice" formed around critical budget issues? Does the organization have a legislative platform? This area is critical because nothing dooms advocacy efforts in state legislatures quicker than lack of agreement among key constituent groups.

Political parties is another arena in your strategy. Not only does this foster contact with elected officials but it provides an opportunity for influencing party platforms, selection of candidates and for working on behalf of candidates (e.g., voter registration, contribution to candidates, campaigning). Once elected, candidates are increasingly accessible to people who have helped them get elected.

There are several ways to inform and put pressure on key decision makers. One is to present testimony before the legislative committees and provide the committee with information and data through brief reports and letters. If done in conjunction with coalitions and with relationships already established, the effect is likely to be greater. Writing letters to the editor of your local newspaper or sending letters directly to elected officials makes them aware of your and your supporters' concerns. Develop a block of voters who will be part of a letter writing campaign, sign petitions, or show up at a legislator's office. The message these people send is "If you want our vote, support our cause." The perceived size of the voter group, the perceived likelihood that they will vote, and the degree of perceived competition for the elected office are critical factors.

Someone needs to be involved in the appropriations process from initial budget preparation to bill signing. Who that is depends on available resources. If your organization belongs to a statewide coalition, you may be able to hire a professional lobbyist. Given enough time, the social administrator can have direct involvement. To have the desired effect, no part of the process can be ignored. The area of concern must be kept on the state agency's agenda as the departments prepare tentative budgets one to two years in advance of the legislative session.

The state agency's budget as proposed to the governor or budget bureau needs to be watched and influenced. The formal budget preparation process within the governor's office can be influenced. The budget bill in the state legislature begins with the governor's budget. Pressure from your interest group and local legislative representation can help fashion the bill. Every step of the legislative budget process can be influenced. In many states there is a legislative budget reconciliation process between the house and senate versions of the budget. One of the authors participated in an early morning (1:00 AM) budget reconciliation committee meeting where top leaders of both houses and parties traded millions of dollars in disputed amendments to forge a budget agreement. Many budget enhancements can and have occurred at this time. A request of $100,000 can be included and overlooked in a $2 billion budget. Of course, the budget reconciliation agreement is still subject to approval by both houses and ultimately the governor's pen.

*Grants and Contracts.* A second funding mechanism is through grants and contracts.

> The essential difference is that . . . contracts spell out more clearly and in greater detail the requirements of the program of work to be conducted under the grant. While a grant might call for a "demonstration of the effectiveness of casework in public housing," a comparable performance contract might specify the delivery of 1,000 hours of casework to 250 clients during the ninety day period. (Lohman, 1980, p. 63)

Grants and contracts can be awarded from state, local, or federal sources as well as private foundations. Grants are often designed to provide seed money for one to three years at which time grant supported activities would need to be funded in other ways if they are to continue. Successful acquisition of grants requires a knowledge of diverse funding sources and highly developed skills in program design.

Despite deficits and cutbacks, government remains a major source of funds. Obtaining these funds needs careful consideration and decision making. Meeting government standards may mean changing the program, adapting the goals to fit the government agency. Is the organization willing to change its goals, its programs? How important is that funding? What kind of constraints would there be on the organization that does succeed in getting a grant or contract? Before we consider these questions you want to know where to find all that money.

To get a glimpse of one state agency's successful exploiting of federal and private grant opportunities, see the case example about the Ohio Department of Mental Health on page 198.

*Read* The Federal Register. *The Federal Register* is the weekly document presenting all federal legislation and appropriations. It is in the library or you can get a subscription. Use this consistently if a considerable portion of the organization's finances are from federal contracts and grants. Since *The Federal Register* publishes thousands of pages each month, the cost and time involved in reading or even skimming this publication is great. You can conserve reading time by being aware that certain announcements appear at predictable times during the year. By using your network of contacts, you can be alerted to the relevant announcements.

People within the network may be competing for the same pots of money, but if they can see it as competition against another section of the country rather than against each other everyone may benefit. The more you can inform others about announcements the more they are likely to inform you. The more proposals generated, the more likely your community will get its fair share.

*Get on your state's mailing list for contracts in specific program areas.* You will then receive a Request for Proposal (RFP) any time funds are available in that area. Some states have better mailing list systems than others and these systems can change quickly. It is not at all unusual for different state agencies or even departments within the same agency to maintain different lists. Occasionally getting included on the list becomes a political question. You need to keep after this with continued contacts and inquiries both with the relevant agency and with administrators of programs similar to yours.

*Become acquainted with local representatives of federal, state, and city programs.* The regional administrative staff of the Department of Health and Human Services regularly calls upon a group of local social service providers when a grant is to be let; she knows what they are doing and the areas in which they could work together. An AIDS service organization works closely with the state and the city's Department of Health and has convinced staff of the need for additional resources from both departments. A great deal of work was done by the local agency so that the new grants would be forthcoming.

*Read the grant or contract application carefully.* Be realistic in your planning and be sure that you can accomplish what is required within the given time lines and the budget restrictions. If the budget requires a matching dollar amount, are there other resources to meet the match? Finally, plan to spend three weeks of intense time in the preparation of the proposal (if you have that much notice).

Competition for most grants is fierce. The agencies who are most successful combine well-developed grant writing skills with many attempts. They simply write more grant applications. Inevitably, the agencies that acquire the most grant awards are the ones with the most grant failures. As Peters and Waterman (1982) wrote:

> Several years ago, we studied the successful versus the less successful wildcatters in the oil business. We concluded that if you had the best geologists, the latest in geophysical technique, the most sophisticated equipment, and so on, the success rate in wildcat drilling in established fields would amount to about 15 percent. Without all these pluses, the success ratio dips to around 13 percent. That finding suggests that the denominator—the number of tries—counts for a great deal. Indeed, an analysis of Amoco, recently revitalized to become the top U.S. domestic oil finder, suggests just one success factor: *Amoco simply drills more wells.* The company's head of production, George Galloway, says, "Most favorable results were unforeseen by us or anybody else. . . . That happens *if* you drill a lot of wells." (p. 141)

We have come to call this the Pete Rose Principle of Management. Pete Rose is well known for having achieved the most career hits in baseball history. What is less recognized is that Rose also had the most at-bats (attempts) and has made the most outs in baseball history. In many facets of human service management, including competing for grants, the number of at-bats is more important than the batting average.

*Consider participating in established programs that might fit your organization.* Your program or organization might fit guidelines for the Job Training Partnership Act, through local Private Industry Councils, or for the Carl Perkins Vocational Training monies, through local school districts or through your state. You might collaborate on federally funded projects through community colleges or four year educational institutions. If you run child care programs or train child care providers, your organization could become a Child Care Food Program Sponsor. If these arrangements interest you, talk with city or state employees in departments which match your organization and find out about the opportunities for funding.

*Be prepared and follow up.* The *record keeping,* the *paperwork,* and the *reporting* are *critical pieces following the award* of the contracts. Establish plans early for preparing these materials to meet deadlines. If you were counting on this grant to assist with cash flow, ask about payment—length of time required, increments, and advances. Few things will get programs in trouble quicker than not filing reports as required or not using funds as budgeted. Needless to say, you must read all of the requirements of the contract and follow them. The program might be producing the greatest positive benefit for clients and be closed due to failure to follow fiscal contractual obligations. For many state and all federal contracts, there are lengthy regulations regulating purchasing, subcontracting, and so on. The social administrator may not understand all of them, but he or she will be held responsible for all of them. Hire consultants where needed. One program that was having difficulty with fiscal matters hired an outside accounting firm to take care of all check writing, fiscal controls, and federal fiscal reports. Nothing was questioned in any subsequent audit.

*Contributions.*  A third funding mechanism is contributions. Contributions involve soliciting private giving from individuals or organizations. President Reagan envisioned contributions as replacing cuts in welfare programs proposed by his administration. In reality, private giving remains a fraction of total human service funds. Contributions range from small donations to multi-million dollar endowments requiring the use of investment managers. Management activities include special fund raising events, phone or door-to-door canvassing, computer-based donor lists, and special requests of corporations. Fund raising campaigns are extremely costly in terms of time and money, and realistic projections of possible donations are therefore required before undertaking such an endeavor.

Contributions from local individuals and philanthropic organizations have long been a major source of funds for social services. Over the years this area, like all others has changed and continues to change. These changes include a decreased proportion of overall social services funding coming from these sources and an increased professionalization of the funding mechanisms used by these sources. For example, the United Way and Foundations use contracts rather than undesignated contributions. Despite the blurred boundaries, this section will include what the social administrator needs to do to obtain funds from foundations and corporations, United Way's individual gifts, and special events.

*Soliciting from foundations and corporations is a traditional and comfortable fund raising strategy for many groups.* Foundation-giving amounts to 6 percent of private giving, while corporations provided 5 percent of the total donated dollar. In 1987, this amounted to more than $8 billion. The largest gifts went to educational and arts organizations, but social service organizations shared quite generously, receiving more than 30 percent of their funding from these sources and from individual contributions. (*Giving U.S.A.,* 1988).

There are four types of foundations:

1. *Independent or family foundations.* Funds for these foundations is from a family or group of individuals. Funds are given to religious, educational, social, or other charitable organizations according to the foundation

interests. A board of directors, perhaps constituted of family members or friends, makes donor decisions.

2. *Corporate foundations.* Corporations make annual contributions from profits to their own foundations. Funds are given according to concerns of the foundation and governance is by a board of directors containing corporate people and/or community individuals. Some companies have local giving committees.

3. *Operating foundations.* These foundations use their resources to fund programs of the parent organization. For example, the Metropolitan Community College Foundation funds projects at the community college.

4. *Community foundations.* These are publicly supported foundations that hold funds for several trusts and small family foundations. These foundations make disbursements in accordance with donor guidelines and interests. There may be boards of directors or committees for each of the trusts, and a larger board that represents the diversity of the community. Some community foundations act as money managers and fund solicitors for groups of not-for-profit agencies. An agency can deposit its small endowment with the foundation and receive the benefit of larger returns due to pooling of funds and professional management. Many of these foundations also solicit funds for a core endowment. The income is then distributed among member organizations according to agreed-upon rules.

You can learn about the giving practices of foundations in your community by being alert to newsletters of other organizations, reading the charitable news in business newspapers, talking to peers, and paying attention to names of business leaders who are acknowledged and celebrated for their community service. Corporations are also well known for making in-kind gifts—the Apple Corporation donates computers, Hallmark donates many of its products to organizations in the Kansas City, Missouri, area.

Both *foundation and corporate solicitation* depend upon careful research. Development staff, volunteers and the director or other staff can be involved in this research. Several steps are involved:

*Everyone involved must be familiar with the agency, its programs, services, capabilities, and plans for the future.* Everyone must be able to define goals, objectives, program target populations, expected outcomes, impact of the organization and its programs, and special qualifications of staff and the organization for its programs. Understanding the budget and being able to define the role of foundation or corporate funding in the overall agency plan is essential. All of this information forms the basis of a foundation or corporate proposal for a specific program or for funding the organization as an entity.

*Donor research can be done formally and informally.* The informal approach is to talk with other, similar not-for-profit agencies and find out who is providing their funding, to whom they have applied, and what the responses have been. Determine who the corporate leaders are in the community, what their interests are, the issues they are concerned about, and who within your organization's leaders or supporters knows them and would be willing to approach them.

The formal approach is to determine if there is a Foundation Center reference collection or a member of the Foundation Center Network—a Cooperating Collection close to you. The Foundation Center was established by foundations to provide authoritative information about private philanthropic giving. (Read, 1986) The network operates through public libraries, nonprofit organizations, and community foundations to provide this information.

A visit to one of the libraries or offices of the Center offers excellent resources to assist you in your research. Most of the network members have collections of private foundation information returns (IRS Form 990-PF) for your view. These returns will tell you how much money the foundation gave away in a specific year (they are usually two years behind the current year), organizations to whom the foundation gave, its officers' and board members' names, and addresses to write for more information. In addition to the returns, many of the centers have giving analyses available by name of foundation or type of program. The centers will have information about national and local foundations, with national information limited to larger foundations. They also will have information about corporate donors, particularly large corporations known for their private giving, or corporations that have their own foundations. Finally, the Foundation Center produces many of its own publications that are an aid to research. Other reference works on funding include:

- *The Foundation Directory* uses COMSEARCH printouts that are issued in four categories: recent grants by broad subject area (24 of them), special focused subject area (65 of them), geograpahic area, and by special topics (foundation assets, annual grants of largest foundations, etc.).
- *Foundation Grants Index Annual* lists grants of $5,000 or more from about 450 foundations. The Foundation Grants Index BiMonthly gives current fund raising information.
- *National Databook* lists 24,000 active grant-making foundations in the U.S.
- *Corporate Foundation Profiles* is a comprehensive analyses of 250 of the largest corporate foundations and summary analyses of 475 others. While this information on national corporations and foundations will be enormously helpful, the network collections will have local resources as well. Many organizations have developed local fund raising guides, listings of local and regional foundations and socially active corporations. Resource librarians will also be extremely helpful in directing you to the information you need. The Foundation Center provides a toll free number (800–424–9836) for information regarding its services, local network member locations, and its publications.

Once you have defined some broad prospects, usually by subject interest area, geographical distribution area, or by the type of support the foundation might give, it is important to review the informal information and include that in your planning. This should allow you to focus your prospect list and to be more aware of the real possibilities of funding.

The research effort is time-consuming and entails much work. It also requires good record keeping. Forms or a computer database for recording information about foundations should be developed by the organization, and should be used consistently. These should be updated when new information is available and used for both informal and formal research.

As the prospect list is narrowed, additional information should be gathered about foundation and corporate application requirements, time lines, and other submission requirements. Some foundation boards meet only once or twice each year and if you have missed a deadline, it would not be worthwhile to submit an application until the next review period. Also, it is important to submit appropriate materials, especially if a foundation requires a specific application package.

*Decide which foundations and corporations would be most responsive to your request.* Generally, you can count on a 30 to 50 percent rate of return, depending upon these factors

- What is your organization's reputation? How well known are you?
- How critical to the community do people perceive your program/issue being?
- What is your organization's previous experience with the foundation donor?
- Who in your organization knows people in the foundation or corporation?

Remember: foundations look at programs and organizations that work on problems of interest to them and at organizations that have demonstrated success and expertise and that can replicate their programs in other locations or can demonstrate collaboration with other agencies.

*Preparation of a proposal allows you to specify your needs and your knowledge of the issues involved in responding to those needs.* Proposal formats vary widely, and the funder may specify a format. If no format is specified, the following may be a useful guideline:

1. *Introduction.* This describes your agency. It tells your organization's history and how familiar you are with the need area, and describes the administrative capabilities and previous experiences. The organization's mission statement should appear in this section.
2. *Problem description.* The problem description section of the program design is included here (see Chapter 2). Identify the population affected and whom you are targeting for service. Indicate an awareness of other programs designed to deal with the problem and their results.

3. *Goals and objectives.* State what you want to accomplish. The goals and objectives section of the program design is useful for this section (see Chapter 2).
4. *Implementation plan.* This is an action plan that gives specific details of what your organization will do, who will do it, and in what time frame.
5. *Evaluation plan.* This describes the mechanisms to be used to monitor the implementation of the program and to evaluate whether or not the goals have been achieved.

*Prepare a cover letter that describes the program and the request in general and asks for a specific grant amount.* The letter is signed by the organization's chief executive officer or board chairperson and is sent on the organization's letterhead with the proposal. Most importantly, the letter sets a follow-up date. For example, "Susan Green, our director, will call you on December 1 to answer any questions about our request, or you may feel free to contact us with your questions at (817) 299-4000."

*Follow up contact with the chief executive.* The development staff member or a volunteer makes the follow-up call. Some foundations prefer not to be contacted once they receive a proposal, but they usually inform you if that is their preference. During the call, it is appropriate to invite foundation staff or directors, or corporate representatives to visit your program site. You may also ask to meet with their staff or board members.

If you are refused (not an uncommon phenomenon since foundations are asked for much more money than they can disburse), contact the foundation about other assistance, ask again during their next funding cycle, and don't give up.

Funding is only the beginning of your relationship with the foundation. It is extremely important to stay in touch on a regular basis, with reports, timely information, and invitations to visit. Once you have developed a relationship with a foundation, it can provide a significant resource to the agency. When one grant ends, another can be requested with the confidence that a first-time asker cannot possibly muster.

*For-Profit Subsidiaries.* The Children's Museum of Denver introduced the idea that you could make your own money to help support your agency. The museum marketed its expertise in designing activities and games for children. Profits from the design business built a bigger, more wonderful museum for the city's children. Nonprofit organizations have also formed subsidiaries that provide employee assistance services (e.g., substance abuse treatment, marital counseling) to corporations at rates above cost. The "profit" is used to subsidize the nonprofit's basic services. In one case, a fast food franchise was purchased and then donated to a nonprofit human service organization that used the franchise to employ clients and to apply the profit to other services. In fact, a particular strength embedded in this approach is the opportunity to create jobs and job training for human service clientele. For-profit subsidiaries of nonprofit organizations have developed thrift shops, set up training and development sidelines, and used their entrepreneurial spirits to support clients in many creative ways. This is a funding option, but proceed carefully.

The Internal Revenue Service is also interested in these money-making schemes. Many for-profit subsidiaries raise tax questions. Knowledgeable attorneys and accountants need to be brought into the discussion early when such ventures are being considered. Watch out, too, for political fallout. The restaurant owner who was a state senator did not listen sympathetically to the lobbying interests of the executive director whose agency operated a for-profit lunch counter.

Choosing the business is a difficult decision. The organization should look at its strengths and at its needs. It also should look at the marketplace and at the experience of other entrepreneurs. You could check out the business "incubators" in the community. These groups provide technical assistance and business start-up assistance. Their staff helps in the development of business plans and consults in risk planning.

You also have to carefully consider who will run the business. Will you be the one in charge? Can you hire a consultant, enlist the help of volunteers, or will other staff be assigned? What happens to other responsibilities while this is being studied or developed?

Financing for business ventures must also be carefully planned. Funding for such ventures cannot be considered a threat to ongoing funding for programs. The agency must be in an excellent cash position to consider a project of this scope and have the ability to secure financing from local banks or friends. Undercapitalization (insufficient cash) may be the leading cause of small business failure. Some business ventures have been donated to agencies—remember those individual donors we discussed earlier.

*United Way Participation.* For many health and social service organizations, United Way provides another cornerstone to funding. United Way funds all of the major national youth organizations, the American Red Cross, family service agencies, some national health agencies, and many newer local agencies meeting specific community needs. Should an agency determine to become a member agency with United Way, there are several tasks to be considered.

*The rules for entry.* What does it take to get in? Most United Ways have a specific procedure and deadlines for new agencies or new programs. It frequently requires "proving" yourself, agency, or program for several years before you are accepted. The United Way represents the mainstream of the community. To become accepted you need to become part of that mainstream, which requires time and persistence.

*Policies for participation.* Once an agency is a member, there are requirements to be met for accountability, reporting, submission of financial audits, agency evaluations, and United Way campaign participation. In addition, United Ways may apply fund raising restrictions to members. Some are as lenient as only restricting activities during the campaign; others allow no corporate solicitation at all, and limit additional fund raising activities as well.

*Funding priorities.* Some United Way offices fund programs that they have determined to be a priority need in the community. If your organization's programs are not within those priority areas, they will not be funded, or funding will be low. In addition, the United Way may only fund by program area, and if you need assistance with overall organization funding, it might be difficult to fit the scheme used by the United Way.

*Understanding the evaluation and decision-making process.* In some United Ways, a group or groups of community people visit the agencies, are given materials that the agencies have prepared, and then they decide the level of funding. In other United Ways, staff makes the decision or there is a very closed process. It is important to know how those decisions are made because that information could influence your decision about participation. Finally, an organization might be concerned about United Way's commitment in the community. Do United Way staff and volunteers represent the community? Is there a commitment to funding new and innovative programs in addition to the community's long-standing programs? How will the new agency fit into the ongoing services funded by the United Way? If the United Way is a major source of funds for your agency or program, there is no substitute for knowing all you can about their policies, procedures, and priorities. Since you are also a member of the same community, you will want to influence these policies, procedures, and priorities. The degree to which you, your staff, volunteers, and board are involved in all levels of the United Way is critical.

**Individual Gifts/Annual Giving.** The development of a donor list, comprised of individuals is often the cornerstone of fund raising for many organizations. Those who comprise an organization's individual donors are the family, the folks upon whom you can count. How do you find them? How do you get them to give?

*Phonathons/telethons.* Board members, volunteers, program alumnae, service club members willing to help out, and others gather together and use donated telephones to call supporters and would-be supporters, to increase membership or fund raise. A battered women's shelter raised $25,000 in supporting memberships through a well-planned telephone campaign. Telephones in an insurance agency office were donated for a month. Several service clubs, volunteers of the program, and board members staffed the phones four evenings each week. The program's director obtained lists of potential donors, previous members, and friends of the organization. A script was prepared for callers who were also provided refreshments. The event was fun and productive. The list of new supporting members was then used as the basis for two direct-mail solicitations. These were conducted six months and one year later with good success each time.

Telethons, which are televised appeals for funds, are generally more expensive to operate and require a great deal of advance planning, entertainment, and volunteers. But when they are done well, they produce excellent results. The Variety Club in one city conducts a telethon for several children's charities. The Club has built support in the community through the participating organizations and their friends, and the telethon is only one event of many intended to support the Club's efforts. Telethons can also succeed when there are local segments of national events, such as the Muscular Dystrophy or United Cerebral Palsy telethons.

*Members/friends.* Many nonprofits have established categories of membership that cost far more than the regular cost of a membership, or they create friends groups that support the organization. The recruitment of these special supporters may be done through mailings to selected lists or to previous members and past individual donors to the organization. When used as part of an overall fund raising strategy, these supporting groups can raise substantial funds for an organization. The supporting and contributing members of one YWCA fund scholarships for teen members. The supporters of a child abuse prevention program commissioned a series of posters that have been sold to generate more than $50,000 in income for the organization.

*Direct mail.* There is much to be said about the use of mailed solicitations to prospective donors; in fact, there have been volumes written about it. Before embarking on a direct-mail campaign, consider that it often requires several attempts at direct mail to establish profitability. Be prepared to barely cover costs or even lose money during a first attempt. Be aware of the rate of return you will need in order to break even and to make money from the solicitation. If your list is a good one in terms of your cause being of interest to the recipient, many on the list are prior donors, and the audience knows and likes the organization, expect no more than a 7 to 10 percent return on your first mailing. If you purchased a list and there are few, if any, relationships between the list and your organization, prepare for a 1 to 3 percent return.

If you can afford it, get help from a consultant or community resource familiar with direct mail solicitation. Contents, preparation, and mailing are time consuming, and there are companies with expertise—and maybe willing to donate their services. The contents of the package should include a letter describing the organization and presenting its case, a brochure about the organization, and a stamped self-addressed envelope which identifies the donor and provides information about categories of support. If a donor can be found to donate the package and mailing costs, every dollar raised is profit. Some foundations fund such efforts because the establishment of a worthwhile individual donor list is a significant step for an organization.

The lists used for solicitation are extremely important. The more related the list to your cause, the more likely you are to receive funds from that list. A Boys Club organization used lists of members of men's clubs and university clubs for a solicitation, which talked of the benefits of club membership and the special significance of the Boys Club in a young man's life. The letter was signed by a socially prominent, highly successful business man. The Boys Club received a 10 percent response rate, with gifts ranging in size from $25 to $1,000, and their leaders considered the solicitation a success.

Timing of the mailing is of great consequence. Many agencies that use direct mail plan a solicitation at mid-year and at the end of the calendar year. It is important that your organization's mailing stand out from the rest, so consideration should be given to a schedule that is different from what others use.

When mailing the appeal, use first class postage, if possible. If you are using a third class bulk mailing permit, use the postage stamp made for that purpose, rather than the not-for-profit stamp containing the permit number. Prospective donors are far more likely to pay attention. First class also buys you either forwarding or a return if the person has moved. This can be an important mechanism for keeping a list up to date.

*Annual giving.* Did you think that you do all of this work only once? The answer is, of course not. The primary reason for building an individual donor list is that it provides opportunities for renewed giving, larger gifts, and special campaigns. A fund raising plan includes a timetable for solicitation of individual gifts, carefully considered to coincide with organizational marketing and other community relations activities. In addition, a record-keeping system must be in place, so that gifts are tracked, acknowledgements are sent and donors are otherwise appreciated as often as they are asked for gifts.

**Special Event Fund Raising.** Last year a local chapter of the American Cancer Society raised $125,000 through an auction, Big Brothers and Big Sisters raised well over $100,000 in its bowlathon, and the Boys Club raised $65,000 through its Steak and Hamburger Dinner (the corporate executives get the hamburgers; the kids get the steaks). All of these and many other special fund raising events in one metropolitan area prove there is still much money to be made. All that is required is a wonderfully clever idea, hundreds of volunteers, sufficient time for planning and implementation of the event, and a great deal of luck. Issues to consider include:

*Time.* Do you have the time to produce the event? The planning of a special event takes a great deal of time, and an astute awareness of community preferences for events, seasons, and dates. The most successful large-scale events are planned for several months, or even the entire year, with pre-event parties and gatherings and much fanfare.

*Staffing.* Do you have the staff to produce the event? Can you hire a consultant, or does the organization have sufficient volunteers to manage the event? If you and your staff assume responsibilities, how much time will be taken away from program or other agency concerns? Special events are very time consuming and have the potential of costing more than they produce.

*Owning it.* The more community involvement in the event, the more likely it is to succeed. Those bowlers for Big Brothers and Big Sisters are people who like to bowl, not necessarily people who care about the organization. But they like the event, and they get involved and pay the fees.

*Creative thinking.* New ideas are not only welcome, they are a necessity. The fashion show featuring 100 years of women's swimwear might work for the YWCA's 100th birthday, but it wouldn't attract an audience for the Comprehensive Health Center.

Is your community's calendar overcrowded? Are your volunteers overtired, overworked, and overwhelmed? Do you have other needs calling to you and no time to plan for a fund raising event? Consider blanketing your community with invitations for a night at home, in front of the TV. A local chapter of the American Red Cross raised almost $10,000 this way, with far less energy and expense than a dinner and reception would have required.

*The invitation list.* Remember all those donor records you have been keeping and those lists you have been collecting? This is the time to use them. But remember, they must also tap special audiences. Golfers may not be well represented in your mailing list. For a charitable golfing event you will need to supplement your list with golfers.

*Specific marketing needs.* No matter what other public relations plans the agency has, the event will take precedence. Marketing needs to begin about three months before the event. These responsibilities can seem overwhelming, therefore, organization and detailed planning are musts.

*Paying for it.* Many organizations ask corporations to underwrite the event, particularly for the first year. Others are able to secure donations for design and printing of invitations and other front-end costs, so that the event supports only its direct costs and the remainder is profit. Some organizations collaborate on special events, sharing the expense, the invitation list, and the profits.

**Fee for Service.** A fourth source of funds are through fee for services rendered.

> When these fees are charged to individual clients, they are often based on sliding scales, with individuals paying differing amounts depending on their financial status (ability to pay). Frequently, fees are paid not by consumers themselves, but by outside organizations, or third parties. Third-party payments can come from insurance companies, Medicare, public agencies purchasing services for clients, or other sources. (Lewis & Lewis, 1983, p. 61)

Service fees from third parties (e.g., private insurance, medicare, medicaid) is a major source of funding for health and mental health services. Consequences of this type of funding may restrict or regulate what kind of service is delivered by whom and for how long are required in order to be reimbursed. Agencies that rely heavily on these fees also tend to eschew the use of indirect services, which cannot be reimbursed (e.g., work with collaterals, public education and consultation, advocacy) and to avoid in-home, in-community client contacts in favor of office-bound settings. This latter consequence is critically important since in-home or outreach services in several fields (e.g., mental health, child welfare) have demonstrably superior results to in-office interventions. To remove nonreimbursable travel time, many agencies demand office-bound interventions. As these dilemmas suggest, management activities would require careful bookkeeping systems, establishment of a sliding fee scale for clients, and constant work with third party reimbursers to influence their regulations to be consonant with what is best for the agency's clients and to set rates at adequate levels.

Fee for service is based on the concept that someone pays for each unit of services consumed. The client may pay the entire cost or only a portion through a mechanism like a sliding fee scale or a copayment. A separate funding source like the state department of mental health may pay through sources such as medicaid. When engaging in fee for service reimbursement, it is critical to determine unit costs. If fee for service is a major portion of your budget, it may pay to contract with an accountant to determine the cost of a unit of service. States that reimburse through fee for service set rates at the state level, which may or may not cover your costs. Rate setting is a constant debate within states and another target for influencing skills.

Through the preparation of the expense budget, managers are able to determine the cost of an individual unit of service. The computation of budget information for determining fees for service depends on the type of budget. Budgets frequently have a section for direct costs and a section for indirect costs. Direct costs include such elements as personnel, telephone, and travel, all directly related to the program. Indirect costs include bookkeeping, agency insurance coverage, and legal fees, which are all used to support all of the programs of the agency. A portion of these indirect costs supports each individual program. The distinction between direct and indirect costs depends on the particular method of accounting. The federal government has very particular rules for indirect cost accounting. Fees for service based upon all costs will keep a program operating. Fees for service based only upon part of the costs will need to be augmented by other fund raising events.

Here are a few considerations in thinking about establishing unit costs for fees for service.

1.  What is the unit of service? Is a unit one hour with a counselor, or is it that hour and six months of follow-up services? Does the unit include travel or record-keeping time?
2.  What indirect costs are included? Should a percentage of mailing and

telephone costs be considered part of the unit, or should our definition be very narrow and include only the direct service?

3. How can it be accurately determined what the number of clients will be? Estimates based upon past experience, future projections, or knowledge of the population you are targeting can be used. Projects that overestimate the number of clients may not produce enough revenue to cover salaries.

4. What value has the unit cost determination for us? If the cost is to be used for establishing program service fees, very careful consideration must be given to assuring that all expenses that relate to that unit cost are included when it is determined. If our plan requires that we compare unit costs for several years, it is important that those expenses included in determining unit costs are the same for each year.

Unit costs are most often used to establish fees for service. Once one knows the cost of a unit of service, it is not difficult to develop a set of guidelines for fees, to be used with funders, clients, and grantsmakers. As an example, the counseling program in our AIDS Services Organization has a total expense of $100,450. It is expected to serve 200 clients in the coming year. Thus, a simple unit cost would be total cost ($100,450)/number of clients (200). In this case, the unit cost would be $502.25 for the year. If you wanted information about an hour of service, you would have to determine the total number of hours the services were available and divide the cost by the number of hours ($100,450/2,080); in this case, the hourly cost is $48.29.

## ALLOCATION OF FUNDS: BUDGETING

The budget is the document that allocates funds within an organization. Management writers and consultants are wont to describe the budget as a primary management "tool" for controlling the organization. Without negating its obvious role as a boundary setter and control mechanism, the performance manager can see the budget as a primary tool for increasing performance. This means that the budget and the process that leads to its creation must be guided by three principles:

1. The budget acts as a vehicle for provoking a review of current performance and strategies for increasing performance.
2. The budget gives prominence to a particular form of efficiency: the proportion of money being devoted to those activities with the most direct link to client benefits.
3. The final budget should be based on and tested against its ability to increase performance.

This section will describe the major budgeting methods and evaluate them against these three principles.

## Types of Budgets

*Line Item Budget.* The most basic and frequently used budget method is the line item budget (Table 5–2). A line reflects the amount of money to be spent on a particular expense category for the organization and the amount currently spent. The principles of line item budgeting serve as a foundation for all other forms of budgeting. The major advantage of line item budgeting is simplicity and expenditure control. The categories are limited and fixed over time, and increases and decreases projected in any given line are usually determined as a small increment of current patterns. Stretch (1980) summarizes the benefits for management control:

> One of the major strengths of the line budget approach is that it provides management with the capacity to have a very precise degree of control over authorized expenditures by specifying the line item categories and their respective amounts explicitly authorized by the budget. Formal authorization to exceed allocated amounts is required. Thus, a high degree of management fiscal control is exercised. (p. 90)

For the performance manager, line item budgets are inadequate tools. First, they provide no basis for comparing program costs with administrative costs, and therefore an important efficiency measure is beyond the reach of the manager. Second, line item budgets encourage stagnant programs. Since there is no outside criterion present for the budget decisions, managers tend to use a small increment larger than current spending levels as the proposed expenditures and the proportion between line items tends to remain the same. Third, there is simply no way to link expenditures to performance as a basis for evaluation or decision making. In short, the line item budget acts as a subversion rather than as a stimulant to creativity and enhanced performance.

*Functional Budget.* While the basic information contained in a line item budget will be evident in the subsequent techniques, each will go beyond this primitive format. Functional budgeting separates two major categories of organizational expenditures: those for program services and supporting or administrative services (Table 5–3). The strength of functional budgeting is to allow the manager to assess the proportion of funds being assigned to these two major functions and thereby develop an approximate measure of efficiency. Again, while an agency can underspend in supportive services to the detriment of clients, personnel, and the agency, as a general proposition the goal is to get as much money into program services as possible. The strategy here is to instigate savings in administrative services.

For the performance manager the functional budget is more helpful than a simple line item budget, but it remains quite limited. The functional budget does not provide a direct link between resources and performance, and therefore represses consideration of strategies, and an assessment of current performance.

**TABLE 5–2. LINE ITEM AGENCY BUDGET**

| 1990 REVENUE | |
|---|---:|
| Contributions | $ 60,000 |
| Grants | |
|    Foundations | 63,000 |
|    Government | 55,000 |
| Special Projects | 25,000 |
| Churches | 15,000 |
| United Way | 30,000 |
| Estates/Memorials | 9,000 |
| Training Fees | 8,000 |
| Merchandise/Salables | 7,000 |
| Interest Income | 2,000 |
| TOTAL REVENUE | $274,000 |
| | |
| 1990 EXPENSE | |
| Personnel | |
|    Salaries | $137,000 |
|    Fringe @ 20% | 31,900 |
| Nonpersonnel | |
|    Professional Fees | 7,000 |
|    Rent | 21,000 |
|    Utilities | 6,500 |
|    Telephone | 4,300 |
|    Supplies | |
|       Office | 3,700 |
|       Program | 8,000 |
|    Small Equipment | 1,800 |
|    Equipment Repairs/Maintenance | 1,800 |
|    Postage | 6,000 |
|    Printing | 10,000 |
|    Staff Development | 5,500 |
|    Publications | 1,800 |
|    Volunteer Training | 3,250 |
|    Travel/Mileage/Parking | 5,500 |
|    Insurance | 7,500 |
|    Promotion | 4,000 |
| TOTAL EXPENSE | $271,500 |

*Zero-Based Budget.* This form of budgeting seeks to link productivity and costs through the creation of decision packages. The procedure requires the manager to start with a base of zero dollars, to analyze and develop alternatives for the next project period, and to assign resources to each level of productivity. See Table 5–4 for an example. Once the decision packages are constructed, managers have before them much of the data to make meaningful programmatic decisions. Zero-based budgeting is particularly strong in helping avoid knee-jerk incremental budgeting and by linking resources to productivity. Its weaknesses are in linking client outcomes to resources because there isn't sufficient knowledge in the field. This budgeting process is also extremely expensive. As Stretch (1980) notes, "costs are the considerable amount of staff and executive time required, plus possible severe

**TABLE 5–3. FUNCTIONAL BUDGET AIDS SERVICES ORGANIZATION**

| | Program Services | | Supporting Services | |
| --- | --- | --- | --- | --- |
| | Teens | Counseling/ Support | Mgt. & Gen./ Fund-Raising | Total |
| **1990 REVENUE** | | | | |
| Contributions | $ 30,000 | $ 20,000 | $10,000 | $ 60,000 |
| Grants | | | | |
| Foundations | 30,000 | 25,000 | 8,000 | 63,000 |
| Government | 35,000 | 20,000 | | 55,000 |
| Special Projects | 15,000 | 7,500 | 2,500 | 25,000 |
| Churches | 5,000 | 8,000 | 2,000 | 15,000 |
| United Way | 12,500 | 12,500 | 5,000 | 30,000 |
| Estates/Memorials | 4,000 | 5,000 | | 9,000 |
| Training Fees | 8,000 | | | 8,000 |
| Merchandise/Salables | 3,000 | 3,000 | 1,000 | 7,000 |
| Interest Income | 500 | 500 | 1,000 | 2,000 |
| TOTAL REVENUE | $143,000 | $101,500 | $29,500 | $274,000 |
| **1990 EXPENSE** | | | | |
| Personnel | | | | |
| Salaries | $ 72,000 | $ 50,000 | $15,000 | $137,000 |
| Fringe @ 20% | 14,400 | 10,000 | 7,500 | 31,900 |
| Nonpersonnel | | | | |
| Professional Fees | 4,000 | 3,000 | | 7,000 |
| Rent | 12,000 | 6,000 | 3,000 | 21,000 |
| Utilities | 4,000 | 2,000 | 500 | 6,500 |
| Telephone | 5,000 | 3,500 | 800 | 9,300 |
| Supplies | | | | |
| Office | 2,000 | 1,000 | 700 | 3,700 |
| Program | 5,000 | 3,000 | | 8,000 |
| Small Equipment | 500 | 800 | 500 | 1,800 |
| Equip. Repairs/ maintenance | 750 | 750 | 300 | 1,800 |
| Postage | 3,000 | 2,000 | 1,000 | 6,000 |
| Printing | 5,000 | 4,000 | 1,000 | 10,000 |
| Staff Development | 2,500 | 3,000 | | 5,500 |
| Publications | 800 | 900 | 100 | 1,800 |
| Volunteer Training | 1,250 | 2,000 | | 3,250 |
| Travel/mileage/park. | 1,500 | 3,500 | 500 | 5,500 |
| Insurance | 4,000 | 3,000 | 500 | 7,500 |
| Promotion | 2,000 | 2,000 | | 4,000 |
| TOTAL EXPENSE | $139,700 | $100,450 | $31,400 | $271,550 |

disruptions to staff routine and the questioning of basic commitments with possible large-scale morale problems." (p. 95) If used as an across-the-board, annual budgeting technique, zero-based techniques will collapse under their own weight much like Planning, Programming, Budgeting System (PPBS) does. (Wildavsky, 1974) Using it judiciously, however, during periods of retrenchment, with discre-

**TABLE 5-4. ZERO-BASED BUDGET AIDS SERVICES ORGANIZATION**

| Degree of Objective Attainment | Decision Package Rank | Level of Effort | Level of Funding Proposed |
|---|---|---|---|
| Unacceptable | 5th/Basic | 8-hour teen hotline volunteers, 1/4 professional supervision | $ 6,000 |
| More Acceptable | 4th/Add increment | 24-hour hotline volunteer staff, 1/4 professional supervision | 12,000 |
| Acceptable | 3rd/Add increment | 24-hour hotline, full-time professional staff, volunteers | 30,000 |
| Exceeds Objectives | 2nd/Add increment | 24-hour hotline, full-time professional staff, 1/2 time volunteer trainer, volunteers | 42,000 |
| Further Exceeds | 1st/Add increment | 24-hour hotline, full-time professional staff, full-time volunteer recruiter/trainer, 1/2 time hotline staff | 66,000 |

tionary funds or with particular program areas (especially where productivity is of concern), could make zero-based budgeting a valuable performance enhancing tool.

*Program Budget.* In both line item and functional budgets, the unit of attention is the organization but most human service agencies operate more than one program. In Chapter 2, program was defined as a collection of activities focused on a single goal. It is through the program that clients receive assistance, that staff find meaning in their work, and that society finds a way to address concerns. If true, the basic unit of budgetary attention for the performance manager must be the program. Program budgets display expenditures by program allowing the performance manager to analyze the relative costs of programs and to further link resources to performance through the use of client oriented program goals (see Table 5-4).

Program budgeting allows comparison of "program expenditures and representative local and national data to determine first, their degree of overall fiscal reasonableness, and second, if any immediate or long-range corrective action seems necessary." (Stretch, 1980, p. 92) An example of the power of this form of analysis was evident in Kansas concerning mental health expenditures. The state of Kansas like most states operates two major mental health programs. (Rapp & Hanson, 1987) The first is state psychiatric hospitals and other safety net services whose primary goal is to stabilize psychiatric symptoms so that return to the community is possible. The second program provides funding for community-based services designed to enhance the integration and quality of community life for persons suffering from severe mental illness. An analysis of state mental health financing policy uncovered that Kansas was spending about 90 percent of its mental health dollars on state and private psychiatric hospital care with the majority being consumed by state hospitals. This data was compared to national data where it was found that Kansas ranked fifty-first in expenditures for community care of the mentally ill among the states and territories but only slightly below average in total mental health spending. This analysis has led to a series of proposals to reallocate money from the state hospital program to community-based programs. This kind of analysis is easily accomplished through program budgets and can lead to major program improvements not evident when using other budget formats.

## Developing the Budget

The development of a sound, accurate budget is an important step for a manager who is looking at an organization's plan for the year. A budget is a financial plan, describing in numbers what will be happening in the organization and in any specific program within the organization.

1. It is based upon projections of income and expense for the program/ organization.
2. It uses the program/organization's needs and available resources as its basis.
3. It looks back at past performance and forward to the availability of new resources for the organization.
4. It should be developed in a process that permits input from staff members regarding their program needs and advice from administrators regarding organizational capacity and political reality.

Program budgeting requires that staff is aware of the program or agency's resources and understands the program's expense and other resource needs. Program budgeting can be accomplished as long as there is an identifiable program design. Staff must examine the design to determine what it will take to make the design operable.

1. Who and what types of people will the program require as staff? What should the organization provide to these staff?
2. Will the program require space of its own? What kind of space is needed and where should it be?
3. Are there equipment needs for this program? Can it share with others or does it need its own? Are donations possible or should we plan a purchase? Can we lease or should we buy?
4. What kinds of supplies and materials are needed?
5. How will we market our services?
6. What kinds of assistance will we provide to clients?
7. Will staff need publications, materials, or other resources to do their jobs well? Will staff need training and development to maintain a high quality of performance?
8. What kinds of insurance or protection does the organization require to assure that this program can operate in today's marketplace?

**9.** If we place this program into an existing organization, what other resource needs must be considered to assure a viable operation?

Each of these questions leads staff to others, questions about fund raising and quality of program, expectations of funding sources and board members, and questions about what is practical and realistic given the capacity of the organization. All of these questions are important in determining what the budget will look like and, in a budgeting process, time should be permitted for considering them and responding to them.

Once the questions have been considered, staff can prepare a budget worksheet. The worksheet contains lines for each commonly used expense item such as personnel, medical insurance, equipment, supplies, and so forth. The program budget contained in Table 5–5 is based upon a design for an AIDS counseling and education program for teens in which three of the four staff members train and counsel teens who will train and peer counsel with other teens. This program will fit into an existing AIDS service organization, will use a part of its space and some of its equipment, but will require some separate telephone service and have some other needs of its own. Examine the worksheet and consider how to respond to the questions stated above.

***The Budget Worksheets—Expense and Income.*** Although there may be many different styles of worksheets, the one seen in Table 5–5 is standard for most budgets.

*Personnel.* All categories of staff would be listed here, including exempt or professional staff (those exempt for payment of overtime hours), support (paraprofessionals), and clerical staff. Also included here are expenses for fringe benefits, such as the employer's portion of Social Security taxes (FICA), worker's compensation insurance (usually purchased with the organization's liability insurance package), unemployment compensation (based upon a salary percentage determined by the state's employment division), the employer's portion of a medical premium, and the employer's payments for any other fringe benefit. All of these line items are added together to provide a total personnel expense.

It should be clear that the person preparing the budget must have very specific information available when completing the worksheet. In order to plan for staff, he or she should be aware that full-time staff work forty hours per week and about 2,080 hours per year. Salary ranges should be consulted to be sure that new staff are hired at appropriate hourly wages. If the program or organization is new, the person preparing the budget should be familiar with market wages in the community for various types of jobs. In most communities, some type of salary or wage survey providing comparable data is usually available. Asking other social service program managers can also provide salary data.

Salaries are listed as the gross wage, and all employee taxes will be part of the gross figure, with the exception of the FICA payment to be made by the employer.

## TABLE 5-5. PROGRAM BUDGET WORKSHEET

**Program Name:** ASO Teen Services                                   **Budget Year:** 1990

**Summary Program Goals:** (1) 3,000 teens from at least 10 area school districts will learn about AIDS prevention, and be familiar with the facts of the disease; (2) at least 25 teens will become peer counselors, after participation in training; (3) at least 5 teens will become part of the training team.

### Expense Budget

| | |
|---|---:|
| PERSONNEL | |
| 1. Teen Program Director | $14,000 |
| Half-time administrator for teens component (shared with counseling program) | |
| 2. 3 Counselors/Educators @ $19,330 | 58,000 |
| Full-time staff in teen program, responsible for education, recruitment, and training of teens | |
| FRINGE | 14,400 |
| FICA, Medical, Worker's Comp, Retirement @ 20% of personnel cost | |
| TOTAL | $86,400 |
| NONPERSONNEL | |
| 1. Professional fees—1/2 audit and projected legal fees | 4,000 |
| 2. Rent—6,500 feet of space at 3030 Walnut @ $6.50 per sq. ft. | 12,000 |
| 3. Utilities—62% of gas and electric service (determined by daily usage) | 4,000 |
| 4. Telephone—Use of 800 number and lines for teen hotline | 5,000 |
| 5. Office supplies—standard supplies for office use | 2,000 |
| 6. Program Supplies—teen program manuals, materials, 5,000 packets for student use | 5,000 |
| 7. Small Equipment—shared rental of postage meter, calculator | 500 |
| 8. Equipment repairs—shared copier and typewriter maintenance agreement | 750 |
| 9. Postage—regular and bulk mail postage for newsletters, recruitment, and recognition event mailings | 3,000 |
| 10. Printing—Printing of letterhead, flyers, program brochures | 5,000 |
| 11. Staff Development—National AIDS meetings for two staff | 2,500 |
| 12. Publications—resource periodicals and books for staff | 800 |
| 13. Volunteer Training—food, rental, and miscellaneous costs of training | 1,250 |
| 14. Travel/mileage/parking—staff mileage and parking | 1,500 |
| 15. Insurance—45% of liability insurance, 50% of officers' and directors' coverage | 4,000 |
| 16. Promotion—PR materials, program video production | 2,000 |
| TOTAL NONPERSONNEL | $ 53,300 |
| TOTAL EXPENSE | $139,700 |

For budget purposes, the employer portion of FICA is figured at 7.65 percent of gross salaries. Unemployment compensation is determined through an "experience rate." The state determines the rate to be paid, depending upon past unemployment claims paid by the organization. If the organization has no prior history of claims, the rate is set at the highest amount, 2 to 3 percent for the first $7,000 or $7,500 earned by each employee. The amount is payable quarterly. Once an organization has proof of its not-for-profit status, the rate is lowered. Other fringe benefits should be figured at their actual annual cost to the organization.

*Nonpersonnel.* These are separate line items for a variety of expenses that the organization or program will have to incur.

- *Professional Fees:* consultant, accounting, auditing, legal, and other fees paid to contract personnel
- *Supplies:* usually subdivided into food, program, office, maintenance, and salable (if applicable)
- *Occupancy:* this includes rental or lease payments for shared or individually leased space, usually figured at a dollar amount per square foot, utilities such as electricity, gas, water, sewer, and telephone service
- *Insurance:* expenses for liability and officers and directors insurance (to protect the organization and the board of directors
- *Small Equipment:* usually equipment costing under $300, such as calculators, tape recorders, lamps, and other minor equipment expenses
- *Equipment Repairs/Maintenance/Contracts:* equipment leases, maintenance contract payments, repairs
- *Postage:* all mailing expenses, including bulk mail or third class and business reply postage
- *Printing:* expenses of printing materials, newsletters, letterhead, business cards, etc.
- *Publication/Advertisements:* resources for the program and classified ads for new staff
- *Promotion/Marketing:* expenses for marketing the program, flyers, brochures, video and slide production, other outreach activities
- *Mileage/Transportation:* reimbursements for staff and/or participants' mileage or other transportation costs
- *Meetings/Dues:* expenses for staff participation in professional organizations and meetings
- *Staff Development/Training:* expenses for staff attendance at conferences, workshops, and other training events

To complete each of the lines of the program budget worksheet, research sources of information. It would be necessary, for example, that staff obtain information from utilities about rates and expected increases. The cost of telephone system installation, ongoing service, and training should be investigated. Staff should examine each in terms of program needs and obtain accurate information to assist in the planning process.

The completion of each raises additional questions to be considered. Will the AIDS education program for teens pay stipends to trainers/peer counselors? At what rate will staff be reimbursed for their mileage? What kinds of and how much insurance does the program need? Can any of the expense items be donated to the program? Answers to these questions will have an impact on the program and on the budget, and each must be carefully examined.

Our expense budget has left out a large category of expense, normally referred to as capital expense. These items are usually equipment and leasehold improvements (facility renovation and repairs) in excess of $300. A separate capital budget is prepared to list and present these items.

If the budget is for a single service program, all expenses are assigned to the types of lines discussed above. If, however, the program is part of an agency, the completed expense budget for the agency would contain expenses for Program Services and for Supporting Services, usually referred to as Management and General and Fund Raising. Each program service (child care, teen services, etc.) would have its own budget. Costs not directly attributable to the program would be included in the Management and General and Fund Raising columns. As an example, the salary of the executive director is split between the two supporting services. That position is responsible for agency management, program oversight, fund raising (including grant and contract preparation and supervision), and for maintaining relationships with the board. The salary will be allocated to the two columns either through the results of a time study that shows how much actual time is spent in management and general activities and how much in fund raising, or through the use of a predetermined formula. If the organization is having a benefit to raise money for a teen program, the costs associated with the fund raising event are charged to fund-raising, within several line items. The organization might charge its liability insurance costs to program services, but charge its expense for officers and directors liability to supporting services, in the management and general column.

In addition to an expense budget, the program staff needs to plan for income (see Table 5–6). A new group of questions emerges for staff to consider.

1. Where will we get our resources?
2. Will we charge fees for service, and on what basis (sliding scale, actual cost, a set fee)?
3. How much can we expect from the fund raising benefit that has been planned?
4. Can we sell a product or otherwise produce earned income for this program?
5. Are there ways we can leverage services with corporations or other organizations to produce revenue?
6. Will this be a membership organization? What types of fees will be charged for membership? If we charge a membership fee, does the income accrue to the program, or is it used in the management and general or administrative portion of the organization?

When all of the questions have been considered, the income worksheet is prepared, by category.

**TABLE 5-6. PROGRAM BUDGET WORKSHEET**

| Income Budget | |
| --- | --- |
| Contributions—Individual and corporate, direct mail | $30,000 |
| Grants—Foundations (Robert W. Johnson, Community Foundation, Foyer Fund) | 35,000 |
| Grants—Government (City, County, and State contracts) | 35,000 |
| Special Events—Dinner Theatre, Art Auction | 15,000 |
| Churches—Christmas appeal, speaker fees | 5,000 |
| United Way—Allocation for teen program, already approved | 12,500 |
| Estates/Memorials—Memorial gifts | 2,000 |
| Training Fees—Fees for training students, paid by School Districts | 8,000 |
| Merchandise/Salables—Sales of T-shirts, buttons | 3,000 |
| Interest income—Interest from seven-day CDs | 500 |
| TOTAL INCOME | $146,000 |

- *Contributions.* The "no strings attached" gifts to the organization or to the program. These gifts may be small or large; they may result from requests or may just appear. Budgeting for them requires that staff be familiar with the organization's ability to garner past donor support, or, in the case of a new program/agency, that staff can predict from community trends how its contribution request will be received.
- *Grants.* These income items are generally the result of specific requests to the granting agency, which may be a public or governmental agency, or it might be a foundation or trust gift. Grants usually require detailed reporting on a regular basis. Again, if we believe we will be awarded these grants or contracts based upon ongoing work or new relationships with the potential funder, those dollars should be listed here.
- *Program income.* These funds are derived from fees paid by clients or third party payers (such as insurance companies). You need to estimate usage of your program based upon past experience or on projections that you believe are reliable.
- *Special project fund raising.* Remember the fund raising benefit? The projected income is listed here.
- *Memberships.* This income line reflects membership fees projected for the fiscal year.
- *United Way.* If you have applied for or are currently receiving United Way funding, those dollars should be listed in a separate category. The separate listing informs others that your program has obtained or is planning to receive these dollars.
- *Interest income.* If your program/agency is endowed, has funds available for investment, or simply has an interest-bearing bank account, the interest should be listed as a separate category of income.
- *Other income.* This may be one line item or several, specific items, which

should be explained in the budget. Other income items might include vending machine income, sales to the public (tee shirts, buttons, or other products), space rental (the office might be rented for meetings, parties, or dances, when our program is not operating), or other miscellaneous items.

The worksheets are now complete. The items have been totaled; the income and the expenses indicate some funds left over. Is that because you are a good planner or because you were overly optimistic about revenues? An additional review of the budget assumptions (the answers to all of the questions previously presented) will help confirm whether you are being fair and conservative. Review the budget and the assumptions that contributed to its development with other staff members, board members, or colleagues. Such information sharing validates decisions and clarifies incorrect assumptions.

If, instead of having excess income, the projected budget indicates a deficit, the social administrator needs to review the budgeting assumptions, consider ways to increase income and/or reduce expense. If the budget cannot be balanced, is it feasible to operate the program?

## Budget Monitoring

The availability of a computer, software, and a knowledgeable person can assure ways of analyzing income and expense and monitoring the budget. (1) *Timely reports* of past income and expense and ways of breaking the annual budget into monthly increments is one way to monitor a budget. With a monthly budget, reports can compare actual operation to budget projections and show any variance, so that staff and board members can operate with accurate information. (2) *Breakeven analyses* is information detailing how many participants, paying what fees will be required to produce the income necessary to meet expenses. (3) *Fixed versus variable expenses* are those incurred whether there are clients or not, such as utilities and rent; variable expenses can be controlled or changed even if we don't have clients, such as program supplies costs or emergency assistance payments.

The purpose of these various budget monitoring systems is to keep the agency functioning within available resources. One of the most difficult management tasks is responding to reduction in funds. During the late 1970s and early 1980s, an entire literature on "cutback management" developed in response to federal budget cuts. When faced with the unpleasant task of bringing expenses in line with reduced funds, there are basically three strategies that can be used.

First, and most commonly used, is the reduction of all items across the board. A 10 percent reduction in funds is shared equally by all organizational units. This is the path-of-least-resistance strategy where equity and simplicity make it the easiest of solutions to implement and for organizational personnel to accept. A second strategy is to reduce costs at the margins for supportive services and supplies: paper, pens, secretarial support, telephones, staff training, travel reimbursements are reduced leaving personnel largely untouched. The short-term relief of knowing jobs will be sustained is often replaced with hostility as staff find they cannot do the job without the basic tools and supports. Some of these savings can hurt clients directly as in the case of reducing travel reimbursement forcing clients to come to the agency for service and in some cases thereby reducing client outcomes.

A third strategy reframes the cut-back crisis and makes it an opportunity. At the risk of sounding like Pollyanna, two prevalent opportunities will have to suffice:

1. It can be an opportunity to increase the resource for the most needed or most effective programs. An agency with a one million dollar budget needs to reduce costs by 5 percent or $50,000. A small and not well-regarded program is being operated for $70,000. By eliminating that program, $20,000 can be added to a higher priority program.

2. Some programs, often civil service based, have a disproportionate number of supervisors, middle managers, administrators, and other specialists. Forced reductions in the budget can be used to eliminate low priority "overhead" positions and even perhaps to add more direct-service personnel. Justification for this form of resource allocation comes from the case study of *The Dana Corporation* and a marvelous study of managers by Martin (1983). This latter study suggests that reducing the number of supervisors improves effectiveness and efficiency.

Position reductions based on seniority, hiring freezes, and across the board cuts remove decisions from the managers' authority and expertise. Instead, managers must examine the organization's mission, recognize marginal investments or programs of limited utility, use rational mechanisms for making choices, encourage the active participation of agency employees, and retain organizational openness. Any such process should place performance and client outcomes at the pinnacle of decision-making criteria.

What must be remembered finally, is that budgeting is a political process. A staff member who develops a budget must be prepared to "sell" it. He or she should have a strong and consistent rationale for explaining income and expense and be able to market the budget and the program it represents to supervisors, volunteers, and board members.

## MANAGING TIME

Personnel costs account for 80 percent to 90 percent of human service budgets. The organization buys the intelligence, skills, and energy of people who are then asked to contribute these to the achievement of the organization's goals. Staff assist clients. Therefore, time may be an organization's most precious resource. The misuse and waste of time can rarely be benign. Mostly it is *toxic* to the ability to help.

The foundation of this section is based on the following assumptions:

1. Time is a precious resource.
2. There is a finite number of minutes in a day, and there is a tremendous amount of work to be done.
3. The amount of work that could possibly be undertaken exceeds the available time.
4. Time is wasted in most if not all organizations.
5. The basic principles of effective time management are simple but difficult to implement.

All of this simply suggests that time is a resource that people can use in conscious ways to improve organizational performance. To accomplish this you need to: know thy purpose, know thy time, and do something about it.

## Know Thy Purpose

The key to using time effectively is the link to performance. This entire volume has been focused on performance. Enhancing performance whether it be through improved information, improved program design, or better use of time must begin by defining performance unambiguously. Knowing your goals means knowing how the tasks you perform every day contribute to client change, organizational productivity, staff morale, resource acquisition, and efficiency. This is not an easy task. Determining the conditions under which the short conversation with Mary contributes to staff morale or wastes time is not always obvious.

What should you and your staff be spending time on is the key question. For performance managers, those personnel from frontline supervisors to the agency executives, their central purpose is to make the work of the frontline practitioners more effective, more efficient, and more satisfying. The principal job is to help those who provide the service. As the discussion of the inverted hierarchy will detail (Chapter 7), this means (1) providing focus and direction, (2) providing the tools, (3) insuring rewards are in place, and (4) removing obstacles to performance. The question might be reframed this way:

1. What should I do to help provide performance direction for my people?
2. What additional tools do my staff need to improve performance?
3. How am I going to make my staff feel like winners?
4. What obstacles to performance can I remove?

The answer to these questions becomes the inventory of goals of the first priority. Each goal could involve techniques of program design, personnel management, resource management, and information management that have been discussed throughout this book.

Planning a day, a week, a month, or longer time period begins with answers to the previous questions, a selection of which answers (or goals) to work on, and some idea of the actions needed. You end with the placement of these actions in your calendar book. Most, if not all, days should have something related to the above (goals) and tasks. They should, in fact, dominate a performance manager's schedule. At the minimum, however, there are precious few reasons why the manager cannot do something to help the staff feel like winners every day.

Since the ultimate purpose of the organization is to assist clients, the performance manager needs to have contact with them. Some of these encounters must be personal, face to face. But communication between clients and managers can occur through client satisfaction surveys, suggestion boxes, or termination interviews. Meetings between clients and managers can be formal as in focus groups, or membership in advocacy organizations, or other scheduled meetings with consumers. They can be informal as the manager wanders the hallways, reception areas, and other places where clients can be found. This direct connection between manager and clients provides an indispensable set of information with which to direct staff, reward staff, and uncover obstacles to improved service.

## Know Thy Time

Once the focus of the social administrator's time has been established, the next step is to identify the obstacles to doing it. The obstacles are legion. Every person in the organization is subject to the interests and demands of other organizational personnel and constituencies from the external environment. Phone calls, meetings, unscheduled visits to your office, and paperwork are often not part of the answer to the question: How did I help my staff today? Controlling these distractions or exploiting them to enhance performance is a difficult task indeed. Personally, we want to be liked and saying "no" is often uncomfortable. Organizationally, the complex relationships that are required sometimes mean that some intrusions must be accepted when it is not central to performance. In a sense it is an investment—I will help you so that later I can expect responsiveness to a concern of mine.

To begin to control time and identify obstacles to its proper use, one must "know thy time." This is the title of the second chapter of Drucker's wonderful little book *The Effective Executive* (1967). Amost every time-management program includes some variation of the idea of at least occasionally keeping a time log. To change your use of time you have to know what is happening to it right now.

There are at least three concrete benefits of consciously determining what you do with your time. First, it helps you to learn about yourself. Everyone's style of work is different. Some people get some tasks completed more quickly and with better quality in the early morning. Others perform best in the afternoon. If your job requires a large quantity of writing and you do that best in the morning, don't let meetings get scheduled in the morning. You can't act on this kind of knowledge unless you know yourself. No one else has this knowledge. By comparing your work habits with how you use your time, you can manage your time better.

Secondly, determining what you do with your time helps you know your job. Everything takes time. All work takes time. Every task you undertake and complete takes time. If you want to alter your job to use time differently, you have to know what you are currently doing with your time. You might be surprised to learn the relative time required for various tasks. Recall is very unreliable. For most people the difference between the time a task takes and the time we remember a task taking is very different.

Third, determining how your time is being used helps you learn about your work environment. In any organization a person's time is not his or her own. Organizations consist of people, people must be attended to, and people take time. Many, perhaps most, interactions with people in organizations are absolutely essential to get the work of the organization completed. On the other hand people in organizations (e.g., in meetings) may also be the largest nonproductive user of time. You can only make judgments about people transactions in your work environment when you are aware of the extent and nature of these transactions.

A time log is a useful device for determining how time is spent. A time log is simply a running record over some period of time (see Figure 5–1). The format and time sequence used in the time log are less important than using the log. Since each work day is often idiosyncratic, a time log should be maintained for at least one week and up to one month. Only in this way can one comprehend patterns of time usage. On the other hand, doing a time log every day is probably not warranted and will in and of itself become a time waster.

A time log can answer some rather important questions:

1. How much time is devoted to tasks identified in the know thy purpose section?
2. How much time is devoted to tasks directly related to performance?
3. How much time is devoted to whom?
4. How much task time is initiated by me or by others?
5. How much time is unambiguously unproductive?
6. How much time is spent in regular meetings? Ad hoc meetings?
7. How many times do interruptions occur by telephone? Visits to my office?

## Do Something About It

Once social administrators know what they want to spend time on and on what they are spending time, action is required to make the two as congruent as possible. This action step will assist others in the organization in managing their time as well as taking control of your own time. To assist others to have the time needed to complete the work, the social administrator needs to find ways for everyone to learn the basic time management principles.

For frontline staff whose efforts help clients, time management revolves around the question of how much time should be spent in direct contact with clients and collaterals, or put another way, how much time should be spent in implementing the program as designed. The assumption here is that clients get helped when they spend time with the staff or when the staff is doing specific client-directed activities. The time management task for frontline staff is how to gain as much direct-service time as possible.

| Early morning |
|---|
| 8:00<br>8:15<br>8:30<br>8:45 |
| 9:00<br>9:15<br>9:30<br>9:45 |
| 10:00<br>10:15<br>10:30<br>10:45 |
| 11:00<br>11:15<br>11:30<br>11:45 |
| 12:00<br>12:15<br>12:30<br>12:45 |
| 1:00<br>1:15<br>1:30<br>1:45 |
| 2:00<br>2:15<br>2:30<br>2:45 |
| 3:00<br>3:15<br>3:30<br>3:45 |
| 4:00<br>4:15<br>4:30<br>4:45<br>5:00 |
| Late afternoon |

**Figure 5–1.** Daily Time Log

234

To help manage the time of frontline staff, the performance manager needs to set a standard for direct-service time. The goal for most organizations should approach 75 percent. The second task is to configure meetings, paperwork, and other activities into the 25 percent of the time remaining. The performance manager must become the guardian and protector of the 75 percent. Not to do so reduces client benefits.

Meetings and paperwork are two large time consuming activities for all staff and most importantly frontline staff. The inverted hierarchy in Chapter 7 contains detailed suggestions on reducing demands of meetings and paperwork to liberate time for clients.

Psychological barriers aside, taking control of the administrator's own time is easier. Once discrepancies between current use of time and desired use are identified, the manager has three choices. First, select those activities that can be removed. Regularly scheduled meetings and paperwork are often fruitful areas for reduction. Other tasks may be suitable for delegation, and thereby removed from the manager's responsibilities. Second, select activities that can be controlled. For example, accepting and returning phone calls can be prescheduled or attend meetings only during the time when relevant issues will be discussed. Third, select those activities that can be better exploited to enhance performance. For example, "coffeepot" conversations can be made into opportunities to help a person feel like a winner. Regularly scheduled meetings can be restructured. Administrative announcements can be minimized and replaced with performance enhancing discussions, problem-solving, and celebrations of successful performance. Telephone calls from external constituencies can be opportunities to educate and refocus their agenda on one that is more helpful to the organization.

# VOLUNTEERS

## Uses and Selection

The vast majority of human services work is done by people with 85 percent of the expenditures devoted to personnel. When agency personnel lament the lack of resources, it is usually the lack of additional human resources to which they are referring. Volunteers are both an underused and misused resource that continues to hold considerable promise for better performance in many programs and organizations. Volunteers can bring new energy, ideas, talents, and resources, such as community goodwill and influence to the agency. They can augment the jobs of agency personnel by providing support services, such as clerical and reception services. Volunteers can be used to perform direct-service tasks that do not require professional training or skills (e.g., telephone contact with clients, transportation for clients, child care for clients when receiving services). Volunteers, with proper training and supervision, can become service providers in their own right. At times, volunteers can be used to make a resource available to clients who otherwise would be inaccessible. In short, community volunteers can be an important human resource for the client-centered agency.

New social service administrators often wonder how to deal with volunteers. Even those who have learned the skills of performance management are not able to see the connections between those who are paid as staff and those volunteer staff who serve without pay. Both groups require equal amounts of care and attention. In a traditional nonprofit social agency, volunteers provide governance and person-power to stretch the capacity of the agency. They serve on boards of directors, raise funds, steward those funds, assist in programs, and, like staff, are an invaluable resource to the organization.

Whatever their responsibilities are to be within the organization, volunteers should be provided with task-directed job descriptions. Before seeking volunteers, the organization must examine its needs and determine the types of expertise that it will require from volunteers. A plan for recruitment should be developed, so that persons possessing the needed skills can be sought. Finally, the organization should have a well planned selection process that permits careful decisions to be made regarding volunteers who are chosen. In some organizations, where volunteers work with children, police checks may be necessary; in other agencies, health testing or some type of certification may be required. In some communities, volunteer centers recruit, screen, and identify volunteers who are then referred to agencies that require their services.

When an organization seeks members for its board of directors, it should be as careful in this selection process as in selecting for staff positions. Seriously consider a matrix of needs and available skills. Again, the process used to recruit and select staff should be in place as the organization seeks these administrative volunteers.

## Orientation, Training, and Rewards

Once volunteers are chosen, they need to be oriented and trained. Expectations should be carefully laid out so that everyone understands what is required of the volunteers and the staff who will be working with them. Volunteer morale is critical for organizations that rely on their energy and participation. An organization must have reward systems in place. Volunteers are to be nurtured, cherished, their work recognized and appreciated, in the same way in which staff are valued. Volunteer recognition events are held in many organizations to show appreciation. Volunteers and their employers are invited to breakfasts, dinners, and luncheons; often, program participants share stories of relationships with volunteers; plaques, small gifts, and expressions of caring are given and volunteers know how important they are, in the life of the agency. Some national corporations such as J.C. Penney recognize community volunteers on an annual basis. United Way often honors community volunteers through picnics and other celebrations.

Most community volunteers work within an agency's program, assisting staff, clients, and other constituents. Depending upon the size of the agency, the volunteer program may be informal, involving only a few people, or it may be highly organized with staff directing and coordinating the work of volunteers. Development and training activities are important and necessary for these volunteers. The learning and utilization of new skills are an important part of the daily reward system that must be in place for volunteers within the organization.

Finally, whatever the position of volunteers in the organization, positive relationships are critical. Everyone in the organization must understand the importance of volunteers and work with them as if they were members of the staff. Their ideas, performance and management styles, and organizational skills can be used to the organization's advantage only if they are treated with respect and cherished as among the agency's most ardent supporters.

## ACQUIRING TECHNOLOGY AND IDEAS

Technologies are the collection of methods used by the organization in order to perform. Hasenfeld (1983) defines it as

> a set of institutionalized procedures aimed at changing the physical, psychological, social or cultural attributes of people in order to transform them from a given social status to a new prescribed status. The term "institutionalized" denotes that the procedures are legitimated and sanctioned by the organization. (p. 111)

Technologies are often codified and reinforced through a variety of organizational statements and prescriptions: program design, procedures and policy manuals, rules concerning documentation, mission statements, job descriptions, and the focus of staff development programs. The program design chapter discusses the selection of intervention technologies, and the information management chapter discusses methods for monitoring compliance of key elements of a technology. This section will focus on the performance manager's role in acquiring technologies.

In the continuous quest for improved performance, the manager is compelled to be vigilant—to constantly look for more powerful technologies. The selection of technologies has great influence over the benefits that accrue to clients. Simply stated, some technologies work better than others. A second performance area influenced directly by the acquisition of technologies is staff morale. A work environment that is dynamic and innovative is most exciting. Learning is a valuable reinforcer for most professionals. Creating such a workplace, rich in learning opportunities, should have a potent effect on job satisfaction.

Acquiring technology and program ideas is intimately related to innovation. The performance manager's constant quest for better performance implies the need for innovation and change. The continuous search is for new and better ways to do the organization's work. With the vast array of forces that demand conformity to existing arrangements, how does a manager create the milieu that encourages creativity and innovation?

## Listen to the Clients

Clients can directly offer suggestions for improved operations and can indirectly tell the staff what it has to do better.

First, properly designed client satisfaction instruments can elicit those things that were helpful or appreciated and things that could have been helpful. Other mechanisms include focus groups where a small group of clients discuss how they experienced the service and suggestions for improvement.

Second, client "failures" are a rich source of direction for innovation. Their failures must be seen as staff failures. One of the outcomes for community programs for people with severe mental illness is to prevent psychiatric hospitalization and increase community tenure. Given the nature of severe mental illness, some clients will periodically be admitted to such a facility for, it is hoped, a brief stay. Much learning can accrue from a systematic review of cases requiring hospitalization through trying to answer the question: Under what conditions could this hospitalization have been averted? A critical appraisal will lead to factors (e.g., resources) that are currently beyond the capacity of the organization or community. But the appraisal will also, with some regularity, uncover factors that the organization controls or influences.

## Create Champions

Every successful innovation—the idea that moves from conception to implementation—has a champion. As Schon states: "No ordinary involvement with a new idea provides the energy required to cope with the indifference and resistance that major technological change provokes. . . . Champions of new inventions display persistence and courage of heroic quality." (Quoted in Peters & Waterman, 1982, p. 200) The creation of champions means the performance manager must encourage, support, and model creativity. He or she must stimulate the search for new ideas. People need to be allowed to try out new ideas in modest ways. And people need to be allowed to fail. In fact, to create champions and innovations requires the celebration of failures.

## Informal Innovation Groups

These are small ad hoc groups of staff or other key players, who brainstorm solutions to difficult and multi-faceted organizational problems. A few guidelines could include the following:

- Keep it small (probably no more than six people).
- Work on a provocative problem. (e.g., Under what conditions could we avert all psychiatric hospitalizations? How can we get all programs to institute and respond to a client feedback system?)
- There are no bad ideas. Participants should have permission to suggest

virtually anything that strikes them without argument or embarrassment.
- All ideas are recorded and good ones assigned for further development.

## Worker/Supervisor Learning Groups

Although individual supervision continues to be the norm in human services, group supervision offers considerable promise for enhancing efficiency, staff morale, and client outcomes. (Rapp & Chamberlain, 1985) Such arrangements focus more on learning and problem-solving than on supervision as usually viewed. The group is a richer source of ideas than any one individual, thereby enhancing the potential for learning. Selected cases can be viewed in depth or systematic attention can be focused on particular obstacles. Team members can receive support and encouragement; successes can be celebrated. (See Chapter 4 for more details on group supervision.)

## Staff Development

Although discussed in depth in Chapter 4, the emphasis here is on the role of staff development in fostering innovation. The use of outside speakers and materials begins to "open the doors" to new ideas from beyond the organization. It is a method for bringing the best new ideas into the organization. In general, the topics and speakers should be directly relevant to the goals of the organization and priority given to people who have "done it," that is, who have demonstrated high rates of client-outcome achievement. The cost of such speakers and the desirability of having a regular parade of such occasions, often means that organizations may have to pool their funds.

## University-Agency Connections

A major underdeveloped resource for most human service organizations are universities. Universities, through their faculty and libraries, are repositories of knowledge. This resource, if structured and channeled correctly, offers an unparalleled source of ideas, technology, and innovation. They are also responsible for training the future professionals. Unfortunately, collaboration has been isolated and that which has occurred is often marked by dissatisfaction and disappointment if not downright hostility. Despite the rather poor track record, there are a few examples of highly productive collaborations. (Moore, Davis, & Mellon, 1985; Davis & Sanchez, 1987)

   The most celebrated arrangement is the case of the county extension office. Through these offices, university agents disseminate the latest knowledge and technologies to farmers. They distribute literature, consult with individual farmers, speak to farm organizations, and occasionally test the new ideas on actual farms using it as an extended laboratory. The problems mentioned by farmers become fodder for future research. Many agricultural gains in the United States have been attributed to this institutionalized arrangement of dissemination and research.

While there is not a comparable structure for human services, there have been some notable examples. (See Talbott & Robinowitz, 1986, for examples in mental health.) Successful arrangements share a number of characteristics.

1. The arrangement provides identifiable benefits to both parties.
2. The relationship is both institutional and personal.
3. Both parties seek to make the other "look good."
4. Both parties are very sensitive to the exigencies affecting the other party.
5. Both parties deliver. Dates and time lines are adhered to and responsibilities are met.
6. Recognition for any achievements is shared.
7. Representatives of each entity have contact with personnel at multiple levels of the other organization.

The performance manager needs to look for university faculty who meet most of the following conditions:

1. They know the most current literature in the field and ideally are a regular contributor to that literature.
2. They share and adopt the goals of your organization.
3. They are willing to commit the time necessary to do the work.
4. They are reasonable, personable, pleasant, and, ideally, enthusiastic.

The specific arrangements could include consultation with various groups of personnel, in-service training and workshops, joint supervision of university students, program evaluation, research, policy analysis and advocacy, management system development, or training.

## THE STRATEGIC PLAN

Developing a plan can be an important process because it becomes an organizational resource. Strategic planning is the process of determining where your organization should be in the future and how you will get there. It helps an organization find the best fit for its mission, its capabilities, and its environment. A planning process can provide a unique perspective to inform an organization's leadership of what it can accomplish, given its overarching goals, the resources that it has and can acquire, and the requirements of the external environment.

An organization that wants to improve its performance and clarify its future direction will find a planning process most helpful. The development and implementation of a strategic plan permits an organization to survive, and perhaps even flourish, with fewer resources. A plan can influence others through its direction and focus. A plan can communicate that the organization is sound and strong. Finally, a plan can build teamwork and a sense of expertise.

The use of strategic planning has become very popular among nonprofit, social service organizations. Yet, there are situations in which the process is of little value. It can be costly, both in time and money, and these costs may outweigh the benefits of planning. If the organization is facing life-threatening problems, such as large deficits or significant staffing issues, these problems should be dealt with first. There must be an initial commitment to using the plan that is developed, and it must be based upon agreed on and accurate assumptions. Finally, in some organizations, there is a preference for using intuition as a mechanism for determining focus and direction, and a formal planning process would not be seen in a positive light. Where does your organization fit? What do you want to be? What are you willing to do to get there? If strategic planning fits your organization, consider the following necessary steps.

## Get Organized

You should be aware at the outset that a carefully designed planning process requires about forty hours of work in a group, in addition to research. Think about your organizational needs and determine if you need outside help to facilitate the process. To organize for the planning effort, get a commitment from your board and staff members, and form a planning team of eight to ten people who care about the organization's future and are willing to give their time and energy to this effort. Explain the requirements of meeting and research time and get commitments to participate. Once people understand the need to plan and have agreed to work, the leadership needs to design a process that fits the organization's needs. Planning may be done in a few weeks, or it can require several months; the process can be formal, with much data collection and analysis, or it can be quite informal, based upon a set of assumptions developed by the team and some outside experts. What does your organization need? Which style of planning fits who you are?

## Take Stock

Perform a situational analysis at the first planning meeting. Look at the history of the organization and its current situation. Examine the organization's mission statement. Does it reflect the desired outcomes for the agency's clients? Have the organization's activities and programs changed? What new elements should be added? Once the team has agreed on wording for the new mission statement, it is important to look at the organization's strengths and weaknesses, the forces inside the organization, and its resources and capabilities. Then the team should examine opportunities and threats, the forces outside of the organization that have an impact upon it. These forces are the needs of clients and other stakeholders, the activities of competitors and allies, as well as social, economic, political, and technological forces in the society. The team is looking at what is needed, as well as what is feasible in the service area, given the climate outside of the organization. Finally, in this step, the team must examine issues that are critical to the agency, given strengths, weaknesses, opportunities, and threats.

## Develop a Strategy

The planning team determines the approach to planning that best fits the organization. Most nonprofits use a combination of approaches:

- The *scenario design*. The team identifies possible major scenarios for the future, evaluates those, selects the one preferred and plans for achieving it.
- The *critical issues approach*. The team lists critical issues and priorities for the organization, then develops mechanisms to resolve each issue and checks to determine that strategies were sound.
- The *goal approach*. The team sets goals, identifies strategies or objectives to meet the goals, selects the best strategy, and then outlines specific plans to accomplish each strategy.

The team should choose the approach or combination of approaches that best fit the organization's style and needs. (Barry, 1986)

## Draft and Refine the Plan

After the format for planning is established, the team meets in a working session, usually a full day, and the first draft of a plan is produced. The team meets again to refine the plan and then presents it to the organization's leadership for its approval.

## Implement the Plan

This is the most significant step, and the one that often gets lost in the process. The organization's leadership is responsible for seeing that the plan is put in place and that its implementation is monitored. Progress on achieving goals should be carefully noted; corrective action should be taken if there are problems. Each year, the plan is updated to maintain the organization's progress and direction.

## Knowing When You Are There

Strategic planning is a way of thinking that is an ongoing process, so the plan is never complete. It is not an end in itself, rather it is a tool to help the organization accomplish its mission, using and managing its resources to the best advantage. When strategies are stated simply, when tasks are manageable, and when there is careful consideration given to the organization's ability to implement the plan, the results of planning can be a vehicle that takes the organization exactly where it wants to go.

# SUMMARY

This chapter completes the trilogy of information, personnel, and resources. It answers the question: What does a manager manage? Resource management involves the acquisition and allocation or use of money, personnel, technology, clients, and community goodwill and influence. In this chapter we have discussed money, time, volunteers, and ideas and provided specific instruction in the acquisition and allocation of these resources so that client outcomes and organizational performance can be enhanced. It is not enough to simply acquire the management skills of the previous chapters. Too often the authors hear: "I cannot do this in my organization." An additional set of skills is required to implement this model in organizations. These organizational change strategies are considered in the next chapter.

# REFERENCES

Barry, B. W. (1986). *Strategic planning workbook for nonprofit organizations*. St. Paul, MN: Amherst Wilder Foundation.

Davis, M., & Sanchez, A. M. (1987). *Interdisciplinary collaboration between state mental health and higher education*. Boulder, CO: WICHE.

Drucker, P. (1967). *The effective executive*. London, England: Pan Books.

*Giving U.S.A.* (1988). New York: American Association of Fund Raising Council, Trust for Philanthropy.

Hasenfeld, Y. (1983). *Human service organizations*. Englewood Cliffs, NJ: Prentice-Hall.

Lewis, J. A., & Lewis, M. D. (1983). *Management of human service programs*. Monterey, CA: Brooks/Cole.

Lohman, R. A. (1980). *Breaking even: Financial management in human service organizations*. Philadelphia: Temple University Press.

Martin, S. (1983). *Managing without managers*. Beverly Hills, CA: Sage.

Moore, D. J., Davis, M., & Mellon, J. (1985). *Academia's response to state mental health system needs*. Boulder, CO: WICHE.

Peters, T. S., & Waterman, R. H. (1982). *In search of excellence*. New York: Harper & Row.

Rapp, C. A., & Chamberlain, R. (1985, September/October). Case management services for the chronically mentally ill. *Social Work Journal, 30*(5), 417–422.

Rapp, C. A., & Hanson, J. (1987, December). *Towards an agenda for mental health in Kansas*. Lawrence, KS: University of Kansas School of Social Welfare.

Read, P. (1986). *Foundation fundamentals: A guide for grantseekers*. New York: The Foundation Center.

Stretch, J. J. (1980, Spring). What human services managers need to know about basic budgeting strategies. *Administration in Social Work, 4*(1), 87–98.

Talbott, J. A., & Robinowitz, C. B. (1986). *Working together: State-university collaboration in mental health*. Washington, DC: American Psychiatric Press.

Wildavsky, A. (1974). *The politics of the budgeting process* (2nd ed.). Boston: Little, Brown.

# CHAPTER 6

# Getting It Done

In this chapter, we discuss the knowledge, skills, and attitudes needed for managers to move the organization to improved levels of client-centeredness and performance. People both provoke and prevent change, and therefore interpersonal influence skills become of paramount importance. After exploring the resistances and obstacles to change, we provide a step-by-step process for instigating such change. The process includes methods for analysis and influence strategies based on the social science and practice research.

In the last five chapters we have discussed the following ideas: Recognizing the complexity of social work, the program design model begins with a theory of change and includes such critical features as expectations of clients and workers as well as the behaviors required to produce the client benefit (Chapter 2). The information management model assumes that you have the data you need to keep your program working for clients (Chapter 3). And finally, the acquisition of resources, their efficient use, the design of work, and the satisfaction of staff are all essential skills for enhancing performance (Chapters 4 and 5). Yet even with these tools and skills, the social administrator encounters frustrations because the program is not operating as designed, the information system is resisted, volunteer recruitment is down, and one staff member cannot seem to be satisfied. So how does the social administrator put management technologies into action successfully?

Social administration like other areas of social work is a difficult and complex process. There are no formulas that guarantee success. This chapter presents approaches to implementing client-centered performance administration.

## COMPLEX ENVIRONMENTS

As it has been seen, human service organizations operate in highly political environments in which multiple constituencies make demands. Nevertheless, these constituencies are necessary if desired levels of program performance are to be achieved. This high level of interdependence is commonly manifested by the amount of time many managers, especially top-level administrators, spend with funders, legislators, related social service agencies, media representatives, community leaders, and personnel from the justice and educational systems. Another common manifestation of interdependence can be witnessed on the front lines as client-service personnel identify a wide variety of obstacles to better client service: uncooperative judges, police, teachers, families, employers, landlords, government bureaucrats, and so on. The inherent interdependence of social administrators and constituents is also demonstrated in the multitude of factors that have been identified as contributing to the social problem in the program design material.

The client-centered performance manager believes the principle purpose of extraorganizational activities is to influence the people who can affect performance, and client outcomes in particular. This should not be seen as a public relations scheme for organizational maintenance. As Miringoff (1980) states it should not be a

> focus on merely "making us look good," whatever the quality of the actual service product may be . . . to concentrate on the packaging and the image or impression of the product, such that the actual substance is ignored. Public relations in the human services, designed merely to maintain the organization, and perhaps to enhance its image by making it "look good" in the eyes of significant elements in its community, can be detrimental to that organization's functioning. The goal of merely "selling" the agency in order to improve its image, increase its grants, give it political clout, or make it competitive with other agencies—in short maintain the organization—can supplant the service goal of public relations. (p. 160)

A performance oriented purpose, on the other hand, will guide the manager in the selection of activities and the way the activities are fashioned and pursued.

## LACK OF POWER

A lack of formally constituted power constrains the performance manager's attempts to influence key players. Power, in this case, refers to the ability to force compliance through actual or presumed control over possible penalties. For example, most agencies have no formal authority to order a judge to behave in a certain way, or a teacher or a worker in another agency. The organization cannot force a legislature or a United Way to increase funding. A university cannot be coerced into tailoring its curriculum to fit the needs of a particular agency.

There are exceptions, however. Some agencies, mostly government ones, are given the responsibility to dispense money for services through grants or purchase of service contracts. Such an agency can withdraw or withhold money for noncompliance. The dilemma is that such an action requires the agency to either find another service provider or to no longer offer the service. These undesirable or not feasible alternatives are made less practical when one considers the political attention and conflict that is likely to accrue. The limits of power are also evident when one considers that when "compliance" has been coerced, agencies and people are quite ingenious in sabotaging or undermining the program or project.

In other situations, authoritative power has been granted to another individual. Most managers are not agency executives, and therefore each has a "boss" or several layers of bosses who have been assigned some level of authority over them. Yet lower-level managers are closer to the service delivery nexus and are often in a better position to identify resource needs, iatrogenic consequences of agency policies, the ineffective or toxic behavior of services delivered from other agencies, and the weaknesses of current service methods and procedures. Without power, social administrators must develop other ways of influencing constituents to make the changes necessary to improve performance.

## RESISTANCE TO CHANGE

Change makes something different. That something could be a policy, a program, a procedure or method, a decision, an allocation of money or staff time, or an organizational structure. Regardless of the specific "something," the ultimate "something" is behavior. A policy or procedure is changed so that the behavior of the relevant parties changes. An increase in staff means that more clients can be served—a change in these new clients' behavior is the goal. An organizational structure is changed so that employees will spend more time with clients or be more efficient decision makers. Behavior is a useful referent for change in another way. Most change occurs over time and involves a process. (Hage, 1980) At each stage, the social administrator is asking someone or some group to behave in certain ways to promote or facilitate the desired change. In other words, the process of change can best be viewed as the increments of behavior change that occur towards the desired end-state, which is also some change in behavior. For example, an attempt by a supervisor to change the intake procedures of another agency may first require agreement by that supervisor's boss to meet on the issue; then to get agreement that the boss should schedule a meeting with the other agency's executive.

Resistance to change refers to those forces or conditions that tend to decrease the likelihood of the change occurring. These resistances can be grouped into three categories: (1) predispositions, (2) objective resistances, and (3) subjective resistances.

### Predisposition

"The general tendency of organizations—and human services are no exception—is toward stability and maintenance of the status quo." (Hasenfeld, 1983, p. 221) Kaufman (1973) also states: "A host of forces thus tend to keep organizations doing the things they have been doing in the recent past, and doing them in just the way they have been doing them. . . . So formidable is the collection of forces holding organizations in their familiar paths that it is surprising that any changes ever manage to run the gauntlet successfully." (p. 39–40) This same proposition holds for individual behavior as well. "A basic assumption is that in most instances people will be reluctant to modify the way they have been doing things unless they are very dissatisfied with the existing arrangement." (Neugeborn, 1985, p. 1985)

This predisposition is reinforced in a vast corpus of procedures, policies, and cultural norms that comprise the organization. These prescriptions provide constraints on the behavior of organizational members that tend to suppress the willingness and ability to change. Many human service organizations are or are becoming vertically differentiated with many layers of authority, specialization, and high formalization. These organizations have a rather low capacity for change. (Hage in Hasenfeld, 1983, p. 233) Much of this increased rigidity comes from a distrust among organizational members. (Kaufman, 1971) Administrators act as if they fear that subordinates will misuse resources and authority without a litany of rules and regulations and careful policing.

Another contributor to the predisposition to resist change is the lack of client focused management to which organizational members ascribe. Therefore, the performance gaps that the performance manager identifies are either not seen by others or are dismissed as relatively unimportant. The fact that much of the organization's external environment does not demand a client-centered perspective further reinforces the predisposition to the status quo.

## Objective Resistances

Objective resistance may derive from such considerations as the financial cost of change, the likely benefits of the proposed change, and any track record the innovation has produced elsewhere. In some situations the change is desired, but the agency does not have the resources to accomplish it. This is especially true in contemporary human service organizations where resources at the fringes are absent; everything is already committed (e.g., time or money). The burden of proof is always on the change agent, and therefore the best possible evidence must be collected.

Technological factors also act as obstacles to change. As Neugeborn (1985) states, "People have an investment in the skills and practices they learned in school or on the job." (p. 187) Nowhere is this more evident than in community mental health as it seeks to convert from a psychotherapeutic model of care for people with severe mental illness to a community-support services methodology or as some would say from social control and rehabilitation to social care. Despite overwhelming evidence of the ineffectiveness of psychotherapy and an increasing accumulation of research demonstrating the efficacy of a community-support approach, the resistance has been at times overwhelming.

The notion of "sunk costs" is appropriate here. For an organization, sunk costs refer to the amount of resources that have been invested in creating and sustaining current practices. For the individual, sunk costs refer to years of training and experience to develop their current style and the associated costs of money, energy, and inconvenience confronted. Proposed changes easily become a perceived threat to one's self-esteem and self-worth.

## Subjective Factors

The failure to account for subjective or human factors is the most prevalent reason for unsuccessful influencing. Too often managers are startled that their rational arguments did not hold sway. "What more evidence could I provide?" This section will identify the most common subjective factors often rooted in human emotions.

*Fear of the Unknown.* Part of the subjective resistance to change is derived from the fear of the unknown. This helps explain why even the most unhappy of employees may still resist a change that seems to address some of their reasons for the unhappiness. Regardless of the dissatisfaction with current organizational practices, at least they are known and predictable. Unfortunately, many proposed changes cannot be conveyed in a fashion vivid enough to elicit feelings of comfort. In addition, many proposed changes are not predictable; despite painstaking and systematic preparations change often provokes unintended consequences. For example, every performance manager will attempt to introduce client-outcome measures into the organization. While the comments from personnel will often be couched in ideological language (e.g., unprofessional, dehumanizing), a fear of the unknown is usually at the root of the problem.

*Self-Interest.* It is a rare individual who will change when it is not in his or her self-interest. Self-interest can involve a person's desire for power, money, prestige, convenience, and security. (Patti, 1980b) Self-interest pertains to not only individuals but organizational sub-units or other organizations. Self-interest is a fundamental basis for resistance to organizational change. (Gummer, 1978; Hasenfeld, 1980; Patti, 1980b). Since self-interest is individualistic by definition, change efforts often must be based on assessments of each individual's interests and view of their world.

*Control.* People and organizations desire control over their work and their environments. Change is often perceived as reducing one's control. In part this relates to a reduced ability to predict; fear of the unknown. Just the act of proposing a change in one's behavior suggests that someone else wants you to change. It conjures up subtle subordination costs (Simon, Smithburg, & Thompson, 1950) whereby the person perceives to be "pushed around" or "told what to do." Therefore change efforts need to pay careful attention to people's security and control needs.

With all of the people involved and all of the types of resistance, it is a wonder that anything gets done. Yet we know as managers, you do get things done. What follows are ideas and an approach which we have gleaned from the experience of others, from the literature and from our own experiences.

# STAGE I: ANALYSIS AND PREPARATION

## Preface: Believe

It is not unusual to find social workers who are cynical and no longer believe that things can change. Believing that it can't happen is a sure path to failure. While belief in change will not guarantee success, it is an absolute prerequisite (please see Chapter 1, section on Healthy Disrespect for the Impossible). There is no magic formula for keeping the faith, but you may find two ideas helpful.

First, look around your organization and see what *has* changed. Actually make a list of changes you have observed. There are changes within all organizations. An organization, at one level, is a collective of people. People are dynamic and in a constant state of change. It may not be the change we want, but simply noting existing changes can help us renew our faith in change.

Second, Ellis and Harper's (1975) rational sentences are useful. In *A New Guide to Rational Living,* they present the idea that we limit ourselves by holding onto beliefs that are not rational. To counter this, they suggest constructing sentences that tell us when we are limited by our own beliefs. For example, "George will learn how to supervise that unit effectively. I need to be patient and persistent." This may sound a little like the childhood story about the little engine that could, but it works for many people.

## Establish the Purpose

Performance managers who seek to be a successful agents of change in all but the most mundane of matters, must do their homework—be prepared. The first task of being prepared is knowing what you want. After years of teaching students and working with thousands of human service professionals, we have come to see that many change efforts are not based on a *clear* idea of outcomes or goals.

There are at least two levels of purpose. The first level relates to some ultimate change desired whether it's the development and design of a new policy or procedure, the acquisition of new resources, or a key player's behavior. The second level relates to all those behaviors the performance manager seeks to elicit along the way. In order for a change to occur, the performance manager needs to get many smaller behaviors changed. Restructuring a meeting, changing intake procedures, adopting a new intervention technology, reducing paperwork, establishing a performance guidance system, acquiring additional program funds, or even changing one critical behavior of a key player does not often occur in one meeting or through one memo. Rather each meeting and each memo has a separate purpose that, if achieved, will move the change process in the desirable direction.

## Select the Focus of Change

Since the number of needed changes are rather infinite and the resources (time, energy, money, etc.) are so limited, the performance manager needs to pick the focus of change carefully. One method is to adapt "the box and whiskers" technique described in the program design chapter. The current arrangement would be described and replaces the social problem in the center of the figure. On the right-hand side, the problems and weaknesses caused by the current arrangement and the benefits accrued are listed in two categories: organization and individuals. This list should in part be based on a consideration of the five performance areas. On the left-hand side, the factors contributing to the current arrangement are listed. These could be organized according to the administrative technologies of program design, information management, personnel management, and resource management. This includes the problems that were to be solved by the current arrangement. This method is useful for organizing the collection of information and the performance manager's thinking.

While you do not want to unnecessarily restrict what you are trying to improve, there are a few key points about what people tend to find easier to accept. We suggest that you consider these points particularly in the way you frame your change focus. People tend to find changes easier to accept when:

- there are obvious advantages to the new way;
- it uses less of a scarce resource;
- it is simple; and
- it is consistent with values, interests, and prior experiences.

Three categories of change that will take prominence over others should emerge. The first category is the behavior of key players external to the organization. In program design, the key players and the minimum behavior necessary for desired client outcomes to occur were identified. More to the point, if these key players do not behave as specified, clients will be hurt or at least not helped. The performance manager needs to pay careful attention to these behaviors and insure that mechanisms are in place to elicit and maintain these behaviors.

The second category includes those forms of change that will naturally lead to other desirable changes. For example, developing and implementing a performance guidance system will change what personnel pay attention to, will set the stage for the exchange of rewards, and will identify problems that were left uncovered before. In a similar fashion, changing the criteria for decisions, or job descriptions, or the organizational structure will produce other benefits. The key is the direct link to one of the performance areas.

The third category involves insuring that the organization has the resources needed to do the job whether its personnel, funds, goodwill, technology, clients, or equipment. It means acquiring those tools needed by organizational members to carry out their assigned responsibilities.

Selecting the focus should result in an unambiguous statement of the change to be made. It should be behavioral and specific so that it is clear if it has been achieved or not. The purpose can be written in terms of a specific product (e.g., a case review system will be implemented that contains at least these three elements).

The purpose can be written in terms of a specific decision (e.g., my supervisor gave permission for me to meet with the judge to develop referral procedures). The purpose can also be focused on specific behavior (e.g., monthly staff meetings will begin with a review of the most recent client outcome reports).

Once the behavior or sequence of behavior (the purpose) has been established the following questions can serve as a check that you have identified a performance oriented focus for the change.

- Which performance area will this behavior enhance?
- How will this behavior improve this performance?
- Is this new way viable?
- What other ways are there to achieve the increase in performance?
- Is this the "best" way to improve performance in this area?

## STAGE II: DEVELOPING THE DESCRIPTIVE MODEL

### Analyzing the Current Arrangement

The better the information you have about current arrangements the better the strategies to accomplish your purpose. There are a variety of reasons why an organization conducts business using its current arrangement. The current arrangement was designed to solve some previously defined problem. There once was a reason or reasons that led to the development, implementation, and adherence to how things are done. What were those reasons? Are the reasons still relevant? To what degree did the arrangement solve the problem it was designed to solve? Is it currently solving the problem?

The current arrangement has produced some benefits but has no doubt caused some problems. What roles do which people play? Who is benefiting from the current arrangement? How are they benefiting? What are the problems? Who is unhappy about the current arrangement and why? Who is uncomfortable about parts of the current arrangement?

In this analysis and description of the current arrangement there are going to be features that you will want to maintain. There will be behavior you will want to reinforce. There will also be people who want things changed. Some of these people will want the same things you want. Others will be unclear on what they want, and others will want things changed in ways that are in opposition to what you want. In all cases, you should identify features or current results that need to be reinforced, left undisturbed, or systematically addressed and identify possible facilitators of change.

For example, you decide that a counseling program would benefit from a different form of supervision. After careful consideration of program design and personnel management elements, you decide that adoption of Harkness's (1987) client-centered menu would enhance client benefits. Your goal is to have the counseling supervisor discuss cases in a supervision session. The supervisor would select questions from the following menu:

1. What does the client want help with?
2. How will you and the client know you are helping?
3. How does the client describe a successful outcome?
4. Does the client say there has been a successful outcome?
5. What are you doing to help the client?
6. Is it working?
7. Does the client say you are helping?
8. What else can you do to help the client?
9. How will it work?
10. Does the client say that will help?

In your analysis of the current arrangement, it is obvious that the supervisor and worker are the key individuals to consider in this change effort. You hypothesize that two of the main reasons for the current arrangement is the agency's emphasis on policy and that the supervisor probably never had the opportunity to observe another form of supervision. You attend a group supervision session and observe that the time is mainly spent with a discussion of changes in agency policy and programs. Near the end of the session a small amount of time is spent on clients. This time is spent on distributing new cases and venting frustrations. Most of the workers appear disengaged and ready to leave. In short discussions afterwards at the coffeepot, workers share the frustrations of all this "policy stuff," and there never seems to be time to get help with cases. In a short friendly chat, the supervisor shares the frustration of having to spend all this time on agency policy and wishes that staff were more helpful. You finish your analysis by concluding that the group supervision format is a feature you wish to maintain. The workers' frustration about not getting enough help with cases and the joint worker and supervisor frustration about the sessions will facilitate change.

## STAGE III: FURTHER SPECIFYING THE NEW WAY—THE NORMATIVE MODEL

You now need to complete the detailed description of your proposed change, your "better idea." Earlier in the process the manager could just define the purpose as a client-focused supervision session using a list of questions that are adapted from Harkness. Now, the manager needs to be more specific as to substance and process of the proposed change. Basically, this requires answering the following three questions.

- Will it offer the maximum likelihood of enhancing performance?
- Who does what when?
- What features and resultant benefits must be incorporated from the current arrangement?

At this stage, the performance manager needs to get very specific and discrete. Most changes require people to perform in specific ways and often in a particular sequence. Answering the "who" question requires considerations of authority, ownership, competence, and predisposition to support the change. Personnel who either have formally constituted authority (e.g., supervisor, agency director, board, etc.) or possess informal authority (e.g., an influential staff member, a relevant specialist, an elite from an external constituency) need to be considered and identified. They usually have to agree to the innovation or to sanction steps leading to it. For the innovation to be adopted and implemented as conceived, a host of people need to "own" it, otherwise seemingly successful efforts can later be sabotaged. Identify the people whose ownership is deemed critical. People who are particularly competent and respected are also sources for answering the "who" question. These people often carry weight in discussions. Their input often tips the decision-making scale one way or the other. And lastly, people who have a predisposition or who are likely to agree and support the change should be identified. They become the core group of support as the innovation winds its way towards implementation.

Once the players have been identified, each person should be assigned the minimum behavior necessary for the innovation to occur. What is it each person has to do for the change to occur?

After this has been completed, an analysis of benefits and costs of your innovation should be calculated. This includes money and time as well as subjective or psychological effects. Be clear—the "better idea" will cause some new problems or exacerbate others. The performance manager should try to predict what these will be. The objections of others usually harbor a problem or dilemma that the innovation may cause. Active and careful listening is indispensable.

Harkness (1987) demonstrated that the use of the client-centered menu improved outcomes by 17 percent. It is clear that the key person is the supervisor and that the key behaviors are discussing cases instead of policy, selecting questions from the Harkness client-centered menu, and expecting workers to brainstorm helpful ideas in case discussions. The workers' concerns about their cases and the current time devoted to case discussions ought not only to be kept but expanded. The benefits include improving outcomes for clients, potentially reducing worker frustrations about their cases, and generally improving the atmosphere during supervision. Costs include the lost time spent on policy and the potential initial loss of self-esteem on the part of the supervisor as she struggles with thoughts about what she has been doing and the need to change her behavior.

## STAGE IV: PLANNING THE ACTION STRATEGY

With the previous analyses completed, the performance manager is ready to plan the action strategy. This involves two tasks: vulnerability assessment and strategy selection. Strategy selection involves use of a collection of behavioral or cognitive strategies. These strategies are discussed in detail later in this chapter.

### Vulnerability Assessment

Since the use of power is usually unavailable to the performance manager, he or she must persuade people. A case may need to be built for each key player. The person who is concerned with cost needs to see that the change will not unduly stretch the budget. The person who is concerned with staff burnout will want to be assured workers will not be overly burdened. In other words, what does the person need or want? What usually motivates them to act? What is the person's expected position or response to the performance manager's idea or proposal? What concerns does the position imply?

Pay attention to the ideologies, values, and past statements of the key players. Find out their relationships with influential people, their self-interests (status, prestige, power), their role models, which people they hold in high esteem, their discomfort or unhappiness with the current arrangement, and the process they use to make decisions. For example, some people require evidence of past success of anything new before supporting it.

The empathy capacity of the manager is important here. Social administration like other types of social work practice requires placing yourself in another person's position to understand his or her behavior. Just as in direct practice, this is a difficult task. It requires knowledge, experience, and practice. It is not possible to put yourself in another person's position without some basic knowledge of that person. Their needs, wants, motivations, and values are categories of basic information needed to understand their position. You can acquire this information in a variety of ways.

1. Determine their academic training. The academic discipline or training of a person provides information about a person's values and world view. Whether this is a result of education or a process of self-selection is not important, people in disciplines and professions seem to share a common view of the world. For example, economists tend to view people as motivated by economic advantage. Psychologists tend to find explanations of behavior within the person. Of course these are simplistic examples, and one must be careful of stereotyping.

2. What do they get excited about? The source of a person's enthusiasm at work clearly provides us with valuable information about the person. What are they working on when they work hard or late? What is it they say they are trying to accomplish?

3. Who do they seem to work well with? People tend to spend time with others

with similar values and motivations. If we know who a person works with and we know more about that person, we have additional clues about the individual's values. Included in this consideration is the person's heroes. Who is it within the profession, area, or agency that the person values, attempts to emulate, or sees as a role model? The important point here is work relationships. We are attempting to discover a person's work values. While a person's social relationships are informative, the focus of administrative empathy is the work world.

4. What demands are placed upon this person by whom? Frequently people behave in specific ways because of the demands other people place on them. Recall the multiple constituent dilemma in Chapter 1. People in social agencies must respond to a large number of constituents. If you systematically identify each constituent and the demands he or she places upon the individual you are trying to convince, you have important information that will help you tailor your case to that particular person.

5. What does this person talk about? Listening to what a person says, the questions they ask, and the work on which they focus tells us a great deal about a person's job values. Listening to people in meetings, in their offices, at the coffee-pot, in the parking lot, at the elevator, and by the mailbox tells us about their language and interests. The ubiquitous memos, letters, and position papers also provide information.

Determining a person's values and motivations, and ultimately their expected position is not solely a cognitive exercise. Frequently the best source of information is working with the person and being observant at the same time. As a test of your knowledge of the person try a role play with a colleague with you playing the role of the person you want to persuade. If you are a convincing representation of that person, you are likely to have an accurate representation of the person's expected position.

## STAGE V: DEVELOPING A CONSENSUS MODEL

The next stage of King and Clelland's (1976) implementation model is negotiating a consensus model. The consensus model is the actual change to be implemented and most often it falls somewhere between the normative and descriptive models. The descriptive model is the current arrangement. The normative model is the ideal state. Since the ideal state is rarely achieved, the next stage is to negotiate a consensus. The result is the consensus model. This model reflects the idea that change is an incremental and interactive process. The key points here are the ideas of negotiating and consensus. Social administration like other forms of social work involves working with people for mutual need fulfillment. Consequently, interpersonal skills similar to or identical to those used by direct-service social workers are also essential for the social administrator. This section will review some of these interpersonal skills.

At the individual level you may be able to get the product or behavior you want. But it is rare to get all of what you want at any one point in time. The social administrator who keeps this in mind is likely to engender less resistance and frustration. It may even be possible that this administrator will be more successful in the long run.

## Some Basics About Negotiating

Social administrators like direct-service workers need to be good negotiators. Much of this chapter has included material often considered to be part of being a good negotiator. Here are additional points to remember about negotiating: preparation, directing the feedback process, the use of questions, and the process of negotiation.

*Preparation.* Like most acts in social work, negotiating begins with careful preparation. Preparation involves both attitudes and behaviors. Two attitudes required by successful negotiators include being prepared to make concessions and the desire to satisfy the needs of the people involved. The negotiation process is no place for a competitive win-lose philosophy. Since you are genuinely interested in improving conditions for clients and working with people for mutual benefit, you should have a give and take attitude. For people to want to perform the behavior required to improve the program each person must have his or her needs satisfied. This desire to satisfy needs leads to making concessions.

When one is involved in the negotiating process and is confronted with a dizzying array of seemingly incompatible needs, it is difficult to see how mutual needs can be satisfied without giving up the very essence of what we are trying to accomplish. The skills required to find common ground are identifying needs/goals and increasing choices. A good place to start is to write down what you think are the compatible and incompatible needs. Make the compatible list as long as possible and the incompatible list as short as possible. Frequently what seems incompatible after closer examination is not so. For example, the teenager who wants to be out from under his mother's control wants the same thing his parent wants: an independent adult free from problems such as drugs. In striving to make the list of compatible needs longer seemingly incompatible needs can be rewritten to demonstrate compatibility. Of course, there is always the possibility that real incompatible needs exist, which would indicate that the change has little likelihood of succeeding. Of course this does not mean ignoring incompatible needs/goals—that would simply result in later failure. But as you work with people, if you can point out that there are more areas of agreement than disagreement, it is easier for everyone to keep working toward consensus.

Once you have your list of what seem to be incompatible needs, you may be able to shorten it by examining the list to determine which ones are really incompatible and which ones only seem to be incompatible. One of the keys to breaking through and finding agreement is to increase choice. Developing as many ideas and alternatives as possible frequently results in finding ways to reconcile incompatibility.

To locate compatibility examine needs/goals in terms of "shoulds" or history. "Shoulds" frequently are not needs but people's reactions to what they think other people want them to do. Likewise goals that have been around for a long time, have not been achieved, and are in constant need of reminding tend not to be real goals. You can also identify superordinate goals. That is, goals that are on a higher level of abstraction. (Gruber, 1986) This is somewhat easier for the social administrator because social work values unify his or her concerns with those of other social workers and frequently unite apparently disparate agendas. Recognition that everyone is attempting to produce the same client benefit can often unite apparently disparate interests.

*Direct the Feedback Process.*  People need to be involved in the change process if they are to agree on something that will affect their lives. They need an opportunity to have their questions answered. They need to help shape the result through incorporation of their expertise. And they need to come to agreement with enough knowledge about the new way that they are not surprised about some aspect that causes them to withdraw their agreement. Consequently, the social administrator developing a consensus must take the responsibility to direct the information and feedback process. Of course, this is a basic direct-practice skill.

Developing consensus among a group of people who may not even be physically in the same place requires communication and often communicating on an intense and persistent basis. The social administrator needs access to key decision makers and other key players on as regular basis as possible. Popping in on a judge or taking advantage of a street corner encounter to change behavior does guarantee success, but as part of a larger pattern of contact and relationship it may lead to success.

The first role for the social administrator in this process is to directly provide both relevant information and feedback. (See Chapter 3 for the principles of the effective use of information and feedback.) Other points of which most people need reminding include the need to be descriptive and factual and not judgmental. Of course, the social administrator also has legitimate opinions that need to be expressed in the "I statement" format.

Another aspect of directing information and feedback is not taking responsibility for doing all of it yourself but making certain others provide both the information and feedback that comes from their expertise and concerns. You need to actively encourage the parties involved to provide information and feedback. This feedback tends to be more useful if it is specific, occurs close to the act or the behavior, and if it can be checked. Also feedback on things that cannot be changed is not very useful. For example the statement, "I don't think clients five years ago would have said that" may be exactly correct, but it is not a useful statement.

Feedback has by its very nature the image of the past. Literature on feedback indicates that under many circumstances it is most useful when it is focused on the future. (Taylor, 1987) Remember that in this consensus building process you are trying to arrive at some ideal state. Keeping that clearly in front of everyone including using feedback is important. "That incident in last month's staff meeting really bothered me and some other staff. I wonder how we might respond differently if that situation seems to be occurring again next month." This example of future oriented feedback tends to be more useful than: "That incident in last month's staff meeting really bothered me. Let's talk about what caused it." A good way to maintain a future orientation is to frequently remind people where this effort is headed, restate different positions, and compare and contrast positions. This can serve to regain the focus, demonstrate expectations for various positions, and indicate the work remaining to arrive at the eventual goal.

One last reminder on directing the feedback process. The quiet person can represent a real challenge. With a large number of people involved and many things occurring at one time, it is easy to forget about the person who seems quiet and uninvolved. Yet this person may very well have the piece of information that could bring everything together in a positive manner. Alternatively, this person may make the statement late in the process or ask the question that destroys the emerging consensus. The lesson is obvious. You must draw this person out in a nonthreatening manner.

***Use Questions.*** The use of questions is yet another generic social work skill that is critical to the success of the social administrator working to build a consensus. The often stated and equally often forgotten old saw that you cannot ask questions unless you listen requires no elaboration. But *thinking* about the purpose of a question is seldom considered. In the negotiating process, questions can have several different purposes. Recognizing this and matching the question to the purpose is a skill worth practicing. We have identified six different purposes for questions.

- To gain attention
- To regain control of the conversation
- To provide information
- To start the audience thinking
- To bring to conclusion
- To obtain information

The purpose of the question affects what happens next far more than the question itself. For example if the purpose is to regain control of the conversation, the subject is of little importance. But if you want information, the subject is critical. Listen to questions and watch their effects on people. Practice using purposeful questions.

The purpose is just one consideration. Questions that do not appear to be linked to anything are very difficult to respond to in a useful manner. Consequently, it is helpful to think about the context and consequences of the question. The context includes the foundation for the question and attending to transitions. A useful technique is to repeat the essence of the statement before as a transition to the question. It is also important to consider the consequence of asking the question. Is there an answer that could be harmful to your purpose? For example, if your purpose is to bring the meeting to a conclusion, you do not want to ask an expansive question like: What other ideas do you have that might be useful? The primary considerations in the consequences are the purpose and not offending the audience or putting the audience on the spot unless that is central to your purpose.

Lastly, the format and sequencing of questions is an important consideration. Questions can be sequenced in either an inductive or deductive manner. That is, they can take a topic and go from general to specific or specific to general. Schulman (1982) talks about this using the metaphor of the funnel sequence of questioning or the inverted funnel. Format of questions should include the oft stated reminder that questions that cannot be answered by a simple "yes" or "no" are more useful. Also the nonquestion is often a good question. That is, a simple statement of reflection or restatement is often useful.

## The Process of Negotiating

The process of negotiating a consensus is a complicated and nonlinear process that this short section could be seen as oversimplifying. The intent here is to remind the reader of the complexity of the process and some skills that the authors have found useful.

*Agenda Setting.* Change is an incremental process in which one seeks to take the other party as far as they can in a given encounter. At times this may mean just getting an issue on the agenda or discussing it in the most general way. The social administrator is always pushing it to the next step and only temporarily stopping when the other party has let it be known this is as far as it goes for now. It means moving verbal commitments to behavior as soon as possible.

Two essential ingredients in the initial process of developing consensus are establishing your expertise and demonstrating personal qualities that will make it easier for others to work with you. Simons (1987) observes that persuasion is influenced by the expertise, trustworthiness, and likeability of the person seeking to persuade. The social administrator needs to establish a track record of trust. He or she must be seen as having a commitment to the organization and clients and having the ability to deliver. It is also helpful if the manager is friendly, outgoing, and liked by those he or she is trying to convince.

Whether the consensus building process is occurring in a meeting or a series of events with different people at different times and places, there are several agenda setting considerations. The social administrator should seek to initiate and limit the agenda, as well as keep people focused on the agenda. We frequently hear people say, "I am not the leader of the group," or "That is not my job." If you are the person concerned with doing something differently, it is your job. Whether you are the nominal leader in a given situation or not makes little difference. In this agenda setting process, you also want to carefully consider who should participate. The goal is to involve the fewest people with the most authority.

*Agenda Maintenance.* As you move from agenda setting to agenda maintenance, you may also need to set time limits and referee them. Remind people of the time limits and negotiate around missed deadlines. The equalization of perceived power may also be important at this time. This may lead to consideration of the location of meetings, the decor of the meeting place, the use of names or titles, where people sit, and the provision of information about people.

As the consensus development process begins you will want to identify and state a mutually agreeable and concise definition of the situation. This in itself may require negotiation. Part of this definition may be the identification of existing areas of agreement. When demonstrating areas of agreement, there is frequently a tendency to push for quick agreement on apparently minor points through some type of formal or informal voting process. Avoid this. People may not think through their position before voting with the apparent majority. Later they recognize their disagreement and withdraw their vote, undermining or delaying the consensus building process. In your position as social administrator and consensus negotiator, you may want to make an early concession. This demonstrates to others that you are serious about developing a consensus and not just pushing your position.

*Avoiding Polarization.* It is not easy for people to alter their behavior. Consequently, tension and anxiety are a natural ingredient in the consensus building process. It is important to avoid polarization. This frequently freezes people in their position making it much more difficult for them to change. Humor is also a useful tool to relieve tension. When humor is used sincerely and frequently in ways that do not belittle participants, it can keep the level of tension from contributing to polarization. Reminding participants of their relationship as a group or of a commonly held value can also help maintain an atmosphere of openness and reduced tension. Some of the participants will also have developed skills in tension reduction and conciliation. Conscious identification and reinforcement of these people will make the process easier. The social administrator does not need to play all of the parts or even write the entire script, but he or she must outline the event and direct the performance.

In extreme cases where people are struck and are still trying to work toward consensus, role reversal can be a useful technique. Being unable to see another position can sometimes be overcome by role playing the different positions and asking people to play a role that is the reverse of their position. With role reversal people can frequently see aspects of their position not previously seen and thus become open to change.

Lastly, as individual events occur and the consensus building process progresses, you need to end each event on a positive note, get agreement and on next steps, and get it in writing. In general, never let the record of a decision remain only in people's memories. There should be a record of that decision that can be referred to if necessary.

## Some Reminders About Groups

Administrators spend a large amount of their valuable time in meetings and working with groups. For this reason we would like to remind you of a few of the essentials about groups. This is no substitute for a thorough study of groups along with experience. However, a summary of a few of the key ideas about groups, along with the consensus building strategies to come later, may assist you in integrating group skills into your administrative practice.

People have an effect on the group and the group or presence of other people has an effect on individuals. Specifying the exact nature of these relationships is still fertile ground for the social psychologist. Nevertheless, it is known that the effect of the group on individuals depends on the

- purpose of the group,
- number of people in the group,
- immediacy of the group members,
- status of the members,
- group norms,
- communications opportunities of the members, and
- cohesiveness of the group. (Wrightsman & Deaux, 1981)

Some people seek out an audience and perform at a much higher level in a group while others shrink from an audience. These effects can be positive or negative depending on a large number of variables including what the group is doing and characteristics of the individual. Although the exact effects are difficult to predict in a given situation, from the social administrator's point of view you need to be conscious of these variables, note their effects in your practice arena, and attempt to account for them in individual situations.

Social administrators frequently find themselves in problem-solving situations with groups. (In fact we suggest later that this is one of the most powerful ways to use groups.) The social psychologists remind us that the result of group problem solving is not necessarily better than individual problem-solving. The effectiveness of group problem-solving depends on the task, characteristics of group members, and the skills of the individual members. These are critical variables to keep in mind as you engage groups in tasks and problem-solving that will be discussed as the first strategy for building a consensus.

The skills required to work effectively with groups are presented in a variety of texts using different organizing schemes. Toseland and Rivas (1984) present a succinct and useful discussion of these skills. (See Table 6–1.)

## Developing Consensus: Behavioral Strategies

Development of a consensus requires a large number of interpersonal skills. This chapter cannot begin to adequately discuss all of these skills, which are probably best learned experientially. The following merely covers the basics.

*Behavioral Strategy 1: Work on a Group Task.* One of the most powerful techniques for developing a consensus with a group of people is to get them involved in

**TABLE 6-1. A FUNCTIONAL CLASSIFICATION OF GROUP LEADERSHIP SKILLS**

| Facilitating Group Processes | Data Gathering and Assessment | Action |
|---|---|---|
| 1. Attending to others | 1. Identifying and describing thoughts, feelings, and behaviors | 1. Directing |
| 2. Expressing self | | 2. Synthesizing thoughts, feelings, and action |
| 3. Responding to others | 2. Requesting information, questioning, and probing | 3. Supporting |
| 4. Focusing group communication | | 4. Reframing, redefining |
| 5. Guiding group | 3. Summarizing and partializing information | 5. Resolving conflicts |
| 6. Involving group members in the communication pattern | 4. Analyzing information | 6. Giving advice, suggestions, or instructions |
| | | 7. Confronting |
| | | 8. Providing resources |
| | | 9. Modeling, role playing, rehearsing, and coaching |

doing a *task*. All too often meetings in organizations are a waste of time. The agenda is unstructured or absent, and the desired outcomes are not specified. Few participants take responsibility for helping structure or lead the meeting. When a meeting operates at an abstract level with vague verbal exchanges, few concrete results can be expected. Although most social workers possess considerable verbal ability, it is this very skill that can become a problem in meetings. Discussing issues or problems on a conceptual level often passes for doing work. Or time is taken up with one person trying to convince another person to agree with his or her position. Influencing others does have a role to play in meetings, but verbal skills can be put to better use if the group is concentrating on doing a specific task together.

For example, you are trying to implement a new program for children with emotional disabilities in a mental health center. When you developed the program design, you struggled with the target and client population because of the lack of definition of an emotionally disturbed child. During your research, you became convinced that because of this lack of definition programs become filled with youth who may be less disabled while those with serious disabilities are denied access. In your design, you developed some preliminary boundaries for the client population, and now you find yourself in a meeting of mental health center staff discussing who should be served by your new program. You could present the results of your deliberations and attempt to get the group to adopt your target population. In this process, you would argue for your conclusion. You might be successful. Or as we have frequently found, you may open the door to a discussion of why your definition is inadequate and must be modified and probably end up with a very general description of a client population that defeats your very purpose.

The task-centered approach in this situation would change the focus by getting the group to do work together rather than engage in verbal argument. In this case you as the instigator might present frequently used definitions of youth with emotional disabilities and point out their inadequacy in implementing a new program. In this process you would indicate how no one is helped by the definition and get the group engaged in developing an intake checklist that will unambiguously as possible determine which youth will be served and which youth will not be served by this program.

If you are successful in getting the group engaged in this task, you are accomplishing several things at the same time. You are building on the group's strength in terms of analytic and verbal ability by directing this into a critically important task. You are developing ownership for the product, which enhances the implementation of the product as intended. You are drawing on the collective practice wisdom of the group, which is bound to be larger than yours. As items for the intake checklist are put forth, you are provided with specific suggestions to reward individuals as well as the group. Consequently the group is going to experience increased feelings of competence and probably cohesion. As the group struggles with the difficulty of the task, you are provided with a natural opportunity to provide the group with information you acquired in your program design efforts.

No single example can demonstrate the richness and variety of this strategy, but the list of benefits is quite impressive. Of course, the group or individual members must have the specific skills required to complete the task. The group may simply not have any history in doing work together, which may make it difficult to engage them in a task. You may also select a task that they just do not have the ability to complete. In either case, it is likely that the original tasks can be broken down into a small task or set of tasks that the group can successfully complete.

It is also frequently the case that part of the task cannot be finished because someone needs to do some other work outside of the group meeting, checking case files or state policy, for example. In this situation the work is delegated to group members. The more that each member can take responsibility for a part of the task, the more the benefits of this approach will be accrued. Voluntering to do a part of the task shows commitment on your part as well. One advantage to the delegation of tasks to be done outside of the group is the natural establishment of the agenda for the next meeting as well as prior commitment to work at the next meeting.

In short, managers who are skilled at translating issues into concrete tasks and involving others in their completion are often quite successful in change efforts.

***Behavioral Strategy 2: Modeling.*** Modeling as an administrative strategy for building consensus is simply doing. Much of what we want people to do is a set of behaviors that are much too complex to explain or attempt to talk people into doing. When a person does (models) the set of behaviors the components of the behavior are demonstrated. This also allows the audience to compare their behavior in similar situations to the demonstrated behavior. Not only the behaviors are demonstrated but the rewards possible or accruing from the behavior are also demonstrated. This includes both extrinsic and intrinsic rewards. Modeling not only demonstrates the rewards available from others but also demonstrates the ways in which the behavior is intrinsically energizing or exciting.

Modeling has several implications for social administrators. The audience has to be able to see the behavioral components, the extrinsic rewards and the intrinsic rewards. The audience has to believe that the rewards would also be available to them. The audience has to believe that they could perform the behavior. These conditions mean that the administrator using modeling must establish the conditions for modeling to be effective. The social administrator must remove any real or perceived barriers to performing the behavior. The social administrator must make certain that the rewards are available to others who perform the same behavior. The administrator must explicitly demonstrate the implicit rewards through demonstrating the excitement or joy felt by performing the behavior.

*Behavioral Strategy 3: Inducements and Rewards.* This strategy comes directly from the various behavioral schools of thought. People exhibit behavior they believe to be rewarding. There are two ways this happens. Conditions are established that assure the person of being rewarded. Or behavior is exhibited and rewards accrue, which increases the frequency of the behavior. Of course the link between the behavior and the inducement or reward must be explicit. In addition for inducements and rewards to work, they must be valued by the person and must be perceived as fair and not patronizing.

This strategy is yet another instance where the administrator must know what people value and what specific individuals find rewarding. (The personnel management chapter includes consideration of common job values and the reward-based environment.) The administrator must explicitly link the inducement or reward to the desired behavior. In many behavioral models, this is emphasized through temporal placement of rewards and behavior. Given the environment in which administrators operate, "being there" when the behavior occurs is unlikely. Consequently, the administrator needs to be explicit in the link between the inducement, the reward, and the desired behavior. Linking rewards that come from the social administrator to rewards that normally occur within the environment also enhances their effect. Again, being explicit about intrinsic rewards and creating a reward-based environment is a large part of this strategy. An important task for the social administrator is to make the reward-based environment an expectation of everyone in the workplace and to clearly define the performance that results in rewards.

*Behavioral Strategy 4: The Broken Record.* There is no more indispensable ingredient to successful influencing than persistence or what Fairweather, Sanders, and Tornatzky (1974) call perseverance. The performance manager simply does not give up and is always searching for a different way to influence. The performance manager keeps the issue on the organizational agenda until it's resolved. The broken record strategy is one manifestation of interpersonal persistence. If you keep the measurement of client outcome, for example, on the agency agenda, it is more likely to occur. A meeting has many diversions. The persistent focusing of the group on the task frequently results in a more productive session. This may take the form of repeating a question each time the group becomes diverted: "Where do you think we might begin in developing client-outcome measures that will give us the feedback we need on our good efforts." If you can find several different ways of asking the same question, it might be received more kindly by the group. But if you cannot find other ways of asking the question, it works to simply be a broken record and repeat the exact sentence.

## Developing Consensus: Principles Underlying Effective Persuasion

In trying to influence others, a person may use persuasion, inducement, or constraint. (Gamson, 1968) "In contrast to inducement or constraint which requires the manipulation of consequences contingent upon the target's response, persuasion involves changing the way an individual or group perceives a set of alternatives through the provision of new information." (Simons, 1987, p. 244) Or as Larson (1983) puts it, "The process of persuasion involves your presenting good reasons for a specific choice among probable alternatives." (p. 281) The following material on the principles of persuasion was reproduced from Simons' article "The Skill of Persuasion: An Essential Component of Human Services Administration" (1987).

Theory and research on persuasion is concerned with identifying the characteristics of messages that persons find appealing, with discovering the nature of communications that are perceived to contain "good reasons" for adopting the position being advocated. Based upon the findings of several decades of research, the following appear to be effective principles of persuasion.

Simons (1982, 1985, 1987) has conducted an extensive review of the social psychology literature on cognitive strategies for persuasion and influence. While these are presented as additional discrete strategies, their best use is in combination with other strategies such as doing work with a group. It is also natural to think of cognitive strategies to be the exclusive realm of oral interchanges, but they are also useful with other communication channels such as memos and reports. We will review several of these strategies by describing the strategy and providing an example within the context of social administration. This is no substitute for learning and practicing these experientially. Social administrators are encouraged to practice each of these with another person who can observe the use of the strategy and its effect on the audience and provide feedback.

*Cognitive Strategy 1: Emphasize Advantages or Rewards.* People are constantly processing the information available to them and making decisions as to how they might best satisfy their needs and achieve their goals. Hence, the probability that individuals will change their behavior in response to a communication is increased when the message provides information indicating that the change will enable them to more effectively satisfy their needs and desires.

Several studies show that a target audience is more apt to adopt a favorable attitude toward a behavior or procedure when they perceive it to have a relative advantage over existing or alternative practices. (Coleman, Katz, & Menzel, 1966; Leventhal, 1970; Rogers, 1983) Rogers (1968) notes that the advantages or rewards associated with an action may not be economic or material. The benefits of adopting the line of action being advocated may be largely psychological, leading to an increase in prestige, status, or satisfaction. People must have sufficient reason for modifying their behavior or for adopting a new procedure. One good reason for doing so is because the new approach yields rewards at a level unavailable through existing practices or alternative action.

***Cognitive Strategy 2: Make It Comprehensible.*** The action being advocated must be presented in a language that is readily understood by the target audience. Technical jargon should be avoided if possible. People will not adopt a line of action that they do not fully comprehend. Simple, easily understood ideas are more likely to be accepted than complex and hard to follow arguments. (Glaser, Abelson, & Garrison, 1983; Rogers, 1983; Zaltman, 1973) Comprehension can sometimes be augmented with graphs, charts, or through site visits where the audience can view the innovation in action. Clarity and comprehension are important in addressing a person's fear of the unknown.

***Cognitive Strategy 3: Show Compatibility of Values.*** There is substantial evidence that people are more apt to accept an idea if it is perceived as consistent with their present beliefs, values, and ways of doing things. (Rogers, 1983; Zaltman, 1973) For instance, Woolfolk, Woolfolk, and Wilson (1977) found that students who were shown identical videotapes of a teacher using reinforcement procedures evaluated the teacher and the technique more favorably when the videotape was described as an illustration of "humanistic education" than when it was labeled behavior modification. And, Sanders and Reppucci (1977) reported that the reaction of school principals and superintendents to a program proposal varied if the program was identified as employing a behavior modification approach. Such studies are a clear demonstration of the ways an audience's receptivity to an idea can be destroyed by using words or phrases the group perceives as representing beliefs or practices that are contrary to their values.

Various groups, whether human service agencies, funding bodies, or civic organizations, are often committed to a particular socio-political ideology. An idea is more apt to be accepted or assimilated by a group if it is perceived to be compatible with the assumption, principles, and procedures that make up the group's ideological orientation. (Glaser, Abelson, & Garrison, 1983) Compatibility promises greater security and less risk to the receiver while making the new idea appear more meaningful. (Rogers, 1983) Enhancing organizational performance, client centeredness, and client outcomes comprises an attractive ideology and set of values that can be difficult, but far from impossible, to disagree with.

***Cognitive Strategy 4: Cite Proven Results.*** An audience is more apt to accept an idea if its consequences have already been observed. When people can see the positive results of an action or procedure, they are more likely to adopt it. (Glaser, Abelson, & Garrison, 1983; Rogers, 1983) Given this finding, a stepping stone approach is often the most effective way of selling an idea. First, a small group is persuaded to test the procedure. The positive results obtained in this demonstration project or pilot program are then cited in persuasive communications designed to promote the idea across a broader population.

***Cognitive Strategy 5: Allow for Trialability.*** The target group will perceive less risk if the new idea can be tried on a piecemeal basis prior to wholesale adoption of the procedure. (Rogers, 1983; Rogers & Svenning, 1969) As Glaser, Abelson, and Garrison (1983) observe:

> The extent to which a proposed change is known to be reversible if it does not prove desirable may affect its adoption. Not all innovations can be discarded later with impunity; the bridges back to the status quo may have been burned. Situations in which the user need not "play for keeps" provide more opportunity for innovation. (p. 61)

People are reluctant to commit themselves to a line of action that does not allow for a later change of mind. An idea is more apt to be adopted if it can be broken into parts that can be tried one step at a time, with the group having the option of discontinuing the new procedure at any time if they should decide that it is not producing the anticipated results. (Rogers, 1983) Often influencing efforts can be buoyed if the performance manager has already implemented the practice in his or her domain, thereby modeling its implementation and effects.

***Cognitive Strategy 6: Link Message to Influential Others.*** Consistent with the predictions of balance theory (Heider, 1958), several studies indicate that people tend to adopt the same attitude toward an object or idea as that held by someone they like and that they tend to adopt the opposite attitude toward an object or idea as that held by someone they dislike. (Tedeschi & Lindskold, 1976) In this way, individuals maintain cognitive balance.

These findings suggest that an idea is more likely to be accepted if it is linked to people that the target audience likes. The most direct method for doing this is to have someone the audience likes or respects deliver the persuasive appeal. When this is not feasible, reference might be made to influential others as part of the persuasion message. For instance, if a city council member is known to be a firm supporter of the state governor, the governor is known to have the same views on an issue as the social worker who is trying to influence the council member, this information could be presented to the council member. This general tactic can be used whether the favored person is the president, a movie star, a well-known expert on some topic, or the person's colleague, friend, or spouse.

The social worker might cite individuals when information about whom the target audience likes or respects is lacking. This strategy is based on the extensive body of research indicating that people tend to be attracted to people they perceive as similar to themselves. Thus, when attempting to persuade a landlord to make repairs, the worker might name other landlords who have made such repairs; when attempting to persuade a principal to institute a drug education program, the worker might cite principals from other schools in the city who have begun such programs, and so forth.

*Cognitive Strategy 7: Avoid High Pressure Tactics.* Research based upon reactance theory shows that when individuals feel pressured to select a particular course of action, whether through the promise of rewards, the threat of punishment, or intense appeals, they tend to increase their valuation of alternatives to the position being advocated. (Brehm, 1966; Wicklund, 1974) High pressure tactics create a boomerang effect. The use of pressure to persuade people to adopt an idea frequently creates resistance and a determination to act in a manner contrary to the proposed action. Human beings value their freedom and will resist attempts to circumscribe their choice or self-determination. Therefore, messages should be presented in a manner that minimizes any threat to the person's feeling of freedom. Phrases such as "It's your decision," "But, of course, it's up to you," and "Think about it and see what you want to do" serve this function; whereas words such as "must," "should," and "have to" are likely to arouse resistance. (Brehm, 1966)

*Cognitive Strategy 8: Minimize Threats to Security, Status, or Esteem.* Change agents often commit the "rationalistic bias" of assuming that people are reasonable beings who, when presented with the logic of a new and better approach, will recognize its merits and embrace it without hesitation. (Zaltman & Duncan, 1977) Events frequently fail to unfold in this fashion. People's logic and reason is often distorted by less rational processes. A defensive emotional response may cloud sound judgment. Emotional defensiveness may be produced because a group fears the new procedure will signal a diminution in their prestige or power. (Bright, 1964; Berlin, 1968) Those persons who have benefited the most from existing practices are likely to be threatened by a change in procedures. Other individuals may fear that the new approach will devalue their knowledge and skills and that they will have a difficult time learning the new procedures. (Bright, 1964; Glaser, Abelson, & Garrison, 1983) In still other instances, people may be reluctant to adopt a course of action because they feel they will lose face with their friends or some constituency.

The wise agent of change will construct his or her communications in a manner that alleviates such threats. Whenever an idea might be interpreted as threatening to the target group's security, esteem, or sense of competence, these fears should be discussed and objectively examined as part of the communication process. By acknowledging and evaluating these concerns through the two-sided approach discussed below, defensiveness may be reduced and reason allowed to prevail.

*Cognitive Strategy 9: The Two-Sided Argument.* This strategy recognizes that there may be several points of view on any point of discussion. To use this strategy you present the other position or positions first and then present the position you would like supported. The presentation of the other positions is more effective when it is accompanied with clear appreciation for each position. The advantage of this strategy is that it demonstrates understanding and appreciation of the other positions. It tends to reduce defensiveness and preempt counterarguments.

Here is how this works. You are clearly convinced that it is essential to have some type of client-outcome measure for your program. The program has been operating for several years without any measure of client change. The program is apparently successful since no one has perceived a problem or has pressured the program to make changes. You decide to engage the direct-service workers in a task group to develop a client-outcome measure. Several weeks of discussion have occurred, but there remains a lack of agreement on whether to even try to design such a measure. The task at this meeting is to get approval to go ahead. A two-sided argument strategy for this scenario might go like this:

> We have devoted several hours of discussion over the last several weeks to discussing the desirability of instituting a client-outcome measure. The task today is to decide whether we are going to go ahead with it. There seem to be two positions on this issue. The first position is that it is not desirable either because it is not needed or would have negative side effects. More specifically, such a policy is not needed because workers know the degree of progress being made on each case. The negative side effects might be as follows:
>
> 1. It is another worker task and another piece of paper to have completed.
> 2. Some clients will not want to complete it and will find it intrusive.
> 3. It could disrupt the natural flow of the service interchange.
> 4. Administrators could use the information as part of performance appraisals and other evaluations.
> 5. If the data does not look good, it could threaten our funding.
>
> These reasons for not instituting a client outcome measure are astute and could very well come to be. This is why I want to design the procedure with you and not with top-level administrators who are not asking for it nor would they know or appreciate these possible negative consequences.
> Here is another position on whether to go ahead.
>
> 1. We are doing good work and an appropriate outcome measure would help show others that this is true.
> 2. With the hectic job environment in which we work, it is easy for each of us to "lose the forest in the trees," get caught up in the crisis cases, and thereby become frustrated. Such a measure could provide perspective and a reminder of what's going well.
> 3. A client-outcome measure would also *provide us* feedback on how well we are doing and perhaps point to areas of improvement.

**4.** Ron pointed out that he has worked in two agencies where such a system was in place, and it was quite useful to the teams. It led to identifiable program improvements and an increased exchange of good news. All things we have uniformly stood for.

My own position is that it depends. There is precedence for systems having both sets of results. But I would like to go ahead and design a system that will produce the positive consequences and avoid the negative ones. If it cannot do this, we'll drop it. But we will not know if it can be done unless we start designing the specifics. So I recommend we begin the design process. What are your opinions?

Woven into this monologue are several ideas. First, the task before the group is made clear. Second, the contrary position is detailed first, and its credibility is established. Third, the group's wisdom is acknowledged and the opinion that they are the best people to work on it implied. Fourth, the supportive position is described and a specific person recognized. Fifth, threats to security and control are attenuated by suggesting that a decision to go ahead is not a fait accompli and everyone will continue to be involved in designing it correctly. The reader may also notice how the monologue also introduced compatibility of values, cited proven results, and allowed for trialability.

***Cognitive Strategy 10: Cognitive Dissonance.*** In this strategy when a person senses a contradiction between a behavior and an attitude, they tend to want to change to resolve the dissonance. That is, if they are aware of a contradiction between a behavior and an attitude, they are likely to change the attitude or the behavior to bring the two in line with each other. There is a danger in using this strategy. Some people when they see that there is a contradiction point it out with an attitude of "I got you." Some people think about this strategy as confrontation with a negative emotional component. Our experience is that by including a negative emotional component in the delivery resistance results or increases. One definition of confrontation is to compare two things by placing them side by side. The challenge is to place the two contradictory items side-by-side within a relationship that engenders change rather than resistance. This strategy may also be used in a more active way by inducing or rewarding a person or group to perform an action that is in the direction of the desired position without examining attitudes that would contradict this behavior. When the audience sees that there were rewards from the behavior despite its contradicting their original attitude, they are more likely to bring the attitude in line with the behavior.

Using the same example of implementing a client-outcome measure, someone might resist the task based on the idea that the use of such a measure is too intrusive for the client. You might use this strategy:

Bill, I understand your concern about not being overly intrusive into clients' lives. I think the way we respect clients is one of the strengths of this program. I have also heard you, like the rest of us, express concern about clients getting what they need from the program. It seems to me that we can accomplish both things. I think we can find or develop a measure that lets our clients tell us how we are doing without being intrusive, and in any case no client will be required to complete the instrument.

***Cognitive Strategy 11: Specify the Consequences of a Stance.*** With this strategy the audience is involved in exploring the consequences of a position through logical reasoning. When the consequences of the desired position are seen as more beneficial or more likely to satisfy a need, then the audience is more likely to move toward the desired position. This strategy is essentially thinking through positions and their consequences. It is more common than unusual to adopt a position without systematically thinking through the consequences. After all, we are all busy people with workloads that seldom allow time for reflection. This strategy works best when the audience describes their position and the anticipated consequences of this position. The leader's job in this situation is to help clarify the position and the consequences. The leader also has to assure that negative or possible undesired consequences are identified. In other words, the leader must have done his or her homework and be a skilled interviewer. When the position and consequences are clear the leader points out how these consequences are not as desirable as those emanating from the desired position.

***Cognitive Strategy 12: Weight of the Evidence.*** While specifying the consequences of a stance relies on logic, weight of the evidence relies on documentation. You present all of the evidence for your position, and this suggests to people that they might adopt a new position based on the evidence. Comparing the evidence for one position to the evidence for another position can also be used. Similar to a courtroom analogy the position with more evidence tends to be sustained. Just like in court you need to consider the nature of evidence. In court there are specific rules of evidence. In the area of the social programs, evidence tends to come from empirical literature, theoretical literature, and the experiences of others.

In the example above you might be able to use the weight of the evidence to counter the argument that the measures will be intrusive. Part of this might be to have Bill share the bases for his concern about client-outcome measures being intrusive. Separate from this you would share your evidence for the efficacy of your position. It might go something like this.

> I have been looking into the literature about programs like ours, and I have found that positive outcomes for our clients are based on a theory of change that says that parents are less likely to abuse their children when they know how to discipline their children and view the children more positively. There was a good article on this in the last issue of *Social Work,* which I copied so each of you could have a copy to read. You will see that I copied a second article by Walter Hudson about his scale that measures parents' attitudes toward their children. You will notice that he found the scale to have very good psychometric properties. He also found that a wide range of parents could complete the scale in just a couple of minutes

and that they found it to be very helpful. I also had occasion to call Dr. Hudson and ask if he knew of any program like ours that was using this scale. He gave me the name of a program in Arizona that is doing very much the same thing we are and is using the "parents' attitude toward their children" scale. I gave them a call and they said they found it to be very helpful in getting feedback from clients. The director gave me the name of a worker who would be in the office at this time and would be happy to talk with us about how she uses the scale and how parents respond to its use. Shall we give her a call?

## STAGE VI: MAINTAINING THE NEW WAY

It will come as no surprise to most people that the longest part of this chapter and the most difficult management behavior is the development of consensus. It is also clear by now that in many ways the implementation of change is a never-ending, iterative process. The consensus that becomes the new way falls short of the ideal. In the process of change so much is learned that the normative model changes. The end of the road moves further ahead of you. All of this is true and at the same time the social administrator needs to keep in mind that each incremental step must be maintained and used as a building block for the next step.

There is no better way to maintain a change than to generously reward people for their behavior. The personnel management chapter lists rewards directed toward staff that are valuable with other constituents. The last chapter will supplement these ideas with a few additional ones. A reward-based environment needs to exist around any implementation effort to maintain that change and move toward continued improvement.

## SUMMARY

The complexity of human service organizations and the environments in which they are embedded means that change will be fraught with difficulty. In this chapter, we describe the processes and strategies for instigating organizational change so that client-centeredness and organizational performance is enhanced. The development of these skills requires years of concerted practice and experimentation by the manager. This chapter could serve as a reference guide to developing these skills.

## REFERENCES

Berlin, I. N. (1968). Resistance to change in mental health professionals. *American Journal of Orthopsychiatry, 69*, 109–115.

Brehm, J. W. (1966). *A theory or psychological reactance*. New York: Academic.

Bright, J. R. (1964). *Research, development, and technological innovation: An introduction.* Homewood, IL: Irwin.

Coleman, J. W., Katz, E., & Menzel, H. (1966). *Medical innovation: A diffusion study*. New York: Bobbs-Merrill.

Ellis, A., & Harper, R. A. (1975). *A new guide to rational living*. Englewood Cliffs, NJ: Prentice-Hall.

Fairweather, G. W., Sanders, D. H., & Tornatzky, L. G. (1974). *Creating change in mental health organizations*. New York: Pergamon.

Gamson, W. A. (1968). *Power and discontent*. Homewood, IL: Dorsey.

Glaser, E. M., Abelson, H. H., & Garrison, K. N. (1983). *Putting knowledge to use*. San Francisco: Jossey-Bass.

Gruber, M. L. (1986, Fall). A three-factor model of administration effectiveness. *Administration in Social Work, 10*(3), 11–14.

Gummer, B. (1978, September). Power politics approach to social welfare organization. *Social Service Review, 52*(3), 349–361.

Hage, J. (1980). *Theories of organization*. New York: Wiley.

Harkness, D. R. (1987). *Social work supervision in community mental health: Effects of normal and client focused supervision on client satisfaction and generalized contentment*. Doctoral dissertation, University of Kansas School of Social Welfare, Lawrence, KS.

Hasenfeld, Y. (1980, December). Implementation of change in human service organizations: A political economy perspective. *Social Service Review, 54*(4), 508–520.

Hasenfeld, Y. (1983). *Human service organizations*. Englewood Cliffs, NJ: Prentice-Hall.

Heider, F. (1958). *The psychology of interpersonal relations*. New York: Wiley.

Kaufman, H. (1971). *Administrative Feedback*. Washington, DC: The Brookings Institute.

King, W. R., & Clelland, D. (1976). The design of management information systems: An information analysis approach. *Management Science, 22*(3), 286–297.

Larson, C. U. (1983). *Persuasion: Reception and responsibility* (3rd ed.). Belmont, CA: Wadsworth.

Leventhal, H. (1970). Findings and theory in the study of fear communication. In L. Berkowitz (Ed.), *Advances in Experimental Social Psychology, 5*. New York: Academic.

Miringoff, M. L. (1980). *Management in human service organizations*. New York: Macmillan.

Neugeborn, B. (1985). *Organization, policy and practice in the human services*. New York: Longman.

Patti, R. J. (1980a). An overview of organizational change. In H. Resnick & R. J. Patti, (Eds.), *Change From Within* (pp. 3–32). Philadelphia: Temple University Press.

Patti, R. J. (1980b). Organizational resistance and change: The view from below. In H. Resnick & R. J. Patti, (Eds.), *Change From Within* (pp. 114–131). Philadelphia: Temple University Press.

Rogers, E. M. (1968). *Diffusion of innovations* (3rd ed.). New York: Free Press.

Rogers, E. M. (1983). The communication of innovations in a complex institution. *Educational Record, 48*, 67–77.

Rogers, E. M., & Svenning, L. (1969). *Managing change*. Washington, DC: U.S. Office of Education.

Sanders, J. T., & Reppucci, N. D. (1977, October). Learning network among administrators of human service institutions. *American Journal of Community Psychology, 5*, 269–276.

Schulman, E. D. (1982). *Interventions in human services* (3rd ed.). St. Louis: C.V. Mosby.

Simon, H. A., Smithburg, D. W., and Thompson, V. A. (1950). *Public Administration*. New York: Knopf.

Simons, R. L. (1982, May). Strategies for exercising influence. *Social Work Journal, 27*(3), 268–274.

Simons, R. (1985, January–February). Inducement as an approval to exercising influence. *Social Work, 30*(1), 56–68.

Simons, R. (1987, Fall/Winter). The skill of persuasion: An essential component of human services administration. *Administration in Social Work, 11*(3/4), 241–254.

Taylor, M. S. (1987, Fall/Winter). The effects of feedback on the behaviors of organizational personnel. *Administration in Social Work, 11*(3/4), 191–204.

Tedeschi, J. T., & Lindskold, S. (1976). *Social psychology: Interdependence, interaction and influence*. New York: Wiley.

Toseland, R. W., & Rivas, R. R. (1984). *An introduction to group work practice*. New York: Macmillan.

*Webster's Third New International Dictionary* (1972). New York: World.

Wicklund, R. A. (1974). *Freedom and reactance*. Hillsdale, NJ: Erlbaum.

Woolfolk, A. E., Woolfolk, R. L., & Wilson, G. T. (1977). A rose by any other name . . . : Labeling bias and attitudes toward behavior modification. *Journal of Consulting and Clinical Psychology, 45,* 184–191.

Wrightsman, L., & Deaux, K. (1981). *Social Psychology in the 80s* (3rd ed.). Monterey, CA: Brooks/Cole.

Zaltman, G. (1973). *Processes and phenomena of social change*. New York: Wiley.

Zaltman, G., & Duncan, R. (1977). *Strategies for planned change*. New York: Wiley.

# CHAPTER 7

# Integrating Client-Centered Management: The Inverted Hierarchy

In this chapter, we integrate the concepts and skills from previous chapters using the framework of the inverted hierarchy. The inverted hierarchy posits that a manager's job is to help personnel do their jobs more effectively and efficiently. The manager does this by providing the direction and the tools to do the job and by removing obstacles and constraints to performance. Opportunity-finding is presented as a critical set of skills for meeting this responsibility.

The most resilient symbol of management is the organizational chart. Originally devised for the military and borrowed by manufacturing companies during the Industrial Revolution, the hierarchical and pyramidal organization chart (sometimes referred to as a table of organization) is ubiquitous in human service organizations. The basic configuration is portrayed in Figure 7–1. The chart typically includes three types of personnel. The first is line staff, the people who actually make the product or deliver the service. The second type is supervisory and management personnel who are responsible for controlling and coordinating the work to be done. The third type of personnel is support staff who perform specialized roles for the organization like budgeting and accounting, legal services, information systems, housekeeping, and so on. In the pure sense these support personnel have no direct authority over the line and managerial personnel, although they do have control over knowledge and information.

This traditional organizational configuration was designed to enhance the manufacture and distribution of products. Efficiency was the ultimate criterion, and control was the principal function of management. The organizational chart then portrayed what positions existed in the organization, how these are grouped into units, and how formal authority and communication flows among them. (Mintzberg, 1979) This vertical hierarchy depicts the division of labor and establishes that power is centered at the top.

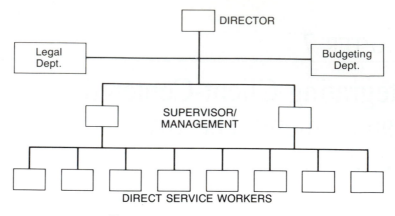

**Figure 7–1.** Hierarchical Organization

The criticisms of this organizational configuration are legion. For the client-centered performance manager, the most pertinent consequence is the inherent separation of managers from frontline workers and clients. Furthermore, the larger the organization, the greater the distance between day-to-day client contact and the policy decisions affecting these clients. "The vertical, one-way hierarchy tends to separate and give precedence to goals of organizational maintenance over client-oriented goals." (Altshuler & Forward, 1978, p. 58) While this seems to occur in business with profound consequences (Peters & Waterman, 1982), human services with its plethora of constituencies makes it that much easier to "forget" about the clients. The typical organizational structure reinforces the tendency to maximize nonresponsiveness to clients and their welfare.

A second implicit consequence of this configuration is that control remains the major managerial function with its implicit assumption that "employees in the trenches" will do badly or inadequately unless their behavior conforms to the letter of policies and procedures and is closely monitored. Unfortunately, many organizational rules (i.e., policies and procedures) were not developed based on the needs of clients but based on the needs of the organization. For example, most "paperwork" was not designed to help frontline workers provide better service but to control who is to receive what form of help for how long in order to please other constituencies. Another problem with rules in human service organizations is that they assume clients are the same or at least similar enough that a rule can be implemented uniformly with rather uniform results. The worker trying to help a particular client knows how farcical this assumption is. The agendas are therefore widely discrepant. Managers seek to control and maintain adherence to the rule book while workers seek to help individuals who are unique. It's no wonder that management in so many human service organizations is seen as irrelevant or as the major obstacle to quality service.

A third consequence of the typical organizational configuration is symbolic. Clients are most often not even included in the chart. The power is at the top and all others are subordinate. Subordinate means "inferior to or placed below another in rank, power, importance, etc.; subservient or submissive." (Webster's New World Dictionary, 1972) These concepts are abhorrent to the client-centered performance manager. The need for a new symbol, a new metaphor for the human service manager is needed.

## A NEW METAPHOR

Human service organizations that are producing superior rates of client outcomes seem to turn the typical organizational configuration upside-down in everyday practice. (Gowdy, Rapp, & Poertner, 1987; Gowdy & Rapp, 1988) It is from this observation that the inverted hierarchy was created as depicted in Figure 7–2. This organizational configuration is a more accurate portrayal of a client-centered organization and has more fidelity with concepts underlying the client-centered performance model of management. First, the pinnacle of the chart is the client and all organizational personnel are subservient. In fact, supervisors are subservient to frontline workers and the "boss" is subservient to supervisors and frontline workers.

The assumption central to the inverted hierarchy is that the principal function of management at any level is not control but *to help the next higher rung do their jobs more effectively.* "Subservient" then relates not only to power and authority but to service. And the service is to help others who want to do the best job possible to do their job better. But how do managers help? There seem to be three major categories of organizational helping:

1. Clearly laying out the job to be done and the expectations of how it should be done.
2. Providing the tools to get the job done.
3. Removing obstacles and constraints to the desired performance.

Many of the managerial concepts and strategies described in this text can be seen as fitting in one or more of these categories. This chapter will attempt to reorganize many of these previous ideas and add others and thereby integrate the content.

With the host of competing, nonclient oriented demands placed on the manager, how can the manager use the skills and strategies identified in the text? The inverted hierarchy requires highly developed skills in finding opportunities to be client- and worker-centered. Opportunity finding becomes the foundation for successful implementation of the inverted hierarchy.

## FINDING OPPORTUNITY: THE FOUNDATION OF THE INVERTED HIERARCHY

The engine or driving force continues to be the continual quest for improved levels of performance and client centeredness. The link between the quest and the strategies of the inverted hierarchy is the manager's ability to find opportunities.

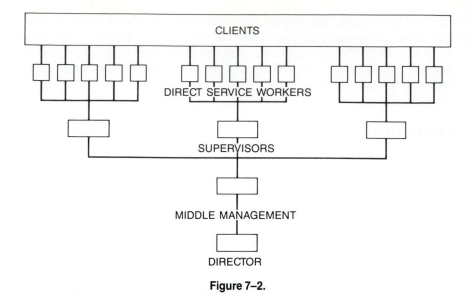

**Figure 7–2.**

Management books and curricula are replete with discussions on problem solving, decision making, and other analytic skills but as Livingston (1975) argues:

> Preoccupation with problem solving and decision making in formal management education programs tends to distort managerial growth because it overdevelops an individual's analytical ability, but leaves his ability to take action and to get things done underdeveloped . . . all too often leads to "analysis paralysis." (p. 99; 100)

More critical to success and performance is the manager's ability to find opportunities. As Drucker (1964) states:

> All one can hope to get by solving a problem is to restore normalcy. All one can hope, at best, is to eliminate a restriction on the capacity of the business to obtain results. The results themselves must come from the exploitation of opportunities. (p. 5)

While these comments were made about business, they equally apply to the management of human services.

Opportunity is defined as "a combination of circumstances favorable for the purpose" or "a good chance or occasion." (Webster's New World Dictionary, 1972) Particularly critical is that an opportunity is relative; relative to the "purpose." This then implies at least a three-step process:

1. Environmental sensing (circumstance)
2. Comparing the sensing to purpose
3. Exploiting those events or circumstances that are favorable to the purpose

Opportunities are potentially present in virtually all situations from writing a memo or getting a cup of coffee to responding to a grant announcement or testifying before a legislative committee. Simply, the client-centered performance manager is highly skilled in exploiting everyday events, tasks, and situations to move the organization and its personnel to higher levels.

## Environmental Sensing

Finding opportunity demands a high level of perceptiveness. The performance manager is constantly surveying the environment for cues. While the range of environmental cues are infinite and rather amorphous, there are five identifiable categories.

The first category of environmental cues are those events that have already been defined as problems by some player. Often these take the form of complaints or dissatisfactions. At times they emerge as messes: a configuration of events and opinions in which the "problem" has not yet clearly emerged. The Chinese character for opportunity is the same as the one for problem. This connotes that embedded in every problem is an opportunity. In terms of sensing, problems are the most straightforward since they are usually communicated orally or occasionally in writing. The difficulty comes when the manager must analyze the contours and textures of the problem so that an opportunity can emerge.

机危

A second category of environmental cues are those of strengths. This includes identifying high performance, locating the factors that have contributed to this performance, influential relationships between people (e.g., staff, key players, etc.), special talents of people, strong client-centered beliefs, and so on. The sensing and storage of strengths is important to the performance manager for several reasons. First, it provides the basis for rewards. Behavior that is rewarded tends to increase in frequency, thereby replacing behavior that is ignored. Second, the performance manager is constantly trying to disseminate "what works" to other organizational units and people who are not using the effective methods. Third, people tend to grow and prosper based on exploiting their strengths. (Weick, Rapp, Sullivan, & Kisthardt, 1989) Once aware of the strengths the manager can facilitate this growth. Fourth, identified strengths can be used by the manager to help turn problems and other environmental cues into opportunities.

A third category of environmental cues concerns inconsistencies and disconti-nuities between events, behavior, and beliefs. The search is for discrepancies and often requires a higher level of conceptual skill than does the search for problems and strengths because the manager needs to find two or more items and often these are not obvious. The inconsistencies are endless, but here are a few, prevalent, general types:

- a person's statements and his or her behavior, an organization's statements and its behavior
- a person's behavior or statements and the organization's purpose
- social work values and a person's behavior

People possess a need for consistency and strive to maintain consistency of attitudes and behaviors or between attitudes and behaviors in order to avoid a psychologically uncomfortable state. (Simons, 1982) Identified inconsistencies, therefore, provide fertile ground from which opportunities can emerge.

A fourth category of environmental cues concerns what others are doing. This includes learning about effective program strategies and interventions, management techniques, and so forth. It also includes learning from seemingly unrelated events and enterprises. The manager, for example, can learn much about public speaking by watching politicians and skilled orators. Similarly, many business management techniques are worth investigating.

The fifth category of environmental cues concerns societal trends, stable societal beliefs and values, and some wisdom about the future. This cluster is by far the most challenging, demanding a high level of intelligence and acuity. The manager is called on here to see the big picture and how the organization and its purpose fits with this picture. A few examples include:

- Expressed concern with the most disadvantaged, most difficult clients
- The over 100-year trend toward normalization of clients and nonsegregation
- The fact that the costs of solving social problems will continue to be a consideration

## Comparing the Sensing to Purpose

The performance manager is constantly comparing circumstances and environmental cues with organizational purpose. It's from this cognitive process that managers identify opportunities. Purpose can best be viewed in terms of the five performance areas: client outcomes, productivity, resource acquisition, efficiency, and staff morale. Layed over these performance areas is the mission to make the organization's services as client centered as possible. In the quest for these, the performance manager seeks to blend the agendas of a variety of internal and external constituents.

## PROVIDING DIRECTION

Managers need to clearly lay out the job to be done and the expectations of how it should be done. This includes clearly describing how a particular employee's job fits into the larger program, agency, or societal context. This cluster of managerial strategies can be subdivided into: (1) vision, (2) program design, (3) managing people, (4) managing information, (5) modeling, and (6) bringing meaning to everyday events.

### Vision

> Vision is the key to leadership. Unless you have a vision of where you're going, you are not going to get there.
>
> > Rev. Theodore Hesburgh, President
> > University of Notre Dame

> Where there is no vision, the people perish.
>
> > Proverbs 29:18

One of the most common elements cited in discussion in leadership is vision. As Henry Kissinger has stated:

> The task of the leader is to get people from where they are to where they have not been. The public does not fully understand the world into which it is going. Leaders must invoke an alchemy of great vision. Those leaders who do not are ultimately judged failures, even though they may be popular at the time.

Human service managers, no less than others in leadership positions, need to develop and articulate a vision of the enterprise. Exceptional managers "deal in symbols and visions and shared understandings as well as the techniques and trappings of their own specialties." (Kanter, 1983, p. 305) The overreliance of management technology can stifle innovation, reduce creativity, and prevent the organization from doing "the right thing." Visions that influence tend to have the following characteristics. First, the vision captures the central reason for the organization's existence and describes the fundamental business of the organization. It defines the client as the penultimate reason for the organization but does so by speaking directly to the interests of not only clients but staff and a larger society as well. Second, it is future oriented and has a timeless quality to it. It invokes feelings of optimism and hope. It has a certain universality of appeal. It is both inspiring and realistic. Third, it uses a language that eschews jargon and professional terminology, and often employs analogy, metaphor, and personification. The use of symbols is prevalent. Fourth, it is personal. It is something the manager owns, and it derives its passion from that ownership.

At its core, a vision establishes and communicates the organization's values. It is shared values that Peters and Waterman (1982) found to be the principal control mechanism in exceptional companies, not hierarchy, and policy and procedures manuals that seem to be the mechanism of choice in human service organizations.

A vision can serve several important functions for the manager and the organization. First, it can act as a guide to managerial and staff behavior. It provides another benchmark for selecting priorities, identifying opportunities, and for making decisions. Second, a vision can act as a tool for unifying potentially disparate agendas of multiple constituencies. The vision is something the manager seeks to share with others. It helps a manager act "integratively, bringing other people in, bridging multiple realities. . . . It outlines a pattern for the organization and its constituents." (Kanter, 1983, p. 305) Third, a vision should answer two important questions. For clients, "Why would I want service from the organization?" For employees, "Why would a person want to work for this program?" It seeks to create a shared meaning. Fourth, a vision is a symbol for the organization and as a basis for developing other symbols. In fact, the vision is quickly turned into symbols by the best managers. (Peters & Austin, 1985) The vision is communicated in myriad ways—it becomes ubiquitous. It is a way of stating what the organization stands for.

A formal mission statement can help communicate the vision, values, and focus of the organization. Decide what the mission is to be and avoid conflicting missions. For example, a girls correctional facility mission is two-fold: to protect society and to habilitate juvenile offenders. This leads to a confusion of values since protecting society can be done simply by removing offenders from society and does not necessarily translate into or incorporate habilitation. If the mission was simply the care, treatment, and habilitation of clients, then protection of society could be inferred as a result of the mission rather than a separate goal or mission.

## Program Design

The program design as described in Chapter 2 helps prescribe the minimum sets of behavior required for goal achievement. A well-done program design provides a variety of direction-setting elements including goals and objectives, the target population, and the service plan. The service plan itself describes where the help will be provided, what the natural flow is of helping phases, what the expectations of clients and workers are, and how emotional elements will be accommodated. It also prescribes the minimum behaviors required of key players for the program to meet its goals. The client-centered performance manager would use this document as a ready source for directing behavior.

## Managing People

Two critical vehicles for setting direction, task analysis, and job descriptions were described in Chapter 3. If done with precision and tied to client outcomes, job descriptions are the most direct source of job prescription for the individual employee. The focus in Chapter 3 was direct-service worker positions, but it is equally important to write supervisory and managerial job descriptions that are precise.

One strategy for developing supervisor job descriptions is to use the inverted hierarchy concepts in the following order:

1. Establish the perspective that a manager's job is to make the job of others more effective and efficient and that there are three clusters of ways this can be accomplished.
2. Take each cluster sequentially and have three to ten people brainstorm a list of ways that cluster could be put into operation.
3. Edit the lists by grouping similar items together and removing ones not seen as relevant.
4. Convert the remaining lists into job description format.

This process has been successfully used in a variety of local and state level human service organizations.

## Managing Information

Many of the information system strategies described in Chapter 4 are tools for organizational personnel to use to get the job done. If "what gets measured gets done," then, the data collected and reported by personnel send a powerful message concerning what is important to the organization. The selection and reporting of client outcomes defines the priority domains of the work. The selection and reporting of those worker behaviors most influential in producing these outcomes establishes the most important behaviors. In this respect, the data helps guide and direct behavior. Feedback when used prospectively directs behavior and provides a tool for improving performance.

## Modeling: Management Behavior as a Resource

The behavior of the manager is an underrecognized and critical resource. For a manager there is no "throw away" behavior. All of the manager's behavior affects others in the work environment.

A powerful technique for directing behavior is the modeling of supervisors and managers. Does their behavior consistently embody the values of the organization? Are they models of client-centeredness? This modeling helps guide others in how to make decisions and how to behave. There is no more destructive element in an organization's culture than supervisors and managers pronouncing one set of values or prescriptions and they themselves behaving in incompatible, inconsistent, or opposite ways.

The modeling of client-centeredness is particularly important. The following are but ten examples that are often within the control of managers:

1. Interact with clients in the hallway, waiting rooms; find opportunities to do so—have an open-door policy for clients.
2. Institutionalize a variety of client feedback mechanisms (e.g., client satisfaction surveys, focus groups, suggestion boxes) and respond to them.
3. Insure client representation on the board of directors or advisory board.
4. Provide membership dues to staff and consumers so they can join consumer organizations and advocacy groups.
5. Arrange for advocacy group representatives to regularly address staff meetings.
6. Donate honorariums to consumer organizations.
7. Talk about clients in every interaction; make them heroes.
8. Insure that the manager's personal staff acts as an extension of that manager in treating clients with the highest degree of courtesy, respect, and dignity.
9. Hire former clients.
10. Involve clients in the design and implementation of program evaluations and share results with them.

## Bringing Meaning to Everyday Events

Another opportunity for providing direction occurs in many of the myriad interactions that fill each day. The most obvious are those in which staff come to you for advice and suggestions. Others are more subtle. A worker frustrated by a client who has not followed through on a series of agreements will have a natural tendency to be angry or blame the client. While acknowledging the frustration, the manager can reframe the client's behavior as being a result of fear or lack of confidence. The manager can emphasize the heroic mission the program has established to work with clients confronting the most difficult situations.

Helping a client complete onerous financial assistance forms can be placed in a perspective that emphasizes the client's need for money and the importance of the worker arranging it. Once the assistance is arranged, the worker and client can begin work on job training or parent education, for example.

Another method of providing and reinforcing direction and bringing meaning to everyday events is to create a book of agency stories. These are short descriptions of events and worker actions that reflect the kind of work desired. Stories can be solicited from workers, colleagues, supervisors, or clients, or can be generated by the manager. New additions could be included in newsletters or posted for some period before being formally entered in the story book. The stories themselves can be used in speeches and training sessions, and made a formal part of employee orientation. It could also be used as a recruitment device for new staff. The story book becomes one source of the heroes and symbols of the organization.


## PROVIDING THE TOOLS

With expectations clarified and a variety of mechanisms established to reinforce them, the tools required to meet the expectations need to be provided. It is often the discrepancy between expectations and tools that causes job dissatisfaction and ineffectiveness. For example, setting ambitious goals for clients and workers and then requiring service on fifty clients at one time.

There are two general strategies. First, the client-centered performance manager seeks to place as many resources as possible in the trenches where the help occurs. In many agencies, especially public bureaucracies, there are simply too many employees who do not provide service as their primary responsibility. Overhead costs should be kept to the minimum, which usually means reducing levels of managerial and staff positions. Second, the client-centered performance manager should constantly be asking employees, "How can I help you with your job?" Furthermore, these responses should be written down and done. An eminently worthwhile question the manager could ask every day while driving home is, What did I do today that made the jobs of my workers more effective or easier? Tools can be placed in three groups: (1) information, (2) structural supports, and (3) tangible resources.


## Information

*Training.*  Am I asking the staff to do something they don't know how to do? The answer is too often yes. Training includes such activities as orientation and preservice training, continuous in-service training, continuing education, and so on. Given the inherent difficulty of human service work and the fact that the lowest credentialed, most inexperienced personnel are placed in direct helping roles, the training imperative is clear. Simply, we cannot provide too much training. (Please see chapter on personnel management for details on training.)

*Technical Assistance and Consultation.*  This refers to the provision of help in the technical application of helping strategies to particular clients or groups of clients. It's one thing to know how to do a specific method of assessment or intervention and another to skillfully apply that methodology to the myriad case situations that a frontline worker confronts. Ready and continuous access to such a resource can help insure that training is applied in practice. The most continuous sources of such help is the immediate supervisor or peers, but access to outside experts is often valuable. The focus of the work is placing individual cases and situations under the microscope. By this we mean the compulsive review of even the most minute details of case situations and helping interactions.

*Interpersonal Feedback.* This includes feedback from clients and significant others, coworkers, supervisors, and upper-level management. Interpersonal feedback provides information concerning some action or actions on the part of the worker. People's behavior is in large part determined by the reactions of others. We grow and learn from what others tell us about ourselves. Therefore, the organizational culture must encourage and facilitate ongoing exchanges, and specific mechanisms need to be established. Focus groups and exit interviews with clients, group and individual supervision, written notes and evaluations, and even coffeepot conversations can be opportunities for feedback.

*Information System Feedback.* Another tool for feedback is data reports provided by the organization's information system. If designed according to the protocols established in the information management chapter, frontline workers would receive critical information on the results of their prodigious efforts.

## Structural Supports

*Caseload Size.* Given the established expectations, a frontline worker's caseload must allow for those expectations to be met. Protective service caseloads of fifty are common as are caseloads of 70 for community mental health case managers. The protection of children and improving the community integration of people with severe mental illness is both too important and too demanding to be prohibited by unworkable caseload size. The simple truth is that the goals we seek to achieve simply cannot be achieved under such a yoke.

Creativity and courage by managers are often needed. For example, a team of four frontline workers is expected to provide case management services to two hundred frail elderly. Instead of having each worker responsible for fifty clients whereby four workers are overwhelmed and only day-to-day crises can be responded to, assign twenty clients to one or two workers and assign the other clients to the remaining workers. This configuration provides at least one worker and 20 clients a chance to receive the benefits promised by the service, although two workers would continue to be overwhelmed.

Reducing caseloads may mean not serving everyone who is eligible or who could benefit from the service. Rather than being seen as irresponsible, this choice is often the most responsible decision. This requires "straight talk" to elected officials, funders, and other constituencies. An analytic process for defining who will be served was described in the program design chapter and would be helpful in establishing reasonable caseloads.

*Interagency Agreements.* The increasing specialization of our service programs combined with the complexity of human life and problems means that clients can rarely have their needs met through one agency. Many client problems are in fact not "client problems" but problems at the transaction between clients and societal institutions (e.g., schools, courts, employers). This means that help is provided by multiple agencies and the targets of change are often institutions not the clients.

The close working relationships between agencies is indispensable for effective and efficient helping. One tool is the provision of interagency agreements. We are not referring to the "Aunt Fanny" agreements with their vague references to cooperation and collaboration, nor are we referring to twenty-six page "continuity of care" agreements. Rather, one- or two-page working documents that detail the reciprocal responsibilities in behavioral language is the recommendation. The document should answer the question: Who will do what when? This is a document which can literally, if needed, be placed on the table between workers of two agencies to guide their work around a client. The section on key players in the program design chapter can be helpful.

*Forms as Tools.* It became fashionable in the late 1970s to describe new forms as "tools." Webster's Third New International Dictionary (1972) defines a tool as "an instrument or apparatus necessary to a person in the practice of his vocation or profession; an instrument by which something is effected or accomplished." (p. 2408) In short, an instrument that helps a person do his or her job. It is unfortunate that the overuse of this metaphor has camouflaged the fact that some forms can, in fact, serve as a rather powerful aid to doing the work.

Forms as tools require that the form is directly related to the specific job a person is being asked to do and some notion about how it is to be done. Furthermore, the form needs to help the worker help the client by identifying the work focus, making specific decisions about clients, and/or as a means of feedback.

The two "forms" ubiquitous in every agency are assessment and case (treatment) plan. These forms should, more than any other forms, be supportive of good helping. For example, a case plan should be designed to have the client goals, the tasks needed to accomplish the goals, time frames for accomplishment, who is responsible, and a place for worker and client signatures. It should act as an *agenda* between worker and client, laying out the areas to be discussed and the agreements needing to be reached. It should be a document that both worker and client can work from and each should have a copy.

To act as a tool, a case planning form must be able to be used with clients. The form should not be isolated from the helping task. In other words, a case plan should be completed with the client, not before or after a client encounter in the worker's office. If workers are not using the case plan with clients regularly, then the form is wrong (it is not a tool), or the work is not being done properly. The case planning form should not include superfluous information requirements unless by adding an item, another form used for documentation can be eliminated. If it is to guide the work, it cannot pose distractions to that performance.

Similarly, assessment recordings should help structure the information collection. It should help a worker and client identify the information needed to develop a case plan and organize it in a way that conclusions and directions become clear. It should not include information that is not going to be used. For example, some agencies still require rather long social histories as part of the assessment process but little of the information is ever used to form a case plan. Assessment should be relevant to the form of help the agency is offering. For example, a genogram (McGoldrick & Gerson, 1985) is of little use to a worker who is offering to help someone choose, get, and keep a job or find housing.

Both case plans and assessments should be designed to be as dynamic as actual helping. Assessment is ongoing—it is not a one-shot event. Workers are learning something about clients with each encounter. Case plans change as situations change and often additional tasks or altered time lines are made weekly. Forms and policies that do not allow or facilitate changes detract from the helpfulness of these documents. For example, agency policies requiring a treatment plan update every three months or six months is simply not reflective of actual helping.

*Helpers for the Helpers.* Many workers have too much to do for too many people. Some of the work involves little skill but is constant, if not predictable (e.g., clients needing emergency transportation, clients needing a reassuring phone call, clients needing specific help in balancing a checkbook). Managers who arrange for volunteers, casework extenders, emergency transportation services, or student help and adequately structure their work may free workers for tasks requiring their skills and assist in managing the workload. The use of task analysis described in the personnel chapter will help guide the meaningful structuring of such roles.

*Supportive Policies and Procedures.* Policies and procedures are important for the control of hierarchical organization. Policies and procedures can also be obstacles to the client-centered organization. Organizations often develop policies and procedures in response to a perceived problem that no longer exists or that is contradictory to expectations the same organization has for its workers. For example, an agency may expect workers to be available for crisis situations after hours but places limits on the use of compensatory time. If the expectation is for an outreach mode of service delivery and yet billable service hours do not include transportation time, major disincentives are created. The best source for identifying organizational anomalies is the workers themselves. If you *listen,* you will be able to identify the areas of change.

## Reward-Based Environment

The personnel management chapter discusses the basic ideas underlying creating a reward-based environment such as creating winners, principles of reinforcement, menus of available awards, getting other organizational members involved. But beyond these ideas is a simple notion that work should be fun!

Ideally the fun should come directly from the work or be symbolic of the work. This does not preclude birthday parties, agency softball teams, or Friday afternoon "Happy Hours." They too can help build camaraderie and make people feel special.

But fun that comes from the work offers the added benefits of increasing performance and making the *work itself* enjoyable.

The authors have been particularly impressed with the results of celebrations and gag awards. An annual conference in Kansas of state and local mental health managers focused on community-based care for people with severe mental illness always includes an "Awards Ceremony" recognizing exceptional performance. Awards have included the following:

- Hospital Buster T-shirts for the programs that have the lowest utilization of state psychiatric hospitals
- An American flag for getting clients registered to vote and involved in elections
- The Reaganomics Award for the program with the most employed clients
- The Bag Lady Award for the program that can scrounge (mobilize) the most community donations (e.g., time, money, jobs, housing, recreation, space, etc.)
- A pair of gloves for the "Hands-On" Management Award for the manager who gets most personally involved in his or her program

These awards not only provide public recognition of meaningful achievement but are a source of much laughter. The power is seen in the response of one mental health center executive director whose agency had not received an award, "What do you think we need to do in order to receive an award next year?"

A major social experiment is currently underway in Philadelphia under the leadership of Estelle Richman. The effort is to close Philadelphia State Hospital and provide community care for these hospitalized patients with psychiatric aides and nurses from the hospital. The work is among the most demanding to be found anywhere with expectations of seven days a week, twenty-four hours a day availability by these case managers. While Richman has removed obstacles, provided resources, and hired quality supervisors, she has also mounted celebrations tied to training events in which gag awards are a routine occurrence. The enthusiasm, joy, and pride is tangible in the staff.

Making work fun and using fun to reinforce the work is also reflected in the case management training program offered by the University of Kansas School of Social Welfare. Under the leadership of Wally Kisthardt, the two-day training includes a sing-along to the song "Case Management Blues," and buttons given to trainees who demonstrate ability in applications of the particular skills. When the training is delivered as part of a new agency initiative, the training team toasts the effort with champagne. Other times, participants are asked to share particularly satisfying success stories or particularly humorous case stories.

Every organization should have a "Perfect Failure Award." One agency calls it the "Boner Award," which is a large bone with a yellow ribbon around it. The nature of human service work means that despite Herculean efforts by workers, clients will still not achieve all their goals and endure other "failures." Given the complexity of social work and the general lack of knowledge linking worker behavior to client benefit, managers must encourage worker creativity. For workers to succeed with clients, they must experiment and risk failure. Celebrating failure encourages the kinds of creativity required of the worker. Workers who do everything correctly and go beyond normal efforts deserve as much recognition as those who achieve "success." Two other highly recommended awards are the "Extra Mile Award" and the "Mission Impossible Award." The former would recognize effort well beyond the call of duty. The latter award would recognize the solution of some chronic or seemingly incorrigible problem (e.g., a client who has made significant gains but who everyone had given up on; getting an uncooperative judge to follow agency recommendations). Such awards would help encourage risk-taking and extra effort by organizational members.

Fun and celebrations should also include clients. Award ceremonies for client achievements, pictures on walls, and alumni involvement in current programs. Why not enshrine the heroes in an agency Hall of Fame? Our social programs should have an element of joy to them. In the study of excellence in community service for people with severe mental illness (Gowdy & Rapp, 1988), celebration and laughter were found to be consistent themes. According to Katy Slayton:

> The number one thing we do is laugh. I don't mean we're ridiculous, I don't mean we spend the day in a gale of laughter, but if I can get to the end of the day and think I've caused somebody to laugh who wouldn't have laughed otherwise I put a star on my chart, so to speak. We've accomplished something. You recognize the little things.

In Hutchinson, Kansas, Cheryl Runyan has two groups that meet weekly in the public library. The focus of one group is to learn to laugh:

> Most of our contact is in the community since that's where the people are. One is a humor group: the main thing is to sit around and laugh. We show Bill Cosby tapes, Candid Camera tapes, we tell jokes. Clients monitor themselves on a ten point scale regarding skills around humor. Most move up the scale over time.
>
>   We do constant praising, with every contact. Our practicum students are drummed into strengths building and praise. We kid and tease. We laugh. That's healthy. But it's not part of the traditional psychotherapy stuff. We relate to people like family, and they relate to us that way. Last year, my father had surgery, clients sent cards, they called. It was wonderful. That's caring. That's what it's all about. We feel good about the program, we have good vibes about ourselves, our clients. It brushes off. If the atmosphere is cheerful you're cheerful. We understand when it's bad. We cry with our clients, too. When we can do all that, they can connect. They're beautiful people. I would trust them to get me places nobody else could.

The prerequisite of recognizing and celebrating achievement is observation and listening. Managers must simply place themselves in a position where they can see or hear incidence of good or superior work and achievement. One cannot hide in an office and still identify performance worth rewarding. The use of client satisfaction surveys, focus groups, information system reports, and contact with key factors are traditional sensing devices.

## Tangible Resources

*For the Worker.* These can vary widely depending on the agency and the particular job, so a few examples will have to do. A classic situation concerns the outreach worker who is expected to do his or her work outside of the agency. Resource supports would include cars, adequate travel reimbursement, liability insurance, a beverage holder and trash bag for the car, clipboards or lap-top computers for recording in cars or parks, a roll of quarters to check in with the agency by telephone, cellular phones or beepers. For many workers, easy-to-use resource guides, rolodexes, adequate office supplies, and so on would help them do their jobs more effectively or efficiently.

*For the Client.* These too can vary widely, but in many agencies access to a fund for emergencies would be critical. These are monies not bureaucratically encumbered (e.g., forms, permissions, meetings, and several layers of review) but almost immediately available for such things as rent deposits, food, clothing, and registration fees for community activities. It could mean a "lending closet," where clients who could not afford to buy could borrow some item like vacuum cleaners, kitchen supplies, furniture, or even fishing poles.

## REMOVING OBSTACLES AND CONSTRAINTS

The third category of managerial behaviors in the inverted hierarchy is the constant and conscientious removal of barriers to performance. In a sense, the lack of any of the previously mentioned behaviors is an obstacle. For example, inadequate job descriptions detailing work expectations is an obstacle. Lack of rewards is an obstacle. This section will not repeat these managerial ideas but rather will focus on a few of the most ubiquitous obstacles in human service organizations. A major theme in this section is "less is more": less paperwork, fewer meetings, fewer priorities, fewer permissions, fewer organizational levels, fewer excuses, less noise. The obstacles will be addressed in two categories: organizational structures and psychological obstacles.

## Organizational Structures

These obstacles are created by the organization, often as an attempt to solve a previously defined organizational problem.

*Hierarchy.* The performance manager must remove needless organizational levels. The goal is to push responsibility, authority, resources, and problem-solving to the lowest possible level of the organization. This can only be done by removing managerial levels whose major purpose is control. The test needs to be: How does this position directly enhance performance? How does it help the people above? What responsibilities are redundant with other levels? Where is authority shared when it could be vested in one person at the next level? In many human service organizations managers are not helping but in fact get in the way. Jobs should be redesigned to be helpful, and the remainder phased out. Not only does this remove an obstacle to performance, but allows the organization to commit the resources to frontline positions where the help to clients occurs. The result is a more efficient and effective organization.

### Case Study

The Badlands Mental Health Center received funds to expand their case management services to people suffering from severe mental illness. For two years, the Badlands program has been producing exceptional results in terms of their goals:

1. Reduce the incidence and days of state psychiatric care (increase community tenure)
2. Improve the vocational status
3. Improve the independent living status
4. Increase social supports

The expansion was sizable enough to warrant a look at the organizational structure. Six organizational levels were proposed:

1. case managers
2. team leaders
3. supervisors
4. program director
5. clinical director
6. executive director

A rough draft of the responsibilities of the first four levels were as follows:

  I. *ROLE OF CM*
     1. Assessment/needs strengths
     2. Development of comprehensive service plan
     3. Linking and referral
     4. Monitoring
     5. Tracking and evaluation
     6. Advocacy on the individual level
     7. Triage caseloads: whom served, how served
     8. Crises intervention and management
     9. Provides required documentation
    10. Maintains contact with client
    11. Provides supportive communication with client around daily living stress and/or individualize goals
    12. Outreach
 II. *ROLE OF THE TEAM LEADERS*
     1. Has responsibility plus authority
     2. Emphasizes supervision over administrative functions

3. Gets rid of stumbling blocks for CMs
4. Provides emergency backup and support
5. Consults daily operation
6. Handles DPS forms, documentation issues
7. Picks up to supervisor staff differences
8. Supervises students and volunteers
9. Goes out with CM on regular basis
10. Identifies needs for in-service training
11. Is minimally involved in resource development except on a one-on-one basis
12. Assists CM in the accessing of existing resources
13. Carries minimal caseload
14. Runs group supervision with other team leaders and supervisor
15. Initiates disciplinary action, including verbal counseling

III. *ROLE OF THE SUPERVISOR*
1. Supervises team leaders
2. Handles disciplinary actions beyond verbal counseling
3. Mediates disputes between team leaders and their staff
4. Handles system negotiations
5. Handles resource development on system level
6. Assists in recruitment of students and volunteers
7. Supervises some students and volunteers
8. Handles some liaison work not carried by program manager
9. Supervises and evaluates team leaders
10. Monitors the quality of record keeping activities of staff (e.g., medicaid requirements)
11. Processes consumer/customer complaints
12. Is involved in special planning projects
13. Recruits, orients, and trains staff (team leaders and case managers)
14. Is involved in systems negotiations by providing input regarding realistic specific problems CM, staff face

IV. *PROGRAM MANAGER'S RESPONSIBILITIES*
1. Actively develops resources
2. Links TMHC management (spearheading, problem solving)
3. Monitors case records (review records for appropriate content)
4. Attends quality assurance meetings
5. Monitors income generation
6. Monitors mental health board contract
7. Attends supervisors meeting
8. Communicates management information to staff
9. Processes consumer/customer complaints
10. Prepares monthly and quarterly reports
11. Provides data for program evaluation and quarterly PE report
12. Is involved in special planning projects
13. Talks at supervisory level with managerial representatives from other agencies about system problems and policy issues
14. Provides input for the development of the budget and prepare budgeting changes throughout the year
15. Plans and decide regarding staff development
16. Assists in the recruitment, orientation and training of supervisory staff
17. Recruits, orients, and trains staff that report directly to him/her
18. Is responsible for caseload distribution, staff meeting caseload expectation, caseload prioritization, screening of caseload, and referrals to appropriate programs

A review of these drafts was led by the executive director using the questions and criteria previously described. Below are some of the points that were made:

1. Some responsibilities were totally unclear (e.g., consult daily operations, handle DPS forms) and were clarified or removed.
2. Nonhelpful roles or responsibilities (inverted hierarchy notions) were removed (e.g., monitors, prepare monthly reports, attend supervisory meetings).
3. Redundant items were removed (e.g., responsibilities centered on students, liaison, resource development).

The result of this analysis was that at least one level (supervisor) and perhaps a second level (program director) was eliminated; responsibilities were written more precisely and almost all were written in terms of helping frontline staff do their jobs better. A side benefit was that the need for more meetings and bigger meetings was reduced. The biggest consequence was that case managers and team leaders (the people closest to the clients) were delegated authority to make decisions and take action commensurate with their responsibilities and to do so without the need for permission from multiple levels of managers.

*Paperwork.* Paperwork is the most onerous task for frontline practitioners, the burden can consume over 35 percent of an agency's time and resources and the benefits accrued to the organization are slight even when identifiable. More specifically, can a link be established between performance and every form now being required of staff? Paperwork within human service organizations has reached crisis proportions with studies and estimates suggesting that over 30 percent of a worker's time is consumed by such requirements. It is a major factor in reduced productivity, efficiency, job satisfaction, and even effectiveness. (See the chapter on information management for additional discussion.) The reduction of paperwork, however, seems particularly incorrigible.

Forms can serve three legitimate purposes. First, forms provide the information needed for documentation, a record of what was done to whom, for instance. This information can help the agency to meet professional standards set by accrediting bodies, to protect the agency against complaints and lawsuits, and to meet requirements for funding. The majority of forms in agencies are devoted to this purpose.

Second, forms can act as tools for staff to help prompt and guide their work and as an aid in supervision. For example, a model of intervention that depends on an assessment of client strengths (Modrcin, Rapp, & Chamberlain, 1985; Rapp & Chamberlain, 1985; Weick, Rapp, Sullivan, & Kisthardt, 1989) requires an assessment device that helps guide the practitioner and client through this process. Requiring social histories, listings and analysis of problems, deficits, and weaknesses, in addition, will not only consume a large amount of time but will distract the practitioner from the desired focus. Client assessment and case planning forms are the most common manifestations of forms for this purpose. (See section on "Forms" earlier in this chapter.)

Third, forms can act as the collector of performance information. Since the chapter on managing information is devoted to this topic, the reader is referred there.

*Paperwork reduction success stories.* The process a manager needs to follow to reduce paperwork varies by purpose so forms for documentation and forms as tools will be treated separately.

Our experience suggests that 90 percent of agencies are overdocumented and/or incorrectly documented. In other words, too much needless information is collected and some valuable information is still missing. Over time some external group (e.g., state or federal government, insurance carriers, accrediting bodies) add and occasionally delete data requirements while internal groups (managers, planners, information system specialists, supervisors) are doing the same. Managers have all too often assumed a passive position as these new intrusions occur by seeing the new demand as nonnegotiable or noninfluenceable.

In contrast, Estelle Richmond, a model performance manager, as Executive Director of the Murtis Taylor Mental Health Center in Cleveland, Ohio, took a radically different strategy. In trying to improve case management services to persons with severe mental illness in inner-city Cleveland, she wanted to confront the need for intensive service with limited resources but did not want to be consumed with unnecessary paperwork. She collected all the forms being used and quickly observed that many were redundant in whole or in part, and others appeared useless. In answer to her question, why are we using this form, her staff most frequently stated that it was required by the Ohio Department of Mental Health, the Cuyahoga County Mental Health Board, the Joint Commission on Accreditation of Hospitals, or all three. Richmond then called each organization, reviewed their requirements form by form. She found that some forms and information were not required at all; other information was required but could be collected much more simply or not as frequently; and other forms and information were negotiable. An example of the latter situation was a form assessing a client's functional status that was required by the state. When Richmond demonstrated that that information in a different format was included in their case assessment forms, they withdrew the demand and thereby eliminated one form. When she was done, the required forms for case management were down to six pages. These six pages were designed to act as "tools" and still meet all documentation requirements. (See case study at the end of this chapter.)

Another example may be called a "Tale of Two State Agencies." In the early seventies, the federal government required state child welfare agencies (among others) to report on the amount of worker time consumed by various activities. The Illinois Department of Children and Family Services met this demand by requiring all workers to complete time sheets on a continuous basis. An expensive computer system was put in and a cadre of data entry people hired to enter the thousands of time sheets each month. The data was never accurate as workers sabotaged the system by recording incomplete or made up data. One office actually Xeroxed copies and sent them in under different names. Despite all this, it met federal requirements.

In contrast, Kansas Department of Social and Rehabilitation Services used a sampling procedure whereby each month a randomly drawn sample of workers was assigned the responsibility to complete the time sheets. While onerous for one month, workers tolerated the demand since it would be quite a while till they had to do it again. The computer infrastructure was radically less expensive and also met federal requirements.

*Strategies for paperwork reduction.* The following are strategies for reducing documentation requirements. First, the manager should establish a benchmark like paperwork can consume no more than 10 percent or 15 percent of frontline staff's time. The burden then falls on management to set documentation requirements that would accommodate such a goal.

Second, the manager can analyze the paperwork demands on frontline staff by creating two lists. The first list contains all of the "assumed" data and forms required by external agencies (e.g., accreditation, granting agencies, legislature). The goal with the first list is to meet (or change) the requirements of the external agencies at the minimum acceptable level. This means the manager talks directly with people from these agencies. What are the minimum requirements? How often must it be completed? What is the intent of the information? What is done with it and why is it important? Many human service agencies are laboring under false assumptions about such requirements. Once this information is gathered, the manager orders people to no longer complete forms above the minimum requirements. Then the manager designs the simplest, least redundant way of collecting it. (The case study of Estelle Richmond at the end of the chapter provides a vivid sample of this process.)

The second list contains the forms and data requirements developed by the agency itself. With this list, the manager tests each data element and each form in terms of its presumed effects on the performance areas. Basically the questions are: How is this piece of information helpful to the work? What decisions or actions need to be informed by this data? If the answers do not meet *explicit* tests of helpfulness, performance, action, and decision, they are automatically dropped. Another approach with this list is to do a zero-based paperwork review in which staff are to pretend there are no requirements and develop needed forms as if the agency is new.

Another paperwork reduction strategy is to exploit the power of the microcomputer. With adequate programming, these machines can remove much of the redundancy of recording and produce reports tailored to a wide range of constituencies, internal and external to the organization. (Taylor, 1981)

*Memos and policies.* While forms seem to be the major culprit, the use of other kinds of paperwork can also needlessly consume resources. Some people overly rely on memos where a phone call would suffice or even be more effective. Others believe memos should include *all* the relevant information, which leads to several pages for each document. They are not only time consuming to write but the receivers also have to devote time to reading, thereby multiplying the time consumed. Proctor and Gamble addressed this by requiring memos to be one page, otherwise the memo would be kicked back. One reason for this policy was that in the mind of Richard Deufree, past president of P&G, long memos restrained action. His invective was often, "Boil it down to something I can grasp." (Peters & Waterman, 1982, p. 150)

Another paper producer is the predilection of many organizations to construct policies as a solution to most organizational problems, which then means having them committed to paper, reproduced, distributed, read, and stored. The nature of bureaucracy, especially public ones, with its concern with equity and rules seems to encourage such practices. In such settings, thick policy and procedure manuals evolve quickly and because of their size, density, and detail, are rarely used. In some human service organizations, separate units are established to design policies. Policies are seen as inflexible prescriptions for behavior and probably should be, but organizations and clients are often not amenable to uniform prescriptions. The pattern is often that a policy is identified as not working, it does not handle all situations or handles them poorly, then a new one needs to be written to help cover these disparate situations. This continues but never seems to apply to all situations. In these cases, a policy is not needed but rather more staff training, better supervision, or a stronger organizational culture in which people will make "correct" decisions and actions as they relate to particular situations.

*Meetings.* Drucker (1967) states that every meeting is a waste of time. "Meetings are by definition a concession to deficient organization. For one either meets or one works. One cannot do both at the same time. In an ideally designed structure there would be no meetings. Everyone would know what he needs to know to do his job." (p. 45)

There is no perfectly designed organization and Drucker realizes that. Meetings are a reality of organizational life and much of our precious time gets spent in them. Keeping Drucker's admonition in mind should be a first step in using our meeting time more constructively. However, this is not enough. You need to know how to diagnose meeting time and what to do about it. The first step is to decide how much intra-organizational meeting time you are willing to tolerate knowing that whatever time spent cannot be used to serve clients. Ten percent of a worker's time seems like a reasonable amount to shoot for. The following are some useful guidelines for the use of meetings.

### When Not to Have a Meeting
1. If the meeting is a substitute for action, don't have it. Can the next steps be taken without the meeting? Could the decision be made without the meeting? The key is knowing the goal of the meeting and determining if the goals could be accomplished in another, more efficient manner.
2. If the meeting doesn't have an agenda, don't have it. This is an old and obvious point, but how many meetings have you attended that have not had agendas? Don't assume someone else has an agenda. If the agenda is not explicit, don't have the meeting.
3. If the meeting does not enhance performance, don't have it. This requires a

clear link between the goals of the meeting and the goals of the organization. If the link is not obvious or seems forced, the meeting is not necessary.

4. If the purpose of the meeting is to convey information, don't have it. Announcements are more efficiently handled by memo.

## What to Do to Prepare for the Meeting

1. Remember the chairperson doesn't do it alone. Frequently people "leave the running of the meeting to the person in charge." Don't do it! Help out. All the behavior expected of someone who is designated as chairperson is also the responsibility of everyone else.

2. Prepare for the meeting. Look at the agenda. Think about the items. Do you need to take something with you. A few minutes of preparation can help save a lot of time at the meeting.

3. Set expectations. For a meeting to run efficiently, everyone needs to know and perform their role. You need to perform your role and also help establish expectations for everyone else. All of the points in this list are expectations for people's behavior. Follow this guide and expect it of others.

## What to Do When the Meeting Starts

1. If the link between agenda items and performance is not explicit, question each item and delete those with no connection.

2. If someone only needs to be at part of the meeting, schedule them accordingly.

3. If the meeting does not begin on time, start it. You don't have to be the chair of the committee to get it going. Just suggest that the meeting begin and keep it up.

4. If someone wants you to come out of the meeting for a phone call or anything else, tell them later.

5. If someone is talking, listen. This is easier said than done. The mind loves to ramble. Test yourself as someone talks. Can you summarize what the person has said? Can you connect what they are saying to the central issue under discussion?

6. If the person talking begins to ramble, don't reinforce their behavior. Use nonverbal behavior consciously: Look away or attend to something else. When the person finishes, bring the group back to the question or agenda.

7. If closure on the point of discussion is evasive, push it. Help to reach closure by reflecting back what has been said, summarize the points or positions presented, probe by asking follow-up questions.

8. If closure on an item is occurring, make certain that the action is explicit. What is the decision? Who is going to follow up? What is the next step?

## What to Do After the Meeting

1. Make certain someone has summarized the meeting and distributed the summary to everyone who needs it.

**2.** Do your part. Take whatever next step you agree to and report back to the chairperson.

## Psychological Obstacles

This entire book is about new managerial methods and new perspectives. Given this, it is logical to identify obstacles that reside in the minds of managers. Many of these are created and sustained by structural features of the human service organization, but etiology is not the concern here. Rather, the concern is that there are personal and psychological stances that greatly impede organizational performance.

The absence of the managerial perspective reflected in the basic principles (Chapter 1) acts as a major barrier. For example, it is simply impossible to manage according to the inverted hierarchy if one does not have a healthy disrespect for the impossible. If you think that you cannot reduce paperwork, you will not. If you think that you cannot arrange training opportunities with such a limited budget, you will not.

*Blaming and Excusing.* Many of the negative descriptors (e.g., complacent, defensive, rigid) of organizations, specific organizational units or people reflect a certain psychology characterized by feelings of impotence and insecurity at its roots. The most prevalent behavioral manifestations are in blaming or excusing. Common excuses for not performing are "not enough money," "not enough time," "not enough staff," "not enough community resources." Blame is often focused on families, court personnel, other agencies, funders, administrators, and most disturbingly on the client. Some human services have even developed professional sounding phrases for blame like "the client is resistant to therapy." Blaming and excusing deflect responsibility from the agency and its personnel and reinforce feelings of impotence.

High-performing managers simply will not and do not tolerate blaming and excusing. The perspective is to identify obstacles that, for example, may be the behavior of court personnel. Obstacles, however, are meant to be attacked, removed, or attenuated. Where excuses and blame lead one to passivity, obstacles are susceptible to analysis, problem solving, and intervention. Every small increment of success can therefore produce an increment of confidence, control, and empowerment.

*Detachment of Personnel.* Organizations unresponsive to employee needs, organizations that place a premium on control and permissions, organizations that ignore or punish extra effort or risk-taking on behalf of clients, organizations that place a premium on form rather than results come to be viewed as the enemy.

Employees, especially those in frontline positions who have the least power and responsibility, often become psychologically detached from these programs or organizations. It is a coping strategy—a protective device to feelings of low worth and hostility by the organization. The organization is not "me" but is personalized as upper management or the board of directors.

The goal for the client-centered performance manager is to have each employee see themselves as the agency. They share responsibility for each success and each disappointment. In their contacts with clients and key players, they realize that they not only represent the agency but they are the agency. Their names could just as easily be placed on the agency letterhead as the executive director. Part of their work identity is the organization much like a part of a person's identity is the family or church.

Strategies for creating such feelings include the constant sharing of credit for agency successes, maintaining nurturing work environments, treating employees as adults by giving them responsibility and authority, permitting autonomy, encouraging risk-taking, learning from failure, encouraging interdependence, creating winners, rewarding risk-taking, and establishing an inspiring vision and concomitant values. The manager can also create other opportunities for linking personal and organizational identities: have frontline workers do some public speaking on behalf of the organization, arrange for workers to do presentations at statewide conferences on the agency's programs, encourage workers to attend board meetings or legislative hearings, involve workers on temporary task forces and work groups, have the organization be a regular source of prestige and rewards for the worker, place pictures of workers in annual reports, include stories of workers in newsletters, regularly ask everyone for their opinions and take them seriously, give frontline workers business cards, fill their offices with agency awards.

### The Case of Estelle Richman: Providing Tools and Removing Obstacles

Case management had been a lower-level priority in this Ohio community mental health center for several years. Case managers were given little support and recognition. In early 1986, the executive director, Estelle Richman, identified case management as a number one priority and became committed to providing case management effectively.

Various organizations and groups who had a stake in the center were first identified: the county mental health board, the agency's board of trustees, agency administrators, and case managers. Each group of stakeholders was seen as a team that needed to interact with another group of stakeholders or team. Ms. Richman acted as a facilitator between the county board of mental health and the agency board of trustees, and between the agency board of trustees and the agency administrators. The case manager supervisor acted as a facilitator between the agency administrators and case managers. Once stakeholders had been identified the process of education began.

Educating the board of trustees was effective due to its simplicity and honesty. First, case management was added as an agenda item every month as part of the director's report. Topics included: meaning of CSP, importance of case management, the need for case management, evaluation based on outcome rather than productivity standards, empowerment versus enablement. The result of this education process was the board's approving a new organizational structure creating a case management unit separate from the outpatient department. The unit was staffed with a supervisor and six case managers.

Secondly, both the executive director and case management supervisor took advantage of every opportunity to attend county and state conferences, workshops, or seminars on case management. Articles, books, and other materials on case management were collected, read, and discussed. Policies and procedures began to develop. Simultaneously with their self-education program, Ms. Richman and her program director began an energetic education program for the case managers. This training included teaching a model for effective case management and making workers feel like stakeholders with a voice in determining how the program would function. After a couple of months, these workers were able to contribute invaluable feedback.

The following items were presented by the case managers and, with Ms. Richman's influence, policies successfully adopted or changed to make the program more effective.

1. *The need for an agency-owned vehicle for the case managers to use if their car was not available.* Ms. Richman requested that the finance committee of the board of trustees approve leasing a car. The committee learned that aggressive outreach was the preferred mode of treatment and availability of an agency-owned vehicle would facilitate this. Further, statistics showed that case managers spent 50 percent of their direct-service time in the field. The committee was impressed by the data and the commitment of "meeting the client on the client's turf" and recommended approval to the board. The leased car arrived two months after the request. The finance committee has continued its support by approving the leasing of a second vehicle.

2. *Punching a time clock acted as a barrier to case management work.* The time clock had been placed in the agency by the board of trustees and all staff were required to "punch in" except the highest level administrators. Data was presented to the personnel committee by the director showing that case managers were frequently needed by clients prior to 9:00 AM and after 5:30 PM. Each time they came in early or left late, special recordings needed to be done. Large accumulations of compensatory time developed. The paperwork flow through the personnel department tripled. The personnel director and Ms. Richman requested that case managers be permitted to work flexible hours. The personnel committee of the board enthusiastically endorsed flexible time and removal of the time clock for case managers. This was achieved in three months. The removal of the time clock for case managers not only removed an obstacle to their work, but became a visible symbol of the organizational importance assigned to case management services, case managers, and their chronically mentally ill clients.

3. *Visual-display pagers became a necessity as case managers spent an increasing percentage of time out of the agency.* Pagers cost the agency $200 per pager plus air-time. The fiscal director had not planned for them in his budget and was apprehensive as to their value. Ms. Richman's program director spent time explaining case management, aggressive outreach, and community resources. The budget director began to understand that case managers working with clients and collaterals in the community were more productive than when in the agency. All sixteen case managers now have their own pagers.

4. *Case managers frequently complained about required paperwork.* They noted that some forms were redundant and others appeared useless. All paperwork not relevant to the client was reviewed by the county mental health board and the agency quality assurance coordinator. All paperwork that could not be documented as necessary by a primary funding body was eliminated. If the only funding body requesting the document was the county mental health board, negotiations were held to eliminate the paper. Frequent reviews of required paperwork are done. An agency goal to maintain documentation time at less than 20 percent remains strong. Clerical workers have been retained to help with nonclinical documentation and routine paperwork.

5. *Caseload size was an immediate problem as the agency sought to do effective case management.* It was apparent that caseload size had to be reduced. The board of trustees made the commitment to shift resources and to hire additional case managers to effect an overall caseload ratio of 43:1 from the original 75:1. With the identification of priority clients three case managers have 10 to 12 clients, 10 have 35 clients, two have 60 to 80 clients, and one has 150 clients. Clients on the 150

caseload require only medication monitoring. Clients on the 60 to 80 caseloads are currently stabilized and working but have periodic needs for support. These caseloads are the next priority to be reduced to 35:1.

6. *Many clients have a payee for their disability checks who is frequently an outside agency with minimal understanding of the mental health system.* The program director and billing coordinator approached Ms. Richman and the fiscal director about the feasibility of the agency becoming representative payee for clients requesting this service. Case managers felt strongly that they would be better able to advocate for clients in the community if the agency was the payee. While very new territory, Ms. Richman and the fiscal director determined that clinically it would be worth the risk. Financially, the agency loses money on this project, but case management successes have far outweighed any fiscal negatives. Currently the agency is representative payee for 100 clients.

In conclusion, the agency has been successful in implementing a comprehensive case management system, and this is due to an executive director who was single-minded in her pursuit, who set the direction (e.g., specify client outcomes, job descriptions, designed model of intervention), provided the tools to do the job (e.g., training, leased cars, pagers, quality supervision), and assertively removed obstacles to performance (e.g., paperwork, time clock, caseload size).

### The Case of Wernert, Hunter, and Ferree: A Persistent Commitment to Excellence for Clients

Thomas Wernert is Executive Director of the Lucas County (Ohio) Mental Health Board, Jack Hunter is the Executive Director of the Ruth Ide Mental Health Center, and Virginia Ferree is the Executive Director of the Zepf Mental Health Center. These three administrators decided to mount a new county-wide initiative to provide case management services to the chronically mentally ill. Their story is one of intelligence, commitment to clients, and leadership. As a team, they took the following steps:

1. They searched the country for the strongest model of case management.
2. They precisely defined the client outcomes they desired: increased community tenure, improved independent living status, increased vocational status.
3. They defined "the business" of intensive case management as being "to increase the independent community functioning and quality of life of the severely mentally disabled in the most dignified fashion possible using the most powerful goal oriented strategies available."
4. They developed uniform job descriptions for case managers and their supervisors that detailed the specific expectations (e.g., amount of client time, amount of time in the community, etc.).
5. They redesigned assessment and case planning forms to be supportive of the case management model to be implemented.
6. Since they did not have the funds to provide intensive case management for all clients, they precisely described which clients would be eligible.
7. They developed an information system to systematically report on client outcomes to all parties in the system.
8. They selected supervisors, trained them, and involved them in the process of designing the system.
9. They created a menu of activities for creating a reward-based environment for case managers and clients.
10. They hit the "podium trail," informing the community of the initiative and clarifying reciprocal expectations.

Once these tasks were completed (about four months), they arranged for intensive training for the case managers and supervisors. This simple listing of steps tends to camouflage the spirit and commitment in which they were done. To be a part of these discussions was to witness the preoccupation these three leaders had with clients, staff, and doing the job the best way possible.

Months later, the triumvirate is still meeting regularly to find problems and successes, assertively revising the earlier decisions when indicated, and to insure that all is being done to make the case management system work. After observing a three-day meeting for this purpose, a first time member of the group stated, "In all my years I have never seen three administrators talk for so long about clients and how we could do better."

## SUMMARY

The inverted hierarchy metaphor integrates the concepts and methods presented in previous chapters. We also introduce new ideas and strategies concerning paperwork, meetings, opportunity-finding, creating a vision, modeling, prevalent psychological obstacles to performance, and other management concerns. Our experience suggests that exceptional client-centered performance managers embody the inverted hierarchy perspective and practice the methods included in this chapter.

With the value base embodied in the management principles of Chapter 1, the analytic program design framework, the skills of managing information, personnel, resources, implementation, and the inverted hierarchy, the social administrator is equipped for effective practice. We are confident that client-centered performance will accrue to managers who conscientiously practice and continue to learn from their practice.

## REFERENCES

Altshuler, S. C., & Forward, J. (1978). The inverted hierarchy: A case manager approach to mental health. *Administration in Mental Health, 6*(1), 57–68.

Drucker, P. F. (1964). *Managing for results*. New York: Harper & Row.

Drucker, P. F. (1967). *The effective executive*. London: Pan Books.

Gowdy, E., Rapp, C. A., & Poertner, J. (1987). *Managing for performance: Using information to enhance community integration of the chronically mentally ill*. Lawrence, KS: University of Kansas School of Social Welfare.

Gowdy, E., & Rapp, C. A. (1988). *Managerial behavior: The common denominator of effective community based programs*. Lawrence, KS: University of Kansas.

Kanter, R. M. (1983). *The change masters*. New York: Simon & Schuster.

Livingston, J. S. (1975, January/February). The myth of the well-educated manager. *Harvard Business Review, 53*, 96–106.

McGoldrick, N., & Gerson, R. (1985). *Genograms in family assessment*. New York: Norton.

Mintzberg, H. (1979). *The structuring of organizations*. Englewood Cliffs, NJ: Prentice-Hall.

Modrcin, M., Rapp, C. A., & Chamberlain, R. (1985). *Case management with psychiatrically disabled individuals: Curriculum and training program*. Lawrence, KS: University of Kansas School of Social Welfare.

Peters, T. J., & Austin, N. (1985). *A passion for excellence*. New York: Random House.

Peters, T. J., & Waterman, R.H. (1982). *In search of excellence*. New York: Harper & Row.

Rapp, C. A., & Chamberlain, R. (1985, September/October). Case management services to the chronically mentally ill. *Social Work, 30*(5), 417–422.

Simons, R. L. (1982, May). Strategies for exercising influence. *Social Work Journal, 27*(3), 268–274.

Taylor, J. B. (1981). *Using microcomputers in social agencies*. Beverly Hills, CA: Sage.

*Webster's Third New World Dictionary* (1972). New York: World.

Weick, A., Rapp, C. A., Sullivan, W. P., & Kisthardt, W. (1989, July). A strengths perspective for social work practice. *Social Work Journal, 34*(4), 350–354.

# Index